Proper Mark Twain

Proper Mark Twain

LELAND KRAUTH

The University of Georgia Press | Athens and London

© 1999 by the University of Georgia Press

Athens, Georgia 30602

All rights reserved

Designed by Kathi Dailey Morgan

Set in Janson by G & S Typesetters

Printed and bound by Maple-Vail

The paper in this book meets the guidelines for
permanence and durability of the Committee on
Production Guidelines for Book Longevity of the
Council on Library Resources.

Printed in the United States of America

03   02   01   00   99   C   5   4   3   2   1

Library of Congress Cataloging-in-Publication Data

Krauth, Leland.

Proper Mark Twain / Leland Krauth.

p.   cm.

Includes bibliographical references and index.

ISBN 0-8203-2106-0 (alk. paper)

1. Twain, Mark, 1835–1910—Ethics.   2. Didactic

fiction, American—History and criticism.

3. Moral conditions in literature.

4. Sentimentalism in literature.

5. Ethics in literature.   I. Title.

PS1342.E8K73   1999

818'.409—dc21   98-51168

CIP

British Library Cataloging-in-Publication Data available

Frontispiece: Mark Twain, 1904. Yale Collection of Western Americana,
Beinecke Rare Book and Manuscript Library.

FOR BARBARA

CONTENTS

ACKNOWLEDGMENTS

Like the luminous novel that it eventually considers, *Huckleberry Finn*, this study was a long time a-borning. The good thing about that protracted gestation is that it enticed many people to help not just the emerging text but the struggling writer. My debts to others go way back and run deep. Although I have discovered a Mark Twain quite different from his, I first felt the excitement of Twain's work as an undergraduate listening to James M. Cox's brilliant lectures. Edwin H. Cady imparted a sense of the complexity of Twain's culture. The scholar to whom I am most indebted, however, is Louis J. Budd. His studies are, as every Twain scholar knows, searching explorations of the writer, his historical context, and the works themselves. His thinking has informed mine at every turn. I want to acknowledge his importance to this study, even as I exempt him from any responsibility for the argument that follows.

I was drawn to work seriously on Twain not only by the vitality of his writing but also by the excellence of the critical commentary it has provoked. (I sometimes think that the next best thing to reading Twain is reading about him.) My indebtedness to that rich body of scholarship is recorded in my bibliography. It is a pleasure to acknowledge some more immediate obligations. I owe a special debt to Alan Gribben not only for his superb scholarship but also for his having suggested that the Elmira College Center for Mark Twain Studies invite me to work there. The Center's former director, the late Darryl Baskin, brought me to the Center first as a scholar-in-residence and then as a teacher of a summer course on Twain, and he somehow made both occasions simultaneously stimulating and soothing. The 1989 State of Mark Twain Studies conference, held at the Elmira College Twain Center, gave me the opportunity to develop ideas that would eventually become chapter 7. The Elmira Center has been crucial to my work in many ways. Gretchen Sharlow, the present director of the Center, has provided information and encouragement. Her invitation to lecture at the Center in 1997 gave me a chance to air some of the ideas set forth in chapter 4, and her hospitality—as it always does—made that visit reinvigorating. A symposium in 1990 at the Mark Twain Memorial, organized by its director John Vincent Boyer, allowed me to work through a brief first version of what would become chapter 3. Through the years I have been kindly received by three editors of the Mark Twain Project, Henry Nash Smith, Frederick Anderson, and the current director Robert Hirst. Two editors at the Project have been especially helpful to me. Victor Fischer listened, located materials, and offered support. Michael B. Frank always managed to find the time to talk Twain with me, and I am indebted to him for his knowledge of Twain, his help at the Papers, his personal encouragement, and most of all, his good humor and humane spirit. He represents our profession at its best. I know I voice what all who know the Twain Project feel when I say that their publications constitute one of the monuments of twentieth-century scholarship.

Several present or former members of my own department here at the University of Colorado at Boulder have been helpful in various ways. My always dear colleague, the late Virgil Grillo, together with his wife, Joanne, got me to Berkeley to work at the Twain Papers. Les Brill long ago read some early versions of my work, and found it good—and said so in ways that made me take heart. At a critical juncture my former chair, James Kincaid, arranged a sabbatical, and I want to thank him even though he didn't include me in his acknowledgment of those who "did nothing" for his grand book, *Annoying the Victorians*—though he certainly could have. Gerry Kinneavy has provided not only unflinching support but also endless good humor; he is a man Mark Twain would have enjoyed. Nan Goodman read a version of the introduction and tactfully gave me such trenchant criticism that I had to rewrite the entire thing. Off and on one whole summer Mary Klages and I met over coffee every other week or so to read each other's work. My debt to her criticism is exceeded only by my gratitude for her steady encouragement. And finally on the department front, my colleague Charles Squier, a renaissance scholar and a renaissance man, often listened to Twain stuff as we hiked, and always found, as renaissance men do, something new and kind to say about it.

Oddly, for years now, my most vibrant sounding board for notions—perhaps "remarks" would be more precise—about Mark Twain has been the economist (and secret Twain aficionado) Craig Davis at the University of British Columbia in Vancouver. His enthusiasm is matched only by his boundless, wild humor, of which Twain himself would surely approve.

A version of the first part of chapter 4 appeared in *Western Illinois Regional Studies* 2 (spring 1979): 52–69; a portion of chapter 1 appeared in *Mississippi Quarterly* 33 (1980): 144–53; and a small part of chapter 6 appeared in *American Literature* 54 (1982): 368–84, copyright Duke University Press. I am grateful to the editors of those journals for permission to reprint.

I also want to acknowledge the help of the editors and staff at the University of Georgia Press. Malcolm Call proves that southern courtesy, abetted by good humor, is alive and well these days.

In "Pudd'nhead Wilson's New Calendar" Twain tells us, "Grief can take care of itself; but to get the full value of a joy you must have somebody to divide it with." I'm afraid that during the long making of this book I haven't let grief take care of itself but have shared it with my family—along with doubt, insecurity, and various forms of plain craziness. Now I want to divide my joy with them. As extended family, Eli and Althea Pearlman have provided understanding and good humor. My daughter Heidi was a writer-in-residence at the Elmira College Mark Twain Center when I was there working on this book, and she gave me then, as she always has, the benefit of her rich intelligence, her creative imagination, and her zesty spirit. My other daughter, Karin, often sustained me, albeit by phone, with genuine interest and an unerring sense of the meaningful in life. My son, Gregory, and his wife, Kathy, have been good-humored supporters. At a desperate moment in the preparation of the manuscript they stepped in and performed computer magic, and in the end they prepared the final electronic copy of the text. Most of all, however, I am grateful to them for bringing into my world my grandchildren, Sam and Sophie. To think of them is to overcome despair; to be with them is to know joy. The endless source of all that is good in my life is my wife, Barbara. Although of a Jamesian sensibility, she has a Twainian whimsy, a Twainian eye for the fraudulent, a Twainian compassion. A superb writer and sharp-minded critic, she has helped everything in this book. For her buoyant spirit, for her capacious imagination, for her supple intelligence, I have no words, only endless love; she has made my existence a life.

ABBREVIATIONS

AD Samuel L. Clemens's autobiographical dictations, MTP.

AI *Huck Finn and Tom Sawyer among the Indians and Other Unfinished Stories.* Ed. Dahlia Armon and Walter Blair. Berkeley: University of California Press, 1989.

AMT *The Autobiography of Mark Twain.* Ed. Charles Neider. New York: Harper and Brothers, 1959.

CE *The Complete Essays of Mark Twain.* Ed. Charles Neider. Garden City, N.Y.: Doubleday, 1963.

CG *Contributions to the "Galaxy," 1868–1871, by Mark Twain.* Ed. Bruce R. McElderry Jr. Gainesville, Fla.: Scholars' Facsimiles and Reprints, 1961.

CH *Mark Twain: The Critical Heritage.* Ed. Frederick Anderson. London: Routledge and Kegan Paul, 1971.

CofC *Clemens of the "Call": Mark Twain in San Francisco.* Ed. Edgar M. Branch. University of California Press, 1969.

CtHMTH The Mark Twain House, Hartford, CT.

CY *A Connecticut Yankee in King Arthur's Court.* Ed. Bernard L. Stein. Berkeley: University of California Press, 1979.

ET&S1 *Early Tales and Sketches, Volume 1 (1851–1864).* Ed. Edgar Marquess Branch and Robert H. Hirst. Berkeley: University of California Press, 1979.

ET&S2 *Early Tales and Sketches, Volume 2 (1864–1865).* Ed. Frederick Anderson, Lin Salamo, and Bernard L. Stein. Berkeley: University of California Press, 1975.

FE *Following the Equator: A Journey around the World.* 1897. New York: Dover, 1989.

FM *Mark Twain's Fables of Man.* Ed. John S. Tuckey. Berkeley: University of California Press, 1972.

HH&T *Mark Twain's Hannibal, Huck, and Tom*. Ed. Walter Blair. Berkeley: University of California Press, 1969.

HF *Adventures of Huckleberry Finn*. Ed. Walter Blair and Victor Fischer. Berkeley: University of California Press, 1985.

IA *The Innocents Abroad, Roughing It*. Ed. Guy Cardwell. New York: Library of America, 1984.

L1 *Mark Twain's Letters, Volume 1 (1853–1866)*. Ed. Edgar Marquess Branch, Michael B. Frank, and Kenneth M. Sanderson. Berkeley: University of California Press, 1988.

L2 *Mark Twain's Letters, Volume 2 (1867–1868)*. Ed. Harriet Elinor Smith and Richard Bucci. Berkeley: University of California Press, 1990.

L3 *Mark Twain's Letters, Volume 3 (1869)*. Ed. Victor Fischer and Michael B. Frank. Berkeley: University of California Press, 1992.

L4 *Mark Twain's Letters, Volume 4 (1870–1871)*. Ed. Victor Fischer and Michael B. Frank. Berkeley: University of California Press, 1995.

LE *Letters from the Earth*. Ed. Bernard DeVoto. New York: Harper and Row, 1962.

LLMT *The Love Letters of Mark Twain*. Ed. Dixon Wecter. New York: Harper and Brothers, 1949.

LOM *Life on the Mississippi*. Ed. James M. Cox. New York: Penguin, 1984.

MTA *Mark Twain's Autobiography*. 2 vols. Ed. Albert Bigelow Paine. New York: Harper and Brothers, 1924.

MTB Albert Bigelow Paine. *Mark Twain: A Biography*. 3 vols. New York: Harper and Brothers, 1912.

MTBus *Mark Twain, Business Man*. Ed. Samuel C. Webster. Boston: Little, Brown, 1946.

MTC1 *Mark Twain: Collected Tales, Sketches, Speeches, and Essays, 1890–1910*. Vol. 1. Ed. Louis J. Budd. New York: Library of America, 1992.

MTC2 *Mark Twain: Collected Tales, Sketches, Speeches, and Essays, 1852–1890*. Vol. 2. Ed. Louis J. Budd. New York: Library of America, 1992.

MTE *Mark Twain in Eruption.* Ed. Bernard DeVoto. New York: Harper and Brothers, 1940.

MTEnt *Mark Twain of the "Enterprise."* Ed. Henry Nash Smith. Berkeley: University of California Press, 1957.

MTHHR *Mark Twain's Correspondence with Henry Huttleston Rogers.* Ed. Lewis Leary. Berkeley: University of California Press, 1969.

MTHL *Mark Twain–Howells Letters.* 2 vols. Ed. Henry Nash Smith and William M. Gibson. Cambridge: Harvard University Press, 1960.

MTL *Mark Twain's Letters.* 2 vols. Ed. Albert Bigelow Paine. New York: Harper and Brothers, 1917.

MTLB *Mark Twain's Letters to Will Bowen: "My First and Oldest and Dearest Friend."* Ed. Theodore Hornberger. Austin: University of Texas Press, 1941.

MTLH *Mark Twain's Letters from Hawaii.* Ed. A. Grove Day. Honolulu: University Press of Hawaii, 1975.

MTLP *Mark Twain's Letters to His Publishers.* Ed. Hamlin Hill. Berkeley: University of California Press, 1967.

MTMF *Mark Twain to Mrs. Fairbanks.* Ed. Dixon Wecter. San Marino, Calif.: Huntington Library, 1949.

MTMS *Mark Twain's Mysterious Stranger Manuscripts.* Ed. William M. Gibson. Berkeley: University of California Press, 1969.

MTN *Mark Twain's Notebook.* Ed. Albert Bigelow Paine. New York: Harper and Brothers, 1935.

MTOA *Mark Twain's Own Autobiography: The Chapters from the "North American Review."* Ed. Michael J. Kiskis. Madison: University of Wisconsin Press, 1990.

MTP Mark Twain Papers. Bancroft Library, University of California, Berkeley.

MTSpk *Mark Twain Speaking.* Ed. Paul Fatout. Iowa City: University of Iowa Press, 1976.

MTTB *Mark Twain's Travels with Mr. Brown.* Ed. Franklin Walker and G. Ezra Dane. New York: Alfred A. Knopf, 1940.

MyMT William Dean Howells. *My Mark Twain: Reminiscences and Criticism.* New York: Harper and Brothers, 1910.

N&J1   *Mark Twain's Notebooks and Journals, Volume 1 (1855–1873).*
Ed. Frederick Anderson, Michael B. Frank, and Kenneth M.
Sanderson. Berkeley: University of California Press, 1975.

N&J2   *Mark Twain's Notebooks and Journals, Volume 2 (1877–1883).*
Ed. Frederick Anderson, Lin Salamo, and Bernard L. Stein.
Berkeley: University of California Press, 1975.

N&J3   *Mark Twain's Notebooks and Journals, Volume 3 (1883–1891).*
Ed. Robert Pack Browning, Michael B. Frank, and Lin
Salamo. Berkeley: University of California Press, 1979.

"OT"   "Old Times on the Mississippi." *Great Short Works of
Mark Twain.* Ed. Justin Kaplan. New York: Harper and
Row, 1967.

P&P   *The Prince and the Pauper.* Ed. Victor Fischer and Lin
Salamo. Berkeley: University of California Press, 1979.

PW   *Pudd'nhead Wilson and Those Extraordinary Twins.* Ed.
Sidney E. Berger. New York: Norton, 1980.

RI   *Roughing It.* Ed. Harriet Elinor Smith and Edgar Marquess
Branch. Berkeley: University of California Press, 1993.

S&B   *Mark Twain's Satires and Burlesques.* Ed. Franklin R. Rogers.
Berkeley: University of California Press, 1967.

TA   *A Tramp Abroad.* New York: Harper and Brothers, 1907.
Vols. 3 and 4 of *The Writings of Mark Twain, Author's
National Edition.* 25 vols. 1907–18.

TS   *The Adventures of Tom Sawyer, Tom Sawyer Abroad, Tom
Sawyer, Detective.* Ed. John C. Gerber, Paul Baender, and
Terry Firkins. Berkeley: University of California Press,
1980.

WIM   *What Is Man? And Other Philosophical Writings.* Ed. Paul
Baender. Berkeley: University of California Press, 1973.

WWD   *Mark Twain's Which Was the Dream? and Other Symbolic
Writings of the Later Years.* Ed. John S. Tuckey. Berkeley:
University of California Press, 1967.

INTRODUCTION

In 1907 Mark Twain appeared to have reached the pinnacle of his career: he was honored before the world with a degree from Oxford. During this year of international acclaim, he gave two speeches which reveal the divergent aspects of Mark Twain that had defined him from the very beginning of his career. The first speech, given in May at the Government House in Annapolis, Maryland, begins surprisingly, "Yes, I have been arrested" (*MTSp* 550). It goes on to record minor criminality, past and present, and then finds its nub in an elaborate account of stealing a watermelon when young, discovering it was not ripe, returning it to its owner, accusing him of perniciously peddling unripe melons, and demanding a replacement, all of which is said to further the moral improvement of the melon owner. Twain ends by saying, "Since that day I have never stolen a water—never stolen a green watermelon" (*MTSp* 554).

Twain's second speech, given in Liverpool, England, at the Lord Mayor's banquet in the town hall, begins graciously, "My Lord Mayor, my Lord Bishop, and gentlemen: I want to thank you" (*MTSp* 577). It immediately wanders off to relate a medley of mishaps, past and present, and then finds its nub in an elaborate expression of gratitude for the reception he has received in England. He gives thanks for the "cordial welcome" given him during the last twenty-six days and offers praise for the ties that bind his country and England: "English blood is in our veins, we have a common language, a common religion, a common system of morals, and great commercial interests to hold us together" (*MTSp* 582). He ends by retelling (and freely reshaping) an anecdote from Dana's *Two Years before the Mast*, the story of how an upstart captain of a small coasting sloop, the *Mary Ann*, hailed a majestic Indiaman—"Ship ahoy! what ship is that, and whence and whither?"—only to be humbled by the reply that suddenly put before him his own insignificance: "*The Begum of*

Bengal, a hundred and twenty-three days out from Canton—homeward bound!" (*MTSp* 582). Gracefully, Twain turns the ships' encounter into metaphors for himself. One hour in twenty-four, he says, he is meek and humble, a mere *Mary Ann*, but during the other twenty-three, "my vain self-satisfaction rides high and I am the stately Indiaman, plowing the great seas under a cloud of sail, and laden with a rich freightage of the kindest words that were ever spoken to a wandering alien, I think; my twenty-six crowded and fortunate days seem multiplied by five, and I am the *Begum of Bengal*, a hundred and twenty-three days out from Canton—homeward bound!" (*MTSp* 582–83).

Both speeches are enlivened by humorous exaggeration, playful self-belittlement, and whimsical turns of speech. The first has a comic surface but a serious undertow, for as he plays with the theft of the watermelon, Twain's language mocks religious instruction, moral reformation, spiritual guidance, and principled action. It toys with the concept of a moral universe and spoofs the idea of an ethical humanity. The second speech also has a comic surface, but in the end there is no disjuncture between surface and substrata, for as Twain expresses his thanks, his language earnestly upholds the religion, morality, and commerce shared by England and America. While its stately close is an acknowledgment of vanity, created in part by a generous reception, it evokes personal splendor, large purpose, age, and the universal longing for home. Both speeches are humorous, but they disclose two very different Mark Twains: one transgressive, the other bounded.

The transgressive Twain is the most familiar and the most studied today. The bounded Twain, on the other hand—the proper Mark Twain—has received little sustained critical attention. To approach the proper Twain we need to consider the improper. There are gradations of impropriety. At the extreme, this Twain is sometimes described as a "cheerful nihilist"—a believer in nothing but the absurdity of life (Hauck 133–66). This Twain is, in the words of one recent critic, "the black hole of American comedy" (Kaufman, *The Comedian as Confidence Man* 187). While such a characterization may be precise in terms of the sheer force Mark Twain has exerted in the galaxy of humor, not to say the universe of literature, it unfairly defines him as a destructive force. But as Leslie

Fiedler has observed, there is often a "positive underside" to Twain's "most negative convictions," a "joyous affirmation beneath his bleakest nihilism" (*Love and Death* xiv).[1]

Most commentaries on Twain do not go so far as to see him as an annihilating force, nor do they limn a Twain who believes in nothing. If Twain's humor was "his kind of primal scream," not one of pain but of "ecstasy," as Louis J. Budd has suggested, then, as he points out, that "transcendent ecstasy" was "directed outward" to become "transactional," "social" ("Ecstasy of Humor" 8). The mainline of Twain criticism has explored this social dimension, but most studies find in the transaction between Twain and his culture chiefly subversion. Here the transgressive Twain not only refuses to conform to conventional standards—he undermines them. Temperate, judicious, and penetrating, Henry Nash Smith's *Mark Twain: The Development of a Writer* (1962) locates the greatness of Twain in a subversive act: the affirmation of vernacular values in opposition to the dominant culture. Focused on the forms of Twain's humor, Cox's brilliant *Mark Twain: The Fate of Humor* (1966) tracks the career of a humorist who subverts traditional values, including at the last the value of the moral sense, through varieties of irreverence. Bruce Michelson's more recent study, the powerful and convincing *Mark Twain on the Loose* (1995), climaxes this interpretative tradition, for he contends that Twain opposes everything in his culture that is (or even just seems to be) "rigid and regulating to mind and identity: any confining orthodoxy, whether political, religious, aesthetic, imaginative, or even biological" (4).

What, then, of the bounded Mark Twain? He lurks around in the margins of most critical commentary, usually as an embarrassment, for insofar as one celebrates Twain on the loose, one inevitably chafes at tetherings—even self-chosen ones. But there is a bounded Twain—the proper Twain who honors conventions, upholds proprieties, believes in commonplaces, and even maintains the order-inducing moralities. (Another way of describing this Twain, one Twain himself was especially sensitive to, is to say that he was a gentleman.)[2] The proper Twain is, as much as the transgressive Twain, a humorist; his confirmations are often comic; his expressions of propriety are often as playful as they are powerful. Far from subverting, however, the proper Twain upholds; instead of contesting, this Twain confirms; rather than questioning, this Twain answers.

Some illuminating recent studies have linked Twain to his culture. Cardwell's biographical study, *The Man Who Was Mark Twain* (1991), explores such things as Twain's obsessive materialism, his misogyny, his fear of and interest in sex, and his persistent racism—all of which were arguably commonplace in his time. Examining chiefly his later works, Gillman's *Dark Twins: Imposture and Identity in Mark Twain's America* (1989) reveals Twain's troubled—and culturally grounded—ideas of racial, sexual, and ontological identity, as well as his insecurity about his role as author. More broadly still, Robinson's *In Bad Faith: The Dynamics of Deception in Mark Twain's America* (1986) argues that, despite his attempts to expose the fraudulence of his culture, Twain himself is caught up in its duplicity and false values. Martha Banta ends a 1991 essay, "The Boys and the Bosses: Twain's Double Take on Work, Play, and the Democratic Ideal," with the playfully self-conscious observation that it is "the purpose of such essays as this to underscore all that is wrong in the world" (511). One might well say the same about the studies of Cardwell, Gillman, and Robinson: they show, perceptively and convincingly, to be sure, a great deal that was wrong with both Twain and America. But Twain was a complex, multidimensional personality, and so there are things right as well as wrong with the Twain who used as passwords the shibboleths of his culture.

Twain lived in—and wrote in response to—a mid to late Victorian culture, one in which "seriousness" was uppermost and "morality" (conventionally defined) was bedrock (Howe 21). Since a humorist inevitably makes fun of the world he or she inhabits, it is not surprising that Twain collided with his culture, transgressing its boundaries. What is surprising is the degree to which he also tried to uphold that culture and locate himself within its precincts. He has been labeled an "outlaw comedian" (Kaufman, "The Comedic Stance" 85), and he has been said to wage "unrestricted war against seriousness" (Michelson 9). However, Twain himself would have rejected such definitions. He worried over his place in Victorian American culture and often tried to align himself with it.

In his richly detailed study, *Our Mark Twain*, Louis J. Budd defines the forces that coalesce to create Twain's public personality: "the shifting triangle formed by the effects of his writings, the personae he tried to create in his other activities, and the image of him haphazardly constructed by the public" (10), and he shrewdly points out that Twain "bursts through any pattern that systematizes him" (23). Without trying to pigeonhole him, then, it is still worth noting that one of the recurrent ways Twain tried to manipulate his image was to promote the sense that he was a figure to reckon with. He engaged in a series of self-definitions that were both strategies for appeasing his culture and honest expressions of how he thought of himself. Astoundingly, but not altogether dishonestly, for instance, he proclaimed in his autobiography that he was a moralist: "I have always preached. . . . If the humor came of its own accord and un-invited I have allowed it a place in my sermon, but I was not writing the sermon for the sake of the humor" (*AMT* 273). However awkwardly this fits Twain's work, it matches nicely the expectations of the genteel culture.

Over and over he insisted that Mark Twain was more than a mere hu-morist. Protestations along this line sound throughout his career. Here are three such moments, which almost span his career, in which Twain aligns himself with the genteel culture by claiming as his own the quali-ties that it cherished. In 1871, during his second lecture tour, he described in a now famous letter the propitious union of opposites appropriate for Mark Twain: "*Any* lecture of mine ought to be a running narrative-plank, with square holes in it, six inches apart, all the length of it & then in my mental shop I ought to have plugs (half marked 'serious' & the other marked 'humorous') to select from & jam into these holes according to the temper of the audience" (*LLMT* 165–66). In 1895, after being Mark Twain for some thirty-three years, he not only continued to insist on a seriousness that would please the most high-minded Victorian but also claimed for himself the kind of tender feeling dear to the Victorian heart: "I maintain that a man can never be a humorist, in thought or in deed, until he can feel the springs of pathos. Indeed, there you have a basis of something material to go upon in trying to comprehend what this impal-pable thing of true humor is. Trust me, he was never yet properly funny who was not capable at times of being very serious. And more: the two are as often as not simultaneous" (Budd, "MT Talks" 11). Finally in 1908, near the end of his career, he also suggested that empathy was funda-

mental to the humorist: "It has always been the way of the world to re-
sent gravity in a humorist. It is a little strange that this should be so, for
an absolutely essential part of any real humorist's native equipment is a
deep seriousness and a rather unusually profound sympathy with the sorrows and sufferings of mankind" (qtd. in Camfield 236). Emphasizing seriousness, pathos, and compassion, Twain aligned himself with conventional nineteenth-century norms for art. He thus defined himself as far
from an "outlaw comedian."

It was difficult for Twain to champion himself, but his creator, Samuel
Clemens, hit on another strategy. (The exact relationship between Clemens and Twain will be taken up a little further along in this introduction.) Clemens found—indeed he seemed to create—a series of confi-
dants who could testify in behalf of the proper Twain. Three such figures
were Mary Mason Fairbanks, Clemens's wife, Livy, and William Dean
Howells. Knowing him well, knowing him as he let himself be known to
them, they thought they saw in him things no one else did. Mrs. Fairbanks, appointed surrogate mother, affirmed, in the rather extravagant
terms typical of her romantic sensibility, the existence of a little-known
"*royal* part" of his nature (*L2* 307, her emphasis). During their courtship,
Livy came to see what she called "the true nobility" of his character
(*L3* 394). With a little help from Clemens himself, she perceived in his
innermost self "a deeper, larger nature" (OLC to Fairbanks, 15 Jan. 1869,
MTP), and she eventually described it to Howells as full of "beauty and
tenderness and 'natural piety'" (*MyMT* 48). Howells also believed in the
finer man a little layer lower in Clemens, defining its essence as "innate
nobleness" (*MyMT* 13). This triumvirate has most often been discussed
as Clemens's self-appointed preceptors—guardians of the conventionally true and proper who schooled Clemens in the art of genteel living
and Mark Twain in the knack of fine writing. But they were more than
his social instructors and literary guides; they became apologists for the
proper Mark Twain.[3]

Fairbanks championed Twain in the pages of her husband's Cleveland
newspaper. Livy, of course, had no public outlet for announcing her sense
of Mark Twain's propriety (and being married to his creator she would
not have spoken publicly of him even if she had), but when Howells

praised him in the *Atlantic* for his "common sense" and his "love of justice" and said that he was "always in earnest," even when he was humorous (*MyMT* 130), Livy was moved to write to him: "We do thank you most heartily for your notice of Mr Clemens book—I have wondered so many times why some one did not take note of certain things in Mr Clemens which seemed to me his strong points, and now you have spoken of them so of course I am particularly pleased" (*MTHL* 1:298). The idea that Mark Twain was misperceived prompted Susy to undertake her biography of "papa," and her sense of his seriousness and tenderness became the approved family view. (It coexisted, as Hamlin Hill has demonstrated [*God's Fool*], with other, less positive impressions.) Revealing how inseparable Clemens was from Twain, even for his daughter, Susy announces early in her biography, "It trobles [*sic*] me to have so few people know papa, I mean realy [*sic*] know him, they think of Mark Twain as a humorist joking at every thing" (*Papa* 106). What she wants people to see instead is "something of his kind sympathetic nature" (*Papa* 107). She also wants to make clear his seriousness: "Papa can make exceedingly bright jokes, and he enjoys funny things, and when he is with people he jokes and laughs a great deal, but still he is more interested in earnest books and earnest subjects to talk upon, than in humorous ones (*Papa* 207). Twain quoted these statements with approval in his autobiographical dictations, and added, "Fifteen years were to pass before any other critic—except Mr. Howells, I think—was to re-utter that daring opinion and print it" (*MTOA* 169). Howells had, often at the instigation of Clemens himself, been making the case for Mark Twain's seriousness, for his moral concern and philosophical bent, since he first reviewed *The Innocents Abroad* in 1869. Unlike Twain's other apologists, Howells was at the center of nineteenth-century literary discourse in America. In reviews, general evaluations, and finally in his own small book, *My Mark Twain*, he insisted that to know Twain well, to know something beyond "his rebellious spirit," was to know that he was "the most serious, the most humane, the most conscientious of men" (*MyMT* 34).

Although he entitled his book *My Mark Twain*, Howells always thought of him as "Clemens." Howells's problem is still with us. Distinguishing Clemens from Twain is nearly as impossible for the critic today as it was for Clemens himself. A comic mask, a humorous public personality, a literary identity, Mark Twain is perhaps best understood as the creative spirit—genius in its root sense—of Sam Clemens. Once named, Mark Twain became inseparable from Clemens, even for Clemens himself. He signed letters alternately "Sam" or "Mark," from time to time put himself down as "Sam Mark," canceling one or the other, and sometimes he signed himself as "S. L. Clemens" with "Mark Twain" written across the "S. L. Clemens" as if in cancellation or duplication.[4] Mark Twain is finally inextricable from Sam Clemens because he manifests himself not only in the literary works but also in the lived life; he creates the person as well as the persona in the text. Insofar as Clemens, histrionic to the core as Howells observed (*MyMT* 52), brought himself into existence day by day, week by week, year by year, not only in his texts but also out of them, the source of that unending creation was Mark Twain. (Who else walked around his dinner table, talking dramatically and gesturing for emphasis with his napkin?) In his fine study of American authors and the literary marketplace, R. Jackson Wilson has defined the authorial presence in a text as a "figure of speech," and he observes that such figures occupy "a dual ground, a footing both in the minds of the people who held them and in the texts in which they are manifested" (9). To Wilson's double landscape one should add a third terrain: the consciousness of the authoring writer. For authors imagine themselves to themselves—and articulate that vision in various ways. However difficult to triangulate, this tripartite configuration seems closest to what confronts us as we look at—and for—Mark Twain. In examining Mark Twain, then, this study will peer not only into the texts but also into the preconceptions of the writer's audience and into the writer's own self-conceiving. And while an effort will be made to distinguish Clemens from Twain—it was, after all, Clemens who married Livy—this study hopes to illuminate Twain even when it scrutinizes Clemens (surely it was the self-creating Twain who beguiled and finally won Livy through "Sam Clemens's" love letters).

Tricky as it is to negotiate the Clemens-Twain symbiosis, there is a further problem: the definition of the Twain persona itself. Many studies—and this is perhaps wise as well as expedient—do not define Mark Twain but simply let the persona subsume Clemens and Clemens inform the persona. Everett Emerson has, however, attempted to pin down the persona:

> Mark Twain: a personage palpably present in his words, an irreverent skeptic, irrepressible, humorous, unpretentious but self-assured, and often victimized, usually by his own illusions. Sometimes there are two different Mark Twains, a "before" version and an "after." Then one meets either a naive and youthful innocent, one who is not very bright, easily misled but well-meaning, *or* an experienced, confident, humorous, perhaps impudent veteran, who knows the world, especially its underside, thoroughly. . . .
>
> He also developed . . . another kind of voice, that of a storyteller, usually an older man and often a Westerner, who has had a long career as a miner, a sea captain, a riverboat man. This narrator speaks in the vernacular and is distinctly antigenteel. He is usually an innocent, or rather pretends to be, and he tells tall tales, but with a straight face. (Emerson, *Authentic MT* x)

This description differs from most only in its thoroughness and careful precision. It reflects both the common emphasis on Twain's vernacular and the equally familiar sense of his subversive humor. It really defines the transgressive Twain: a voice that is skeptical, comic, caustic, vernacular, and antigenteel. Missing here, as in most studies, is the bounded Twain—the proper Twain of conventionality, respectability, and propriety. To insist on the proper Twain is not to deny the transgressive; it is only to add to it, to enlarge the persona.[5] In one sense, the proper Twain is the complete Twain—as in the phrase (perhaps more English than American) "a proper scoundrel" or "a proper statesman."

Since both the transgressive and the proper Twain are humorists, it is worth pausing for a moment over humor theory. Theories of humor's origins necessarily remain speculative, but there is a general belief that the psychogenesis of humor lies in repression. Freud first expounded this notion, suggesting that the humorist became funny by momentarily breaking through repressions to release anarchic impulses in violation of both internal constraint and external social taboo (the former having been in the first place created by the latter). The energy released in this process is discharged as laughter (*Jokes and Their Relation to the Unconscious*). In her recent treatment of Lacan, Susan Purdie has identified a similar dynamic. She argues that humor's seemingly subversive action is a "*marked* transgression" of the "Symbolic Law" that controls identity formation, a breach which affirms in its marking that which it denies (5, her italics). In both these theoretical accounts humor arises from—and depends on—the presence within the humorist of the conventional and of the urge to reject it. The humorist is thus simultaneously an upholder of social norms and a violator of them. Indeed, from a slightly different angle, Frank Stringfellow Jr. has argued that the humorist is more upholder than violator. He sees one particular type of the humorist, the ironist, as "unconsciously expressing his identification with authority at the very moment when he believes himself to be attacking it" (150).

Certainly the location of humor in a core of repression is consistent with what we know of Clemens's early life. He was brought up in the constraining, oppressive faith of a frontier Presbyterianism, and he was further subjected to rigorous social codes arising from his parents', especially his father's, pretensions to aristocracy. Both his worldview and his sense of social behavior were severely determined. But he was restive within these confinements. Insofar as one can see it, his psychic makeup fits the theoretical paradigms of the humorist. But, of course, these paradigms define not just the humorist but all human identity. According to psychoanalysis, every person is divided within between voices of authority and cries of rebellion. What is missing from these otherwise compelling accounts of humor is any explanation of why one person becomes a humorist when so many others don't. (To the degree that we all employ humor at one time or another, we are, in fact, minihumorists acting out of the same psychic machinery.) Here humor theory faces what is still the mystery of individual identity—or perhaps, in the case of the artist, genius.

If we turn from theories of the psychogenesis of humor to speculative formulations of its characteristic effects and consequent social functions, we find a similar division of conjecture over humor as a subversion of the status quo and as a confirmation of it. Perhaps the most striking example of this lies in Bakhtin's interpretation of carnivalesque humor, which, on the one hand, is seen as a mockery of the existing order and, on the other, as a reinscription of the very systems being mocked (*Rabelais and His World*). If such humor turns the world upside down, it may do so only to keep it right side up. Those studies of the distinctly American veins of humor that delineate comic types and see in their aggressive deployment forms of regional, social, or political conflict also leave us with a more or less unaligned humorist. For these traditions themselves often contain contrary positions. To cite a single yet telling example (one most relevant to Mark Twain), while the typical southwestern humorist was a political conservative inclined to disapprove of the lower classes, his interest in the doings of unwashed backwoods bumpkins sometimes becomes a tacit endorsement of them.[6] At the other extreme from studies of specifically American humor are the broad philosophical assessments that treat humor as a universal phenomenon, and these too, as Marcel Gutwirth has shown (*Laughing Matter* 1–28), often split into such warring camps as the irrationalists who disrupt order and the rationalists who maintain it, thereby revealing that humor can serve either function (and perhaps both at once).

Despite illuminating efforts to locate the origins of humor and to define the alignment of the humorist, what studies of humor seem to reveal, especially when they are taken together, is that there is no a priori normative locale for the humorist. Given that the humorist is created by the existence within the self of both the conventional and the unruly (the superego and the instinctual challenges to it), it is not accurate to see the humorist as a de facto subversive. Humor arises precisely from the clash between the orthodox and the rebellious. Whether its upshot, its achieved effect in verbal or written form, is conventional or unconventional depends upon the "texts" thus created. To turn again to Mark Twain, he is a humorist because he is within himself both a conventional person, honoring the voices of authority, and a rebel, trying to outshout them. It is up to the receivers of his humor to decide which side of the conflict is finally heard in the works themselves.

Contrary to most readings, this study attempts to show how much— and in what ways—Twain was on the side of orthodoxy. It also aims to reveal how thoroughly he was the product of his culture. To do this, it will track the manifestations of the conventional in the major texts of the Twain canon. The term *conventional* is, of course, hardly fashionable in contemporary critical commentary, but what comes into view via the term certainly is. For what emerges is "ideology": the set of discourses, values, beliefs, and representations generally current in a society by which most individuals define not only accepted standards and customs but also their collective sense of reality (see Eagleton, *Criticism and Ideology*, esp. chap. 2). To see the proper Mark Twain is to discover in his work his culture's dominant ideology. It is to see that his humor often serves to reinforce prevailing attitudes, commonplace ideas, and traditional values.

Chapter 1 of this study first examines Clemens's battle with and for respectability in the West, then looks at his shaping of a conventional persona, The Moralist of the Main, and finally considers *Roughing It* as a rewriting of his actual western past into a more reputable one. In short, it looks at the formation and early confirmation of the proper Mark Twain. Chapter 2 explores *The Innocents Abroad* and *A Tramp Abroad*, companion texts of a sort, finding in the first expressions of Twain's conventional Victorianism, especially his cultural imperialism, and in the second an equally conventional, though for a travel book a highly paradoxical, celebration of the domestic. Chapter 3 turns directly to Clemens's life, reviewing his famous courtship, for that episode is pivotal in the creation of the proper Mark Twain. In the courtship, Twain fashions an image of Olivia and, more importantly, creates Sam Clemens as an orthodox gentleman in a series of literary performances.

Chapter 4 looks at two interlinked texts, "Old Times on the Mississippi" and *Life on the Mississippi*. In the first, the Wild Humorist of the Pacific Slope writes with a conventionality of outlook and style designed to charm the tamest Bostonians; in the second, Twain defines himself as an orthodox writer—a gentleman with a highly conventional style and humor. Chapters 5 and 6 center on Twain's three major boy-books, examining them in the light of the nineteenth century's dominant literary mode: sentimentalism. Chapter 5 argues that Twain employs this mode in both *Tom Sawyer* and *The Prince and the Pauper* to assert the values traditionally celebrated in sentimental fiction but that, while he affirms these values, he is uneasy about the aesthetic by which he represents them. Chapter 6 continues the exploration of Twain's sentimentality, arguing that *Huckleberry Finn* combines sentimentality with humor to overcome the aesthetic dilemma Twain faced in *Tom Sawyer*. Together, humor and sentimentality create the greatness of this novel and generate its conventional moral cast.

Chapter 7 first defines the later Twain as a traditional Victorian Sage, and then looks at the ways in which this Sagely Twain propounds familiar ideas, from *A Connecticut Yankee* on through *Pudd'nhead Wilson* to the final Mysterious Stranger manuscripts. Chapter 8 unveils Twain as personage in *Following the Equator*, flaunting the respectability achieved in— and by—his writings, and then looks at the published portions of his autobiography, finding in this final major text definitive expressions of Mark Twain's conventionality. The brief coda considers two episodes, one literary, the other a public performance, in which Clemens himself seems to certify the proper Mark Twain. Running through these chapters are several important aesthetic issues: the tension between standard and vernacular diction; the conflict between realism and melodrama; the opposition between humor and sentimentality; and the difference between representation or enactment and didactic presentation. For it is through the negotiation of these contraries that Mark Twain expresses himself— and becomes visible to us—in his art.

When Clemens and his confederates were unable to get the public to see Mark Twain as more than a mere humorist, he became restive with his own persona. As early as 1871, he wrote to his brother Orion: "I lay awake all last night aggravating myself with this prospect of seeing my hated nom de plume (for I do loathe the very sight of it) in print *again* every month" (*MTLP* 57).[7] Susan Gillman has suggested that by 1889 he even wanted "to separate himself from the bulk of his writing" in order to rescue himself from "the taint of humor" (*Dark Twins* 35). Similarly, Hamlin Hill maintains that in his final decade Twain "was struggling desperately to cast off the public image of himself" (*God's Fool* xxiv). Such urgencies reveal how deeply Clemens wanted to be seen as more than the fooling humorist who had caught—and held—the public's eye. What he wanted most, however, as the campaign he waged through Howells suggests, was not to repudiate Mark Twain but to redefine him. He wanted to call attention to the multiple dimensions of his humorous persona, to alert his audience to the respectability and conventionality within Mark Twain.

Who was that audience? Twain himself worried around the question, and his answers varied at different moments throughout his career. By choosing subscription publishing, on the one hand, he clearly sought a broad readership among the middle and lower classes; by appearing in such journals as the *Atlantic Monthly*, on the other hand, he reached for readers among the financial and cultural elite. Well into his career, about 1890, he wrote to the English critic and editor Andrew Lang about the nature and direction of his literary work. Although it is long, the letter is worth considering in some detail, for it reveals largely overlooked aspects of his self-conception as a writer. Twain writes to prompt a defense of his work from Lang—"Help me, Mr. Lang; no voice can reach further than yours in a case of this kind, or carry greater weight of authority" (*CH* 336)—thus hoping to achieve through Lang the kind of careful appreciation he more often provoked from Howells. What he wants in this case is to have his work judged by appropriate critical standards, standards that distinguish between work "written for the Head"—and therefore to be measured by "the cultivated-class standard" or "the culture-standard"—and that written "for the Belly and the Members," which requires other terms of assessment. He insists that he has addressed himself to the groundlings without regard for the more privileged (and his letter is most often read for its egalitarian commitments):

> Indeed I have been misjudged, from the very first. I have never tried in even one single little instance, to help cultivate the cultivated classes. I was not equipped for it, either by native gifts or training. And I never had any ambition in that direction, but always hunted for bigger game—the masses. I have seldom deliberately tried to instruct them, but have done my best to entertain them. To simply amuse them would have satisfied my dearest ambition at any time; for they could get instruction elsewhere, and I had two chances to help to the teacher's one: for amusement is a good preparation for study and a good healer of fatigue after it. (*CH* 334–36)

In his description of his own work as hunting for bigger game, he turns writing into a necessary, manly activity quite at odds with traditional nineteenth-century idealizations of literature. His metaphor tacitly acknowledges the economic purpose of his own writing: he bags his game for his livelihood. Oddly, after this figuring of literary work as killing and feeding, he turns to the genteel notion of literature as education, not to disavow that his work may perform that function but to claim, modestly, peripheral help in the task of such instruction: his work prepares one for study and rests one after it. In such a repositioning Twain reveals that he both resists the conventional notion of literature as a way of learning, of cultivating oneself, and subscribes to it.

Earlier in this letter, he emphatically endorses the ideal of literature as a way to cultural improvement:

> It is not that little minority [the "thin top crust of humanity—the culti-vated"] who are already saved that are best worth lifting at, I should think, but the mighty mass of the uncultivated who are underneath. That mass will never see the Old Masters—that sight is for the few; but the chromo maker can lift them one step upward toward appreciation of art; they can-not have the opera, but the hurdy-gurdy and the singing class lift them a little way toward that far height; they will never know Homer, but the pass-ing rhymester of their day leaves them higher than he found them; they may never even hear of the Latin classics, but they will strike step with Kipling's drum-beat, and they will march; for all Jonathan Edward's help they would die in their slums, but the Salvation Army will beguile some of them up to pure air and a cleaner life; they know no sculpture, the Venus is not even a name to them, but they are a grade higher in the scale of civiliza-tion by the ministrations of the plaster-cast than they were before it took its place upon their mantel and made it beautiful to their unexacting eyes. (*CH* 335–36)

The passage is an extravagant defense of the efficacy of popular art forms. Its insistence bespeaks strong conviction. What is striking, however, is that Twain couches his defense in precisely the terms employed by the genteel. He espouses the notion that art of all kinds functions to advance its devotee—or consumer—upward in a hierarchical scale of civilization. Apparently believing that this is the appropriate function of art, he takes unmistakable pride in those, like Mark Twain, who perform it for the lower classes.

What the letter finally discloses is not that Mark Twain wrote for the masses, The Belly and the Members (which, of course, he did), but that he imagines his audience as one made up of social orders distinctly be-neath him. (As he depicts "the mighty mass of the uncultivated," he evokes not the middle class, that mixed group of men and women newly risen in the economy, a group that included Sam Clemens, but distinctly lower levels of the social order.) The letter thus suggests a fundamental dynamic of Mark Twain's writing: he is empowered by his sense of superiority. The most important revelation, however, is that he conceives of literature (implicitly including his own) as contributing to the improvement of those who read it, as enabling them to advance—in appropriate ways—within the traditional culture. Such a conception is far from the idea and the effect of the transgressive Twain, but it is consistent with, indeed a clear expression of, the proper Mark Twain.

CHAPTER ONE

Moralist of the Main

Sam Clemens's time in the West, 1861–66, was probably the most erratic period in his unsettled early life. It was also one of the most formative. Fleeing the Civil War by lighting out for the Nevada Territory, he entered a world in the making, and in it, by default, chance, and design, he made himself. He discovered his vocation as a writer and his talent as a lecturer. He shaped a personal identity, facets of which were to remain with him throughout his life. And, of course, he found—he created—Mark Twain, his creative persona. His self-fashioning was, however, a hit-and-miss enterprise, for he was often as unsteady as the tumbleweed. He shifted jobs, moved homesites, changed outlook, vacillated in confidence, and suffered mood swings from jubilation to despondency. Complicating the contraries of his life and temperament, he began to live and write with an eye on those who had their eyes on him; he began, that is, a process of mythologizing himself, even though the self to be mythologized was only nascent.[1] Yet for all of its vagary, Clemens's life in the West has a discernible drift to it, and in the early Mark Twain we can see at least the shadowy outline of the figure that would become proper Mark Twain.

The western world Clemens entered was itself remarkably fluid. From the physical state of its camps and towns to its mixed economies to its social order, the West was in flux. This instability offered opportunities, but also posed problems. The economic, social, political, and cultural lines along which one usually lived must often have seemed in the Nevada Territory to have been drawn in sand. The institutions and values of the East were replicated in the West, and those who believed in them often upheld them with a stridency that suggests desperation. But there were also new systems, new values, that vied with the old. Clemens experienced this creative collision, sometimes to his dismay, often to his delight.

Here is a teasing letter home to his mother and sister (with a word about his nephew) written after Clemens had been in the territory for an eye-opening five months: "Pa wouldn't allow us to fight, and next month Orion will be Governor, in the Governor's absence, and then he'll be sorry that his education was so much neglected. Now, you should never despise good advice, you know, and that is what I am giving you when I warn you to teach Sammy to fight, with the same care that you teach him to pray" (*L1* 160). Although he is joking, his play registers a key difference between East and West: the rule of law versus the rule of physical force. Neither was absolute in either region, and Clemens had certainly known violence growing up in Hannibal (Wecter, Brashear, Blair, *MT&HF*). But in the territory, force more often held sway. Significantly, to make the point that Orion is unfit for office in the West by virtue of his upbringing, he evokes the figure of their father, John Marshall Clemens, the lawyer and sometime justice of the peace, known as Judge Clemens. In the town of Hannibal—and in his own home—Judge Clemens was an adjudicator of law and a keeper of the peace. He emerges casually here, but he loomed for his son Sam almost as the eponym of civilization itself, and, as I shall suggest, his father's memory haunted Clemens during his time in the West.

Adjusting to the frontier, Clemens was slow to commit himself to any particular line of work. During his first year in the territory he was, in somewhat slow sequence, Orion's assistant, a noticeable loafer, a grudging, then frenetic prospector, and finally a reporter for the Virginia City *Territorial Enterprise*. It was only after five months of writing for the *Enterprise* that he discovered himself as Mark Twain. Indeed, it was not until 1865, four years after he first arrived in the West, three years after he became a full-time newspaperman, that he would somewhat stagily announce that he had had a "'call' to literature, of a low order—*i.e.* humorous" (*L1* 322). Clemens's work as a reporter put him in intimate contact with the full spectrum of western society, as Twain later explained in his "Roughing It" lecture:

A nice, gentlemanly reporter—I make no references—is well treated by everybody. Just think of the wide range of his acquaintanceship, his experience of life and society. No other occupation brings a man into such familiar sociable relations with all grades and classes of people. The last thing at night—midnight—he goes browsing around after items among police and jailbirds, in the lockup, questioning the prisoners, and making pleasant and lasting friendship with some of the worst people on earth. And the very next evening he gets himself up regardless of expense, puts on all the good clothes his friends have got—goes and takes dinner with the Governor, or the Commander in Chief of the District, the United States Senator, and some more of the upper crust of society. (*MTSpk* 60)

Clemens was well positioned to savor such extremes. He had been bred with an acute sense of social class—his father conducting himself as one of the F.F.V.s, his mother imagining herself a descendant of English royal blood, his childhood community dividing itself along social lines defined by race as well as wealth, lineage, and cultural literacy. But his family's financial misfortunes—John Marshall Clemens had, in Robert Penn Warren's haunting phrase, gone "failing westward"—left Clemens without the means to support the pretensions instilled in him.[2] And this, together with his own early knockabout life as itinerant typesetter and occasional writer, left him déclassé. Faced with the openness of the West, he had two divergent responses: he turned bohemian, defying the strictures of class respectability, and he played the gentleman, honoring the standards of proper society.

In biography and scholarship, the bohemian Sam Clemens is by far the most familiar. (Mack, Fatout, Benson, and Lennon all track this beguiling figure.) He makes exciting copy today, just as he made local news during his actual time in the West. Loafer, drinker, rowdy; frequenter of saloons, theaters, and, in all likelihood, brothels; braggart, vilifier, and hoaxer; he lived loose and fast, both in Nevada and later on the California coast. While his late hours, heavy drinking, flamboyant antics, and verbal as well as literary fisticuffs are accepted lines in the standard portrait of Clemens as a bohemian, his sexual outlook at the time is unclear. Some recent scholarship has emphasized the importance of his male friendships without being able to fix exactly their nature—asexual, homoerotic, homosexual, or homosocial (Hoffman, "Mark Twain and Homosexuality"). What should, I think, be clear, however, is that in his bohemian living Clemens indulged a sexual consciousness (of whatever sort—and with whatever consummations) that was itself in conflict with the circumspection of strict Victorian mores.[3] In all his wayward living, he cultivated a kind of freedom, laying the groundwork for his eventual image as nonconforming rebel humorist. Yet cavorting with the rowdy was by no means the whole of his pastimes. Nostalgically recalling his western days, in later years he paid tribute to "the unforgotten and unforgettable": "Goodman, McCarthy, Gillis, Curry, Baldwin, Winters, Howard, Nye, Stewart; Neely Johnson, Hal Clayton, North, Root—and my brother, upon whom be peace!" (*MTL* 2:773). Revealingly, with the single exception of Steve Gillis, the compositor for the *Enterprise*, this list is a roll call of the most prominent citizens of Nevada. Sam Clemens hobnobbed with the elite. If he drifted outward toward the margins of society one day, he drove inward toward its center the next. In his fine study of pioneer response to western experience, Stephen Fender has argued that Clemens "lost his cultural bearings" in the West (8). Clemens did express conflicting attitudes and cultivate opposing lifestyles, but he understood precisely the world he first inhabited, then reported on, and finally fictionalized. His difficulty was a problem not of discernment or comprehension but of allegiance: he was uncertain whether he wanted to be a reliable citizen or a dissolute larker.

So was Mark Twain. Significantly, the first extant piece actually signed "Mark Twain," the now famous "Letter from Carson City" (*ET&S1* 194–98), is centered on the comedy of social ins and outs. In the letter Twain reports on a soiree at the governor's house, to which he says he is invited, alternately mocking the evening's pastimes—dancing quadrilles, singing sentimental songs, playing gracefully at the piano—and praising them as courtly graces in contrast to the behavior of the crude, party-crashing Unreliable, his caricature of Clement T. Rice, a fellow journalist and good friend. Mark Twain has it both ways: he spoofs the genteel at the same time he makes fun of the vulgar. Exaggerating his own traits for comic effect, he depicts himself as both refined and crude. Thus while he shows himself to be the equal, at least in style and vanity, of the social dandy Horace Smith, Esq. (who shatters a mirror by gazing into it), he also displays himself as a match in excessive drinking for the vulgar Unreliable (he empties the punch bowl). The sketch adumbrates a refined social world and defines the roughs who are out of place in it. Twain's account makes him superior to both, aligned with neither.

Such double-dealing is as characteristic of the early Twain's writings as it was of Sam Clemens's actual living. While the source of his ambivalence must remain conjectural, I want to suggest that he was emotionally in the throes of a belated warfare with his dead father, or more accurately, with the standards of respectability and strictures of authority internalized under the influence of that father. Although Clemens seldom mentions his father directly in his letters or his writings, by a kind of metonymy John Marshall Clemens looms in his consciousness in the infamous Tennessee lands. Purchased by his father to promote prosperity, the property became for his son the "heavy curse of prospective wealth" (*L1* 79 n. 11). He observed ironically that although his father had left "a sumptuous legacy of pride in his fine Virginia stock and its national distinction," he soon discovered that he could "not live on that alone" (*RI* 271). His father's notion had been that, in time, as the land accrued in value, the family could sell it and live on the profit. However, both the increase in value and the prospect of sale had proved to be chimeras—only the taxes were real. While he was in the West, Clemens tried repeatedly to rid himself of this paternal "curse" by selling even at a loss, only to be thwarted again and again by Orion. Significantly, whenever he writes of the Tennessee lands, Clemens becomes angry and turns himself into an object of pity. Most often he imagines that he is deeply impoverished and severely suffering. Complaining to his brother about the lands, for instance, he depicts himself as a "beggar" struggling in an "accursed homeless desert" (*L1* 326) and as an exile in "poverty" desperately "battling for bread" (*L1* 341–42). There is more psychological disclosure than financial truth in these self-dramatizations. They reveal not his actual circumstance but his resentment toward his father.

Throughout his life Clemens recalled his father with respect and barely controlled bitterness. Judge Clemens was apparently an upright man of high principle, rigid discipline, impeccable honor, and irascible temper who deported himself as a southern gentleman.[4] To his son he was also a cold, intimidating man. Though few, Clemens's recorded recollections of his father are remarkably consistent. Here are four that range in time from 1870 to 1906:

> He was a stern, unsmiling man, and hated all forms of precocity. ("Wit-Inspirations of the 'Two-Year-Olds'"; rpt. *CG* 55)
>
> My father was a refined and kindly gentleman, very grave, rather austere, of rigid probity, a sternly just and upright man. (*FE* 351)
>
> Stern, unsmiling, never demonstrated affection for wife or child. . . . Silent, austere, of perfect probity and high principle; ungentle of manner toward his children, but always a gentleman in his phrasing. ("Villagers," *AI* 104)
>
> He was a proud man, a silent, austere man. (*AMT* 23)

Clemens acknowledges his father's moral rectitude at the same time he links it to an appalling emotional reserve. Stern, austere, rigid—these are the remembered, defining traits. They are, of course, antithetical to the character Clemens assumed in the West when he chose to live in his bohemian mode as a warmhearted, warm-blooded, luxury-loving, easy-going good fellow. And in contrast to the "unsmiling" father who was "always a gentleman in his phrasing," Clemens not only smiled at the world through Mark Twain but also articulated his experience of it in dialects that were anything but gentlemanly. His conduct and writing in the West seem to constitute a rebellion against all that his father represented as it was embodied in the socioeconomic power structure of the region. But, of course, the only way to finally defeat a father, at least according to both Freud and Lacan, is to become him.

Anger at the father may account for the violent hostility Clemens sometimes levels at authorities in the West. To be sure, the style of much western journalism was itself a harsh one that often employed ridicule and invective, but Mark Twain's version of this mode is often unaccountably savage. His disgust and outrage seem at times to exceed their occasion. Here, for instance, a description of the San Francisco police court moves from factual measurements to virulent—unprovoked—condemnations not only of the criminals and their friends but also of the court officials themselves:

> The room is about 24 × 40 feet in size, I suppose, and is blocked in on all sides by massive brick walls; it has three or four doors, but they are never

opened—and if they were they only open into airless courts and closets anyhow; it has but one window, and now that is blocked up. . . . There is not a solitary air-hole as big as your nostril about the whole place. Very well; down two sides of the room, drunken filthy loafers, thieves, prostitutes, China chicken-stealers, witnesses, and slimy guttersnipes who come to see, and belch and issue deadly smells, are banked and packed, four ranks deep—a solid mass of rotting, steaming corruption. In the centre of the room are Dan Murphy, Zabriskie, the Citizen Sam Platt, Prosecuting Attorney Louderback, and other lawyers, either of whom would do for a censer to swing before the high altar of hell. (*CofC* 155)

Anger at his father, turned against the self by guilt, may also explain Clemens's otherwise puzzling flirtation with suicide early in 1866, after the success of his Jumping Frog tale when his prospects were improving.[5] At about the time of his threatened self-destruction Mark Twain wrote a "Letter from Sacramento" in which he dramatizes a disagreement between a hotel keeper and himself as a conflict between a father and son. In the sketch, after he has overslept, dreaming of being "a happy, careless schoolboy again," Twain blames his landlord, and the two exchange sarcasm and insult as Twain tries to "out 'sass'" the "old man," but the landlord defeats the guest he insists upon calling "my son" by ironically suggesting his indolence, an accusation that resonates gently with Clemens's bohemian life (*Gold Miners & Guttersnipes* 197–98). The sketch is light, but it may betray some of the emotional conflicts at work in Clemens. An internal strife with all that his father represented may also account for a curious piece Clemens published in the *Call* a few months after he arrived in San Francisco. Reporting on the Mechanics' Fair, he fixes upon a "voluminous and very musty old book" on display there; from it he cites just one passage, that describing the trial of Charles I: "The chapter which gives the names of the members of the High Commission before which Charles I. was tried and condemned to death, is racy with comments upon the bad character, the ignominious pursuits, and the former social obscurity of those gentlemen" (*CofC* 112). Clemens believed that Gregory Clement (he habitually misnamed him Geoffrey), a member of that High Commission, was his ancestor, and he proudly identified with him throughout his life.[6] Given his own loose living, he must have enjoyed reading of his presumed forebear's "bad character,"

"ignominious pursuits," and "social obscurity." And, of course, his assumed ancestor's regicide is a classic ritual whose implications were probably not lost on Clemens: it not only dethroned lawful authority and subverted the social order but also enacted a symbolic slaying of the father.

In May 1864 Clemens himself upset the social order of Carson City
in what has been called "the most damaging incident" of his "western
career" (Pettit 30). He managed to offend simultaneously the ladies of
Carson City—along with their husbands—and the staff of the Gold Hill
Union, a rival newspaper; in the process he embarrassed himself publicly
and provoked at least two challenges to a duel. His motives remain
obscure (Clemens himself called part of his behavior a "drunken jest"
[*L1* 287]), but his emotional condition at the time was shaky at best. Even
his authorized biographer Paine, given to protection and adulation, notes
that in the Nevada Territory Clemens was "high-strung and neurotic,"
increasingly restive and contentious (*MTB* 1:238).

In brief, what transpired was this.[7] While the editor of the *Enterprise*,
Joseph Goodman, was on holiday in California, Mark Twain assumed
the editorship of the paper. In an editorial he proceeded to accuse the
ladies of Carson of diverting funds raised at a ball from the U.S. Sanitary
Commission to a secret Miscegenation Society, and at the same time he
charged the employees of the *Union* with defaulting on their pledges to
the Sanitary Fund. Both parties demanded retractions. Twain tried to
placate the ladies privately though Orion's wife, Mollie, and through a
friend, Mrs. W. K. Cutler. When these efforts failed, he printed an apology to the women without signing his name. However, when the *Union*
staff defended themselves in strong terms, he played the role of the fiery
southern gentleman: he fired off a series of notes demanding satisfaction
on the field of honor. He was in a paradoxical position, however. His joke
on the ladies was the jest of a vulgarian; his response to the *Union* was the
thrust and parry of an offended man of honor. But not even Mark Twain
could so outrageously have it both ways on such public issues: he could
not acknowledge insults to very proper ladies at the same time he claimed
"the satisfaction due to a gentleman" (*L1* 292).

He decamped, catching the stage off the Comstock to San Francisco.
Far from being uncertain of the proprieties of the West, he understood

them perfectly; he understood that for once playing both rascal and respectable citizen had put him in an untenable position.

After he left the West, he retold the tale of his departure from Nevada three times: as a part of his "Roughing It" lecture given in 1871–72 (an abbreviated version of which appeared in the book *Roughing It*); as a story, "How I Escaped Being Killed in a Duel," published in 1873; and as an incident of note in his autobiography recorded in 1906. In not one of these retellings did he so much as suggest his violation of social decorum; he repressed his racial and sexual joke on the ladies. (Of course, by the time he wrote all three versions, he had resolved his conflict between bohemianism and respectability in favor of the latter.) In all three accounts he increases the fictional drama by moving himself onto the field of combat—in reality, he never set foot on the field of honor—and in all three, bloodshed is averted when he dupes his rival into thinking that he is a crack shot when in fact, or at least in his fictive version of it, he literally cannot hit the side of a barn door. Twain uses fancy and humor to conceal and dispel the confusion, aggression, and embarrassment of his actual conduct, inventing new events and exaggerating the real ones until they are ludicrous. In his final revisioning of the aborted duel, however, he gives it a more serious—and more revealing—cast.

In the autobiographical dictations he creates a context that seems to disclose long-hidden feelings about his fiasco. In this last retelling he approaches the tale circuitously. As a kind of prefiguration of how he is expected to act, he relates the history of an earlier duel between the rival editors, Goodman of the *Enterprise* and Thomas Fitch of the *Union*. By a series of associations he moves from Goodman to his second, a major called Graves, then to the zealot of manifest destiny, William Walker, under whom the major served, and finally to Angus Gillis, another soldier under Walker and the father of Sam Clemens's own second, Steve. All are seriously heralded as men of great courage—"brave to the very utmost limit of that word" (*AMT* 113). Twain venerates not only Walker, who led filibusters first into Sonora and then into Nicaragua where he reestablished slavery, but also every man who campaigned with him.[8] He even attributes to the major a "mysterious quality" in the "eye" that signifies commanding courage and empowers its possessor to quell opposition (*AMT* 114). Although a steely-eyed brave man is a cliché, Twain is wholly serious, citing his friend Bob Howland, the onetime marshal of Aurora, as another man who possessed the "mysterious" eye (*AMT* 114).[9] In all this, Twain betrays a genuine admiration of conventional masculine bravery that is notably absent from the other two accounts of the duel. The elevation of such conventional bravery places his own conduct in an ironic light, for, of course, he evades his duel through a ruse and decamps rather than carry out his own campaign.

The emotional and psychological bearing of Twain's digression is further revealed by his treatment of the elder Gillis. (After escaping from his own duel, Clemens lodged for a time in the Gillis home in San Francisco.) Had he reminisced of Steve, his own second, his remarks would have been natural enough. But he focuses instead on the father, creating this emotion-charged tableau: "The father made the campaign under Walker, and with him one son. They were in the memorable Plaza fight and stood it out to the last against overwhelming odds, as did also all of the Walker men. The son was killed at the father's side. The father received a bullet through the eye" (*AMT* 113). Courage thus becomes in Twain's final account a matter of a son emulating his father. Looming behind the array of valorous men—except for Goodman, all proud southerners—and specifically embodied in the elder Gillis (who served, as Clemens's landlord, *in loco parentis*) is no doubt the real father, John Marshall Clemens.

Twain created two extended fictional portraits of his father, first as Judge Griswold in the unpublished novel "Simon Wheeler, Detective" (whose earliest material may have been written in the Nevada Territory—see *S&B* 205–6), and then later as Judge Driscoll in *Pudd'nhead Wilson*. Both of these southern gentlemen, pillars of their communities, uphold the duel and enjoin it upon surrogate sons. Indeed, Judge Driscoll not only denounces the nephew he has raised as his son (or rather, the person he thinks is his nephew) for refusing to challenge someone who has insulted him but actually issues the challenge himself and exchanges shots on the field of honor. In drawing these versions of his father, Twain seems to have felt that Clemens had betrayed some part of his heritage when he evaded his duel.

But that is only half of his feeling. If to some degree he is guilty over failing to fulfill the manly role assigned by fathers—southern fathers—to sons, to risk death with equanimity, he is also angry and resentful about the role itself. He is, in fact, rebellious. In both fictions he mocks the judges who believe in the *code duello* as arrogant, pretentious fools who are deceived by an antiquated code into violating their own humanity. In the later autobiography when he describes the stand of the Gillis father and son, he mentions that the father "received a bullet through the eye," and adds, the "old man—for he was an old man at the time—wore spectacles, and the bullet and one of the glasses went into his skull" (*AMT* 113). Twain's tone here is respectful. The mutilation, tantamount to castration, since the eye has been singled out as the sign of manliness, is presented as a part of the general picture of the father's bravery. In all published versions of the autobiography, the account of the wounding ends at this point. But in the original dictation Twain continued, and his tone changed radically: "but often, in after years, when I boarded in the old man's home in San Francisco, whenever he became emotional I used to see him shed tears and *glass*, in a way that was infinitely moving" (AD, 19 Jan. 1906, MTP). Twain himself canceled this passage and two additional sentences extending the joke. He suppressed his mockery of the father whose brave conduct was a tacit rebuke to Clemens's own actions.[10]

Skipping town, leaving Nevada to relocate in San Francisco, Clemens evaded those actions, extricating himself from his immediate difficulties, but he did not escape his emotional disturbances, nor did he resolve his conflict between loose and proper living. On the West Coast, he continued to pose as a bohemian and he continued to play the gentleman. If anything, both postures were intensified. He spent time in the saloons and theaters frequented by the free-spirited, enjoying their patrons and pleasures (upon at least one occasion drinking to such boisterous excess he was jailed). And he visited luxury hotels, fashionable resorts, and the offices and homes of the well-to-do, enjoying the comforts and pastimes of those privileged by wealth and rank. He slummed and he climbed.

The extant documents from this period make it clear, however, that there was a common link between these divergent lives, for Clemens's affected bohemianism, like his posturing as a reputable member of society, was a part of a steady drive upward within the class hierarchy. The coterie of flamboyant personalities that made up San Francisco's bohemia centered on such writers as Bret Harte, Charles Warren Stoddard, Prentice Mulford, and Joaquin Miller.[11] Associating with them, Clemens advanced Mark Twain's career, finding in their journal, *The Golden Era*, an outlet for more extended, more various, indeed more literary writing. Such publication was a step up the ladder of literary respectability. And the climbing Clemens soon went even higher, at least in his own estimation, abandoning some bohemian friends in the process. To his mother and sister he explained:

> I have engaged to write for the new literary paper—the "Californian"—same pay I used to receive on the "Golden Era"—one article a week, fifty dollars a month. I quit the "Era," long ago. It wasn't high-toned enough. I thought that whether I was a literary "jackleg" or not, I wouldn't class myself with that style of people, anyhow. The "Californian" circulates among the highest class of the community, & is the best weekly literary paper in the United States—& I suppose I ought to know. (*L1* 312)

Clemens did seek out the "highest class." In language calculated to alarm his mother by provocatively asserting his lack of respect, he informed his family of his social maneuvering:

> I called on Rev. Dr. Wadsworth last night with the City College man, but the old rip wasn't at home. I was sorry, because I wanted to make his acquaintance. I am thick & [*sic*] thieves with the Rev. Stebbings, & I am laying for the Rev. Scudder & the Rev. Dr. Stone. I am running on preachers, now, altogether. I find them gay. Stebbings is a regular brick. I am taking letters of introduction to Henry Ward Beecher, Rev. Dr. Tyng, & other eminent parsons in the east. (*L1* 368)

Here his slangy language not only teases his mother but also masks his pride; there is truth as well as humor in his account. Clemens did cultivate acquaintance not only with clergymen but also with merchants, writers, lawyers, governors, judges, and senators; he courted the influential and the prominent. Unable to sail on the new steamer Ajax when it inaugurated regular service between San Francisco and Honolulu, he reported home that the ship had "52 invited guests aboard—the cream of the town—gentleman & ladies both, and a splendid brass band" (*L1* 329). He seems for a moment as enthusiastic about the band as the passengers, but after explaining that he had to turn down his own invitation to make the trip, he expresses his regret in terms that underscore his social admiration: "Where could a man catch such another crowd together?" (*L1* 330).

In keeping with Clemens's inconsistent but recurrent movement toward respectable middle-classdom, Mark Twain's writings began to change. Although he continued to turn out news reports (straight and burlesque), personal narratives, outlandish parodies, reviews of cultural events as well as fashions, advice columns, character sketches, short fictions, and personal attacks on rival journalists (his playful send-ups of Dan De Quille and the Unreliable gave way to his truly vitriolic assaults on Fitz Smythe), he often struck a new note. That note was the sound of serious social criticism. Increasingly he turned his humor toward what was wrong in civic life, attacking corruption in private as well as public institutions and in the men (they were all men) who ran them. He became, in the words of Edgar M. Branch, the finest critic of Twain's western writing, an "amateur muckraker," the "public's watchdog," a "trustee of the general good" (*Literary Apprenticeship* 142). Self-conscious about his new role, Twain trumpeted himself as "the Moral Phenomenon" and "the Moralist of the Main" (*MTB* 1:274).

Both sobriquets were partly jokes. Clemens's living, as well as Mark Twain's writing, was so notoriously wayward as to make any insistence that he was a staunch guardian of morality outrageously comic. Twain played with the idea. Offering to fill an editorial vacancy on the *Californian*, he facetiously insisted that what the journal needed was "a good Moral tone" and that he was the one to provide it:

What you want is Morality. You have run too much poetry; you have slathered . . . too many frivolous sentimental tales into your paper; too much harmful elevating literature. What the people are suffering for, is Morality. Turn them over to me. Give me room according to my strength. I can fetch them! Let me hear from you. You could not do better than hire me. I can bring your paper right up. You ought to know, yourself, that when I play my hand in the high moral line, I take a trick every time. (*Gold Miners & Guttersnipes* 168–69)

The language of the ring-tailed roarer, "Give me room according to my strength," and of the gambling shark, "I take a trick every time," playfully undermines the very posture of moral authority Twain is claiming. And yet in his West Coast journalism he did exercise such authority; or perhaps more accurately we should say he did "play" the "high moral line."

His muckraking journalism is curious stuff, for his diatribes against corruption mix the personal with the principled, silliness with outrage, and even connivance with ethics. Often his moral point seems to keep shady company. His "Daniel in the Lion's Den—and Out Again All Right," often taken as an attack on the San Francisco stock market, reads more like a ribbing of chums who will enjoy the joke than a serious critique of illegal trading. (Clemens himself tried hard to cage the right wildcat stock.) His attacks on the police for their mistreatment of the Chinese, heralded as a sign of his emerging humanity, are full of racist epithets that dehumanize the very people he is defending. Even his celebrated attacks on law officers and judicial procedures, famed examples of his "moral" satire, often seem to be personal vendettas against individuals rather than high-minded exposés, just further instances of his familiar verbal dueling, turned now from newspaper rivals to public officials. Of course, much of the oddity of Twain's reform writing simply reflects the nature of western journalism. As various scholars have pointed out, it was pretty rough-and-tumble writing even when it took up ethical issues, and western journalists worked in a precarious world of bribery, intimidation, political pressure, social retaliation, commercial blackmail, and even the threat of physical violence. It was a world, as one scholar has put it, permeated by "the ethic of might makes right" (Berkove 6). Locating Mark Twain's real motives and principles in any given piece of his reform writing is, then, as chancy as prospecting itself. His work was variously determined (at times, overdetermined) as he responded to and out of local politics, personal relations, professional conflicts, petty resentments, genuine principle, momentary pique, and even passing whim. As he became the Moralist of the Main, what he seems to have done is to discover that there was power in morality. By assuming postures of righteousness, purity, and principle, he tapped a source of authority that strengthened an instinctive urge for dominance. In one early sketch he pointedly announced that he had a "talent for posturing" (*ET&S1* 185). As Mark Twain, Clemens had frequently postured as one of the roughs; now as the Moralist of the Main he posed as ethical reformer.

Twain uses multiple voices in his early humorous pieces—the voices of polite refinement and vulgarity, for instance, or of sagacity and idiocy—but his moral satires are largely univocal. The voice in them is one of irritated conventionality; it varies in tone with the seriousness of the topic from annoyance to indignation to outrage. The less serious the issue, the more colloquial Twain's language is likely to be and the more idiosyncratic the posture of rebuke; the more serious the issue, the more formal the language and, significantly, the more conventional the moralistic stance. In a piece like "Socrates Murphy," one of his "Answers to Correspondents," which is sometimes taken as a serious attack on pretension, Twain deploys an aggressive vernacular—he calls it "this rough-shod eloquence of mine"—backed by completely individual authority to denounce the straw man Murphy for humming aloud at the opera: "I can tell you Arizona opera-sharps, any time; you prowl around beer-cellars and listen to some howling-dervish of a Dutchman exterminating an Italian air, and then you come into the Academy and prop yourself up against the wall with the stuffy aspect and imbecile leer of a clothing-store dummy, and go to droning along about half an octave below the tenor, and disgusting everybody in your neighborhood with your beery strains" (*ET&S2* 203).

In his reply to the "Moral Statistician," a somewhat more serious piece sometimes seen as a critique of self-righteous purists who bolster their prohibitions with facts and figures, he rails against the Statistician's objection to such "vices" as smoking, drinking, wearing expansive hoop-skirts, and playing billiards in terms that are highly personal but only guardedly vernacular: "I don't want any of your statistics. I took your whole batch and lit my pipe with it. I hate your kind of people. . . . In a word, why don't you go off somewhere and die, and not be always trying to seduce people into becoming as 'ornery' and unlovable as you are yourselves, by your ceaseless and villainous 'moral statistics'?" (*ET&S2* 189–90). While placing "moral statistics" in quotation marks enforces the challenge to the Moral Statistician's real ethics, putting "ornery" in quotation marks betrays an unwillingness to depart too far from standard English and so lose the authority embedded in it. And in an entirely serious attack on the mistreatment of prisoners and the misuse of public monies, "What Have the Police Been Doing?" Twain uses very few colloquialisms—beyond the then semistandard *ain't*—and no distinctly personal self at all. His tone veers from facetious to sarcastic, and when he makes his central criticism of the way the police have handled a man accused of stealing some flour sacks, he does so by means of an archly phrased rhetorical question couched in a language and syntax of studied formality: "Ah, and if he stole flour sacks, did he not deliberately put himself outside the pale of humanity and Christian sympathy by that hellish act?" (*MTC1* 197). Twain intensifies his condemnation of the police here by appealing not only to a general humanity but also to Christian charity. Both are, of course, thoroughly traditional norms. His other attacks depend on equally conventional values, as he evokes virtue, care, efficiency, safety from insult, due process, and even work as the standards by which to judge the police. His irony thus unfolds through a morality so familiar and stylized as to be clichéd: "I know the Police Department is a kind, humane and generous institution" (*MTC1* 197).

As Moralist of the Main, Twain upholds mainstream morality. Appropriating uncontestable social norms, he asserts himself with vigor. He assumes a stance (and tacitly invites his audience to be impressed by it) either as one against the many—the many Socrates Murphies and Moral Statisticians of the world—or as one against the more powerful, the police and courts. The moral standards he applies, however, are absolutely conventional. Whatever the impulse underlying such work, it clearly aligns Mark Twain with the respectable. (Who among the proper could object to the moral norms he deploys?) The conventionality of his moralism appears not only in admirable postures but also in problematical ones. There has been a tendency to find in the early western Twain signs of the much later Twain, to convert the Moralist of the Main into the champion of democracy, equality, and humanity that appears so forcefully in the last decade of Clemens's life and Mark Twain's writing.[12] But whatever his fervor for morality in people and public offices, the western Twain remained a sexist, racist, and elitist. Of course, this too makes his moralism a part of the main.

He views women through the bifurcated lens of his age as either whores or angels. His reporting took him to the jails on the one hand and to society events on the other; in the first he discovered actual women drunks, thieves, street-brawlers, and prostitutes; in the second he imagined he saw frail vessels of culture. His adulation of the goodness of the latter seems proportional to his disgust with the impurity of the former. Whenever he writes of respectable women, Twain casts them in stereotypical terms as delicate, vain, flighty, and weak. He elevates them along the lines—the narrow, confining lines—of traditional Victorian ideas of gender: women are admirably pure, ethereal, and noble, citadels of virtue and spirituality; and he denigrates them in equally traditional ways as irrational, emotional, and vulnerable, weak creatures to be guarded, cared for, and protected by men. He laughs gently at them. Sexist by modern standards, conventional for his time, his early depictions of women are part of the stock-in-trade of male humor.[13]

His treatment of nonwhite races is no more enlightened. Although Clemens shed his southern sympathies in pro-Union Nevada, he did not give up his prejudices against African Americans. He continued, as Arthur Pettit has shown, to pepper his talk and Twain's writing with "nigger jokes" (Pettit 41–43, 127–30). If in time he was to become, in Howells's memorable phrase, "the most desouthernized Southerner" (*MyMT* 35) he knew, that time lay far ahead. If anything, in the West he deepened his inbred sense of racial superiority, finding Native Americans, Chinese immigrants, Pacific Islanders, as well as free blacks, inferior. He sometimes expressed tolerance for such groups, sometimes accorded them a place in public affairs, and sometimes advocated their humane treatment, but he consistently held them to be less "civilized" than white men.

White men of the better class, that is. Without bothering to worry over the dividing line between his own loose living and the conduct of others, he condemned lower-class drunks, loafers, and brawlers, as well as criminals of all sorts. His class bias constantly informs his rhetoric of vituperation. As he lambasts his various antagonists, both real and feigned, he stigmatizes them by describing their dress, speech, and actions as those of the lower social orders. He depicts his opponents as given to flashy (or worse, stolen) clothes, to slangy (or worse, profane) speech, to crude (or worse, violent) behavior. In playful jibes at friends as well as savage attacks on enemies, he uses derogatory terms for the lower classes, thereby revealing an apparent alliance with the upper. At the same time, however, he makes fun of the upper classes. He spoofs their pastimes, laughs at their pretensions, and mocks their institutions and values. Consistent in his gender and racial prejudices, Twain vacillated in his treatment of classes, just as Clemens wavered in his living.

IN THIS PERIOD OF self-fashioning, the long foreground to his appearance as the best-selling author of *The Innocents Abroad*, Mark Twain is most fully formed in his letters from the Sandwich Islands. Clemens himself recognized the significance of these letters, for he planned to turn them into his first book (*L2* 3), to make them in effect the first extended appearance of Mark Twain before a national audience. Commissioned by the Sacramento *Union* as a roving correspondent sent to the islands to scout out business prospects, Twain ended up writing a series of twenty-five letters, including a news report of the *Hornet* shipwreck. The letters effectively mix travel narrative, description, personal reflection, statistical information, business analysis, and humor.

Perhaps most notable is the outlet Twain invents for his humor. He creates the fictitious fellow traveler, named as commonly and colorlessly as possible, Brown, and makes him an uncouth vulgarian given to antisentimental observations, delight in the hardships and mishaps of travel, insistence on the crude aspects of life, and indulgence in low living. The creation of this traveling companion has been commented on only briefly, but it has provoked disagreement. Rogers sees it as a positive development in the evolution of Twain's burlesque (30–31), while Sloane finds it retrogressive (*Literary Comedian* 73–74). Whether gaining or losing in terms of comedy, by creating Brown Clemens purges the grosser, more transgressive elements from his narrative persona, Mark Twain; he reforms himself into a reputable person.

He speaks with confident, indeed strident, authority. Henry Nash Smith once suggested that Twain's voice and outlook in these letters were tuned to his audience of businessmen (*Development* 14), but, in fact, Twain is writing for a broader audience, one as mixed as the literate California society itself. What happens in the letters is not that Twain meets the expectations, interests, and standards of one class of readers but that he seizes the latitude in his loosely defined assignment to exert more coherently than ever before his nascent respectable self. His sense of personal superiority, his sexism (with its strain of prudery), his racism, his classism, and his stance of moral principle all coalesce to create an imperiously conventional Mark Twain.

His letters reflect this growing main-street morality. The grandest news event during his stay in the islands was the death of Princess Victoria Kamamalu Kaahumanu, and Twain seized the occasion to record her funeral rites in detail. In discussing the princess herself, he was duplicitous, adjusting his account to meet the standards of middle-class decorum. Suppressing his personal feelings and even omitting aspects of the public funeral, he turned a native princess into a Victorian lady and an exotic island rite into a very proper ceremony. On the one hand, he praises this princess in line to have become queen as if she were a refined gentlewoman, citing her artistic talents, her religious devotion, and her charitable works, while on the other, he excludes from his account any acknowledgment of the actual celebration of her sexual prowess. In the privacy of his notebooks, however, he scandalized himself by noting not only the presumed cause of her death but also her alleged sexual appetite: "Pr. V. died in forcing abortion—kept half a dozen bucks to do her washing, & has suffered 7 abortions" (*N&J1* 129).[14] Although he knew that the natives' honorific funeral songs celebrated the Princess's sexual capacity, he omitted any mention of this in his letters to the *Union*. He simply turned the real woman into his notion of a proper woman.

In his other letters, he either ignores the character and circumstance of the native women or remarks on them from highly traditional western (male) perspectives. He teasingly observes them as erotic objects, loosing a male gaze as formidable as that of the heroic fighter he was later to imagine in his autobiography. He is content with, indeed largely oblivious to, the subservient positions of women, but he moralistically condemns their nude bathing and apparent sexual promiscuity (culturally, the latter often involved socially accepted rites of hospitality). In general he ignores the native women, or reifies them into objects of male desire, always judging them in highly conventional ways.

While he puts the native women into traditional Victorian molds, praising or damning them in terms of how well they fit, with the men he expresses a fairly consistent contempt born of his sense of racial superiority. He repeatedly designates them by the then derogatory term "Kanaka." With equal contempt, his racism extends to the Chinese as he argues for their use as "coolies" to create cheap labor. Revealingly, he compares both groups to African American slaves: on the islanders— "As soon as we set sail the natives all laid down on the deck as thick as Negroes in a slave pen" (*MTLH* 195); on Chinese workers—"The hire of each laborer is $100 a year—just about what it used to cost to board and clothe and doctor a Negro—but there is no original outlay of $500 to $1,000 for the purchase of the laborer" (*MTLH* 260).

His sense of class is also at work throughout the letters, from his careful demarcation of the classes assembled for his ship's arrival—"a mixed crowd" of "Chinamen," "foreigners," "the better class of natives," and "'half whites'" (*MTLH* 26)—to his later attention to the divisions on the inter-island schooners between "quality folks" and "natives" (*MTLH* 195). His account of the legislature is full of admiration for the Nobles— "able, educated, fine-looking men"—and skepticism about the Commons—"Kanakas" with a "gift of gab" (*MTLH* 110). He clearly approves of the autocratic rule of the king through his ministers and the Nobles, despite his avowal of "republican notions" (*MTLH* 107). Anticipating the reactionary conservative argument he would later make in "The Curious Republic of Gondour," he endorses the king's replacement of universal suffrage with qualifications that restrict voting to those "possessed of a hundred dollars worth of real estate" or who have "an income of seventy-five dollars a year" (*MTLH* 106). His racism, his elitism, and his prurience combine in this aside that coyly hints at one benefit of miscegenation: "If I were not ashamed to digress so often I would like to expatiate a little upon the noticeable fact that the nobility of this land, as a general thing, are distinguishable from the common herd by their large stature and commanding presence, and also set forth the theories in vogue for accounting for it, but for the present I will pass the subject by" (*MTLH* 110).

It is not surprising, then, that Twain is also an imperialist. He is more than ready, to borrow a phrase from his much later anti-imperial years, to see the American eagle "go screaming into the Pacific" (MT interview, New York *Herald*, 15 Oct. 1900; rpt. Zwick 5). He believes in the moral, religious, economic, and racial superiority of America, and he advocates its domination in the Pacific. He celebrates the American influence in the islands: "The great bulk of the wealth, the commerce, the enterprise, and the spirit of progress in the Sandwich Islands centers in the Americans" (*MTLH* 132), and he urges an increase in the American presence: "let the Islands be populated with Americans" (*MTLH* 21). His jingoism even leads him to champion the American missionaries. Though he expresses mild reservations about their theology of salvation and damnation as well as some of their puritanical imperatives, he lauds them for having raised the islands not only "from idolatry to Christianity" but also "from barbarism to civilization" (*MTLH* 60). In a panegyric, he celebrates America itself as having found "the true Northwest Passage" in the islands, one that will open to it "the bursting coffers of 'Ormus and of Ind,'" the vast "Oriental wealth" fabled in story and legend. Imagining that California will soon be the "depot" and "distributing house" of these riches, he cheerfully uses the language of empire to define its future greatness: "California has got the world where it must pay tribute to her" (*MTLH* 274).

Twain's rhapsodic evocation of Oriental treasure soon to be channeled to America reflects something besides a knowledge of Milton (he quotes the opening of Book 2 of *Paradise Lost*), grandiose vision, and rhetorical extravagance. He was thinking about the Far East, about China and Japan at the time, because the U.S. ministers to those countries, Anson Burlingame and General Van Valkenburgh, had arrived in the islands, and Burlingame in particular had taken Clemens up. He befriended him, helped him to interview the survivors of the *Hornet* disaster, entertained him socially, and encouraged him in his writing, asking, according to Clemens, to be given "pretty much everything" he "ever wrote" (*L1* 344). He even invited Clemens to join him in China, where he promised he would welcome him into his home as well as into his official ministry, and aid him in advancing financially. Many years later in his autobiography, Clemens attested to the importance of Burlingame in his life: "Mr. Burlingame gave me some advice, one day, which I have never forgotten, and which I have lived by for forty years. He said, in substance: 'Avoid inferiors. Seek your comradeships among your superiors in intellect and character; always *climb*'" (*MTA* 2 : 125, Twain's emphasis). An admonition as banal, not to mention as snobbish, as this hardly seems sufficient to change or direct a life, as Clemens suggests it did for him. He had surely heard such "wisdom" before, and as I've pointed out, he certainly had begun to live at least halfheartedly in accord with such notions on the California coast as he played gentleman and courted the world of power and privilege. What made Burlingame seem so important? [15]

He was a former congressman from Massachusetts who had won national fame for his apparent willingness to meet the fiery Preston S. Brooks in a duel after Brooks had violently caned Charles Sumner into insensibility on the floor of the U.S. Senate in 1856. Burlingame was appointed U.S. minister to China in 1861 and served in that post until November 1867 when he resigned to clear the way for his appointment by the Chinese government as its ambassador at large, empowered to negotiate treaties with foreign governments.[16] Clemens flirted with the idea of joining Burlingame in China, and later in 1868, a somewhat better known Mark Twain supported the treaty Burlingame arranged between the United States and China, loudly proclaiming in the New York newspapers the greatness of both the treaty and the diplomat who negotiated it.[17] When Burlingame died in 1870, Twain eulogized him in "A Tribute to Anson Burlingame" published in the Buffalo *Express*, and over thirty years later he memorialized him in his autobiographical dictations. In all his recollections of Burlingame, Clemens praised him extravagantly.

Understandably, given Burlingame's reputation, Clemens recalls him as a brave man, as the "Congressman from the West" (though born in New York State, Burlingame had lived in Ohio and Michigan and Clemens no doubt enjoyed the sense of regional kinship) who stood up to the "bully" Brooks and agreed to duel with "rifles at short range" (*MTA* 2 : 124). Clemens could not have known it, but Burlingame was less than ready to fight his duel, having first apologized for the speech that incited Brooks, and then, when the press began to accuse him of cowardice, having agreed to fight only at a place he knew to be inaccessible to Brooks.[18] Significantly, when they met in Honolulu, the man famous throughout the nation for his willingness to duel and the man infamous on the Comstock for his refusal to duel discussed such affairs; they talked in particular of Sherrard Clemens, a third cousin of Sam's in Virginia who had been wounded in a duel (*L1* 343–44). Apparently they shared, man to man, a sense of martial pride, perhaps in the process repairing Clemens's own. In his recollections, however, Clemens stresses not Burlingame's bellicosity but his tenderness. In the autobiography he recalls him in the language most often reserved for Victorian love: "He had beautiful eyes; deep eyes; speaking eyes; eyes that were dreamy, in repose; eyes that could beam and persuade like a lover's" (*MTA* 2:124). In his "Tribute" he commends him for his "education and culture," for his justice, liberality, and social grace, and for his "great heart warm enough to feel for all" (*CE* 3). Burlingame was, he insists, "a great man—a very, very great man" (*CE* 3).

Such overestimation may well reflect the fact that in Burlingame Clemens found an approving surrogate father. Burlingame lavished praise and affection on him, accepted him uncontingently, and even opened to him, munificently, the prospect of wealth. (All this contrasts strikingly with the real father.) Reminiscing of Burlingame's acts in his ministerial court, of his role as "judge," Clemens admires a severity far more extreme than any he had experienced, witnessed, or imagined in his actual father. Having convicted an "American ruffian" of murder, Burlingame, Clemens reports with approval, immediately gave the order to "take him out and hang him" (*CE* 5). But where the severe real father, John Marshall Clemens, was austere, cold, and unemotional, Burlingame was, at least for Clemens, a figure of warmth and love. In the language of Victorian sentimentality he recalls him as a friend of large "charity," of "chivalrous generosity," a man with a face "children instinctively trust in, and homeless friendless creatures appeal to without fear" (*CE* 3). Surely disclosed here is the emotional significance Burlingame had for Clemens. To be befriended, indeed "fathered," by such a man was no doubt to feel absolved of past misdemeanors as well as encouraged in future undertakings. Under the benign aegis of this imagined man, Clemens could be reconciled with the ghost of his real father and with the world of propriety he represented. In Burlingame he found a "father" he could not only embrace but also emulate.

At the very least, the encounter with Burlingame solidified Clemens's drive away from the bohemian toward the respectable. That drive is evident in his treatment of the past in some of the personal letters he wrote during and just after his time in the islands. Two letters to his childhood friend, Will Bowen, who, like Clemens, had become a Mississippi river pilot, are especially interesting in this regard. In the first, written in May 1866, some six weeks before his meeting with Burlingame, Clemens hazily evokes the past to bridge a falling out between the two old friends and then goes on to suggest that, were they together now, they could go island-hopping "for a year" and have "a merry hell of a time" (*L1* 338–39). The letter has a gruff, old-boy's jocularity to it. In his next to Bowen, one written twelve days after his return to San Francisco, Clemens dwells on his past on the river, and his tone throughout the letter, though still hearty, is less coarse.

As he turns to his past, he not only recalls it but also reconfigures it. He reminisces about his river days in ways that reflect flatteringly upon his past self, first praising the pilots' masculinity—"I know that in genuine *manliness* they assay away above the common multitude"—and then defining their essential character in even more revealing terms: "It is a strange study,—a singular phenomenon, if you please, that the only real, independent and genuine *gentlemen* in the world go quietly up and down the Mississippi river, asking no homage of any one, seeking no popularity, no notoriety, and not caring a damn whether school keeps or not" (*L1* 358, Clemens's emphasis). Looked at in the context of Clemens's present, this is a paradoxical accounting. Indifference to respect, popularity, and notoriety, conjured up as past glory, conflicts with his present struggle as Mark Twain to achieve just these. On the other hand, attributing gentlemanliness to the pilots conflicts with the realities of the past (pilots were not true gentlemen) but coincides with Clemens's—and Twain's—own reorientation in the present. The first may reflect a longing for lost stature and independence; the second reveals the new importance to Clemens/Twain (he signed this letter, "Sam Mark," lining through "Sam") of being a gentleman.

To award himself the status of gentleman in his days as a pilot, he simply rewrites the past. Significantly, the figure who seems to make such revision not only necessary but also possible is again Anson Burlingame, who emerges in the letter itself. Right after his discussion of pilots, Twain tells Bowen that the American ministers to China and Japan arrived in the islands while he was there. He reports with transparent vanity that he and the two dignitaries "just made Honolulu howl" (*L1* 359). But where in his earlier letter to Bowen he had imagined the two of them having "a merry hell of a time," here he apologizes for having gotten "tight once" (*L1* 359). He waxes moralistic: "I know better than to get tight oftener than once in 3 months. It sets a man back in the esteem of people whose good opinions are worth having" (*L1* 359). Clemens is clearly gripped here by conventional standards of good conduct, by a keen awareness of public scrutiny, and by a strong desire for social approval from the "better" class. He is a long way from not giving a damn whether school keeps or not.

JUST AS HE REWROTE the past of his piloting days in his letter to Will Bowen, inscribing his present values onto it, so on a much larger scale five years after he completed his time in the West, he rewrote his western experience in *Roughing It*. That book, in fact, forms a climax to Twain's western self-fashioning.

Roughing It is best understood as a palimpsest. Over the actualities of his western life, recorded with varying authenticity in the letters and early writings, Twain inscribes a newer version. He erases or obscures several things in the process, most notably Clemens's excessive drinking, his sexual interests, and his violence. In his rewriting, Twain never drinks to excess, although the "boys" have a few from time to time and a vulgarian like Jim Blaine gets soused to a wonderful loquaciousness. Sex, which was only hinted at in Twain's western writing, usually in sly observations about such things as dancing, women's attire, and native bathers, is completely eliminated except for one passing acknowledgment that brothels prospered in the flush times. Twain goes out of his way, in fact, to insist, contrary to the facts, that women were absent on the frontier. And when he does stage the arrival of a woman, what he calls that "rare and blessed spectacle," he carefully transforms the ensuing male voyeurism into a respectful reverence (*RI* 392–95). Twain's verbal and literary violence, for which he became famous in the West, is also expunged from the new record. As he erases these aspects of his past, Twain occludes many of the emotions that once possessed him: abandon, intense desire, rage, and periodic despair, among others. He replaces them with a pervasive tone of good-humored equanimity. Given the extensive transformations he undertakes in writing *Roughing It*, it is no wonder that he expressed relief over Howells's favorable review of the book. Twain's terms of gratitude betray not only a sense of guilt but also some suspicion of false identity: "I am as uplifted and reassured by it as a mother who has given birth to a white baby when she was awfully afraid it was going to be a mulatto" (*MTHL* 1:10–11). Rewriting the past in *Roughing It*, Twain mitigates his loose behavior, improves his character, and bucks up his emotional life. Significantly, there is no demonstration of a flamboyant bohemian lifestyle. He effects all this remaking chiefly through his humor and his narrative voice.

James Cox has perceptively analyzed how Twain's humor transforms Clemens's past. He points out that *Roughing It* is "the exaggeration, the tall tale of Mark Twain" (*Fate* 97). Just as Bemis converts his embarrassment and the annoyance that accompanies it into a comic entertainment in telling the tale—tall, to be sure—of the buffalo that climbed a tree, so Mark Twain transforms Clemens's less than heroic past into a humorous narrative that exaggerates the facts to create a pleasurable amusement. On a personal level, such a process purges whatever was embarrassing or humiliating, whatever aroused distress or engendered outrage. It makes acceptable to author and audience alike that which might otherwise be objectionable. For Cox, the motive of this form is "the narrator's conversion of his humiliation, failure, and anger into a tall tale which will both move and rouse the listener—move him to laughter and rouse him to skepticism" (*Fate* 103). As an explanation of the function of Twain's humor in *Roughing It*, this is hard to improve on. But Twain's reconfiguration of the past is even more complex, for it is achieved not only by his humor but also by his seriousness. And the force of the narrative often drives toward persuasion as much as skepticism.

Roughing It is a compound of reminiscence, anecdote, history, description, information, portraiture, monologue, dialogue, and personal commentary—to name only the most prominent of its parts. (Howells would eventually suggest that Twain's characteristic form was the "scrapbook" [*MyMT* 167–68].) What holds these diverse elements together is the narrative voice that articulates them. Following the lead of Henry Nash Smith, most critics have seized on the book's first paragraph and therein—and thereafter—seen the narrator as an innocent, or more complexly as a combination of innocent tenderfoot and experienced old-timer (*Development* 53). Twain does from time to time present himself as an earnest striver, a youthful dupe, or a bumbling failure, but these are momentary poses. Innocence is not really central to the text as a whole. It is, in fact, a posture assumed infrequently, and it is deployed inconsistently from first to last (thereby defeating attempts to read the book as a tale of initiation).[19] The pose of innocence is, I believe, most accurately understood as a rhetorical stance, as a style of discourse adopted for isolated comic effects; it could well be defined as an extended—or repeated—joke. The true narrative voice, heard from the opening "Prefatory" to the closing "Moral," is not that of an innocent, or of an experienced man recalling his former innocence, but rather the voice of a practiced writer, conscious of, indeed self-conscious about, his writing, his written text, and his audience.

This voice of the writer at work is the voice Twain first sounded to the full in his letters from the Sandwich Islands. *Roughing It* is informed by the same prejudices and assurances evident in those screeds (with the notable exception of the strident imperialism that rang so loudly there), but there are also some new dimensions. In general terms, as he wrote *Roughing It* Twain drew upon three major sources: first, for the overland trip, Orion's memorandum book of the journey; second, for the mining episodes and life in Virginia City as well as San Francisco, his own newspaper articles; and finally, for the Sandwich Island section, his previously published letters.[20] Using these documents in succession to rewrite the past, he came progressively closer to the more conventional self of the letters from the islands; as he did so, there was less and less he needed to obscure or conceal. Put another way, more of the original shows through the palimpsest. To be sure, the Sandwich Island letters are heavily revised—cut by perhaps as much as a third—but after expunging his account of future business prospects (now both outdated and largely irrelevant), and after eliminating the character Brown, thereby removing all the vulgarity and crudity, he worked chiefly to improve the writing itself. He refined his own prose, extending and intensifying its poetic effects until they matched or surpassed his recent efforts at the picturesque in such newly written passages as his descriptions of the South Pass, Lake Tahoe, and even Lake Mono. In doing so he makes the new version of his old self something of a genteel traveler.

While Twain rewrites Clemens's past, purging drunkenness, sex, and violence, at the same time he intensifies his sensitivity to landscape—he not only preserves but even extends two aspects of Clemens's sometime former self: he maintains his stance as a gentleman and his posture of moral superiority. Twain thus imposes on the whole of *Roughing It* a posture of propriety by which Clemens had lived only sporadically. This is not to say that he is smug or snobbish or priggish in the text, nor is it to suggest that his narrative is straitlaced, pedantic, or affected. But his voice of the writer writing is predominantly conventional. Despite the flippant remarks, ironic observations, and outlandish assertions (the wild humor for which the book is most often read), his narrative flows along familiar lines of value even as it takes note of what is radical in the West. And the bottom of the channel is often a bedrock of traditional morality.

Reflecting much of the actuality of the West, especially on the mining frontiers, Twain's text presents a destabilized world. It is, as various critics have pointed out, an anarchic world—a world in which traditional authority collapses (see, for instance, Wadlington).[21] Sacred and profane texts—scriptures, histories, fictions—prove unreliable; the legal system is incapable of justice; economic organization is chaotic; businesses go bankrupt; social hierarchies fall apart; and political institutions are corrupt. The West is unstable in part, as Lee Clark Mitchell has pointed out, because of its "bewildering language" ("Verbally *Roughing It*" 74). Even the regnant nineteenth-century metaphysic, a belief in Divine Providence, seems to be called into question in such episodes as Jim Blaine's drunken rambling, with its unconsciously ironic insistence that "Prov'dence don't fire no blank ca'ridges, boys" (*RI* 366), and the Reverend Erickson's desperate translations of Horace Greeley's scrawled correspondence, with its dark message: "Creation perdu, is done" (*RI* 486).[22] The central illusion by which the United States knit itself together, the American Dream, is first traduced by the fraudulence recorded in the book and then shattered by the multiple failures it limns (Hill, "Introduction," *RI* 7–24). In the face of the prevailing disorder and randomness, however, Twain neither adopts the self-serving, self-preserving strategies of the Trickster (Wadlington) nor yields to a bitter cynicism (Robinson, "Seeing the Elephant" 44–45), although from time to time his narrative toys with both. In the absence of reliable authority, he simply becomes his own, authorizing himself as he authors his book. His power turns out to be at one with extremely conventional norms.

He writes into *Roughing It* as counterbalance, if not solution, to the disturbances of the West a grammar of conduct. With seriousness as well as humor, he judges the world as a man of righteousness, purity, and principle—that is, as the Moralist of the Main. He espouses such ordinary values as nonviolence, honest dealings, fairness, and decency. He expects good manners and good speech. He associates bad character and conduct with the lower classes and good with the upper.

One episode in particular encapsulates Twain's moral visioning along class lines. When he and his companions are forced by a flood to lodge at Honey Lake Smith's, an inn on the Carson River, they encounter the "stalwart ruffian" Arkansas (*RI* 201). This coarse, rowdy, drunken lout swaggers through the inn, belligerently accosting everyone, trying to provoke a fight; he intimidates the crowd into docility and the innkeeper into cringing, apologetic sycophancy. The scene is wonderfully comic as Arkansas, longing for a fight, gropes in his drunken befuddlement to find offense where there is only irrelevance. But as his verbal violence reaches its climax, Twain embeds an irony in Arkansas's rant that gives moral point to the whole encounter. "Come out from behind that bar!" Twain has Arkansas rage. "*I'll* learn you to bully and badger and browbeat a gentleman that's forever trying to befriend you and keep you out of trouble" (*RI* 204).

As a representative man of the West, Arkansas is for Twain the inverse of a gentleman. His dialect, his vulgarity, his intoxication, his crudity, his violence, his insistent self-assertion, his coarseness, and his utter disregard for others epitomize the antithesis of the true gentleman as Twain had come to imagine him. The moral man is everything that Arkansas is not. It is no wonder, then, that shortly after this fracas Twain says, "Life in the inn had become next to insupportable by reason of the dirt, drunkenness, fighting, etc." (*RI* 206). Lest my emphasis on this one, clearly comic, scene seem undue, consider another moment in which Twain directly affirms the importance of the gentleman. The comic rendering in the Arkansas incident of a deeply felt perception of Twain's is matched by one of his altogether serious disquisitions. Chapter 48 is a well-known diatribe against the jury system, at the center of which is an invidious class consciousness. Twain objects to the reliance upon "desperadoes," "low beer-house politicians," "barkeepers," and illiterate "ranchmen" as jurors, and calls instead for "a gentleman of high social standing, intelligence and probity" (*RI* 321).

This bias in favor of the upper classes is at work throughout *Roughing It*. In fact, after the graceful overture sounded in the first chapter, his class consciousness emerges at once in the second. The memorable mosquito-smashing Sphynx, who rains "the nine parts of speech" on him and his companions for "forty days and forty nights" and buries them "under a desolating deluge of trivial gossip" that leaves "not a crag or pinnacle of rejoinder projecting above the tossing waste of dislocated grammar and decomposed pronunciation," finally offends Twain by claiming social equality: "When people comes along which is my equals, I reckon I'm a pretty sociable heifer after all" (*RI* 9). Twain's irony here arises from his acute class consciousness. As he re-creates his western experience, he repeatedly uses speech, dress, and manners to define class. The wonderful portrait gallery of vernacular speakers—the Sphynx, Arkansas, Scotty Briggs, Jim Blaine, Captain Ned Blakely, Jim Baker—is really a rogues' gallery of scamps and deadbeats, and despite all of his interest in them, Twain finally lets their substandard language stigmatize them.[23]

From his account of the overland stage service to his observations on the political system of Utah to his careful rendering of the social strata of Virginia City to his comments on California society to his delineation of Hawaiian life and government, he registers class. He tends to approve of the upper classes as long as they exhibit the values of a traditional morality, and he applauds the appearance of that morality whenever he encounters it. He admires, to cite a single—and quite unexpected—example, the character of any stage conductor who is "a good deal of a gentleman" (*RI* 36). What impresses him about the upper classes, besides morality, is power. Although he is perplexed by Brigham Young's polygamy, he admires his absolute control, and so his attitude toward him is finally somewhat ambivalent. He has a similar difficulty with Slade, the desperado turned division agent, whose courtly manners seem to belie his reputation as a killer, and whose killing is at least sometimes the agent of law and order. Twain's general outlook, however, is caught in the encounter with one of the Mormon Destroying Angels. The Destroying Angels are, he explains, "Latter-Day Saints who are set apart by the church to conduct permanent disappearances of obnoxious citizens." But while the one he meets is "murderous enough, possibly, to fill the bill of a Destroyer," it bothers Twain that he doesn't fit the social bill for an angel: he lacks good clothes, dignity, and manners (*RI* 86).

As he envisions it, indeed as he had truly experienced it, the West is rife with contradiction. Westerners believe themselves superior to easterners, while easterners hold themselves above westerners, often failing to grasp the contempt leveled at them. Twain explains,

> Perhaps the reader has visited Utah, Nevada, or California, even in these latter days, and while communing with himself upon the sorrowful banishment of those countries from what he considers "the world," has had his wings clipped by finding that *he* is the one to be pitied, and that there are entire populations around him ready and willing to do it for him—yea, who are complacently doing it for him already, wherever he steps his foot. Poor thing, they are making fun of his hat; and the cut of his New York coat; and his conscientiousness about his grammar; and his feeble profanity; and his consumingly ludicrous ignorance of ores, shafts, tunnels, and other things which he never saw before, and never felt enough interest in to read about. (*RI* 119–20)

Twain tells us that for a time he longs to be a westerner, but that time passes quickly in the narrative because, at bottom, his attitudes and values are those of the "civilized" East. He is clearly critical of the raw towns that pass for civilized settlements (see his descriptions of Carson City and Unionville), and he is clearly disgusted by the low life that takes place in them—by the "swearing, drinking and card playing," not to mention the fighting and killing (*RI* 200). He measures both habitat and inhabitant by cleanliness. A cabin or a town is as good as it is clean and orderly, and a person is as good as he is clean and well dressed. Despite his anti-Mormon inklings,[24] Twain can't help admiring Salt Lake City:

> Next day we strolled about everywhere through the broad, straight, level streets, and enjoyed the pleasant strangeness of a city of fifteen thousand inhabitants with no loafers perceptible in it; and no visible drunkards or noisy people; a limpid stream rippling and dancing through every street in place of a filthy gutter; block after block of trim dwellings, built of "frame" and sunburned brick . . . and a grand general air of neatness, repair, thrift and comfort, around and about and over the whole. (*RI* 89–90)

Even his humor often arises from an espousal of highly conventional attitudes most often associated with the privileged classes. When he bottoms out of mining, for instance, and is compelled to take work at quartz milling, he creates this comic account:

> I will remark, in passing, that I only remained in the milling business one week. I told my employer I could not stay longer without an advance in my wages; that I liked quartz milling, indeed was infatuated with it . . . that nothing, it seemed to me, gave such scope to intellectual activity as feeding a battery and screening tailings, and nothing so stimulated the moral attributes as retorting bullion and washing blankets. (*RI* 237)

Twain's humor here depends on the assumption that intellectual exertion and moral cultivation are not only at odds with labor but desirable activities superior to it. In his wonderful summary of the Comstock during flush times he deploys yet another unexpected traditional cultural value as a pivot for his irony when, after itemizing all the drinking dives, flamboyant fraternal organizations, gambling dens, and overflowing jails, he adds that there is "some talk of building a church" (*RI* 281–82).

Irony operating in terms of such conventional norms shows up everywhere in *Roughing It*, revealing Twain's conservative bias. He is not a solidly orthodox person, of course, and he enjoys, or so he says, the San Francisco earthquake precisely because it creates social chaos: gentlemen and ladies appear in the streets in "queer apparel" or "without any at all"; prominent citizens presumed to be in church dash out of "saloons in their shirt-sleeves, with billiard cues in their hands"; models of fashion are caught in nothing but "a bath-towel"; and ministers, preaching to their congregations, suddenly let fear overcome faith to run out of church, the best place "to die," into the streets, crying "outside is good enough" (*RI* 400–402). But while he plays with such disruptions of social order, he is finally in favor of traditional hierarchies. That is why he objects so to the nabobs. His tales of nabobs pillory them for their ignorance and want of manners. To his dismay, their sudden wealth gives them a kind of social mobility and some kinds of power, but they lack personal merit and culture. Twain is distressed by them because, while they ascend suddenly into the sphere of the privileged, they lack a proper sense of social behavior (see esp. chap. 46).

This cuts to the ironic center of the theme of success in *Roughing It*. Clemens in his actual western days and Twain in his rewriting of them wanted to get rich quick. He acknowledges as much in his text, exaggerating for comic effect his frenzied scheming and multiplying his failures. The book is an extensive record of defeat and a curious commentary on the American mania for striking it rich. Critics have long noted that this emphasis on failure makes *Roughing It* something of an anti-Ben Franklin story (Cox, *Fate* 90–93). Where Franklin wrote of moving from one triumph to another on his way to wealth, Twain records blunder after blunder on his way to desperate poverty. However, Twain's text is more than just an anti-Franklin lesson, for it suggests a paradoxical dynamic of failure/success. Again and again the narrator fails because he is lazy (Lynn, *Southwestern Humor* 161–69), but many of the failures create pleasurable moments of indolence. The famous Lake Tahoe episode is probably the central, defining episode in this regard. The ironic pattern of the action is this: pleasurable idleness creates failure, which in turn yields even more delightful idleness. Paradoxically, then, loss is gain. Twain links to this dynamic his understanding of the end of the drive for riches. While great wealth creates security, offers upward social mobility, and endows its possessor with power, it is also desirable in Twain's account because it gives one leisure and the means to enjoy oneself.

Twain's dream of success in this text is finally a dream of bourgeois comfort and pleasure. When his narrator thinks that he has become a millionaire through the Blind Lead, he envisions a house in San Francisco. He describes it to his fellow prospector, Higbie: "Brown stone front—French plate glass—billiard-room off the dining-room—statuary and paintings—shrubbery and two-acre grass plat—greenhouse—iron dog on the front stoop—gray horses—landau, and a coachman with a bug on his hat!" (*RI* 261). The vision is ironically shattered by Twain when the narrator realizes that he owes the butcher six dollars, but it stands nonetheless as one version of the ideal; it is the goal for which all the western hardship and conniving and struggle are undertaken and endured.

Twain leaves himself at the end of *Roughing It* well short of this dream. The text ends, after the success of his lecturing, with a foreshortened, comic account of his return home, where children have grown up into adults and adults have departed or turned criminal, and with the briefest allusion to his participation in the famous *Quaker City* European excursion (*RI* 542). The last reference is designed to evoke for his readers the success of *The Innocents Abroad*, and so a kind of literary triumph looms momentarily between the lines. Against this he places the final moral: "If the reader thinks he is done, now, and that this book has no moral to it, he is in error. The moral of it is this: If you are of any account, stay at home and make your way by faithful diligence; but if you are 'no account,' go away from home, and then you will *have* to work, whether you want to or not" (*RI* 542). Hamlin Hill glosses this perceptively: "What we can hear quite distinctly is the home-bound and diligent author of the early 1870s renouncing his own earlier life as 'no account'" (Hill, "Introduction," *RI* 19). We can also hear the sound of the proper Mark Twain. In *Roughing It*, Twain has not only renounced an earlier life but also redefined it. As he rewrites Clemens's western life, he falsifies it, fabricates it, and tells a significant truth about it. Put simply, that truth is that he aspired in the past—and still aspires in the present—to be a man of respectability and consequence, with all that that aspiration entails, from the proprieties of conduct to the values of the upper class to the pleasures of a sumptuous brownstone home.

CHAPTER TWO

Victorian Traveler

About halfway through what would prove to be his time in the West, Clemens, then in San Francisco, reported to his friend and former colleague on the Virginia City *Territorial Enterprise*, Dan De Quille, that he had the "Gypsy" and that it might kill him (*L1* 304). As it turned out, his urge to travel more nearly saved him. It impelled him to become a roving correspondent, first for the Sacramento *Union*, then for the *Alta California*, reporting in unplanned succession on the Sandwich Islands, his trip via the Isthmus of Panama to New York, his impressions of that city, then of St. Louis and neighboring towns, and finally—and most spectacularly—of his excursion on the *Quaker City* to Europe and the Holy Land. These were only the beginnings of his travels. He crossed the Atlantic twenty-nine times, shipped into the Pacific twice, and sailed three oceans, encircling the globe. On shore—or rather shores—he was equally mobile, crisscrossing every continent he touched. No one has logged all the miles, but in the end they were nothing short of cosmic.

Clemens's experience of travel was paradoxical: at times it afforded him ease, comfort, and peace (see Harris, *Escape from Time*); at times it maddened him (see, for instance, *MTHL2* 645). The importance of travel for Clemens—and for Mark Twain—was immense. Psychically, "perpetual movement" may have functioned for him, as Richard Bridgman has argued, as "the answer to the precariousness of life" (*Traveling* 149); artistically, as Robert M. Rodney has maintained, it seems to have broadened his outlook, quickened his social conscience, and generally brought him to "maturity" as a writer (284–85); and philosophically, as Forrest G. Robinson has suggested, it deepened, if indeed it did not create, his sense that "all reality is a human construction" ("Innocent at Large" 28). Whatever the cumulative effect of travel for Clemens, in his early years travel writing became crucial to the ongoing process of creating Mark Twain. In his first two travel narratives, *The Innocents Abroad* and *A Tramp Abroad*, companion texts of a sort, Clemens fashioned Mark Twain as a conventional Victorian traveler, thereby extending and solidifying the respectability tried out sporadically in the western writings.

BEFORE TURNING DIRECTLY to these further extensions of the proper Mark Twain, it is useful to look briefly at two things: first, the general nature of Victorian travel writing and, second, the particular circumstances that may have urged Clemens himself to travel abroad.

Given the prosperity of industrialized Victorian England and, after the Civil War, the booming American economy, thousands of newly affluent people went abroad in the second half of the nineteenth century. Twain did not exaggerate when he described himself in the days just before his departure as "drifting with the tide of a great popular movement" (*IA* 24). The reasons for that movement ranged widely from the desire to restore oneself (especially for some Americans after the trauma of the war) to the longing for high culture to the hope for social advancement to the need to escape from home to the prospect of economizing by living abroad (Stowe 5; Steinbrink, "Why the Innocents Went Abroad").

What kind of travelers were these English and American Victorians? Or more to the point here, what kind of travel writers were they once they turned from the trip itself to their accounts of it? The answer is surprisingly simple: their interest, as the great English Victorian writers repeatedly testified, centered on the assessment of foreign cultures. Dickens described his concern as the examination of the "general character" of a people and the "general character of their social system" (285), and Trollope similarly said he liked to study "the political, social, and material condition" of the countries he visited (*An Autobiography* 2:202). Cultural analysis was uppermost,[1] but as recent scholarship has amply demonstrated, such analysis was anything but neutral. The typical Victorian travel writer was a cultural imperialist, defining and defending himself or herself by disclosing the superiority of his/her homeland (see Pratt, Spurr). This act of control, simultaneously one of self-stabilization and cultural validation, lies at the heart of Victorian travel writing. Its animating energy is simply confident judgment, and this kind of judgment is the keynote of Mark Twain's first travel book.

In his incisive study, *Haunted Journeys: Desire and Transgression in European Travel Writing*, Dennis Porter insists that "at their deepest level, all travel books begin, whether or not the fact is acknowledged in the text: at home" (170). Clemens's home circumstances, the conditions that launched Mark Twain on his first European and Near Eastern journey, have seemed almost too obvious to merit consideration. He had the "Gypsy," he needed new material for his *Alta* correspondence, and he wanted to see more of the world. (He deeply regretted not being able to accompany Anson Burlingame to China.) Yet there were other desires at work as well.

His writings between the time he left California in December 1866 and the day he departed on the *Quaker City* cruise in June 1867 reveal a strong preoccupation with relations between the sexes. Twenty-one of the twenty-six letters he published in the *Alta* during this period concern women to one degree or another. His focus shifts from illicit affairs to polite social activities and women's fashions to theatrical displays of female nudity to prostitution (the last letter in this series records a bar woman's direct proposition). The person—or rather the persona—in this correspondence seems more than a little moved by scopophilia.[2] To turn from the published pieces to the private correspondence from this transitional period—one that Everett Emerson has termed "the turning point" (*Authentic* 42)—is to see a quite different kind of desire. Clemens appears in his private letters as a person with considerable knowledge of the world who is angling for positions, flaunting connections, and generally seeking to obtain and exert influence. He appears as a man interested in power.

Both the seeming desire for vicarious erotic pleasure and the more palpable longing for power are satisfied not just in Clemens's actual trip abroad but in the act of writing of it. Power is garnered and manifest in the act of writing itself, an act that inscribes the self on the blank face of existence, as well as in the special kind of writing he undertakes. As he fulfills the unstated formula of the travel genre, the act of judgment, he exerts enormous authority. And as he travels he is able to observe women around the world and to treat them, as we will soon see, to his satisfaction. Such realizations made Clemens's first excursion abroad, or more accurately, Mark Twain's imaginative re-creation of it, a pleasure trip of the first order.

However it struck the thousands of readers who first made *The Innocents Abroad* a best-seller, Twain's text has been viewed by recent critics as an amalgamation of "contradictions" (Messent 24). While such tensions may at first seem to be the expression of Clemens's own conflicted temperament, scholarship on the genre of travel narrative has increasingly revealed that the form itself relied on oppositional strategies. As the travel narrative evolved from the Renaissance tour aimed at perfecting the individual for public life to trips undertaken, individually or in groups, in quest of aesthetic pleasure, the form changed from one in which the personality of the traveler was repressed, subordinated to the account of factual information, to one in which the personality of the traveler was flaunted, its idiosyncrasies put self-consciously on display (Batten 80–81). The performing self of nineteenth-century travel narratives more often than not defined itself against earlier travelers—and against the conventions of travel writing—often casting these antagonisms as the difference between a true traveler and a mere tourist (Buzzard 4). Many of Mark Twain's oppositions are thus inherent in the very form he employs.

If manifest contradictions appear in *The Innocents Abroad*, equally apparent are the ease and certitude with which Twain's narrative voices its very oppositions. That ease and certitude bespeak a kind of wholeness. The text is firmly centered in the persona Mark Twain (there is, as most critics have recognized, no telling where the persona leaves off and Clemens enters in). Florence has argued that the persona is "multiform" (65), a "kaleidoscopic, thoughtful, inclusive presence" (90), yet the chips in that kaleidoscope seem to fall along patterned lines as Twain plays out the roles of Bohemian and Gentleman first tested in the West. The persona Mark Twain oscillates between such postures as scoffer at propriety and defender of refinement, ignorant Philistine and appreciative connoisseur, fiery democrat and conservative capitalist, free-living rowdy and rule-abiding traveler. Twain uses these contrasting postures both humorously and seriously, and while it is seldom acknowledged, the moments of seriousness in the text far outnumber those of comedy. Many of the most infamous examples of humorous irreverence, sudden sallies of flippant opinion, are themselves embedded in contexts of earnest argumentation. Thus, to take only two examples, the iconoclastic dismissal of "The Last Supper" as a "mournful wreck" (*IA* 150) is followed by a lengthy discussion of aesthetic standards (the "mournful wreck" remark serving in context as a kind of journalistic attention-getter), and the wild query to the "sons" of Italy, "Why don't you rob your church?" comes as the deliberately inflammatory climax to a searching series of reflections on the economic and political condition of Italy (*IA* 203). In his illuminating analysis of *The Innocents Abroad*, Cox has suggested that Twain's humor is so recurrent, and so deflationary, that it eventually calls into question all expressions of sincerity, engendering in the reader a skepticism that threatens to undermine the book's moments of seriousness (*Fate* 54–55). The opposite seems to me more nearly the case: the seriousness itself is so pervasive, and so convincing, that the turns of humor, whether irreverent, self-denigrating, sarcastic, or farcical, appear as mere play—as momentary departures from a prevailing steadiness, what we might call short comic side trips on the serious grand tour.

To perform the act of judgment that lies at the center of Victorian travel narratives, Twain, like other American travelers, assumes and constructs in *The Innocents Abroad* a "superiority based on class, race, gender, and national identity" (Stowe xi). Creating such a self, he is empowered to pass manifold judgments on the societies he encounters. Like the typical Victorian traveler, he judges foreign cultures, confirming his preconceptions of "the other," in order to maintain cultural hegemony. In *The Innocents Abroad* he performs this fundamental Victorian act over and over again. Bennett Kravitz has pointed out that Twain uses American "geography" as an "ideological construct" to measure the older worlds he traverses (30), but this is only one of several key tactics Twain employs to ensure his cultural domination. As he performs the characteristic act of Victorian judgment, he aggressively assesses the cultures he encounters in terms of progress, hygiene, women, morality, and religion. And his judgments, the very lifeblood of his text, turn out to be as Victorian—as conventional for a Victorian—as the act of judging itself.

The pattern of his assessments emerges as early as the *Quaker City*'s first landfall at Fayal in the Azores. Within two short chapters (5 and 6) Twain dissects the anatomy of the Portuguese community: taking in the land, its villages, towns, and roads; explaining the local economy; touching on the governmental organization and politics; defining the religious outlook; and above all evaluating the people themselves in terms of their intelligence, knowledge, hygiene, and morality. With variations, this kind of scrutiny is repeated again and again in his travels. What Twain does is quite simply to judge the societies he encounters in terms of a thoroughly conventional Anglo-American ideology of civilization; he ranks a people on a dual continuum of modernization and morality, finding them more or less developed, more or less virtuous. His characteristic way of seeing is encapsulated in the tableau he creates when he reports on the International Exposition at Paris: "Napoleon III., the representative of the highest modern civilization, progress, and refinement; Abdul-Aziz, the representative of a people by nature and training filthy, brutish, ignorant, unprogressive, superstitious—and a government whose Three Graces are Tyranny, Rapacity, Blood. Here in brilliant Paris, under this majestic Arch of Triumph, the First Century greets the Nineteenth!" (*IA* 101).

This is a classic example of the Eurocentric, racist thinking—fantasizing, really—that was characteristic of Victorians. The imagined contrast is nothing less than a lurid configuring of civilization versus savagery, a contrast deployed throughout the nineteenth century to legitimize aggressive imperialist ventures (Pratt, Spurr). Such envisioning is habitual with Twain. While on the surface it seems to affirm a progressive set of political, economic, social, technological, and moral ideals, it actually functions in public terms as an argument for the extension of western culture and in personal terms as a safeguard for the self against the threat of the Other.[3] The dark underside of the vision is repeatedly manifest in Twain's travel narrative. Judging foreign communities, he pointedly degrades their people. He calls the citizens of Fayal, for instance, "unclean" people who "lie" and "cheat" (*IA* 45), and insists that they are "slow, poor, shiftless, sleepy, and lazy" (*IA* 44); he denounces those who greet the ship, "men and women, and boys and girls" as "ragged, and barefoot, uncombed and unclean, and by instinct, education, and profession, beggars" (*IA* 41). Struck as he first encounters a foreign world, this note of emphatic degradation is sounded throughout Twain's text. Here are just three of many examples:

Civita Vecchia is "the finest nest of dirt, vermin and ignorance we have found yet, except that African perdition they call Tangier, which is just like it." (*IA* 205)

The Arabs of Palestine are "infested with vermin, and the dirt had caked on them until it amounted to bark. . . . The lame, the halt, the blind, the leprous—all the distempers that are bred of indolence, dirt, and iniquity— were represented in the Congress in ten minutes, and still they came!" (*IA* 375–76)

The people of Endor "do not mind dirt; they do not mind rags; they do not mind vermin; they do not mind barbarous ignorance and savagery; they do not mind a reasonable degree of starvation." (*IA* 431)

Notable here is Twain's linking of dirt with intellectual and moral limitation: ignorance, iniquity, and even savagery are all signaled for him by filth. For Twain, as for other Victorians in America as well as England, hygiene is a sign of morality.[4] Twain's vehement attacks, his insistent but often unfounded debasements of foreign people, erect protective barriers between his culture and alien ones—and between himself and various manifestations of the Other.

As he judges his way through Europe, the Near East, and the Holy Land, Twain looks repeatedly at that most enticing expression of the Other to the male eye: women. J. D. Stahl has perceptively observed that Twain's anecdotes often "reveal a subtext of sexual curiosity and anxiety" (39). His traveler's gaze is a traditionally male one, and it seems to arise in part from the scopophilia suggested so strongly in his preexcursion writings. This, too, is conventional for a Victorian traveler (a male one) in at least two ways. On the one hand, from at least the eighteenth century on, English-speaking travelers had journeyed to the continent to satisfy erotic desire, either through direct sexual encounter or through vicarious voyeurism (on the erotics of travel, see Porter, *Haunted Journeys*). As John Pemble has shown in *The Mediterranean Passion*, southern Europe in particular became the playground for such self-indulgence. But the conventional male attention to foreign women involved even more than illicit desire. In a special issue of *Ethnohistory* devoted to travel writing, Caroline B. Brettel has argued that nineteenth-century travelers had a "fixation" on women because they found in them both the "most exotic manifestation of 'the other'" and a "dramatic contrast to the Victorian ideal of womanhood" (132). Women became, in the eyes of the typical traveler like Mark Twain, not only the object of desire but also the measure of civilization.

The more elegant and refined, the more delicate and graceful the women he saw in his travels were, the more Mark Twain was inclined to find worth in the society of which they were a part. He is moved to an approval of France by its "stylishly dressed women" (*IA* 78), and again in Italy, a country he generally faults for its poverty, politics, and Catholicism, he finds Genoa a blessed place because of its "beautiful" women who are, he observes, "as dressy, and as tasteful and as graceful as they could possibly be without being angels" (*IA* 128). The terms of his encomium reflect his traditional Victorian idealization of proper womanhood. These women of high fashion promenade nightly, and Twain's delight in them seems to arise from the fact that their dress for public display artfully unites sexuality with propriety, thus bridging a dangerous Victorian divide. His enchantment with fine womanhood, both in itself and as an index to civilization, reaches a kind of climax and his ideal of the woman finds its apotheosis when he sees the emperor of Russia's daughter, "the modest little Grand Duchess Marie" (*IA* 311). "Fourteen years old, light-haired, blue-eyed, unassuming and pretty," she is, Twain says, a "weak, diffident schoolgirl" (*IA* 311–12). But then he imagines, without a shred of evidence, that her "gentleness," if addressed to her father, could wield "tremendous power" (*IA* 312). This fantasy both enshrines female innocence and endows it with the moral force to guide civilizations. It reveals the bent of Twain's deepest feelings about women. The young grand duchess is a kind of Becky Thatcher projected from the depths of his psyche onto the lawns of the czar's summer palace.

When he sees—or thinks he sees—purity in foreign women, he praises them and their homeland. When he glimpses—or imagines—impurity and flaws in the women of other cultures, he attacks them and their country. At issue in this simple duality is no doubt Twain's own purity, a purity put in jeopardy by his strong attraction to women. Not surprisingly, then, in *The Innocents Abroad* he both recoils from the impure and seeks it out; he is both innocent and not. The Victorian prude in him moralizes against Petrarch for loving Laura (another man's wife) and celebrates Heloise's uncle for arranging the castration of Abelard (a fit return for seduction), while the "Other Victorian" in him longs to see the notorious cancan and revels in bawdy Italian peasant girls. When he witnesses the cancan, Twain dramatizes his ambivalence with self-conscious humor: "I placed my hands before my face for very shame. But I looked through my fingers" (*IA* 108). He is careful, however, to restore a proper morality to this episode at the end by comparing the dance to an orgy of devils and witches (*IA* 109).

His chance encounter with risqué peasant girls is quite different. He presents the meeting as one that shatters his illusion of their picturesque innocence, and refrains from giving it a moral gloss, thus releasing a momentary delight in sexual waywardness (see chap. 19). His apparent internal conflict, his delight in and objection to overt female sexuality, generates moments of odd humor. In Constantinople he recalls with indignation old slave marts in which girls were sold "as if they were horses." Then he pens a burlesque "Slave Girl Market Report" whose humor depends on the very reduction of women to commodities that has incensed him (*IA* 290–91). Stranger still, when he takes a bath in Milan and calls out for soap, which an obliging servant woman attempts to bring him, he creates a parody of female helplessness, with himself as the endangered: "Beware, woman! Go away from here—go away, now, or it will be the worse for you. I am an unprotected male, but I will preserve my honor at the peril of my life!" (*IA* 148).

The playful gender-crossing here posits a very pure Mark Twain. His most frequent inhibited response to conflicted desire, however—one typical of male travelers—is to debase the very objects of that attraction. Having dreamed (with the help of travel books) of beautiful, alluring grisettes, he seeks them out in Paris only to insist that the "dozens" of them he sees are all "homely": "They had large hands, large feet, large mouths; they had pug noses as a general thing, and mustaches that not even good breeding could overlook; . . . they were ill-shaped, they were not winning, they were not graceful; I knew by their looks that . . . it would be a base flattery to call them immoral" (*IA* 120). Here the objects of his desire are made too ugly to merit illicit engagement. Similarly, though he is intrigued by veiled Moorish, Turkish, and Arabian women, when he actually manages to glimpse some of these exotic women, these "houris," as he calls them, he finds them "dusky hags" (*IA* 482), associates them with filth and vermin, and explains such customs as a "kiss of welcome" by insisting that "a man would not be likely to kiss one of the women of this country of his own free will and accord" (*IA* 433). Through such debasements he secures himself against the disruptive force of his own desire, for in his travels he seems to hold sexuality itself in opposition to both personal morality and true civilization.

While recognizing that the Mark Twain of *The Innocents Abroad* is a highly critical traveler, John C. Gerber points out that it is "not easy to pin down the central principles of Twain's criticism" (*Mark Twain* 34). (Gerber goes on to observe that Twain is always annoyed by "pretension or hypocrisy" and always outraged by "injustice or cruelty" [34].) It is curious that this Twain who passes judgments so frequently and so strongly should seem so elusive. Individual passages of criticism are always clear and emphatic, but it is hard to compute their sum. Some passages do seem to have more general import than others, however—to move us closer to Twain's general outlook. Here, for instance, Mark Twain, judge without portfolio, complains mightily about what seems to strike him as the most abject human condition—life without principle:

> *They* [the inhabitants of rural villages in Italy] have nothing to do but eat and sleep and sleep and eat, and toil a little when they can get a friend to stand by and keep them awake. *They* are not paid for thinking—*they* are not paid to fret about the world's concerns. They were not respectable people— they were not worthy people—they were not learned and wise and brilliant people—but in their breasts, all their stupid lives long, resteth a peace that passeth understanding! How can men, calling themselves men, consent to be so degraded and happy? (*IA* 164, Twain's emphasis)

The comic fling of the final word does not really change the force of the indictment. Twain condemns these people for existence at the subsistence level. His valuation predicates something like a normative scale of humanity that elevates respectability, learning, wisdom, and thought itself as the higher expressions of the human. Its final sentence also evokes the familiar Victorian notion, one that would be of particular importance to Twain throughout his career, that manhood depends upon the exertion of one's higher faculties, upon the exercise of thought and spirit.

Often, however, Twain's criticism takes a more distinctly moral turn. He faults his fellow pilgrims for not having gentleness, charity, and tender mercy (*IA* 356), and on the other hand, when he is moved to praise Dominican friars for risking their lives to aid cholera victims, he celebrates what he calls "the charity, the purity, the unselfishness" that are "in the hearts of men like these" (*IA* 205). These are two of his most impassioned adjudications, the one critical, the other celebratory, and in both cases he invokes traditional Christian virtues—the so-called soft or sentimental ones. It has become commonplace to say that at the level of culture such attributes were often used in the nineteenth century to rationalize, to disguise, the realities of harsh and competitive capitalism (Douglas 12). For Twain personally, they no doubt eventually came to function this way, but at the time of *The Innocents Abroad* he was a long way from being a practicing capitalist himself. His insistence on soft virtues both reflects his latent religious outlook and provides a moral gloss that covers, or at least mitigates, his own combativeness. What his censure and praise reveal is that beneath the playfulness or the rancor of his judgments, Twain's moral outlook is almost stodgily traditional.

So is the idea of civilization he upholds. The heart of civilization, for this Mark Twain, as for Victorians in general, is predictably religion and the morality that derives from it. His quarrel with excessive piety—or outright sham—in either his fellow travelers or in the institutions he encounters conceals somewhat the extent to which he values religion and judges nations in terms of it. Much of his dissatisfaction with Italy comes from his sense that Catholicism has not fostered a moral society, and his denigrations of non-Christian cultures betray a similar suspicion that their religions have not created an ethical people. This concern for the religious foundation of conduct is relatively new. While the western Moralist of the Main was at one with prevailing social norms, he was not concerned with their grounding in (or possible opposition to) religious belief, though he did praise the imposition of Christianity on the Sandwich Islands. Perhaps the trip to old Christian cultures and to the Holy Land altered the focus of his moral reflections; perhaps travel itself provoked a reassessment; or perhaps there was a personal crisis brewing. In any case, the persona of *The Innocents Abroad* is deeply attuned to the nature and consequence of religious belief.

His time in the Holy Land is thus of special importance to him. Most critics have found a falling off in the Holy Land sections, but the importance of that part of the journey for pilgrims and sinners alike (and, of course, the sinners were not really very sinful) was immense. All were disappointed. As Dewey Ganzel has observed, they came "looking for a Sunday School supplement; they found a near-desert Middle Eastern country, and they preferred the image they brought to the one they found" (246). Twain himself finds the landscape intolerable, and he creates a litany celebrating its hellishness: "The further we went the hotter the sun got, and the more rocky and bare, repulsive and dreary the landscape became" (*IA* 442); "The ghastly, treeless, grassless, breathless canons smothered us as if we had been in an oven" (*IA* 477). And so on in passage after passage. The land of the Holy Land is repugnant: desolate, blistering, arid, empty, stultifying. Twain faces in the landscape the possibility, perhaps the likelihood, that life itself is a void, for the blankness of the terrain suggests the emptiness of existence, the nothingness of human life. He projects his uneasy sense of meaninglessness, futility, and inevitable death:

> Gray lizards, those heirs of ruin, of sepulchers and desolation, glided in and out among the rocks or lay still and sunned themselves. Where prosperity has reigned, and fallen; where glory has flamed, and gone out; where beauty has dwelt, and passed away; where gladness was, and sorrow is; where the pomp of life has been, and silence and death brood in its high places, there this reptile makes his home, and mocks at human vanity. His coat is the color of ashes: and ashes are the symbol of hopes that have perished, of aspirations that came to naught, of loves that are buried. If he could speak, he would say, Build temples: I will lord it in their ruins; build palaces: I will inhabit them; erect empires: I will inherit them; bury your beautiful: I will watch the worms at their work; and you, who stand here and moralize over me: I will crawl over *your* corpse at the last. (*IA* 387)

The rhetoric of this reflection—its contrived (and clichéd) eloquence—should not discount its emotional honesty and intellectual impact. Twain wrote passages of this sort throughout his career, for he seems to have enjoyed their craft and felt their truth. While the conventional language and images here are cast in a stylized prose, the controlling idea is still powerful. Vagueness, abstraction, and convention conspire to soften the vision, but it registers not only the vanity of human endeavor but also the deathly end of human life itself. Robinson has suggested that Twain's divided narrator may entertain the possibility of "oblivion" as "the release from the intolerable burden of consciousness" ("Patterns of Consciousness" 55). But the awareness of annihilation becomes the counterpoint to Twain's interest in faith, creating yet another—and most profound— division in consciousness.[5]

In a study that deserves more currency than it has received, James D. Wilson has argued that Twain is the only member of the *Quaker City* excursion for whom the pilgrimage to the holy shrines of Christianity, the sacred places of origin, "becomes genuine" ("Religious and Esthetic Vision" 161). It seems authentic in part because it is tempered by the honesty, not to say the skepticism, with which Twain views the religious worlds he discovers. While his fellow travelers react out of unthinking, predetermined reflex, he does try, as he says in his famous preface, to see "with impartial eyes" and to write of what he sees "honestly, whether wisely or not" (*IA* 3). Ironically, by the time he reaches the Holy Land, what he has seen—and candidly testified to—is the corruption of religion by superstition, commercialization, and worldly politics. In his scrutiny of France and Italy, he finds religion so encumbered with material embodiments as to have lost all inner truth. In saying so, he knows that he seems to lack a proper reverence for sacred things; his defense is not that he is concerned with true spirituality (for this would smack of sanctimony and self-complacency) but that he is honest. With somewhat uncharacteristic coyness he signals what he truly believes is his unique eminence as truth-teller: "But more than all, I wished that old Diogenes, groping so patiently with his lantern, searching so zealously for one solitary honest man in all the world, might meander along and stumble on our party. I ought not to say it, may be, but still I suppose he would have put out his light" (*IA* 275).

Twain is nowhere more truthful than in his personal notebooks, the jottings that recorded both the trip and his impressions of it. The notebooks are remarkable for their nonliterary quality. They are largely factual notations of the places and scenes of his journeying and lists of potentially useful biblical passages. They no doubt reflect, as their editors point out, the professional journalist who needs only a brief memorandum to trigger an extensive travel letter (*N&J1* 373). Among the welter of factual information and the extensive listings, however, one also finds such entries as these, often given parenthetically after some place: "well authenticate" (*N&J1* 431), or more simply (and grammatically) "authentic" (*N&J1* 439). They reflect the continuing desire to separate the real from the fraudulent, but that effort itself raises an epistemological problem that actually underlies the whole of Twain's judgmental traveling: how does one know? Two other brief notebook entries give further focus to the issue. Of Jacob's well Twain records first this: "Well 90 ft deep—solid rock" (*N&J1* 431) and then later this: "This well, these mountains, yonder city were looked upon by the Savior" (*N&J1* 476). The first entry reflects facts, or what we might call Twain's rational empiricist bent; the second is the product of faith, or what we might call his intuitive idealist disposition.

The Innocents Abroad is anything but a philosophical text, of course, so Twain does not directly argue the epistemological issue, but one can see him in the grips of its dilemma. What he does do, however, is to make his many judgments from *both* perspectives. He is famed (and sometimes defamed) as an empiricist who measures the world by his direct experience. He sometimes judges such things as popular ideas, standard history, all manner of art, and a range of values by their fidelity to facts, to things as they are as he observes them and understands them through his reason, thus giving ascendancy to direct, sensory experience. He determines truth through pragmatic testing. At the same time, though, in his first travel narrative he also evaluates the world in terms of his abstract conceptions of it. He sometimes judges ideas, history, art, and values not by their correspondence to facts but by their approximation of his own intuitive constructs, thus placing a premium on the inner workings of the mind. He calculates truth through mental imagining. Paradoxically, at least from a philosophical point of view, he tells the truths he so prides himself on in terms of both things as they are in empiric reality and things as they are in idealist reality.

This conflict in Twain's way of knowing reaches a kind of climax in the Church of the Holy Sepulcher in Jerusalem. Of all the scared shrines in the Holy Land, this is the one most potent with meaning for him, yet as it turns out, that meaning is encumbered by the usual transparent shams. Most of the holy spots pointed out within the church have "nothing genuine about them," since they are "imaginary holy places created by the monks" (*IA* 455). Twain meets such fraudulence in part by feigning belief in the unbelievable. In the famous Tomb of Adam lament, he burlesques the kind of emotion that a true shrine might engender. He also makes fun of the imagined effort of a true believer to verify his convictions though empirical experimentation. The Church of the Holy Sepulcher is said to contain a short column that, according to tradition, "marks the *exact centre of the earth*" (*IA* 450). Twain invents a tale of a "sceptic" who seeks to prove this allegation by standing above the column at noon to see if the sun "gave him a shadow." No shadow is cast, Twain explains, because it was a cloudy day—"the sun threw no shadows at all" but the skeptic is nonetheless convinced. Twain observes with mock innocence: "Proofs like these are not to be set aside by the idle tongues of cavilers. To such as are not bigoted, and are willing to be convinced, they carry a conviction nothing can ever shake" (*IA* 451). Twain's fanciful tale has multiple targets: he spoofs the claim that the pillar marks the center of the earth, satirizes the credulous who believe such nonsense, and makes fun of those who would prove a matter of faith by experiment. In this case the issue attested to by faith, the centering of the earth about the column, is not to be credited, but neither is the empirical method, however misapplied, in matters people choose to believe.

But complicating this comic rendering of idiotic faith posing as scientific demonstration is Twain's own curious effort to validate his idealist intuition that the place of the Crucifixion is authentic. Of all the shrines in the church, this spot alone moves him.[6] As he tours the church, he is made uneasy by three things: by the renown of the place (it is, he says, "the most sacred locality on earth to millions and millions of men, and women, and children, the noble and the humble, bond and free" [*IA* 457]); by the fact that it is dominated by non-Protestant Christianity (all "sects of Christians [except Protestants] have chapels," he observes

[*IA* 447]); and by the presence within the church of so much that is palpably fraudulent. Ironically in this holy of holies, religious faith is put to the test by religious sham.

Perhaps because of his uneasiness, Twain takes refuge for most of the chapter in the impersonal "one/he" and the general "we." The "I" emerges to do only two things. First, to joke: Twain pretends to seize the sword of King Godfrey of Jerusalem and turn it against a native: "I tried it on a Moslem, and clove him in twain like a doughnut" (*IA* 449–50). (The burlesque lament at the tomb of Adam is also a first-person performance, of course.) Second, to record his response to "the very spot where the Saviour gave up his life" (*IA* 455): "I climbed," he says now of himself, "the stairway in the church which brings one to the top of the small inclosed pinnacle of rock, and looked upon the place where the true cross once stood, with far more absorbing interest than I had ever felt in any thing earthly before" (*IA* 456). This is perhaps as close as Mark Twain comes during his trip abroad to affirming a religious conviction through a traveler's conventional gesture. The extravagance of the claim that this is the most engrossing sight he has ever witnessed is softened by the cliché used to express it—"absorbing interest"—and bolstered by the flat narrative of his ascent to the viewpoint that proceeds it. But before he can thus quietly feel the reality of his faith, Twain tries to shore it up through rational thought. He tries to authenticate the place of the Crucifixion—to explain why this place, unlike so many other holy ones, is to be believed in, why it "affects him differently" (*IA* 455)—by arguing that Christ's fame at the time of his death would have made the spot "a memorable place for ages," that the cataclysmic events accompanying the death (storm, darkness, earthquake) would have fixed the execution and its locality "in the memory of even the most thoughtless witness," and that— here he borrows openly from Prime—people would then "transmit the story to their children" for hundreds of years (*IA* 455). This struggle to back faith by rational analysis (and presumed facts) may betray a gnawing doubt, or it may only be an effort to reclaim for a troubled faith some authentic site in the face of so many false ones. Ironically it reveals at the climax of his religious journeying the dilemma of relocating the very grounds of belief. In this, as in so much else, Mark Twain is a very Victorian Traveler.[7]

ALMOST ELEVEN YEARS separate *The Innocents Abroad* from Twain's next full-scale travel book, *A Tramp Abroad.* They were years in which Clemens exchanged the semi-vagabondage of his early life for a settled domesticity. They were also years in which he resolved the problem of his career by committing Mark Twain to authorship (and occasional lecturing) with notable success, publishing *Roughing It* in 1872, *The Gilded Age* (written with Charles Dudley Warner, of course) in 1873, and *Tom Sawyer* in 1876, along with three volumes of miscellaneous sketches. The three long works all reveal further dimensions of the proper Mark Twain visible in the first travel book: *Roughing It*, as we've seen, mocks a wayward western past while idealizing conventional goals and values; *The Gilded Age* unleashes a traditional moral satire at the manifold corruptions of commercial and political life; and through a haze of nostalgia *Tom Sawyer* celebrates a naughty but exciting childhood—a time dear to the heart of the Gilded Age. All these texts, while stamped with the humor and idiosyncrasy of Mark Twain, are compatible with New England respectability.

The glaring exception to this series of orthodox literary performances is Twain's Whittier birthday speech. Given in December 1877, at the celebration arranged by the *Atlantic Monthly* to honor Whittier on his seventieth birthday as one of the great American poets, that speech misfired. It seems today so fraught with latent antagonism toward eastern respectability and its canonical writers that it has become "a kind of primal scene of Twain criticism" (Lowry 24). It raises the pivotal issue of Mark Twain's relation to the dominant culture of the genteel East. Clemens cast the tale as a conflict of cultures, as Mark Twain's report of an ignorant western miner's account of his overnight encounter in his own cabin with three rowdy deadbeats pretending to be Emerson, Longfellow, and Holmes—three of the cultural patriarchs of New England assembled at the birthday banquet to pay tribute to Whittier. At the end of the story Twain tries to explain to the exasperated and deceived miner that the three roughs who drink, swear, cardsharp, and steal are not the poets they pretend to be but "impostors," only to have the miner challenge the identity of Mark Twain. "Ah!—impostors, were they?" the miner exclaims. "Are *you?*" (*MTC1* 699).

The shocks to Twain's audience, to the newspapers that reported the event, and to Clemens/Twain himself have been amply documented. And by all accounts, Twain, with more than a little help from Howells, exaggerated, indeed fabricated, the extent of his failure.[8] In an illuminating analysis of the speech in terms of the culture's shifting conception of authorship and the changing authority of the literary itself, Richard Lowry locates in Twain's response this collapse: a failure to "figure an authorial identity capable of grasping the authority to face an audience" (27). This nicely centers the key issue in the dynamics of Twain's self-presentation. Not all of his protective layers of narrative structure (the miner—Twain—Clemens) could separate the teller from the tale in this case, especially when the teller stood before his audience. (Twain is far less noticeable when one reads the sketch, and Clemens, having been displaced by—or more exactly, having become—Mark Twain, is invisible.) To counter the irreverence of the tale he pretends to have been told, Clemens seems to have thought that a sophisticated audience would get Mark Twain's joke, seems not to have perceived either the sketch's covert hostility or his audience's latent anxiety about the profession of letters he sported with, and seems, most of all, to have assumed that Mark Twain would be understood as a proper person. Yet he miscalculated the public perception of Twain, which was still that of a wayward humorist, and, most telling of all, Twain himself failed to generate propriety within his text. Before his speech and certainly after it, Mark Twain was suspect.

Although no one has, one might well argue that Twain's overreaction to the minor failure—or modest success—of his speech actually reveals his affinities with the very writers targeted in his speech. He not only apologized cringingly to the three eminent writers with whom he had toyed but also denigrated himself as a heedless "savage" (qtd. in Smith, *Development* 99), a term he usually reserved for those whom he saw in his travels as inferior to Anglo-Americans. He felt that he had so offended that he should even withdraw his next scheduled publication in the *Atlantic*, the rather lightweight burlesque of sentimental love stories mockingly entitled "The Loves of Alonzo Fitz Clarence and Rosannah Ethelton." "It will," he insisted to Howells, "hurt the Atlantic for me to appear in its pages, now." Accounting his blunder immense, he considered a complete retreat: "I feel that my misfortune has injured me all over the country; therefore it will be best that I retire from before the public at present"

(*MTHL* 1:212). Surely such distress bespeaks a concern for decorum that in itself suggests a kinship with the genteel writers he was presumed to have offended. Critics have surmised that the fiasco of the speech was the cause of—or at least one of the major spurs to—the trip he took to Europe from April 1878 to September 1879, the excursion that provided the basis for *A Tramp Abroad*. That narrative was designed to lay to rest any doubt of Mark Twain's propriety.[9]

Twain deliberately entitled his second travel book to recall his first. Warily, he anticipated the critical comparison he sought: "And you see," he explained to Joseph Twichell, "this book is either going to be compared with the Innocents Abroad [*sic*], or *contrasted* with it, to my disadvantage" (*MTL* 1:350). His struggle to compose the book—"a life-and-death battle" (*MTHL* 1:286), he called it—is probably better known than the book itself. With characteristic volatility he switched his mind about it again and again in the long process of its making, hotly railing against it one moment as a "most infernally troublesome" work (*MTHL* 1:290), modestly praising it the next as "no dead corpse of a thing" (*MTL* 1:350). He eventually made *A Tramp Abroad* surprisingly original in form and not so surprisingly conventional in value. How well he succeeded may be indicated by the fact that *A Tramp* proved to be Mark Twain's most popular book in England, selling an astonishing 174,250 copies between 1880 and 1910 (Welland 235). While the Mark Twain of *The Innocents Abroad* had freely judged civilizations, measuring them in terms of their progress, morality, hygiene, women, and religion, the persona of *A Tramp* is circumspect with criticism. In his notebooks Twain fretted about being seen as caustic and irreverent: "Say very little on this delicate subject," "put that into somebody else's mouth," "Put these things in the mouth of critical foreigner" (*N&J2* 54, 57). To solve his presentational problems, he considered inventing travel companions—the Grumbler, John, Haggerty, Harris—to express his critical moods, and while he did make some use of a fictive version of Joseph Twichell, his real companion for part of the trip, he actually ended up venting such invective as the book contains in his own voice.

That voice, the Twain persona in this text, is notably different from that heard in *The Innocents Abroad*. It has been likened to the narrator of

Roughing It because it often assumes "the stance and the language of the feckless lazy man" (Gibson, *Art* 66), but the persona is more than idle and linguistically easy about his indolence. The Mark Twain of this text is a genteel tourist, the very type of traveler often attacked in his first travel book. The actual circumstances of Clemens's trip abetted, if they did not dictate, this self-representation, for unlike his tour with the *Quaker City* pilgrims, his trip abroad to create his second travel book was an excursion encumbered by a considerable household. With him were his wife, Livy, his two daughters, Susy and Clara, and Livy's friend Clara Spaulding, as well as a nursemaid, Rosina Hay, and a valet and baggage agent, George Griffin. While Twain seldom acknowledges this traveling household, he does note in passing that he is a participant in the pastimes of affluent middle-class tourists, in particular their entertainments and arts of self-cultivation. He reports on dressing, dining, and polite social conversation; on music appreciation, opera attendance, and poetry translation; on tourist shopping, art collecting, and even cooking. While there is a fair measure of amusement over these genteel diversions (especially, of course, over the opera), Twain is generally more tolerant than satiric. The pressures that animated his first travel book, strident self-assertion, contentious judgment, are largely absent from the second. Twain appears on the whole as a conventional, complacent, and prominent traveler—so prominent that he could remind himself: "I needed to come to a country where I was unknown" (*N&J2* 163)—in short, a bourgeois tourist.

Twain's voice is so controlled by his conventional role that his humor is often tame, flat, and self-consciously coy. He is innocuously naughty: "But of course we were dead tired, and slept like policemen" (*TA* 1:295); "We have the notion in our country that Italians never do any heavy work at all, but confine themselves to the lighter arts, like organ-grinding, operatic singing, and assassination" (*TA* 1:154). Often he is whimsical: "the horse leaned up against a fence and rested" (*TA* 1:106); "It seemed to me that if I owned an elephant that was a keepsake, and I thought a good deal of him, I would think twice before I would ride him over that bridge" (*TA* 2:88). His voice becomes so genteel it sometimes cloys: "I have been strictly reared, but if it had not been so dark and solemn and awful in there in that lonely, vast room, I do believe I should have said something then which could not be put into a Sunday-school book without injuring the sale of it" (*TA* 1:116).

A Tramp Abroad opens, as most readers have noticed, by not going anywhere. Having introduced himself as a pedestrian tourist, to be accompanied on his travels by his agent, Harris, Twain suspends his narrative. He enlarges upon a series of seeming irrelevancies (though what they are irrelevant to is at this point only the idea of a travel book) that range from operas to duels. What seems to be taking place in these curiously disjunctive episodes and disquisitions is a process that Richard Bridgman sees as fundamental to all Twain's travel narratives: an indulgence of the self's deep (often suppressed) vagaries that turns the text into a casual stroll through the landscape of the mind (*Traveling* 1–13). In this case what seems to mark that landscape of the mind are Twain's anxieties about his own professional competence, concern with his creative process, and frettings over his authorial identity. In short, embedded in a number of these initial wanderings, severely refracted, are Twain's feelings about writing itself.

Print, the very medium of his expression, and fame, his desired goal in writing, are both evoked in his longing to visit "the birthplace of Gutenberg," a longing defeated by the fact that the site has not been memorialized (*TA* 1:10). His writerly inclination to attitudinize in the familiar mode of a romantic traveler—"I . . . presently fell into a train of dreamy thought" (*TA* 1:21)—is comically contested, he reports, by three scornful ravens who squall "insulting remarks" at him, to which he responds by refusing to "bandy words with a raven" (*TA* 1:23). More important, the ordeal of writing is suggested as he tells—or more accurately, retells—the famous bluejay yarn, a tale which points out the difficulty the bird, significantly a wordsmith who can phrase whatever he feels in fine language, in "rattling, out-and-out book talk" that is "bristling with metaphor" (*TA* 1:25), has filling a house with acorns, a difficulty that is obviously analogous to Twain's own compositional struggle to fill his two-volume travel book. Most revealing of all, however, is his gratuitous retelling of the German legend of the Knave of Bergen. In that tale a masked figure appears at a coronation ball, charms the empress as well as the other royal guests by the "grace of his manner" and his "fine conver-

sation," only to be exposed at the unmasking hour as the lowly execu-
tioner of Bergen (*TA* 1:13). The king is outraged at the insult brought to
his queen by the Knave's criminal audacity and at first condemns the ex-
ecutioner to death, but then he hears—and finally accedes to—the in-
genious plea that the only way to eradicate the shame and disgrace is to
knight the Knave. The legend of the Knave of Bergen seems to register
Twain's feelings of past insubordination and present guilt. But the central action of the tale is one of triumphant exculpation: the Knave is not
just vindicated; he is knighted and thereby given public title to an inner
grace. The fable becomes an empowering fantasy that suggests both
Twain's personal sense of self and his authority as a writer. However he
may have appeared when he gave his Whittier birthday speech, Twain
unmasks himself here as a noble figure.

Critics have generally given *A Tramp Abroad* short shrift, finding it the
least successful of Twain's travel books. It is usually faulted for its "shapelessness," "silliness," "digressions," and general lack of "plan" (Emerson,
Authentic 104–6; see also Cox, *Fate* 151, and Geismar 57). Yet one can
discern a kind of plan, one that actually makes use of shapelessness, silliness, and digression. Twain describes himself in the book as a "literary
pioneer" (*TA* 1:97), and it seems to me that whatever the shortcomings
of his narrative, he does engineer an original travel book. *A Tramp Abroad*
is one of Twain's most daring and innovative travel pieces, simply because
he does in it what no one had done before: he writes a travel narrative in
which *nothing happens*. The audacity of his enterprise is matched by its
difficulty. To make nothing the something of his book he had to impro-
vise emptiness, to invent misses, lacks, and vacancies, to exploit the un-
seen, the unencountered, the unexperienced. In sum, he has to narrate—
for a full two volumes—nothing.

The book's curious opening is of a piece with its general design. At the
outset he announces his excursion abroad as a three-part undertaking.
With casual deadpan he depicts himself as an adventurer committed to a
pedestrian tour in Germany and the Alps, as a novice painter devoted to
improving his art, and as a philologist determined to master the German
language. And then he subverts these activities.[10] He not only fails to
learn German but does not even try within the narrative (he relegates his

whimsical account of the language to appendix D); he never studies paint-ing, a point driven home comically by the proud exhibition of his hope-less sketches, which have the look not just of the amateur but of the school-child; and, of course, he never walks on his pedestrian tour when he can take a cab, train, cart, boat, coach, raft, or wagon. At times his insistent repetition of his nonperformance of these tasks becomes tedious, but that is just the point: repetition creates the sense that nothing is going on. One running joke is that when he tries to travel as a proper tourist he fails because he is an inveterate bungler. His narrative becomes, in some of its most engaging episodes, an account of what he does not see—the very opposite of a conventional travel book. He misses one sight after another, by going to the wrong place, by failing to arrive in time at the right one, or by falling asleep at the crucial moment of spectacle. He uses such tac-tics to further the sense of non-event. The famous attempt to see an Alpine sunrise, the climax of volume one in the original two-volume edition, is a virtuoso imagining of defeated tourism. The effort fails because Twain and Harris sleep through one sunrise after another, then mistake a sun-set for a sunrise, and finally peer steadily west on their final day as the sun rises gloriously in the east. Somewhat too self-consciously announcing the drift of *A Tramp Abroad,* Twain reports that Harris tells him "a man might travel to the ends of the earth" with him "and never see anything" (*TA* 2:35).

Some of the strategies Twain hits upon to keep nothing happening are obviously strained. Adventure by proxy is a case in point. When he at-tends the opera, climbs mountains, visits landmarks, and even bows to other travelers through the agency of his companion, Harris, the point is right but the presentation is flimsy. At times he responds to nonevents in peculiar ways: he laments that a young girl does not fall off a bridge into a mountain gorge (*TA* 2, chap. 7), and he complains about not find-ing the corpse of an earlier traveler presumed to have slipped off a preci-pice (*TA* 2, chap. 6). Yet Twain also manages to create a couple of meta-phors worthy of the heroically perverse design of *A Tramp Abroad.* To imagine, as he does, climbing Mont Blanc by telescope and descending from Riffelberg to Zermatt by glacier is to have nothing less than Alpine conceptions of nontravel.

In *A Tramp Abroad* Twain spoofs several popular kinds of travel writing. The first sentence signals his burlesque intent: "One day it occurred to me that it had been many years since the world had been afforded the spectacle of a man adventurous enough to undertake a journey through Europe on foot" (*TA* 1:9). The humor here depends upon the fact that pedestrian tours—and written accounts of them—had become a small fad, not at all something the world was uninformed of. In the course of his book, Twain broadens his joke to include at least three forms of travel writing: the account of a pedestrian tour, a form made famous by Bayard Taylor in *Views A-Foot;* the narrative of a boat trip on a river, reported at length in one instance by Twain's neighbor, Charles Dudley Warner, in his popular *My Winter on the Nile;* and the report of an Alpine climb, celebrated by a host of people but perhaps most sensationally by Edward Whymper in *Scrambles amongst the Alps in the Years 1860–69.* Twain subverts pedestrianism by never walking when he can ride; he mocks river travel by depicting his raft trip as a perilous sea voyage; and he explodes Alpine climbing by turning his ascent of Riffelberg into a lunatic extravaganza. In many ways the Riffelberg episode is the premature climax to *A Tramp Abroad.* The burlesque is overlong and often heavy-footed, but it functions as Twain's culminating assault upon all manner of Victorian venturing: the Alpine climb, to be sure, but also the pampered tourist tour, the true geographic exploration, the scientific expedition, the romance fictions that heroicize such outings, and the over-stuffed personal narrative of travel adventure. Twain aims his burlesque erratically at all of these forms (which is in part why it is such a feeble episode). At the same time, however, he completes his pioneering effort: he encapsulates the underlying intent of his *Tramp* by exposing it as a shotgun blast antitravel book.

Twain's effort to write an antitravel book, or a travel narrative in which nothing happens, is nicely realized in the famous lost-sock episode. That episode also reveals the normative center of the text. The sock escapade dramatizes Twain's heroic struggle on a sleepless night to navigate in the dark on his hands and knees the encumbered space of his own hotel room to locate a missing sock without disturbing the sleep of Harris. He describes the quest as an "exploring tour" (he ends up traveling forty-seven miles according to his pedometer) in which he gets lost but persists in seeking his way (and sock) until he has shattered the wall mirror, knocked over an umbrella three times, scraped a picture off the wall, collided with enough furniture for two households, and broken the lamp, candlestick, and water pitcher, finally awakening the entire hotel as well as Harris (*TA* 1:114–17). Thus "travel" reaches its comic nadir. To create this ludicrous episode, Twain fictionalized a real event from Clemens's trip, substituting Harris for Livy, and giving up in the process the best comic line: "Are you hunting" for the sock, he reported Livy's saying, "with a club?" (*MTL* 1:348). What the farcical sock excursion disrupts is domestic tranquillity, and ironically domesticity, the very antithesis of travel, becomes the heart of *A Tramp Abroad*.

Domesticity is, of course, a thoroughly conventional nineteenth-century value. Caught up in a curious, mobile-domesticity abroad himself, Clemens has Mark Twain praise Alpine homes as sanctuaries rather like the one he left behind at Hartford—or, since that home was often touched by the turmoil of the world, like the always idyllic retreat at Quarry Farm: "And yet those far-away homes looked ever so seductive, they were so remote from the troubled world, they dozed in such an atmosphere of peace and dreams,—surely no one who had learned to live up there would ever want to live on a meaner level" (*TA* 1:280). The wistful note struck here is repeated in the book whenever the rest of home is encountered—or imagined. Twain's fondness for the home shapes his vision. When he does upon occasion manage to observe some scenery in his nontraveling (usually through inadvertence rather than intent), he domesticates it. An Alpine valley becomes "a sort of little grass-carpeted parlor" (*TA* 2:56), a mountain meadow seems "about as big as a billiard table" (*TA* 2:60), and a curved trail cut into rock-face appears "like the roof of a narrow porch" or a large house's "gallery" (*TA* 2:76). He thus miniaturizes the immense and makes familiar the exotic, taming the wild, controlling the unknown, keeping the foreign safely within the purview of his own domestication. Like a good Victorian, Mark Twain makes the home define the world.

For all of its warped originality as an antitravel travel book, *A Tramp Abroad* is Twain's most conventional travel narrative. It contains no sustained challenge to the status quo, no serious criticism of culture, no wrestling with philosophical and religious uncertainties. The ordinariness of the book is nicely indicated by the treatment of time. Where time was seen as an annihilating power in *The Innocents Abroad*, sweeping away whole civilizations as well as individuals, time in *A Tramp Abroad* is just a nuisance, the annoying sound of clocks that wake one from comfortable domestic slumber. Amusingly, Twain observes that seventy or eighty years ago, "Napoleon was the only man in Europe who could really be called a traveler" (*TA* 2:40). His point is that things have changed so that now everyone goes everywhere, but the joke also reflects his earlier sense—a feeling wholly absent from *A Tramp Abroad*—that travel was a matter of invasion, conflict, and conquest. In his notebook he observed, "The funniest things are the forbidden" (*N&J2* 304), but he avoids everything that could possibly be construed as taboo, and his book is finally not very funny. The forbidden was on his mind, however, as he confided to Howells how much of European life he detested and as he wrote and delivered in the safe, all-male confines of the Paris Stomach Club his bawdy speech on "The Science of Onanism." The forbidden was even close to home, *in* the home, in fact, for he seems to have had a code language for sexual intercourse that curiously appropriated the terms of adventurous travel: "And when I get there," he would write to Livy, "remember, 'Expedition's the word!'" (*LLMT* 186). But the forbidden, whether social, intellectual, or sexual, was self-censored from his book.

Even when he takes up again the quarrel with the Old Masters ("Old Masters," he told the Stomach Club, was a euphemism) first launched so stridently in *The Innocents Abroad*, he does it in a partial spirit of repentance, "to see if I had learned anything in twelve years" (*TA* 2:243). While he registers some aesthetic objections, to indicate his more educated self he now concedes many notable achievements. And he declaims against nudity in a way that would satisfy the most prudish Victorian. Significantly, what is at stake for Twain as he reflects on crudity in literature as well as art is his own character as writer. (His narrative thus circles back at its near close to the issue raised, albeit obliquely, in its opening.) Should he venture to describe the lewd, he realizes that he would cause a furor: "What a holy indignation I could stir up in the world—just to hear the unreflecting average man deliver himself about my grossness and coarseness, and all that" (*TA* 2:268). But, of course, he stirs no consternation at all.

PERHAPS THE MOST important review of Twain's *A Tramp Abroad* was the one Howells published (unsigned) in the *Atlantic*, the very magazine from which Twain feared he had barred himself through the imagined disaster of his Whittier birthday speech. Howells praises the book extravagantly. With perspicuity he detects a certain "homesickness" at work in Twain, but generally he finds the text alive with deep feeling and the spirit of truth (*CH* 82–83). He suggests that the book has a "serious undercurrent" in which Twain attacks "matters that are out of joint, that are unfair or unnecessarily ignoble" (*CH* 82–83). Betraying the moral bent of his own thinking, as well as his sense of what will appeal to his Victorian readers—and Mark Twain's, Howells stresses not Twain's humor but his seriousness, arguing that the book provides "something for our reflection and possible instruction" (*CH* 84). He thus finds the book edifying as well as entertaining; he calls it delightful, charming, immensely amusing, and delicious (*CH* 83–84). What Howells is doing, besides reading with one eye closed, is rehabilitating Twain; he is attempting to restore the reputation both he and Twain believed the Whittier birthday speech had tarnished. As his saccharine adjectives indicate, he is genteelizing Mark Twain, but he is not falsifying the book; his reconstruction of his friend is perfectly consistent with the general tenor of *A Tramp Abroad*. Howells simply celebrates some of the conventionalities truly at work in Mark Twain's text. In doing so (to the great delight of Livy as well as Clemens), he announces in effect that Mark Twain is not the unpredictable writer he appeared to be in the Whittier speech, a tramp at odds with his culture, but a thoroughly proper fellow, indeed a sensible and instructive traveler writer. Or to put the effect of Howells's review in the terms of Twain's own narrative, Howells confirmed that Mark Twain was not a masked knave but an honorable knight.

CHAPTER THREE

Man of Letters

Whatever his attraction to—and recoil from—the foreign women he saw on the *Quaker City* excursion, Sam Clemens was, so the story goes, transfixed by the mere image of Olivia Langdon, the woman who would eventually become his wife. With a precision that invites belief, Mark Twain tells the beginning of Clemens's love story this way in his autobiography: "I saw her first in the form of an ivory miniature in her brother Charley's stateroom in the steamer *Quaker City* in the Bay of Smyrna, in the summer of 1867, when she was in her twenty-second year. I saw her in the flesh for the first time in New York in the following December. She was slender and beautiful and girlish—and she was both girl and woman. She remained both girl and woman to the last day of her life." He goes on to praise Olivia for her "absolutely limitless affection" and her "perfect character," and having noted both of these, he observes, "It was a strange combination which wrought into one individual, so to speak, by marriage—her disposition and character and mine" (*AMT* 183, 185). It is generally acknowledged that the marriage of Sam and Olivia was a crucial event in Clemens's life, perhaps the single most decisive one, as it wed him to home and family, to eastern gentility, and to middle-class respectability, creating in the process the center of love, acceptance, responsibility, and conventionality out of which Mark Twain would create his greatest works.

In her incisive study of the courtship of Sam Clemens and Olivia Langdon, Susan Harris outstrips previous scholarship, creating a fresh sense of Clemens, a new view of Langdon, and a compelling interpretation of the essential dynamic between them. She shows that Clemens was more conventional, more traditionally middle class, more at one with his culture, that Langdon was more intellectual, more playful, more knowledgeable, less prudishly Victorian, and that, confronting the potential chaos of life, the two "complemented each other, alternately anchoring while the other wandered" (Harris, *Courtship* 134). Her analysis is so thorough and convincing that additional commentary may seem superfluous. Yet to grasp the proper Mark Twain we need to look again at this pivotal event in Clemens's life. For in his courtship Clemens laid claim to an inherently good character and to a range of proprieties; that is, he announced as his the attributes that manifest themselves in the proper Mark Twain. Indeed, the intertwining of private self and public persona is especially tangled here, for the character traits Clemens claimed as his were enacted by Mark Twain in "Sam Clemens's" love letters.

FAR MORE THAN MOST courtships, Clemens's was conducted through correspondence. After seeing Olivia's image—perhaps—while abroad, he met her in person in New York in December 1867, but he did not actually single her out for a visit until August 1868. When he did, however, after less than two weeks with her, he proposed, only to be rejected. Sent away, Clemens nonetheless obtained permission to write to Olivia—as a brother to his sister—which he proceeded to do in 184 letters.[1] Clemens's love letters are conspicuous as performances, but they are not therefore insincere, for as Harris has observed, Clemens writes himself into the roles he assumes; his letters are acts of "self-creation" (*Courtship* 79). Most critics have tended to view the letters as private documents created by Clemens, while Mark Twain conducted his public life in print and on the lecture platform. But insofar as the creative part of Clemens was Mark Twain, the letters may also be seen as expressions of that pseudonymous self. Clemens's love letters are doubly interesting then: as testaments to essential traits in Clemens/Twain and as performed texts of Twain.[2]

Even as it transpired, Clemens scripted his pursuit of Olivia, creating an extended and varied literary performance, a kind of Mark Twain production. The postures he assumes for himself—and imparts to others— reflect a wide range of genre from conversion narrative to success story to sentimental love tale. At his most extravagant he even invokes fairy tale and romance. Olivia was, he wrote, his "matchless little princess" (*L2* 320), his "ineffable princess of fairy-land" (*L3* 137), and he was, by virtue of her love, "Knighted & Ennobled" (*L3* 87). He described the newly married state of this "princess" and her "knight" in hyperbolic terms, again drawing on forms of fabulous fiction: "We are about as happy in our Aladdin's Palace (I think it is a little more tasteful & exquisite in all its appointments than most palaces are,) as if we were roosting in the closing chapters of a popular novel" (*L4* 74). Writing to friends in the West, he announced his marriage by suggesting that it was fiction turned fact, a fairy tale come true: "I have *read* those absurd fairy tales in my time, but I never, never, never expected to be the hero of a romance in real life as unlooked-for & unexpected as the wildest of them" (*L4* 60–61).

Clouded for him, if not for later critics, by his mystifying rhetoric, by his insistence that he was living a "romance in real life," is the fact that the courtship of Sam and Olivia was in many ways both prosaic and conventional. Almost exactly halfway through the courtship Clemens wrote—with unromantic, matter-of-fact delight—to his family that in undertaking not to love but to convert him Olivia would "unwittingly dig a matrimonial pit & end by tumbling into it" (*L3* 85). Unacknowledged by Clemens is the fact that most of the courtship's central protocols were conventional. The concern for religious compatibility, the deferral to parental approval, the solicitation of character references, the careful calculation of economic competence, and the protracted engagement itself—all these were in keeping with the usual practices of Victorian courtship.[3]

While he forgot it in proclaiming his romance "unlooked-for and unexpected," Clemens had long toyed with the idea of matrimony. Provided that he could find the right woman and create the proper situation, he seems always to have intended to marry. His conception of marriage was closely tied to his feelings about class and sexual behavior. More than five years before he even met Olivia Langdon—and took the full measure of her privileged estate—he was insisting to his sister-in-law, Mollie, that she could not possibly emigrate to the Nevada Territory until she could live in "a handsome house" and "boss" her own servants: "You know it is all very well for a man's wife to talk about how much work she *can* do—but actually *doing* it is a thing that don't suit my notions. That part of the business belongs to the servants. I am not married yet, and I never *will* marry until I can afford to have servants enough to leave my wife in the position for which I designed her, viz:—as a *companion*" (*L1* 145). Clearly Clemens aspired to some degree of luxury as a part of, indeed as the precondition for, married life. Again with typical middle-class Victorian thinking, he imagines his wife as a companion, a social, intellectual, and perhaps even spiritual friend, exempt from domestic labor. Obliquely suggesting that she is to be a sexual companion as well, he explained to Mollie, with what must be playful candor slightly out of control (men did not discuss such things with their sisters-in-law), that his spouse could not do ordinary domestic chores: "I don't want to sleep with a three-fold Being who is cook, chambermaid, and washerwoman all in one." And with an invidious but conventional bit of Victorian class discrimination he added, "I don't mind sleeping with female servants as long as I am a bachelor—by *no* means—but *after* I marry, that sort of thing will be 'played out,' you know" (*L1* 145). The notion of a man's sowing his wild oats before his marriage was yet another Victorian commonplace. Coming from Clemens, who was usually reticent about sexual matters, it is a bit startling. But like the idea that his wife should be a lady exempt from domestic work, it formed the backdrop for his courtship.

Clemens—or more accurately his creative self, Mark Twain—depicts himself and his situation with a vividness normally found only in fiction. His very first letter to Olivia sets the pattern. Dramatically dating it "Midnight," the dark end of the day on which he had announced his love only to be repulsed, Clemens deploys a series of tropes contrasting the richness experienced in loving Olivia with the depletion suffered in being forced to give her up: "The world that was so beautiful, is dark again; the hope that shone as the sun, is gone; the brave ambition is dead." He affirms in intense, slightly exotic rhetoric the great worth of his love despite the fact that it is unrequited: "Yet I say again, it is better for me that I have loved & do love you; that with more than Eastern devotion I worship you; that I lay down all of my life that is worth the living, upon this hopeless altar where no fires of love shall descend to consume it." And he depicts his solitary state in an extended image of reckless sea journeying: "Being adrift, now, & rudderless, my voyage promises ill; but while the friendly beacon of your sisterly love beams though never so faintly

through the fogs & the mists, I cannot be hopelessly wrecked" (*L2* 248).
Clemens courted Olivia with such blatant artifice as this, and his tactic
almost inevitably raises questions about his honesty—questions which
hinge in large measure on style.

There are actually three styles discernible in the love letters. First,
there is what may be termed an elevated style, a highly figurative, intensely rhetorical mode; second, there is an exclamatory style, marked
by plain language, enthusiastic declaration, and insistent repetition; and
finally, lacing the two together, there is a conversational style, one that ap-
proximates the idioms and rhythms of ordinary speech. The contrast between the elevated and exclamatory styles is enormous, as the following
examples illustrate.

Elevated:

> For I *do* love you, Livy—as the dew loves the flowers; as the birds love the
> sunshine; as the wavelets love the breeze; as mothers love their first-born;
> as memory loves old faces; as the yearning tides love the moon; as angels
> love the pure in heart. (*L3* 143)

Exclamatory:

> I love you, Livy—Livy dear—Livy love—I love *you* Livy—
>
> _____
>
> _____
>
> I kiss you, Livy—on forehead, cheek & lips.
> I *love you, Livy.*
> I love only Livy—nobody but Livy. (*L3* 102)

For most readers, the exclamatory style seems more convincing than the
elevated. It works through accumulation, repeating, varying, and intensifying a single thought as if the writer is so gripped by his emotion that
he can only proclaim it again and again. It persuades in part by appearing to be a completely artless outpouring of passion. (In fact, it is crafted—
from its simple opening through its careful modulations and intensifica-
tions, manipulated by line spacing, to the close that repeats the opening
declaration and adds exclusions.) In contrast, Clemens's elevated style
works through obvious artifice, compounding figures of speech in ele-

gant elaboration of its idea, as if the writer is as enchanted by the writing as he is enthralled by his emotion. The elevated style is not emotionless, however; the emotion is just realized—subsumed—in the figures.

At issue here is something of real importance not only in the love letters but in Mark Twain's writing generally. Twain often employs an elevated style to express beautiful scenes, soft emotions, heartfelt moralities, or high-minded principles. In the lecture he gave most often during the period of his courtship, for instance, "The American Vandal Abroad," he alternated between lofty utterances and humorous observations.[4] More often than not, however, critics find his elevated passages suspect. Because they flow gracefully in set patterns and gather in smoothly much that is conventional, the elevated passages are judged glib and fake. Twain's inclination to burlesque the high style also seems to sanction its dismissal. But the fact is that he is most often sincere; his strong emotions simply find expression *through* convention and artifice. (Even his famous profanity is itself a matter of artfully employed conventions.) Clemens scripted such major events in his life as love, loss, anticipation, and death in the highly conventionalized elevated style. If to modern eyes his renderings sometimes seem sentimental, that is partly a result of a cultural shift in taste. In *Sincerity and Authenticity*, Lionel Trilling has tracked such a shift, along with a change in moral perspective, as sincerity gave way to authenticity in western culture. The Victorian age on the whole preferred the elevated style, however, and had no trouble in finding it sincere. For that era there was in the elevated style, to borrow Trilling's formulation, "a congruence between avowal and actual feeling" (2). When Elizabeth Barrett Browning asked, "How do I love thee?" and proceeded to count the ways in extravagant figures, she used the eloquence of her era. Yet she loved Robert as genuinely as Clemens did Olivia.

IN HER FIRST LETTER to Clemens after she had rebuffed his sudden declaration of love, Olivia carefully included a picture of herself, thereby ensuring that he would continue to have an image of her, that she would in a sense be with him even though he had literally been sent packing. It is an odd, revealing gesture on her part, one that seems to signal the ultimate outcome of their relationship just as the game they would play of

brother/sister, student/mentor, neophyte/initiate was first getting under
way. Photographs became a major aspect of their courtship. "The picture, the picture, Livy!" (*L2* 341), Clemens exclaimed more than once,
and the two worried over getting the right kind (they tried daguerreo-
types, porcelains, and ferrotypes). What they sought was the perfect
likeness—a picture of the other that would be, as Clemens put it while
recommending a ferrotype, "*human*" (*L2* 291). As they exchanged photo-
graphic images, Clemens drew a series of fancy word paintings. He created two indelible portraits: one of Olivia and one of himself.

The portrait of Olivia he created is a familiar one: "You are all good,
& true, & generous & forgiving & unselfish—all things that are a glory
to womanhood meet & blend themselves together in the matchless mosaic of your character" (*L3* 240). He declared that she was an angel on
earth who inspired in him awe and reverence. Responding, for instance,
to one of the many portraits she sent him, he exclaimed in January 1869:
"Oh, Livy darling, I could just worship that picture, it is so beautiful. . . .
It is more than human, Livy—it is an angel-beauty—something not of
earth—something above earth & its grossness. There is that deep spiritual look in the eyes—that far-away look that I have noted before when
I wondered in my secret heart if you were not communing with the inhabitants of another sphere, a grander, a nobler world than ours" (*L3* 61).
When Olivia complained of his excess, he defended it as a problem in
writing: "distempered language" with "no voice to modulate it" (*L2* 315).
But he persisted in his idealizations. Indeed, he went even further, making Olivia not just an angel but the object of his adoration, the "focus
of his worship" (Harris, *Courtship* 80; also Hoffman, *Inventing MT* 148).

As his use of the angel figure suggests, Clemens deliberately exploited
highly conventional tropes in his love letters. He made use of equally conventional ideas. The courtship letters are filled with references to classic
English authors. Shakespeare, Pope, Scott, Sterne, Keats, Byron, Young,
Tennyson, Dickens, and Arnold all appear, but two authors in particular
seem to frame the courtship: Coventry Patmore and Elizabeth Barrett
Browning. Although he vacillated in his enthusiasm (first it was "an exquisite book," then he found he did not like it as he had before [*L2* 274,
314]), Clemens generally affirmed the value of Patmore's *Angel in the*

House. At times he found in it "the soul & spirit of what I have been trying to tell you with tongue & pen" (*L2* 313), and he compared Olivia herself to Patmore's heroine: "Honoria is a great-souled, self-sacrificing,
noble woman like you (I can see you in everything she does) & she is so
happy in the weal of others & so compassionate of their woes. And she is
so thoughtful, & so tender, & so exquisitely womanly" (*L2* 343). As even
Clemens's interpretation makes clear, Patmore upheld the traditional notions of True Womanhood. As much as he borrowed and endorsed Patmore's vision of the perfect woman, just so much did he condemn Elizabeth Barrett Browning. In *Aurora Leigh* Browning offered a contrasting
sense of True Womanhood by creating a woman liberated from domesticity and conventional femininity to follow intellectual and artistic pursuits. Olivia liked *Aurora Leigh* (see *L2* 268, 274, *L3* 26, 95, 241, and *L4*
72), and while it is impossible to determine exactly what she admired, it
is hard not to believe that she was impressed by the figure of a strong,
independent woman. Clemens's dismissals of Browning are playful, but
they are also persistent. He calls her "the Widow Browning" and insists
that her book is full of "dark & bloody mystery" (*L3* 241). He also labels
her "old Mother Browning," again patronizing her and suggesting an
asexuality (mothers are always sexless) at odds with his own sexual energy—and probably Olivia's as well. Provocatively he terms Browning's
poetry "marvelous ravings" (*L3* 95), as if she were a lunatic. To be sure,
this was a game he played with Olivia: inciting her by assaulting one of
her favorite writers. But some animus seems to lurk beneath his play.
Olivia sometimes returned as good as she got. Eleven days after their
wedding, she added to a letter Clemens had written to Mary Mason Fairbanks the request that she come stay with them, and then she teasingly
included—for Clemens to see—the suggestion that when she visited they
would "make Mr Clemens read aloud to us in Mrs Browning—Felicity
to us—but what to him?" (*L4* 72). Whatever Browning may really have
been to Clemens, certainly her idea of a true woman was in conflict with
his own.

The opposition between Patmore and Browning, at its simplest a contrast between an angel in the house and a woman in the world, becomes
explicit in Clemens's courtship letters. Laura E. Skandera-Trombley has

shown that Olivia grew up in a community alive with ideas of new roles
for women (see esp. chap. 6). Olivia herself seems to have entertained
during her courtship some hope that she could play an active role on the
public stage of life. Her desire becomes apparent in several of Clemens's
letters to her in which he argues against such a life for her. Shortly after
their formal engagement he wrote, "No, no, darling, it makes me uneasy,
these thinkings, these longings & aspirings after a broader field of useful-
ness." To keep his angel in the house, he mustered three arguments. First,
in what must have been a deeply troubling thought for her, given her history of illness, he suggested not only that she was too frail to enter the
world but also that even thinking of it undermined her health (*L3* 117–
18). Second, exploiting her own religious outlook, he argued that God
had defined her role in life, her "calling," apart from action in the world:
"*Don't* grieve, Livy, that you cannot march up & down the troubled ways
of life *fighting* wrong & unfettering right, with strong fierce words &
dazzling actions, for *that* work is set apart for women of a different formation to do, & being designed for that work, God, who always knows
His affairs & how to appoint His instruments, has *qualified* them for the
work—& He has qualified you for *your* work, & nobly are you performing it. Therefore, be content." Finally, shifting from arguments against
her considering an active life in the world, he championed the good she
did within her own restricted sphere of home and family: "But Oh, Livy
dear, how little you appreciate yourself! You are a living, breathing sermon; a blessing delivered straight from the hand of God; a messenger,
that, speaking or silent, carries refreshment to the weary, hope to the de-
spondent, sunshine to the darkened way of all that come & go about you.
I *feel* this, in every fibre of my being. And the sound, real good conferred
upon the world by the model & example of such a woman as you, is not
to be estimated at all." Clinching his case for Olivia as a powerful force
for the good within her limited world, he extolled her influence by comparing her to one of history's most prominent women—one that Mark
Twain would come to idolize: "In your sphere you are as great, & as noble,
& as efficient as any Joan of Arc that ever lived" (*L3* 63).

As Clemens idealized Olivia, he manipulated her into accepting his notions of her future life. Apparently she did not challenge current defini-

tions of the proper role for women, but she did, as Harris has maintained, "seek to equalize the demands for upright moral behavior on men as well as women" (*Courtship* 97). She insisted that Clemens be both moral and religious. In a now famous letter to his sister, Clemens explained the conditions of his courtship: "I love—I *worship*—Olivia L. Langdon, of Elmira—& she loves me. When I am permanently *settled*—& when I am a Christian—& when I have *demonstrated* that I have a good, steady, reliable character, her parents will withdraw their objections, & she *may* marry me—*I* say she *will*—I intend she *shall*" (*L2* 295). Most commentaries on the courtship have focused on Clemens's efforts to reform in order to secure Olivia's love (and win the approval of her parents). As Jeffrey Steinbrink puts it, "Clemens gamely undertook a personal reconstruction that was intended to make him a conventionally 'better' individual—more religious, more regular in his habits, more refined, more comprehensively civilized" (*Getting to Be MT* 2).

In his attempts to reform, Clemens accorded Olivia a crucial role. Cox has summarized the stratagem: "He offered himself as the repentant prodigal begging to be reformed and asking to be schooled in the tender refinements which only Olivia could teach" (*Fate* 71). But, in fact, this is only half—and perhaps the least significant half—of the plot he created in his courtship. In his letters he actually presented himself in two roles. In the foreground was the figure familiar to criticism, the repentant sinner, a changing person struggling to mend his ways, to achieve moral growth, and to become a true believer; in the background, however, was a figure largely unnoticed in criticism, the true gentleman with a fixed character, instinctively able to exert proper values, to express fine feelings, and to achieve some good within the world. This figure reflects the Moralist of the Main (at his best) and embodies some of the conventionalities of the Victorian traveler Mark Twain. It is impossible to gauge which of the twain Clemenses most beguiled Olivia—they were closely intermingled—but in the course of their courtship, the background was foregrounded, the improving person receded, the constant man of character emerged. By the end Olivia was confronted most often not with the becoming person who might arrive but with the established one who was there from the beginning.

Clemens courted Olivia most powerfully by displaying for her not what he might become but what he already was. He wooed and finally won her by persuading her that his constant self was worthy of her love. The fully formed self he revealed to her had three key dimensions: he presented himself as a Man of the World, a Man of Feeling, and a Man of Letters.

As a Man of the World, Clemens wooed Olivia with financial as well as literary figures. His business affairs—lecturing, seeing *The Innocents Abroad* through the press, looking for a newspaper to buy into—were both natural and performative parts of his correspondence. He paraded numbers before Livy—the number of people in his lecture audiences, the number of dollars he made, the number of illustrations his book would have (and their cost), the number of copies to be printed, the number of copies sold, the number of important people he knew—judges, governors, congressmen, foreign ministers, clergymen—the number of places he had visited, the number of social invitations he received. In all this he attempted to show Olivia and her parents that he was a substantial, upcoming man of affairs. He was also careful to show that he was or would be a moral businessman. He denounced the Cleveland *Herald*, for instance, as a "trimming, time-serving, policy-shifting, popularity-hunting, money-grasping" paper that would "do a great many things for money which I wouldn't do." He preferred, he said, a more "high-principled paper" (*L3* 96). He went out of his way to impress upon Olivia his involvement in business and his engagement with the world. When her mother wrote to the one friend the Langdons had in common with Clemens, Mary Mason Fairbanks, her now famous disturbed letter inquiring about his moral character—"what I desire is your opinion of him as a *man*"—Mrs. Langdon conceded that he was "a man of genius" who possessed "a high order of intellectual endowments" and had "standing among men" (qtd. in *L2* 286).

Clemens also presented himself to Olivia as a Man of the World in a more profound sense. He claimed with perfect legitimacy that his experience—his varied careers and extensive travel—had shown him the moral character of the world:

And moreover you can always say, with every confidence, that I have been through the world's "mill"—I have traversed its ramifications from end to end—I have searched it, & probed it, & put it under the microscope & I *know* it, through & through, & from back to back—its follies, it[s] frauds, & its vanities—all by personal ***experience*** & not through dainty *theories* culled from nice moral books in luxurious parlors where temptation never comes & it is easy to be good & keep the heart warm & one's best impulses fresh & strong & uncontaminated. (*L2* 290)

Latent here is the idea that would later germinate in "The Man That Corrupted Hadleyburg": that temptation is valuable. His distinction between theory and practice was probably in part a ploy designed to give pause to anyone inclined to judge him who had less experience than he did. In truth, however, Clemens had been through the world's mill, especially during his time in the West, and he had finally chosen to be a moral man as his culture defined morality. Arguing the value of worldly experience was problematical. When he suggested in one letter that some young college boys would "be all the better men for sowing [their] wild oats" while they were young (*L3* 131), a variation on the idea he had playfully expressed about himself in explicitly sexual terms to his sister-in-law, Mollie, Olivia quickly objected; and he retreated, acknowledging that breaking God's laws at any time was wrong. But in the very act of conforming to Olivia's strict view of morality, he made again his case for experience: "I was *right*, as far as I went—for I only thought of sowing them being the surest way to make the future man a steady, reliable, *wise* man, thoroughly fitted for this life, equal to its emergencies, & triple-armed against its wiles & frauds & follies" (*L3* 153).

Clemens's depiction of the world here and elsewhere in his love letters is tinged with the kind of melodrama exploited at large in the then popular sentimental novel. Within four years he would, of course, write his own version of such a novel, *The Gilded Age*, in which he burlesqued conventions of the sentimental form at the same time he confirmed the genre's sense of the world as dangerously ensnaring, fraudulent, and wicked. To Olivia he insisted not only that he knew the tricks of life but also that he was steeled against them. He suggested further that manliness consisted in part in being ready and able to bear pain. "Of old," he told her, "I am acquainted with grief, disaster & disappointment, & have borne these troubles as became a man" (*L2* 247). Some of his utterances

on the theme of manly suffering sound like bad speeches from sentimental fiction. When Olivia suggested that she might keep something from
him to spare him sadness, for instance, he wrote: "What! you suffer alone,
to save *me* sorrow! No, no, Livy, I could not be so selfish, so unmanly, as
to wish that" (*L3* 61). And with a melodramatic flourish, he declaimed
that he would protect her "purest heart": "God give me grace to love &
honor, to cheer & shelter it all the days of my life till I die! And when any
harm shall threaten it, any pain, or sorrow or affliction brood in the air
above it, Heaven give me heart to say, Lord let the blow fall on me—not
her" (*L3* 137). Through such extravagant posturing, Clemens conveyed
his serious belief that it was his role to buffer his future wife from the ills
of the world, to sacrifice himself to spare her, to bear for them both with
fortitude and cheer whatever misfortune might befall. It was a highly conventional notion of gentlemanly conduct.

To show in full what manner of man he was, Clemens not only released but actually flaunted his tenderness. He made sure that Olivia saw
that he was a sensitive man, a Man of Feeling. He revealed his gentleness
chiefly through the elevated style. Such a style was thought to bespeak a
poetic self; its very artificiality suggested the intricate workings of sensitivity and signaled the triumph of instruction and self-cultivation over
lumpish human nature. Like all styles, the high one was grounded in a particular social group—in this case, the New England cultural elite (Brodhead 1–12). The conventionality of its rhetorical patterns and tropes
functioned to evoke approved values, shared ways of feeling. By adopt-
ing such a style, Clemens implied that he was a part of the respectable
middle-class culture; he attested to his character by the very way in which
he wrote. A stylistic virtuoso, he was fluent in the elevated style. At one
point in his letters, he displayed for Olivia the paleness of life without
her: "I would not part with you for all the kingdoms of the earth & the
glory thereof. And I pray that when you die, my widowed heart may
break & its pulses cease forever. For what would existence be without
you? There would never be joy in the sunshine any more; nor melody in
music; nor gladness in the summer air; nor splendor in the expiring day;
nor sublimity in the sea; nor beauty in the rainbow; nor worship in the
grateful incense of the flowers" (*L3* 263). To reflect on the eventual death

of one's beloved was not uncommon at the time; such morbid rumina-
tions expressed "the mortuary imagination of Victorian America," which
found its rationale in death rates (Douglas 210). The decorativeness of
Clemens's passage (and there are many like it in the correspondence) actually reinforces the implicit point that he feels deeply, that his is a delicate heart. The morbidity of the idea of Olivia's death is quickly bypassed
as the utterance hurries into its stately listing of loss. The real invitation
here is not to think of death or even separation but to revel for a moment
in a pleasing melancholy.

For Victorians, sensitivity, gentle emotions, and tender-heartedness
were valuable not only in themselves but also as impulsions to humani-
tarian action. From the very first in his letters, Clemens arranged to
let Olivia see that he was compassionately concerned for the suffering.
When he was still writing to her as his "honored sister," he reported on
a visit made with Joseph Twichell to an almshouse in Hartford: "Heaven
& earth, what a sight it was! Cripples, jibbering idiots, raving mad-
men; thieves, rowdies, paupers; little children, stone blind; blind men &
women; old, old, men & women, with that sad absent look in their faces
that tells of thoughts that are busy with 'the days that are no more.' I have
not had anything touch me so since I saw the leper hospitals of Honolulu
& Damascus." Clemens then reported that he helped Twichell "preach
& sing" to these people—"I helped in the singing, anyhow" (*L2* 268). To
demonstrate his sympathy for others, he arranged during his courtship
to give several benefit lectures, proudly reporting to Olivia that one of
them, his talk for the Cleveland Protestant Orphan Asylum, had raised
$807. (The Man of the World thus conspired with the Man of Feeling.)
These activities were not lost on Olivia. Two months before they were
to marry, on a day of such winter beauty, domestic comfort, and affianced
love that she felt "like dancing," she wrote to Clemens: "I am so richly
cared for, that I cannot but have a tender yearning for those whose backs
seem almost broken with the heavy load under which it [*sic*] is bent—we
are happy, my dear, therefore we are the better able and must be the
more ready to help others—and I know that you are" (qtd. in *L3* 394).

A gentleman's tender feelings were often linked to his religion, making
him susceptible to conversion, deepening the hold on his convictions, and

impelling him to act in the light of his faith. When Clemens's own belief was most dubious, he displayed his fine feelings in highly suggestive religious contexts. In the third month of their correspondence, he wrote to Olivia about a friend from his Nevada days, the Reverend Franklin S. Rising. He told her, among other things, of a return voyage they made together from the Sandwich Islands during which the clergyman "tried earnestly" to bring him "to a knowledge of the true God." Clemens explained to Olivia that when Rising wanted to hold services on board the ship but lacked a choir, he himself said, "Go ahead—I'll stand by you—I'll be your choir." Knowing only one hymn, however, "Oh, Refresh Us," Clemens's effort was slightly comic: "Only one—& so for five Sundays in succession he stood in the midst of the assembled people on the quarter-deck & gave out that hymn twice a day, & I stood up solitary & alone & sang it!" (*L2* 333). The tale suggests a kindness in Clemens that must have augured well to Olivia even though his faith was suspect. But his notebook entry for the actual event reads succinctly: "Rev. Franklin S. Rising preached, & the passengers formed choir" (*N&J1* 144). The importance of the discrepancy lies not in what it reveals about Clemens's willingness to stretch the truth (even the proper Mark Twain could do that) but in what it demonstrates about the entire courtship correspondence: just how thoroughly literary it is. Clemens imaginatively reshaped fact into amusing narrative, pretty picture, and moving speech. He capped his tale in this instance with yet another creation designed to reveal him as a man of appropriate tender feelings: "For his [Franklin's] wanderings are done, now; his restless feet are still; he is at peace. *Now* the glories of heaven are about him, & in his ears its mysterious music is sounding—but to me comes no vision but a lonely ship in a great solitude of sky & water; & unto *my* ears comes no sound but the complaining of the waves & the softened cadences of that simple old hymn—but Oh, Livy, it comes freighted with *infinite* pathos!" (*L2* 334). This is worthy of Dickens (who probably inspired some of it). The passage conveys a tender pathos, signaling Clemens's own sensitivity. Should the tale have recalled for Olivia the voice of the sea in *Dombey and Son*, the echo could only further confirm through flattering comparison the fine feelings it seems contrived to display.[5]

Of all the roles he assumed in the courtship correspondence—the changing role of Prodigal, the fixed postures of experienced Man of the World and tender Man of Feeling—by far the most important was that of Man of Letters. It was, finally, the most vivid, the most palpable of the selves he asserted because it was the medium through which the others were realized. As a Man of Letters in his love letters, Clemens created the unmistakable sense of himself as a writer. He did so partly by writing with literary artistry of his love and his experiences but more importantly by fashioning a series of literary set pieces, small exercises in genre, like his rehearsal of pathos over the death of the Reverend Rising. Such mini-works came easily to him. Sometimes he turned out occasional pieces for Olivia: at Christmas, a religious meditation; on Valentine's Day, a love note; for New Year's Day, a panegyric on change. More often he found his personal circumstance occasion enough. He wrote a miniature essay on friendship, distinguishing it from mere acquaintance; he created another on nature in its irritating as well as magical aspects; and he tossed off a melancholy and nostalgic one on separation from home. He worked up a small adventure story about boating in a storm, and entertained Olivia with a little comic extravaganza about walking in the rain with a faulty umbrella. Several times in the correspondence, he created dream tales tinged with Gothicism. Not all of these are finely polished or even completely finished, but they nonetheless all bear the stamp of an incipient literary set piece. They display Clemens as a Man of Letters.

Perhaps the most daring of Clemens's creations as a Man of Letters is his representation of his own religious uncertainty and rational skepticism. Early in the courtship when his position was most precarious, his character most severely on trial, he confessed to Olivia that he seemed not to be "making a progress toward a better life worthy of any one's faith, or hope, or regard" (*L2* 309). The avowal invited encouragement from Olivia even as it risked her disapproval. However, he followed the confession with a bit of self-dramatization that transliterates his personal state into a literary one, into a lurid stock vignette of Victorian despair. The shift is signaled by the self-conscious summarizing phrase, "And so": "And so,—forth I drift into the moonless night of despondency. . . . *What is there in my heart but sinking confidence—what in the earth I stand* upon but graves—what in the air about me but phantoms—what in the firmament above my head but clouds & thick darkness, closing the gates of heaven against me?" (*L3* 309–10). A passage like this sends two contrapuntal messages: spiritual impotence and artistic empowerment. Whatever misgivings about her suitor's salvation it might have precipitated in Olivia, it confronted her again with the indubitable fact that Clemens's fixed character, as opposed to his struggling spiritual one, was not only deeply feeling but also richly creative. By casting his religious difficulty in flourishes of literary melodrama, he displayed both his sensitivity and his power *as writer*.

Clemens's role as writer—the core of his identity—enabled him to negotiate all the difficulties of his provisional courtship. It even empowered him to acknowledge, less than a month before his marriage, his interest in scientific challenge to religious orthodoxy: "I have been reading some new arguments to prove that the world is very old, & that the six days of creation were six immensely long periods. For instance, according to Genesis, the *stars* were made when the world was, yet this writer mentions the significant fact that there are stars within reach of our telescopes whose light requires 50,000 years to traverse the wastes of space & come to our earth." He immediately softens this correction of Genesis by turning it into a literary minidrama, a sentimental rendering of homeless stars and departed peoples:

> And so, if we made a tour through space ourselves, might we not, in some remote era of the future, meet & greet the first lagging rays of stars that started on their weary visit to us a million years ago?—rays that are outcast & homeless, now, their parent stars crumbled to nothingness & swept from the firmament five hundred thousand years after these journeying rays departed—stars whose peoples lived their little lives, & laughed & wept, hoped & feared, sinned & perished, bewildering ages since these vagrant twinklings went wandering through the solemn solitudes of space? (*L4* 12)

In an epistolary moment like this, religious doubt is subsumed by literary performance. Or to put it another way, the Man of Letters covers the tracks of the Prodigal Son.[6]

That he turned his letters into literary exercises was apparent to Olivia as well as to Clemens himself. She spoke of him to Mrs. Fairbanks as one who wrote "letters" for the *New York Tribune* (OL to MMF, 26 Oct. 1868,

CtHMTH), thereby linking his private correspondence to her with his public role as writer. When Mrs. Fairbanks, perceiving the literary nature of his letters to her, persuaded him to publish an extract from his Christmas note in her husband's newspaper, Olivia wrote to her expressing her pleasure that the world would thus get a chance "to know something of his deeper, larger nature" (qtd. in *L3* 42).[7] That nature was for Olivia largely a serious one. What of the comic Clemens? What of Mark Twain? Lurking in most commentaries on the courtship is the feeling that Clemens misrepresented his character by appearing more earnest and proper than he actually was and by suppressing his irreverent humor. Both notions are false. Clemens may have created an exaggerated picture of himself, but he was all that he made himself out to be: experienced in the world, sensitive to human affairs, and endlessly creative. And while it is rather infrequent, his humor is by no means absent from his love letters.

Naturally he teased Olivia.[8] Teasing her was, he told her, a way to keep up his spirits when he was away from her. He did not make fun of her person as much as he did her writing, laughing gently at her spelling and occasionally complaining a bit about her tone. Sometimes he was simply silly. "Why," he asked, propounding what he called a "magnificent conundrum," is "Livy's room like a motion to adjourn? *Answer*—Because it is always in order" (*L3* 126–27). At the other extreme, he jested in rough ways that recall his early western humor. When one of the local sponsors of his lecture failed to deliver a letter from Olivia, he assured her: "If it were not wicked, I could cordially wish his funeral might occur tomorrow. However, I have bribed a man to find & bring me his body, dead or alive—& that letter" (*L3* 114). Despite the fact that his spiritual character was on trial, he played irreverently, as in this report to Olivia on his Sunday in church:

> The young man who went with me got tired of the sermon early. He evidently was not used to going to church, though he talked as if he was. Toward the last he got himself down till he was resting on the end of his backbone; & then he propped his 2 knees high against the pew in front of him; he stroked his thighs reflectively with his palms; he yawned; he started twice to stretch, but cut it short & looked dejected & regretful; he looked at his watch 3 times; & at last he got to belching. I then threw him out of the window. (*L3* 381)

Clemens no doubt shocked Olivia with his humorous play, and he no doubt delighted her as well. As we've seen, he toyed repeatedly with her favorite writer—"Get your Browning ready," he warned her, "for lo, I come like a lamb to the slaughter!" (*L2* 274). To Olivia and her family, he repeatedly joked about lying: "When I delude people they don't KNOW it—& consequently it is no sin" (*L2* 298). And he made making fun of his future father-in-law a standard part of his courtship. Having sent his wedding clothes to the Langdon home, for instance, he instructed Olivia about their handling: "Now your mother must unpack them & put them away for me & be sure not to let Mr. Langdon go wearing them around" (*L3* 391). Even early in the courtship as the damning replies to Mr. Langdon's inquiries into his character were arriving, Clemens kidded Olivia's father—"pure vanity" and made fun of him to her: "I hardly like to tell on him,—but Livy you ought to have seen what sort of characters he was associating with" (*L3* 115). Jervis Langdon apparently flat-out liked Clemens, smoothing the way for him to pursue his courtship as best he could, and Clemens clearly liked and admired Olivia's father, finding in him a nature akin to that he so respected in Anson Burlingame. Once again Clemens had found a surrogate father ready to steer him into realms of respectability.[9]

Clemens also teased other members of the Langdon family. He offered to write a memoir for his sister-in-law-to-be in which he would mix together congratulations from notable people, sublime conundrums, some poetry, and something incomprehensible from Browning, all intended to "'hive' the gentle reader" (*L3* 241). Taking advantage of her seriousness, he set traps for Olivia and played tricks on her, "selling" her in the style of a frontier humorist until his conscience was pricked to apology. At times his humor even bordered on aggression, as it did when he promised Olivia he would write to her close friend Mrs. Brooks, who he felt had slighted him: "Well, all right—I will write her a good hearty letter, & shake hands, & offer right cordially a 'warm nook' by our fireside— and when she comes, Livy, I'll make it about the warmest nook that ever *she* got into, to pay for this!" (*L3* 137). Solemnity and frolic cohabit in the courtship correspondence, for Clemens's humor was not alien to but a basic part of the respectable figure he cut in his letters. He enjoyed "hiving" the gentle reader of his love, and he knew that she could not help being entertained. He penned a poem for her saying so: "A little nonsense now & then / Is relished by the best of Livys" (*L3* 127). Having confided to his sister the trials of his courtship, the tests of faith and character set by Olivia and her parents, he told her in secrecy, "They all like me, & they can't help it" (*L2* 295).[10]

To see the humor in the courtship is to realize the honesty of Clemens's self-presentation and to measure the confidence he had in his rectitude. Because he knew he was at bottom a proper person, a man worthy of Olivia's love, he was free to be funny even about such sacred things as truth, manners, friends, and family. While the letters are dominated by tender emotion, for Clemens—and in fact for Mark Twain—humor and sentiment were not antithetical but complementary. In his love letters, Clemens could be a humorist precisely because he tapped—indeed, sometimes pumped dry—the springs of pathos.

With more pathos than humor, he imagined for Olivia their future life together, and the vision confirmed the constant character he asserted throughout the courtship letters. He really created two views. The first pandered to Olivia's religious feeling, while affirming the bonding of their love: "Let us hope & believe that we shall walk hand in hand down the lengthening highway of life, one in heart, one in impulse & one in love & worship of Him—bearing each other's burdens, sharing each other's joys, soothing each other's griefs—&, so linked together, & so journeying, pass at last the shadowed boundaries of Time & stand redeemed & saved, beyond the threshold & within the light of that Land whose Prince is the Lord of rest eternal. Picture it, Livy—cherish it, think of it" (*L3* 12). The closing injunction to "picture it" betrays that he is fashioning yet another literary piece, a fine word painting done in the style of moralized allegory, of their life together through time. While the first picture posits in its vague and generalized way a movement through the world, down "the highway of life" that Clemens as a man of experience knew so well, the second evokes a life of retreat into a harmony consecrated by love:

> But when we are serene & happy old married folk, we will sit together & con other books all the long pleasant evenings, & let the great world toil & struggle & nurse its pet ambitions & glorify its poor vanities beyond the boundaries of our royalty—we will let it lighten & thunder, & blow its

gusty wrath about our windows & our doors, but never cross our sacred
threshold. Only Love & Peace shall inhabit there, with you & I, their willing vassals. And I will read:

> "The splendor falls on castle walls,
> And snowy summits old in story"—

& worship Tennyson, & you will translate Aurora Leigh & be gentle & patient with me & do all you can to help me understand what the mischief it
is all about. And we will follow the solemn drum-beat of Milton's stately sentences; & the glittering pageantry of Macaulay's, & the shuddering phantoms that come & go in the grim march of Poe's unearthly verses; & bye &
bye drift dreamily into fairy-land with the magician laureate & hear "the
horns of elfland faintly blowing." And out of the Book of Life you shall cull
the wisdom that shall make our lives an anthem void of discord & our deeds
a living worship of the God that gave them. (*L3* 25–26)

In most ways a clichéd version of the ideal Victorian fireside, the picture
is interesting as a ploy and a projection. Olivia is given the attractive role
of interpreter of Holy Scripture, the moral guide for their wedded life.
But the love of the word of God is outweighed in the passage by the love
of the words of men and women. Literary texts vie with the sacred one,
and Clemens's own part in their future life is as reader of secular scriptures. The passage encapsulates—and climaxes—the fixed character he
announced throughout the correspondence: as Man of the World, he
knows it well enough to shun it; as Man of Feeling, he responds sensi-
tively to the varied moods of great writers; and as Man of Letters, he both
honors the texts of others and creates in the passage itself his own.

Clemens's serenity and assurance here are offset by the anxiety and insecurity expressed in one of his final letters to Olivia. Ostensibly the report of a dream, the letter seems to show how he actually felt about himself as the suitor of Olivia Langdon. Although somewhat long, it is useful
to see the whole story it tells:

And honey, I had such a vivid, *vivid* dream! I thought you had discarded me,
& that you avoided me so carefully that for several days although we were
under the same roof & [I] often caught momentary glimpses of you or your
dress, I could not get speech with you. And to add to my misery, I always had
a glimpse of a rival when I had one of you. He was *always* with you, & I seemed

to understand that he was an old rejected lover of yours (but not W.,) who had patiently waited, knowing that he could regain his place in your love if he could but get with you in my absence. Once I thought I was going to catch you alone, for I saw you hasten into a private room. I ran to it, but only to see you with glad face & beaming eyes throw yourself into a seat close to that hated rival—whose perfectly imbecile face I then saw for the first time, & from that moment merely despised instead of hating him.

Well, that very afternoon I caught you alone for a few moments, & ah, yours was the saddest, saddest face that ever was. But you were in the toils of that man & could not escape. Your face said that there was no more *true* happiness for you on earth—nothing but a feverish fascination, & then a vapid, vacant existence, then Death. It broke my heart to see this fearful thing in the darling old face I was still worshipping. I pleaded with you—supplicated you—beseeched you—but you put me gently aside, & said you knew you were drifting to certain wreck, but it could not be helped—it was too late—if this man had *only* been kept out of the way but a month or two longer all would have been well—but henceforth you & I must travel different paths in life, & from this moment these paths must diverge & never come together any more forever. You would "think of me sometimes, & hold me in regard as an esteemed acquaintance." I seized your hand, & said, "O, Livy, I loved you with such infinite tenderness!"

Then the tears sprang to your eyes & you threw your arms about my neck. But only for an instant. Then you sprang up & said "No!—it is over for all time!" And you fled away & left me prostrate upon the floor. (*L3* 423–24)

Through simple bifurcation of self—the urge to divide his identity being endemic in Clemens—he is both himself and his rival. As rival, he is an intruder, a wily corrupter, a mesmerizing violator who will bring certain ruin to Olivia. This dark furtive presence is sinister, and the image of him recalls Clemens's recurrent references to himself in the love letters as a thief, robber, or highwayman (for his sense of criminality, see *L2* 266, 290, 328, 345, 349, 357, and *L3* 137). His lifelong propensity for guilt manifests itself in this criminality. (He held himself responsible for his brother's death, his son's, and Susy's, and blamed himself for the largely imagined familial suffering brought on by his bankruptcy.) Here, however, the threat posed by his illicit self is sexual. Having celebrated Olivia for her purity with an obsession that suggests an opposing desire, he emerges in the dream as one who traps her in his "toils," instills in her a "feverish fascination," and leads her toward "certain wreck." The melo-dramatic terms honor the prudish Victorian sense of sex for a woman as destruction, but they also seem to project Clemens's own guilty feelings about the imminent consummation of his courtship. The ruin he brings is absolute: "a vapid, vacant existence, then Death." In all this, the dark psychic underside of Clemens's self-conceiving expresses itself at last within his love letters.

One comes upon this late letter with a sense of revelation almost as lurid as the letter itself: a feeling of "ah ha, here is what Clemens really felt; here is the real self beneath all the protestations of gentlemanly char-acter." To rest content with that discovery alone, however, is to misread the dream. And it is to misread it—or perhaps more accurately to half-read it—along familiar biographical lines. For of course Clemens had a sense of his inner darkness, of that self-loathing, socially subversive other within him that Kaplan has tracked so closely throughout the life. What is finally surprising about the dream tale, then, is not Clemens's role as destroyer but his part as rescuer. If the first betrays a latent desire, self-doubt, and fear, the second confirms a belief in his genuine probity. As rescuer, he embodies traditional proprieties, tender manliness, and true love, the very qualities he laid claim to during the courtship. And far from ruining Olivia, he offers the hope of "*true* happiness." In this dream he has dreamed a better self as well as a lesser one.

There is a closing frame for the dream tale in which Clemens says (improbably) that he lay abed for an hour, eyes closed, thinking that the "awful calamity" was real. Between full wakefulness and sleep, he first ex-periences "unspeakable misery" and then a cosmic grief: "And I compre-hended that in losing you the very universe had gone from me & black chaos was come again." When he opens his eyes and knows that "it was only a hideous dream," he experiences "ecstasy." While this coda cele-brates Olivia and affirms his love for her, it also revivifies that proper self left in the dream "prostrate upon the floor." It reasserts not only the real-ity of his good self—the other is the figment of nightmare—but also its potency, for in the closing frame he is empowered to dissolve the "ghastly" dream "forever" (*L3* 424).

Although approaching Olivia as supplicant for her moral approval as well as her love (the latter seeming to be contingent upon the former), Clemens was, in fact, a kind of rescuer. In time (certainly not all at once) he liberated her from narrow religious orthodoxy, freed her from limited, if privileged, social circumstances, and lifted her out of the ordinary. He replaced the snippets of her commonplace book with the living presence of a literary personality. To put it more positively still, he opened to her a larger and more mercurial existence. This widening brought Olivia disequilibrium and loss, as well as gain, as the terrain of her life shifted, so Clemens was something of a destroyer, too.

Olivia's rescue of Clemens was even more profound. The terms he used in his first letter to her which seem falsely melodramatic—he is "adrift and rudderless"; she will be his "friendly beacon"—are not far from the mark in the long course of their marriage. Olivia became a steadying center; she confirmed in Clemens that fine part of his nature which was paradoxically indispensable to his creativity yet always suspect. Given these reciprocities, Clemens's celebration of their oneness was a reasonable feeling: "But I am blessed above my kind, with *another self*—a life companion who is *part of me*—part of my heart, & flesh & spirit—& not a fellow-pilgrim who lags far behind or flies ahead, or soars above me" (*L4* 18). He wrote this less than a month before their marriage, and it reveals how far he has traveled in the course of their correspondence. Gone now is the self-belittlement, apology, and promised reform of the early letters. The change was effected as the constant self superseded the improving one—with Olivia's approval. Or to put it another way, while the prodigal self kept right on returning, never to arrive, Clemens's constant self made himself at home in Olivia's love.

The oneness he felt with her, a sense of union that clearly empowered him, extended to his creative performances as Mark Twain. Explaining to her a conversation he had with Twichell, he wrote, "I wanted him to understand that what we want is a *home*—we are done with the shows & vanities of life & are ready to enter upon its realities—we are tired of chasing its phantoms & shadows, & are ready to grasp its substance. At least *I* am & 'I' means both of us, & 'both of us' means I of course—for are not we Twain one flesh?" (*L3* 103).[11] Through the pun on his pseudonym, he incorporates Olivia into his literary identity.[12] In an important sense, the first work to emerge from this reorganized creative self is the courtship correspondence itself. While it is clearly literary, it confounds any easy definition by genre. Overall it suggests an epistolary novel in which three interlinked dramas are played out: the drama of the prodigal self's return; the drama of the constant self's recognition; and the drama of love that depends upon the first two. Whatever the form of the letters as a whole, the important point is that Olivia informs their creation not just by being their recipient but by being assimilated into Clemens's—or since it is a matter of the writer, into Mark Twain's—narrative stance. The proprieties she stood for become a part of *his* outlook.

CHAPTER FOUR

Writer on the River

The marriage of Sam Clemens and Olivia Langdon was by all accounts a strong and a happy one. Their first years together, though racked with difficulties, were years of individual growth as well as mutual adjustment, and many of the accommodations they made, the reciprocities they created, were to stay with them throughout their married life, making it a haven for them both. For Mark Twain the decade of the 1870s was a period in which he was coming into "full maturity" (Budd, "Editor's Notes" 144). Twain seemed, as one critic has observed, "ready to authenticate a personal style, an authorial signature, and to attempt works of magnitude" (Cardwell, *Man Who Was MT* 39–40). In his finely tuned study of the evolving Twain persona, Steinbrink has traced how from 1868 to 1871 the persona, while retaining expressions of "the anarchic or rebellious," incorporated "increasing moral responsibility, respectability, and even piety" (*Getting to Be MT* 50, 18). Certainly the courtship and subsequent marriage intensified some of the proprieties already present in Mark Twain—proprieties evident in the Moralist of the Main and the Victorian Traveler.

Perhaps the most pivotal work to emerge soon after Clemens's marriage was "Old Times on the Mississippi." That work is important for several reasons: first, it is a highly personal text; second, it opened to Twain as never before the realm of river and boyhood home that was to become the center of his greatest works; and third, it presented Twain to a new and highly respectable audience. "Old Times" was, of course, followed by—and literally incorporated into—the later *Life on the Mississippi.* The two texts are, among other things, about writing, for as almost every critic of them has noted, Twain associated piloting with writing, turning his accounts of river work and life into a kind of oblique commentary on his

103

own creative process. Yet key dimensions of Twain's identity as writer in these texts have remained largely unexamined. While there has been a great deal of attention to memory, language, and innocence, little has been said about Twain the writer's authority, gentility, and style, including the style of his humor. Together, these go a long way toward defining the "authorial signature" of Mark Twain.

THROUGHOUT HIS LIFE Clemens sought ever higher levels of social status, and Mark Twain became his ladder upward. Perhaps reflecting his small-town origins, he conceived of writing itself as a "trade that elevated one socially" (Ziff 260). In any case, when Mark Twain first appeared in the pages of the prestigious *Atlantic Monthly*, Clemens himself seemed to have achieved a new level of respectability (and, incidentally, thereby fulfilled some of the promise of his courtship). The publication of Mark Twain in the *Atlantic*, first unobtrusively with the short piece "A True Story," then on a large scale with the seven-part "Old Times on the Mississippi," is sometimes taken as a symbolic turning point in the history of American letters: as that moment at which the high walls of refined literary Boston were breached, a new, vigorous voice of the West was heard, and the vitalities of American writing thus passed irrevocably from the pens of the genteel into the hands of the common (Kaplan, *Great Short Works* xi–xii). The moment is made the more dramatic and suggestive by the fact that Twain was initially rejected by the standard-bearing *Atlantic*. When he submitted the comic and slightly irreverent "Some Learned Fables, for Good Old Boys and Girls," the cautious Howells declined it on grounds that it was likely to offend religious readers (*MTHL* 1:24). What he accepted instead, "A True Story," was a brief dialect rendering of a former slave's misfortunes, a touching, nonhumorous piece which Twain himself described as "rather out of my line" (*MTHL* 1:22). On the face of it, Twain had been welcomed into the *Atlantic* as a serious writer of pathos and turned away as a skeptical humorist.

But the accepted and well-received "Old Times" series itself contains moments of derision potentially offensive to scrupulous religious readers. Twain remarks, for instance, that the chills suffered by homeless backriver families during floods are "a merciful provision of an all-wise Providence to enable them to take exercise without exertion," and later in the series he again mocks Providence for answering profane, prayerful exclamations while leaving the genuine pleas "neglected" ("OT" 35, 76). Such facetious quips and ironic observations are as irreverent as anything in the rejected fable for "Good Old Boys and Girls." If we ask why Howells approved such passages, the answer is surely because the "Old Times" sketches are on the whole so proper. The prevailing point of view in them is so conventional it can assimilate brief sallies of irreverence.

Criticism of "Old Times on the Mississippi" has generally overlooked the nature and extent of the series' conventionality. Critics have been preoccupied with those parts of "Old Times" that anticipate the world of *Huckleberry Finn;* they have focused almost exclusively on what Smith has usefully termed the "Matter of Hannibal" and the "Matter of the River" (*Development* 72). But "Old Times on the Mississippi" encompasses more than a version of Hannibal and a discovery of the river. Failure to see the other perspectives and concerns that also give shape and point to the sketches not only distorts them but also makes them appear badly disjointed, for the last two sketches have little to do with the river of Twain's boyhood and nothing at all to do with Hannibal.

Although he sometimes adopted Howells's conventional terminology, Twain originally conceived of his "Old Times" sketches as a series of "papers" (*MTHL* 1:34). (He calls them that repeatedly in the series itself.) The term *papers* is suggestive as a key to both form and authorial stance. Presidents, generals, eminent scientists (and the like) issue "papers," documents of authority which do not necessarily have a narrative element but which derive their interest from authenticity. "Papers" purport to be from and about the "real" world. Twain, who prided himself on his precise knowledge of piloting and insisted that it was an exact science, approached the writing of "Old Times on the Mississippi" with the authority and command of one issuing "papers." The form can—and in Twain's case does—include narrative and dramatic anecdote, but it is fundamentally factual. So absorbed was he with his knowledge of his subject, Twain did not even mention humor to Howells when he first proposed the series. When Howells discerned a "sort of hurried and anxious air" in the first paper and attributed it to nervousness over an *Atlantic* audience (*MTHL* 1:46), Twain replied, "It isn't the Atlantic audience that distresses me; for it is the only audience that I sit down before in perfect serenity (for the simple reason that it don't require a "humorist" to paint himself stripèd and stand on his head every fifteen minutes)" (*MTHL* 1:49). "Perfect serenity" is more than bravado. In successive installments of the papers, Twain would increasingly exercise his license not to be a clowning humorist.

Of course, much of the beguiling charm of "Old Times on the Mississippi" does reside in its humor. The boy whose grandiose daydreams of celebrity as a clown, a minstrel, and a pirate only give way to an even more improbable plan—to complete the exploration of the Amazon—is unforgettably comic. His capacity for naive foolishness as a cub seems as endless as it is funny. What is less apparent than the humor itself, however, is the fact that the humor is made possible by Twain's sense of eminence, his stance in this case as the author of "papers." Feeling especially secure in his role as authority, Twain is free to acknowledge the failings of his past—his ignorance, his romanticism, his youthful vanity—by turning them into comedy. In general it is true that Twain's successful humor depends on his sense of superiority. When he is uncertain of his position, his humor can become flat, strained, gauche, or shrilly aggressive, as if he were unnerved or struggling to achieve parity through the humor itself. But when he writes with a secure feeling of superiority to the world he envisions, then his humor is at its best.

While Twain approached his "Old Times" with the confidence of the expert issuing papers, he established his superiority within the papers in three ways: first, by displaying his expertise; second, by exaggerating the naiveté of the cub, thereby implying his own vast difference; and third, by lacing his account with concerns far beyond the cub and his limited world. These tactics not only ensure superiority for Twain, releasing his good humor. They also announce his preeminence to his audience, inviting their admiration and approval.

The end of the first paper is a definitive enactment of Twain's superior authorial stance as well as his essential propriety. Up to this point, the presence of the superior Twain is felt only rather vaguely behind the narrative of the boy's ambitions. But at the conclusion of the first paper, lest

Twain or his audience have any doubt about the matter, the eminent Twain emerges. The revelation is sudden and emphatic. Having described the boy's infatuation with the night watchman, Twain closes by defining the watchman, not as the boy sees him, but as he really is: "It was a sore blight to find out afterwards that he was a low, vulgar, ignorant, sentimental, half-witted humbug, an untraveled native of the wilds of Illinois, who had absorbed wildcat literature and appropriated its marvels, until in time he had woven odds and ends of the mess into this yarn, and then gone on telling it to the fledglings like me, until he had come to believe it himself" ("OT" 8). Although Twain says that he discovered the watchman's true character "afterwards," the perspectives he brings to bear on the watchman exceed the experience not only of an enlightened cub but also of a seasoned pilot. The terms of deprecation Twain uses reflect neither the Matter of Hannibal nor the Matter of the River but what we should probably call the Manner of Boston. In Twain's dismissal of the watchman, from the stock pejoratives, "low" and "vulgar," right down to the belief in the pernicious influence of bad literature, the values and attitudes are those of genteel Boston.[1] Denouncing the watchman as a "low, vulgar, ignorant, sentimental, half-witted humbug" actually creates an antonymous identity for Twain; implicitly he is the opposite: a cultured, refined, informed, unsentimental, intelligent man of substance. Is it any wonder that he assured Howells he sat before an *Atlantic* audience with "perfect serenity"?

The Manner of Boston shapes "Old Times on the Mississippi" in important ways. It dictates, for one thing, the material Twain chooses to include in his papers. The series has sometimes been criticized for its falsification of the river trade (DeVoto 100–114; Ferguson 212). Twain is guilty in particular of ignoring the vice rampant on the steamboats, many of which were floating saloons, gambling dens, and whorehouses. His suppression of these seamy aspects of river life is itself a sign of the Manner of Boston. Even more indicative of Twain's propriety, however, is the way in which he does touch briefly upon such low life. He locates it not on board his steamboat but on the rafts and trading scows that also ply the river, and he always speaks of it disdainfully. When his steamer shaves off the steering oar of an unlit scow, for instance, Twain's reflection is charged with moral indignation: "And that flatboatman would be sure to go into New Orleans and sue our boat, swearing stoutly that he had a light burning all the time, when in truth his gang had the lantern down below to sing and lie and drink and gamble by, and no watch on deck" ("OT" 33). By placing vice on the lesser craft of the river, Twain not only preserves the illusion of the purity of steamboat life but actually enhances it. Observing in the Manner of Boston, he makes discriminations throughout "Old Times" in terms of ethical and cultural as well as commercial values. The proper Twain consistently associates the steamboat with superior wealth, art, intelligence, and morality. His contempt for men of inferior character on "small-fry craft" is so great he is occasionally betrayed into tasteless humor ("OT" 34). Flood victims, to his unsympathetic eye, become "roosting" male "miserables" ("OT" 35). And when his mighty steamboat just misses eating up (the metaphor is Twain's) a "Posey County family, fruit, furniture, and all," he facetiously regrets that they veered off in time, "doing no serious damage, unfortunately, but coming so near it that we had good hopes for a moment" ("OT" 33).

Such encounters between the elite and the insignificant on the river are invariably marked by what Twain calls "no end of profane cordialities" ("OT" 34). While his elegant, euphemistic way of putting it, with its calculated incongruity, suggests a supercilious amusement in keeping with the Manner of Boston, Twain's attitude toward swearing is actually mixed. The point is especially interesting, both because profanity was such a touchstone of vulgarity for the genteel and because Twain was so fond of it. He makes the "hard swearing" of raftsmen articulate their essentially low character, even as he turns it into humor in such strokes of hyperbole as "those people . . . cursed us till everything turned blue" ("OT" 34, 33). But Twain also uses profanity to mark the heroic stature of the denizens of the steamboat. He recalls with admiration that when the mate on the *Paul Jones* gave "even the simplest order," he "discharged it like a blast of lightning, and sent a long reverberating peal of profanity thundering after it" ("OT" 6). Profanity of this order is a nearly godlike attribute, and it is not surprising, then, that Bixby, the suprahuman pilot, is described as a "gunpowdery chief" who explodes "with a bang" of red-hot profanity and goes on "loading and firing" until he is "out of adjectives" ("OT" 17). The key to the difference between profanity as a mark of ignorant vulgarity and profanity as a sign of heroic character seems to be the artfulness with which it is uttered. The night watchman swears, but his profanity is "so void of art" that it is "an element of weakness rather than strength" ("OT" 7).

For all of his attention to profanity, and it is one of the recurrent motifs in the papers, Twain always touches on it in delicate circumlocutions, that is, in the Manner of Boston. He carefully maintains his own propriety. His treatment of profanity is either pointedly condescending, when profanity is a stigma, or humorously exaggerated, when it is the mark of a demigod. In both cases Twain's perspective is notably distant. It is only the untutored boy of the opening who is enthralled by the mate's "perfect" profanity and wishes he could "talk like that" ("OT" 6–7).

Although freighted with large segments of factual information, the first five "Old Times" papers are dominated by the process of the cub's initiation. The cub's initial tasks are to discover his own ignorance, to overcome natural laziness, to disabuse himself of inveterate romantic illusions, and, most demanding of all, to learn the river up and down by day and by night in all its ever-shifting detail. Formidable as these assignments are, the cub makes surprisingly quick progress, even in memorizing the river. For the real struggle at the heart of the cub's education is his effort to master not the intricate river but his own truant character.

The pattern of initiation in "Old Times" has often been noted, and one critic has carefully described three stages of the process (Mills), but what has not been taken into account is the fact that the initiation is presented as a matter of moral correction. The Manner of Boston is implacably moral, and Twain emphasizes the moral dimension of the cub's learning. "My complacency," he has the cub remark, "could hardly get start enough to lift my nose a trifle into the air, before Mr. B—— would think of something to fetch it down again" ("OT" 17). Over and over the moments of instruction are precipitated by the cub's insurgent pride: "My self-complacency moved to the front once more"; "I went gayly along, getting prouder and prouder"; "I vaingloriously turned my back . . . and hummed a tune"; "I got to tilting my cap to the side of my head, and wearing a tooth-pick in my mouth at the wheel" ("OT" 22, 24, 29). At such moments, Mr. B——, as much moral preceptor as mere informant, subjects the cub to ridicule and humiliation, to private and public censure, designed to check an errant egotism. The climax of it all comes in the now famous end of the fifth paper when the cub, once again "brim full of self-conceit and carrying . . . [his] nose as high as a giraffe's," is tricked into thinking he is about to ground his boat in deep water ("OT" 50). While everyone on board secretly watches, the cub panics at the false soundings that drop below "mark twain," the signal, of course, for *safe* water, and begs his engineer, "Oh, Ben, if you love me, *back* her! Quick, Ben! Oh, back the immortal *soul* out of her!" The cub is thus taught to trust his knowledge over appearances and to retain his courage in the face of danger, but the "humiliating laughter" that surrounds him also chastens his pride ("OT" 51). The moral point would not have been lost on Twain's Victorian readers, especially those who were following in the same issues of the *Atlantic* Henry James's *Roderick Hudson*, a critical portrait of a romantic egotist whose pride, like the cub's, is also rebuked and who suffers an even more serious fall.

The moral emphasis in the cub's initiation accounts, I think, for the fact that he does not appear in the final two papers. The natural culmination of the narrative line should be the complete transformation of the backsliding cub into the steady pilot. The problem for Twain, though, is that he wants to extol piloting, to herald its "Rank and Dignity" in ways that are incompatible with a fully initiated, that is to say, wholly chastened and humbled cub ("OT" 52). Further, insofar as the cub is an extension of Twain, it would be personally—and publicly—vain to laud his estate, a terrible breach of the Manner of Boston.

To preserve the propriety of his moral perspective, then, comic though it is, Twain simply drops the cub and dissociates his personal history from the concluding praise of the pilot's profession. This glosses over the contradiction between the humility exacted from the cub and the vainglory permitted the pilot. But the shift does not occur smoothly. There is a break between the humorous moment, at the end of the fifth paper, when the cub's pride is most fully and publicly rebuked, and the serious protracted elevation of piloting that follows in the sixth paper and to a lesser degree in the seventh as well. Twain brilliantly bridges the moment of reduction and the ensuing glorification with one paragraph of disarming candor, after which the strongly personal note is never again sounded. Ironically, the change in moral pressure is covered when Twain confesses, indeed professes, the *pride* he felt as a pilot. "If I have seemed to love my subject," he says, "it is no surprising thing, for I loved the profession far better than any I have followed since, and I took a measureless pride in it" ("OT" 52). Then lest his "measureless pride" be taken for the kind of conceit censured in the cub, Twain explains that it stems from the independence inherent in the job of piloting. He celebrates that independence, then the power, and finally the prominence of the pilot, but as he moves toward the acknowledgment of "personage," the personal Twain recedes into the decorous impersonality of the informed authority imparting observed rather than lived experience. With the cub eliminated, the personal self disengaged, Twain is free to extol piloting without appearing arrogant. He is free to observe that pilots fail to show "embarrassment in the presence of traveling foreign princes" because they alone share the same "grade of life" ("OT" 53).

In his 1866 letter to Will Bowen, Twain lauded the pilot in ways that falsified his actual character; but the terms he used then anticipate those later deployed in "Old Times on the Mississippi": "It is a strange study,— a singular phenomenon, if you please, that the only real, independent & genuine *gentlemen* in the world go quietly up & down the Mississippi river, asking no homage of any one, seeking no popularity, no notoriety, & not caring a damn whether school keeps or not" (*L1* 358, Clemens's emphasis). In "Old Times" this idea—minus the mild profanity—would first become the assertion, "a pilot, in those days, was the only unfettered and entirely independent human being that lived in the earth," and then it would swell into the extended comparison of the pilot's freedom to that of kings, editors, clergymen, and writers ("OT" 52). Apart from the more elaborate quality of the later version, the most significant difference is Twain's omission of the term *gentlemen*. While the letter reveals how much value Twain attached in 1866 to the idea of being a gentleman, his failure to ascribe gentlemanliness to the pilot in "Old Times" suggests that by 1874–75 he had lived into a richer sense of the concept. His newer understanding of what it means to be a gentleman is embodied in the Manner of Boston, which pervades the "Old Times" papers. With a touch of condescension in keeping with that manner, Twain speaks of "ornate and gilded" pilots and notes that in St. Louis and New Orleans many did nothing but "play gentleman, up town" ("OT" 54, 53).

Although the cub disappears from the final two papers, the seven parts of "Old Times on the Mississippi" form a more unified artistic and thematic whole than has been generally recognized. The series has a structural unity, achieved in part by the balance between parallel but contrasting elements of the first five and the last two papers. The first and seventh papers, the opening and closing of the series, are balanced opposites. Both begin with elaborately descriptive, picturesque set pieces, and both end with comic denigrations of minor characters—the watchman in the first instance, Stephen in the second. The opening set piece is the familiar and justly celebrated description of a steamboat's electric effect on the sleepy river town that was Hannibal. The less well known parallel scene that opens the last paper is an extended description of steamers leaving New Orleans amidst singing, flags, cannon shots, and huzzahs. The two pictures are similar in their patterned design, as Twain notes in both not only such natural events as the exchange of freight and passengers but also such small things as the cries of the boatmen, the burning of pitch, and even the slopes of the two levees. The passages are pointedly similar in some of their observed details, and they are rendered in the same practiced literary style, designed to achieve through minute particularity a striking pictorial effect. However, the worlds they depict are antipodal and mark the extreme limits of life along the river. The first is a "dead" town "drowsing in the sunshine," whereas the second is New Orleans, a sprawling, energetic city with "two or three miles" of busy waterfront ("OT" 1, 68). While the sleepy town is brought momentarily to life by the arrival of a single "cheap, gaudy packet," life flows *out of* New Orleans onto the numerous steamers that leave the wharf in "stately procession" ("OT" 1, 69). The distance between the river town and the port city is the gulf between a stagnant waystation and a center of civilization. The general movement of the "Old Times" papers is away from the byways back to the source.

Significantly, however, Twain is superior to both the dead town and the wide-awake port. He laughs at the scrambling New Orleans passengers as much as at the little town's dozing clerks and fragrant drunkard. Twain's authorial stance, upon which the humor as well as the information in the papers depends, transcends the reach of civilization posited within the series. It goes beyond New Orleans to New England—to Nook Farm and Boston.

In a letter to his sister, Twain once insisted with youthful cockiness that the centers of importance in America, the only places "to be gravely considered by thinking men," were centers of "intelligence, capital & population" (*L1* 310). The overall movement of the "Old Times" papers is toward a center that possesses intelligence, capital, and population, together with the concerns and values natural to them. New Orleans stands within the papers for a superior way of life, for a denser, more complex civilization. As the papers move toward that civilization, the narrative consciousness itself expands, becoming more sophisticated, more learned, and more discriminating. The papers thus enact and uphold the value of an enlarged awareness. This is, I think, the overarching theme of "Old Times on the Mississippi." The emergence of the fully mature Twain in the last two papers is in its way a fulfillment of the need for learning and growth manifest humorously in the cub of the preceding papers. The expansion of narrative perspective through which the papers evolve from the personal and parochial to the general and broadly informed is the fullest expression of the meaning of the series.

The subjects considered by Twain in the final two papers are treated in a manner that expresses Twain's informed outlook. He creates contexts that extend well beyond the limited world of the river. Thus the pilots' association is seen in the light of national monopolies;[2] the profession of piloting itself is now considered not only in terms of the river trade but also in view of the economic forces at work in the country at large; steamboat racing yields a sense of history; and the river's natural tendency to shorten itself through cutoffs is used to evoke the vast sweep of time.

The world created in the concluding papers is a post-initiation world of knowing, working, and earning; it is a gilded version of a Ben Franklin world in which the ways to wealth are the valued ways of life. In contrast to the arena of the cub's constant failing, this is a world of consummate success. Twain devotes most attention to the organization, rise, and

triumph of the pilots' association. He takes obvious pride in the requirements set by the association for new apprentice pilots, requirements
which underscore the fact that piloting is a reputable profession: "The
applicant must not be less than eighteen years old, of respectable family
and good character; he must pass an examination as to education, pay a
thousand dollars in advance for the privilege of becoming an apprentice"
("OT" 65). Twain delights in the struggle between the association and
the captains, owners, and nonunion members, revealing a fondness for
the inevitability of the outcome that anticipates his later attraction to de-
terminism. But his chief emphasis is on money, the money sacrificed in
forming the association, the money exacted from its belated confederates,
the money finally earned for its members.

Twain, who was keenly aware of the importance of capital, as he told
his sister and demonstrated in his life, is in fact attentive to financial matters throughout the "Old Times" papers. In the very first paper, lost in
the aura of the boys' grand illusions, displaced by their joyful celebration
of the pilot's "glory," is the rather unromantic fact that Twain calculates
the status of the pilot in terms of cash: "Pilot was the grandest position
of all. The pilot, even in those days of trivial wages, had a princely salary—
from a hundred and fifty to two hundred and fifty dollars a month, and
no board to pay. Two months of his wages would pay a preacher's salary
for a year" ("OT" 4). In the course of the series, Twain notes the cash
value of steamboats, cargo, property, and even men, for money becomes
a measure of a man's standing. (The benighted watchman, as one might
expect, makes a paltry six dollars a week.) Twain's casual remark that the
pilot earned a princely salary "even in those days of trivial wages" anticipates his exultation in the last two papers over salaries of four, five, and
even eighteen hundred dollars a month. The cub of the opening, who is
shown not only as impecunious but also as improvident, throws into relief both the enormous affluence and the skillful financial manipulations
recorded in the concluding papers.

When he wrote "Old Times on the Mississippi," Clemens was, of
course, newly established in his lavish home at Nook Farm, carefully locating himself vis-à-vis the world of New England gentility. As a man of
property, he had become ever more staunchly a man of propriety, and so

had Mark Twain. The series undoubtedly reflects that present time of prosperity as well as the old flush times on the river. Twain's interest in money is a notable aspect of this authorial perspective, an important yet overlooked element of the "Old Times" papers. It reveals a norm that was central to but seldom acknowledged by the audience of *Atlantic* readers. When he ushered his friend into the *Atlantic*, Howells himself was most worried not by possible religious improprieties but by the question of what *to pay* so noted and popular an author as Mark Twain ("Recollections" 601). Had it been more blatant than it is, Twain's attention to money would no doubt have struck some of his readers as vulgar; but as it is, recurrent but not obsessive, the effect of Twain's monetary valuations is simply to keep his papers solidly in touch with the real world.[3]

That real world encompassed both his present life in Hartford and his past on the river. Twain's task at this point in his career seems to have been, as Smith once put it, "nothing less than establishing his own identity . . . by working out a continuity between his adult life in Hartford and his remote childhood in the small town on the west bank of the river thirty years in the past" (*Development* 74). The split in the "Old Times" papers between the first five and the final two indicates that Twain was not able to make his past and present fully congruent. But the papers do point toward one form that reconciliation was to take, as Twain tries to pilot his way between the proper Manner of Boston and the crude Matter of Hannibal and the River.

While the final two papers are expressions of Clemens's present self, even tacit affirmations of the need for such a mature, civilized self, Mark Twain locates in them symbolic figures from Clemens's earlier past. Chief among these is the pilot, Stephen, and Twain's treatment of him reveals the struggle to align past and present. His characterization of Stephen is a balance between fond affection and mild criticism:

> He was a gifted pilot, a good fellow, a tireless talker, and had both wit and humor in him. He had a most irreverent independence, too, and was deliciously easy-going and comfortable in the presence of age, official dignity, and even the most august wealth. He always had work, he never saved a penny, he was a most persuasive borrower, he was in debt to every pilot on the river, and to the majority of the captains. He could throw a sort of splen-

dor around a bit of harum-scarum, devil-may-care piloting, that made it almost fascinating. ("OT" 55)

The attractions of Stephen—his achievement as a pilot, his goodheart-
edness, his endless talk, his wit and humor, his irreverent independence,
and his easygoing, comfortable ways—are the charms of Sam Clemens's
own past, the past Mark Twain was appropriating for his fiction. The
flaw in Stephen's character, his financial irresponsibility, is similarly a
vexed point in that past. While Twain is amused by the ingenuity with
which Stephen evades his debts, he cannot wholly condone it. (Twain
himself was always serious about money, if not always shrewd.) But when
he is moved by the pressure of his Bostonian Manner to rebuke Stephen
in the final paper, he simply calls him "careless" and "wayward" ("OT"
76). The gentleness of his terms of disapproval suggests his basic acceptance. Twain manages to reconcile his past and present, to both censure
and tolerate Stephen, by seeing him as little more than a grown-up child
whose irresponsible acts are, like Tom Sawyer's, taken as little more than
harum-scarum pranks.

The ending of "Old Times on the Mississippi," one more reminiscence
of Stephen, seems at first not only casual but peripheral. Twain himself
spoke to Howells of the close as a "postscript," yet he felt it was "necessary" (*MTHL* 1:85). His instincts were sound. Anecdotal as it is, the ending draws effectively upon major aspects of the papers, for in telling the
last tale of Stephen, Twain brings into focus at the close precisely that
propriety which informs the series as a whole.

The concluding humorous story turns upon Stephen's decision to pay
off all his many debts in alphabetical order. To this announcement, the
much persecuted and long put-off Yates replies "with a sigh": "Well, the
Y's stand a gaudy chance. He won't get any further than the C's in *this*
world, and I reckon that after a good deal of eternity has wasted away in
the next one, I'll still be referred to up there as 'that poor, ragged pilot
that came here from St. Louis in the early days!'" ("OT" 78). The evocation of a pilot passing to his heavenly reward is an appropriate vision
with which to close the "Old Times" papers; it elevates the pilot and provides a kind of emotional closure. The idea of wayward Stephen default-

ing throughout eternity is a fine comic invention. But it worried Twain. He, not Howells, was afraid that his final bit of comedy might give offense to his *Atlantic* readers, presumably because it was set in heaven (*MTHL* 1:85 n. 2). He need not have worried, of course. The moral perspective and monetary norm at work in the joke are conventional enough to outweigh any indelicacy in treating God's elect comically. No one objected when he envisioned poor ragged Yates eternally unrepaid by the lovable deadbeat Stephen, especially when that unreliable rascal served as the butt of humor and so by contrast as another and final measure of the proper Mark Twain.

EIGHT YEARS AFTER "Old Times," Mark Twain published *Life on the Mississippi*, a text that assimilated the earlier papers, confirming their personal and ideological perspectives at the same time it provided new revelations of self and new expressions of value. The confidence, superiority, and propriety evident in the original papers are, if anything, intensified in the later book (the proper Twain is even more proper). But, operating out of them, Twain adds two significant dimensions to his evolving text: he gives further definition to himself—the self first sketched in the papers as both pilot and expert; and he undertakes new and different cultural evaluations.

When he incorporated the "Old Times" papers into *Life on the Mississippi*, however, Twain created a seeming disjuncture in his text between a youthful, or somewhat youthful, distant past and an immediate adult present. This was just one of many compositional oddities. If *Life* is, as James M. Cox has suggested, "in many ways" Twain's "most characteristic performance" ("Introduction," *LOM* 9), it is also one of his most problematical. Is it an account of the past, as at least the "Old Times" sections initially suggest, or of the more recent present of Twain's famous return to the river in 1882? Is it personal narrative or factual documentary? Is it travel writing, history, or sociological tract? Is it about the river or the civilization along its banks? Is it a celebration of progress or a lament over change? Is it nostalgic or realistic, pessimistic or hopeful? The book itself provokes such questions, for Twain's subject, form, outlook, and values all seem not just unsettled but often contradictory.[4]

In one sense this is precisely what makes it his "most characteristic performance." Its amplitude, variety, and contrariness, its seriousness, humor, and sentimentality, its unmatchable mix of narrative, history, story, fact, legend, observation, anecdote, critical analysis, yarn, and reminiscence—all these, especially all these *together*, seem to identify Mark Twain. How did he come to express himself so fully? Not to be underestimated is the fact that he had long dreamed of writing a river book. As early as January 1866, he seems to have been planning one (see *L1* 329). Intermittently throughout the 1870s, he urged Howells to make a river trip with him, so that he could gather material for his book. He seemed confident that it would be an important work: "When I come to write the Mississippi book, *then* look out! I will spend 2 months on the river & take notes, & I bet you I will make a standard work" (*LLMT* 166). As Horst Kruse has shown in his meticulous account of the making of *Life on the Mississippi*, the notion of a "standard work" was central to the conception and composition of the book (Kruse, *MT and "Life"* 5–15). It reveals Twain's aspiration to make his mark in high culture by creating a serious, definitive study. To write a standard work is to describe, define, and evaluate with consummate authority; again, it is to write with the command of an expert issuing papers.

It was therefore quite natural for Twain to incorporate his "Old Times" papers into his "standard work." With no acknowledgment that they were written some seven years earlier, Twain assimilates the "Old Times" papers into *Life* wholesale, turning them into chapters 4–17 of his new text. However, he bridges the original papers and the ensuing new narrative in revealing ways. In chapters 18 and 19, "I Take a Few Extra Lessons" and "Brown and I Exchange Compliments," he stages a conflict between the cub and the tyrannical pilot Brown—a fictive representation of the actual William Brown, a man Twain "hated above all other men" (Branch, "The Pilot and the Writer" 35). It is worth noting that the cub Twain presents in these additional chapters of education is not the heedless, romantic innocent he has shown earlier but a shrewder, more mature version, a cub who has "served under many pilots" and has become "familiarly acquainted with about all the different types of human nature that are to be found in fiction, biography, or history" (*LOM* 152). This is a cub initiated into more than piloting. Significantly, the conflict with Brown is dramatized as a matter of class and ethical conduct. Twain has the despotic, "ignorant, stingy, malicious, snarling" (*LOM* 152) Brown rage at the cub for his social status, as well as his standing on punctilio: "You've had no *orders!* My, what a fine bird we are! We must have *orders!* Our father was a *gentleman*—owned slaves—and *we've* been to *school.* Yes, *we* are a gentleman, *too,* and got to have *orders!*" (*LOM* 154). The cub is revealed here—with Twain's apparent approval—as a gentleman, and his gentlemanliness is defined in particularly southern terms: it is a matter of birth, education, and slaveholding. After he has protected his brother Henry by knocking Brown down, the cub uses the true weapon of a gentleman against him: "But I was not afraid of him now; so, instead of going, I tarried, and criticised his grammar; I reformed his ferocious speeches for him, and put them into good English, calling his attention to the advantage of pure English over the bastard dialect of the Pennsylvanian collieries whence he was extracted. He could have done his part to admiration in a cross-fire of mere vituperation, of course; but he was not equipped for this species of controversy" (*LOM* 158–59). This encounter reveals emphatically the working of Twain's class consciousness. Just as he has Brown's dialect signal his coarse and violent character, so he has the cub's correct Standard English announce his status and secure for him the victory and honor of a gentleman.[5]

Most commentaries on *Life* have recognized that the curious narrative (usually described as a travel book) focuses time and again in one way or another on its narrator, Mark Twain. He is its principal character and the true center of interest. As Brodwin has put it, "this oddly constructed work" offers "a complex, mediatory version of Twain himself" ("Useful & Useless River" 197). The Twain that emerges in the transition between the "Old Times" papers and the extended text is not, of course, the pilot, although the Twain of *Life* continues to be knowledgeable about steamboats and the river. Twain had defined himself in terms of piloting in the first five of the "Old Times" papers, and he no doubt valued that identification partly because he associated the pilot with "social status" (Burde 879). Yet, as we have seen, Twain recognized that pilots were not true gentlemen (not among the social elite). When he links the "Old

Times" papers to *Life* through the conflict with Brown, Twain explicitly claims for himself precisely the social standing he denies mere pilots: the status of a gentleman. This is just the beginning of his self-definition, however. In the next chapter, a four-paragraph one entitled "A Section in My Biography," he defines himself further, adding to the social standing of gentleman a professional identity: he is "a scribbler of books," "an immovable fixture among the other rocks of New England" (*LOM* 166). Neither the playful self-belittlement of "scribbler" nor the joke about being one of the "rocks" belies the pride expressed here in his profession as writer. Indeed, the comic metaphor of being among the rocks of the region suggests a strong satisfaction in his stability. "Scribbler" echoes— some eighteen years later—Clemens's avowal of vocation to Orion as a call "to seriously scribbling to excite the *laughter* of God's creatures" (*L1* 323), but now his scribbling is not aimed at the creation of humor; now he is a maker of books. To the stance of expert about piloting assumed in the "Old Times" pieces, the role of one knowledgeable enough to write a series of *papers*, Twain thus adds the posture of professional writer. And as he had employed the Manner of Boston in those papers, he now appropriately identifies himself as both a gentleman and a fixture of New England.

Defining himself as a writer, indeed as a New England one, Twain further distances himself from his old—and now superseded—profession as pilot. In a letter to Howells, he speaks directly of the difference between pilot and writer: "All the boys [the river pilots he had known] had brains, & plenty of them—but they mostly lacked education & the literary faculty" (*MTHL* 1:78). It is Mark Twain who has that faculty and who by the time he writes *Life* has exercised it so successfully that a steamboat has been named after him, as he dramatically points out in chapter 28. (He is so famous, of course, that he is unable to travel incognito.) Contrary to those interpretations that see Twain as suffering "confusion about his identity" (Burde 888), Twain not only knows who he is but goes out of his way to announce his identity: he is a writer. It is no doubt the easy, satisfied, indeed prideful acceptance of this identity which enables him to create his "most characteristic performance."

Since he declares so pointedly that he is a writer, it is wholly fitting that Twain should disclose the origin of his creative identity. Late in *Life*—in the most famous moment in a book of moments—he offers a much-debated account of how he got his pseudonym. In brief, he explains that when he was a pilot on the river he once wrote a burlesque of the river notices (those factual reports on river conditions published for the benefit of pilots) that the aged pilot Isaiah Sellers issued under the penname "Mark Twain." His burlesque, he says, reduced this patriarch of the river to embarrassed silence. Years later when he was a fledgling journalist in the West, he confesses he added theft to injury by confiscating the pseudonym itself.[6] Bridgman remarks, "If ever there were a case of symbolic patricide, this was it" (*Traveling* 115), and G. Thomas Couser glosses the symbolic act: it "seems to bring about the death of the father figure on which his own accession to full authorship depends" (78). Two fathers, the literal progenitor and the literary precursor, are conflated here. Insofar as Sellers is a surrogate for the real father, Twain's tale of his antagonism anticipates the veiled hostility toward that father expressed in his western writings—a conflict largely resolved, as I've suggested, through identification with Anson Burlingame (and after him, albeit briefly, with Jervis Langdon). But Clemens does not just slay the father here; he becomes him, and as he does so, he assumes not only the name of his precursor but also his authority and his respectability. (It is appropriate that the actual leadsman's cry, "Mark Twain," is after all the signal for safe water.)[7] Twain's tale of origin thus posits the very conventionality upon which the entire narrative of *Life* rides.

That narrative seems capricious, but in fact the book has a recognizable form. *Life on the Mississippi* is best understood, I think, as what Northrop Frye has defined as the *anatomy*. As he describes it, the anatomy is a loose-jointed narrative, full of ideas and theories, marked by the free play of fancy, by realistic analysis, by stern moralizing, and by a humor that inclines to caricature; it is encyclopedic in its display of information, digressive in its inclusion of wide-ranging subject matter, and wayward in its development (Frye 308–14). An anatomy is typically animated by caustic criticism (Frye argues that the form derives the Menippean satire), and certainly Twain fills *Life* with emphatic judgments. As Budd has observed, in *Life* Twain leaves "a trail of serious opinion, mostly with constructive praise for any sign of rising industry, but also with flickering sarcasm for any vestiges of the cotton kingdom" (*Social Philosopher* 89).

Twain functions, in fact, as a critic at large. He tends to measure the river civilization in terms of "progress, energy, prosperity" (*LOM* 172); he actually reviews towns and cities in precisely the terms he touted to his sister in his 1869 letter: "intelligence, capital and population." Increases in these are for him not only desirable as advances in themselves but also as catalysts for "the liberalizing of opinion" (*LOM* 266). However, the core of Twain as anatomizing critic may be most fully revealed in one of the passages written for but finally not included in the published text. Defending Mrs. Trollope, of all the foreign tourists to the Mississippi the one he likes best, he defines her character in explaining her outlook: "She was holily hated for her 'prejudices;' but they seem to have been simply the prejudices of a humane spirit against inhumanities; of an honest nature against humbug; of a clean breeding against grossness; of a right heart against unright speech and deed" (*LOM* 219–20). However well they fit Mrs. Trollope, these character traits of humane spirit, honest nature, clean breeding, and right heart seem to describe Twain's conception of the ideal critic, and they disclose just how typically Victorian that conception is. They also come close to defining Twain himself as critic, for he tends to view the river world through a lens of conventionality that not only values population, wealth, and intelligence, as well as more enlightened opinion, but also a humane spirit, an honest nature, clean breeding, and a right heart.

While his criticisms range widely, Twain has a recurrent concern, almost an obsession: the nature and significance of good writing. Just as he identifies himself within the extended text of *Life* not as pilot but as professional writer, so he turns the subject of writing into a central feature in his anatomy. The importance of this act is revealed by its very oddity. One might expect anyone composing a standard work on the river to deal with its geography, history, traffic, economy, society, and so on, but not with writing. Yet Twain's attention to writing becomes one of the major thematic centers of the book.

Strewn throughout his narrative, like so many buoys in the river itself, his remarks on writing keep popping up, guiding the reader into a perception of him as knowledgeable literary craftsman. He sets himself up as nothing less than an authority on writing. He holds forth at length on

proper grammar, criticizing southern "infelicities" (*LOM* 316) and "blasphemous" usages, yet coyly announcing, with his eye on Scripture, that
"no one, either in the world or out of it," has ever written "blemishless
grammar" (*LOM* 196). Predictably he tends to tolerate departures from
correctness when they are made by gentlemen and to condemn them
when they are the mistakes of the lower classes. But he is absolute in his
conviction that whatever unconscious errors are created by the habits of
a community, all people "may justly be required to refrain from *knowingly*
and *purposely* debauching their grammar" (*LOM* 196). He objects to a
wide range of idiomatic expression: "Like the flag officer did," "I did n't
go to do it," and "Where have you been at?" (*LOM* 317)—confusing, as
Sewell has pointed out, what is regional and what is national, largely because he has a "conservative picture of Standard English" (22).

He is free with his opinions on the kind of content that will "interest
the general reader": accounts "full of variety, full of incident, full of the
picturesque" (*LOM* 265). He confidently announces the difficulty of creating authentic feelings: "And, mind you, emotions are among the tough-
est things in the world to manufacture out of whole cloth; it is easier to
manufacture seven facts than one emotion" (*LOM* 198–99). And he explains why a good writer will often turn to facts, especially numerical facts:
"Sometimes, half a dozen figures will reveal, as with a lightning-flash, the
importance of a subject which ten thousand labored words, with the same
purpose in view, had left at last but dim and uncertain" (*LOM* 209). In
even broader terms he articulates his own ideal of what good writing
should accomplish. Twice in the text (and once more in an unpublished
part of the manuscript) he repeats this stock explanation of the power
of successful literature: it creates "a realizing sense" of its subject (*LOM*
337, 259, 370).

Although he lays out an ambitious structure for his book (only to violate it), he says little about structure in general, probably because his own
narrative is as full of turnings as the river. Yet he is acutely self-conscious
of his digressive mode. Sometimes his awareness borders on apology, as
in this transition: "Here is a story which I picked up on board the boat
that night. I insert it in this place merely because it is a good story, not
because it belongs here—for it does n't" (*LOM* 267). More often it reg-

isters as a cavalier insouciance: "I desire to depart from the direct line of my subject, and make a little excursion" (*LOM* 360). On the one hand calling for an adherence to rules (especially those of strict grammar and usage) and on the other exempting himself from constraints of coherent narrative, Twain presents himself within his text as a writer masterful enough to follow or depart from general guidelines at will. But the most significant thing is that the guidelines he does set up, the rules he insists on, are all thoroughly conventional.

In his initial chapter he casually observes that books are accustomed to "use, and over-use" the word *new*—to use it so often in reference to America that "we early get and permanently retain the impression that there is nothing old about it" (*LOM* 41). Although his immediate concern is to evoke a sense of the country's antiquity, the pause over language is significant. He is, of course, fussing over stale words and hoping to find fresh-baked ones, but implicit in his observation is the sense that language mediates between the self and the world, that it creates reality. However, this idea is not entirely sustained when the cub learns to read the river. (Twain wrote of that learning before he recorded the remarks about new and old words, but eventually placed it after them.) To be sure, the ordinary passenger does see the "reality" of the river through the language of romantic travel narratives, but the cub comes to apprehend the river through a curious combination of direct experience (he encounters snags, reefs, wrecks, and so on) and intuition (he must know the river "by the shape" in his "*head*" ["OT" 18]), neither of which is linguistically mediated.[8]

When Twain elsewhere deals explicitly with the formation of the writer, he seems to suggest that the writer acquires knowledge of his subject in a way similar to the cub's. Describing the making of the "native novelist," Twain locates the writer's empowerment in "*absorption;* years and years of unconscious absorption; years and years of intercourse with the life concerned" ("What Paul Bourget Thinks of Us," *MTC2* 166).[9] "Intercourse with the life concerned" evokes direct experience, while "unconscious absorption" suggests a kind of intuitive grasp of reality. Having learned the river, the cub—analogue for the developing writer—abandons a vague, romantic rhetoric for precise, realistic descriptors. And when Twain the writer in *Life* turns from pronouncements and proscriptions about good writing to attacks on bad, he calls for the same shift in language the cub undergoes.

He wants writers, particularly southern ones, to give up false, inflated words. He suggests that while bad writing was the norm in the North as well as the South "forty or fifty years ago," the South still suffers from it. The problem, illustrated in literary periodicals, is "wordy, windy, flowery 'eloquence,' romanticism, sentimentality" (*LOM* 328). The terms in this volley of invectives are revealing: to move from "flowery 'eloquence'" to "romanticism" to "sentimentality" is to see writing as language, philosophical orientation, and moral as well as emotional attitude. Writing for Twain is thus linked to broader cultural discourse. Given this feel for the far-reaching import of writing, it is not surprising that his critique comes to include most of southern culture. His sense of bad writing dovetails with his general dissatisfaction with southern culture; he finds both afflicted by the artificial—the inflated, pretentious, or fraudulent (for his views of the South, see Pettit, Rubin, and Turner). In the face of such falsification, Twain, as both critic and master writer, calls for the genuine. Just as the cub must jettison romantic rhetoric for a sparse, utilitarian terminology, so Twain urges the South to strip down all exaggerated aspects of its culture, all expressions of the "old inflated style" (*LOM* 328). By exposing what is false in its cultural discourse, Twain seems to hope to do nothing less than reconstruct the South. If Clemens the cub had ambition to ride the river in glory as a steamboatman, Twain the writer has an even grander agenda.

SINCE HE SETS HIMSELF up as master writer, Twain all but begs us to consider his own writing in *Life on the Mississippi*. While the book invites such scrutiny, it also provides a special context in which to review his style. Twain lards his text with the texts of others; he fills his book with the voices and narratives of other speakers and writers. As Cox has observed, noting that Twain names one pilot Rob Styles, he "does indeed *rob styles*, showing us, by implication," an "outlaw writer operating as a literary highwayman" ("*LOM* Revisited" 113). Whether as outlaw or, more likely, since he is performing as a proper writer, as authoritative literary collector, Twain re-creates the voices of steamboatmen like Rob Styles, Uncle Mumford, and the pilot of the *R. H. W. Hill* who experiences battle for the first time; passengers like the gentleman who reports on the Darnell-Watson feud, the Irish vender of sappy literature, and Mr. H., who explains upper Louisiana and Arkansas mosquitoes; past informants like Karl Ritter, a murderer, Mr. Manchester, a medium, and the nameless man who reports on Vicksburg under siege; local eccentrics like Henry Clay Dean, the Hannibal carpenter, and the lunatic archangel; and no end of "authorities" from the early explorers to the river historians to foreign travelers. Various critics of *Life* have called attention to the unreliability of many of these narrators; indeed, collectively they seem to enact what Brodwin has called the "overall theme" of *Life:* "mutability and the deceptiveness of human affairs along the river" ("Useful & Useless River" 206). But these narratives, which vary stylistically from the stilted to the coarse, have yet another function: they serve as contrasting styles by which to measure Twain's own.

Twain's style is remarkable. Pellucid, vigorous, and above all flexible, it moves gracefully between the formal and the conversational. Its language likewise runs the channel between the conventional and the odd. Given its variety, no single passage is entirely representative, but it is worth looking at one or two nonetheless.

In chapter 29, "A Few Specimen Bricks," there is a good specimen passage. Beginning, as he often does, with a geographical location, Island 37 in the river between Tennessee and Arkansas, he recalls the Murel gang, reputed to have hidden there, and then creates an extended comparison between Murel and Jesse James. Since he is engaged in comparing, the paragraph has a somewhat more balanced structure than many, but it is not atypical in this book in which the past and present, old times and new, cubs and pilots, North and South, steamboats and railroads, bad writers and good, are compared.

> There is a tradition that Island 37 was one of the principal abiding places of the once celebrated "Murel's Gang." This was a colossal combination of robbers, horse-thieves, negro-stealers, and counterfeiters, engaged in business along the river some fifty or sixty years ago. While our journey across the country towards St. Louis was in progress we had had no end of Jesse

James and his stirring history; for he had just been assassinated by an agent
of the Governor of Missouri, and was in consequence occupying a good deal
of space in the newspapers. Cheap histories of him were for sale by train
boys. According to these, he was the most marvellous creature of his kind
that had ever existed. It was a mistake. Murel was his equal in boldness; in
pluck; in rapacity; in cruelty, brutality, heartlessness, treachery, and in general and comprehensive vileness and shamelessness; and very much his superior in some larger aspects. James was a retail rascal; Murel, wholesale.
James's modest genius dreamed of no loftier flight than the planning of raids
upon cars, coaches, and country banks; Murel projected negro insurrections
and the capture of New Orleans; and furthermore, on occasion, this Murel
could go into a pulpit and edify the congregation. What are James and his
half-dozen vulgar rascals compared with this stately old-time criminal, with
his sermons, his meditated insurrections and city-captures, and his majestic following of ten hundred men, sworn to do his evil will! (*LOM* 211–12)

From the first sentence to the last, Twain moves his prose from impersonal ("there is"), matter-of-fact statement to highly personal exclamation that has the force of a rhetorical question to which all will assent.
Embedded early in this process, in the third of the ten sentences, is the
actual use of the personal "we" as both a momentary grounding in experience and a kind of springboard to the central comparison. As is often
the case in *Life*, Twain corrects other texts, in this instance the "cheap
histories" he found hawked on trains. The basic sentence pattern is a vigorous subject-verb-object (repeated in the main clauses of the compound
sentences), but the complements are sometimes multiple, and within the
simple sentence structure there are many repeated and extended prepo-
sitional phrases that make the syntax seem elaborate. In keeping with the
comparative act, Twain exploits balance and antithesis. His careful punc-
tuation in particular exerts a rigorous control, marshaling parts into ordered sequences and balanced oppositions. Although it dips toward the
conversational at least once—"had had no end of Jesse James"—the diction is essentially Standard English. It is the cultured diction of conventional writing, and at times for certain effects Twain even elevates it toward the distinctly stuffy. All in all, the passage conveys a sense of vigor,
precision, and unwavering control.

But within his staid structures, Twain plays. The language he deploys creates surprises, tensions stretched to contradictions, and unplumbed moral ironies. Consider these fine tunings. Having begun with stately diction—notable in the circumlocution, "principal abiding place," and the cliché, "once celebrated"—he pits "Murel's Gang" against yet another inflated phrase, "colossal combination," only to deflate the decorous terms by the small shocks of the concrete nouns he uses to define the actual members of the combination: "robbers," "horse-thieves," "negro-stealers," "counterfeiters." A similar surprise is achieved by the use of "business" to describe the activities of these cutthroats and cheats. And then Twain turns his playful irony in another direction; he explains that Jesse James has been "assassinated" by an agent of the governor, letting the pejorative connotations of the term hang in the air as he hurries on to complain, ever so slightly, of the result: dead, James is "occupying a good deal of space in the newspapers."

Twain continues his verbal dance between high and low, abstract and concrete, moral and immoral, as he undertakes his correction of pulp history. He archly overstates its mistaken notion that James was "the most marvelous creature of his kind that had ever existed." His correction is a tiny tour de force. The sentence that begins "Murel was his equal in" moves brilliantly from qualities that anyone might long to possess (especially in the era of the self-made), "boldness," "pluck," to horrifying traits, "rapacity," "cruelty," "brutality," to the puffy and vague moral abstraction, "general and comprehensive vileness." Twain tops this with the mind-boggling assertion that Murel was James's "superior in some larger aspects." Apart from the small comedy at work in "superior," the phrasing leaves one groping to imagine a larger villainy than the ones just listed. The short, summarizing sentence, "James was a retail rascal; Murel, wholesale," pivots effectively between the long ones that proceed and follow it. Its key terms recall the earlier "business." Again Twain exploits the language of the paradoxically sentimental, go-ahead age when he condescendingly explains that James "dreamed of no loftier flight" than raiding cars, coaches, and banks—"country" banks at that. The comic ironies latent in Twain's language are unnecessary when the historical truth is itself a joke; then all Twain need do is report it: "this Murel could go into a pulpit and edify the congregation."

Having pointed out in his own dogmatic comments on writing that "half a dozen figures will reveal, as with a lighting flash, the importance of a subject," Twain displays numbers to help bring his comparison of the two criminals to its climax. The contrast between the paltry and the great in crime is measured by the difference between a "half-dozen vulgar rascals" and a "majestic following of ten hundred men." Even as "vulgar" condemns James's gang along curious social lines, "rascals" seems to trivialize their criminality. Twain's linguistic counterpoint to this debasement is the distinctly odd elevation of Murel as a "stately old-time criminal"—an elevation that is exploded in the extracts from a "forgotten book" about Murel that Twain adds immediately after his own account. His language dignifies Murel; indeed, "majestic following" evokes kingship and its loyal nobility. But his final phrasing is lurid to the point of ludicrous, his own brand of pulp melodrama: "sworn to do his evil will!"

Twain's style registers and contains the outlandish content. It arrests everything it examines. The formality of the language, the traditional syntax, the controlled energy of the sentence arrangement, and the emergent aura of certainty—all these suggest the traditional style of polite writing, a style still in bondage to the devices of eighteenth-century prose. One function of such a style in the nineteenth century, as William Veeder has pointed out, is to create "security." It is a style sanctioned by the great writers of the past; it says, in effect, "This is how educated gentlemen wrote in the most gentlemanly of times" (56). Twain's style is thus very much in keeping with the general propriety of his outlook. But within the confines of this style, as we've seen, he plays. What Twain creates in a passage like this is not information (though there is a bit of that), or analysis (though there is a lot of this), or even ethical evaluation (though he argues for superior villainy), but entertainment. The passage is animated by its jarring application of moral terms to immoral men, of business terms to predatory acts, of the language of kingship to criminals. The basic premise, that one cutthroat is superior to another, is both striking and sensational. And Twain pursues his notion through a mildly humorous series of minor linguistic disruptions. The disruptions are, however, assimilated by the conventional style. Writing within tradition, Twain is free to pilot his way somewhat erratically, to amuse without offending. Or to put it another way, because his style certifies his propriety, he is free to toy with impropriety.

A brief look at one other passage will make clear just how freeing, how enabling, Twain's traditional style is. Chapter 27, "Some Imported Articles," begins with a description of the river's solitude. The paragraph is a carefully crafted one in which Twain attempts to "manufacture" some emotions "out of whole cloth."

> We met two steamboats at New Madrid. Two steamboats in sight at once! an infrequent spectacle now in the lonesome Mississippi. The loneliness of this solemn, stupendous flood is impressive—and depressing. League after league, and still league after league, it pours its chocolate tide along, between its solid forest walls, its almost untenanted shores, with seldom a sail or a moving object of any kind to disturb the surface and break the monotony of the black, watery solitude; and so the day goes, the night comes, and again the day—and still the same, night after night and day after day,—majestic, unchanging sameness of serenity, repose, tranquility, lethargy, vacancy,— symbol of eternity, realization of the heaven pictured by priest and prophet, and longed for by the good and the thoughtless! (*LOM* 198)

The cloth from which he cuts this piece of prose is colored deep purple. If anything, his style here is even more conventional than that of the other passage. His diction at once betrays the effort to elevate and prettify as "flood" is used instead of river, "tide" substitutes for water, "league" replaces mile, and "chocolate" fills in for brown. The elevation of language, the insistent repetition, the mannered phrases, the elongated, cadenced syntax, the compiling of adjectives, and the gaudy threads of abstract nouns—these stylistic features make the passage a match for the best of the romantic style he has objected to throughout *Life*. It is his version of "wordy, windy, flowery, 'eloquence.'" And it is good. Quite good. Of its kind.

Such a passage reassures the reader that Mark Twain is a reliable writer, even at times a grand one. In such a passage he out-genteelizes the genteel. He surges beyond the trifling aesthetic effusions of the passenger of "Old Times" to read the lonesome river metaphysically as nothing less than "symbol of eternity." But, of course, it is just here, as his meditation enfolds into itself the perceptions of religion, that he turns it all not into but toward a joke: for as he says, such empty stasis is longed for only "by the good and thoughtless." Just as he concluded "Old Times" by playing with eternity, so he here challenges—humorously, to be sure—a prevailing conception of afterlife. The joke does not destroy the elegant mood created to lead up to it; somehow that mood survives. The passage remains moving. But the irreligious joke remains as well. The key to this double-dealing is the style, which is simply so conventional, and so effective within its conventionalities, that it covers the subversive. To see this is to begin to see the power of Mark Twain as a writer.

Twain out-styles the competition he enters so obviously into in his text. Despite their varied appeal (and his acknowledgments of it), the other speakers and authors in his text are straw artists, one and all. Compared with the writers of the formal style, Twain creates a style that is freer, easier, looser, more flexible, even more graceful *within* the traditional conventions. Compared with the writers—and speakers—of the dialect style, Twain creates a style that is obviously more complex, more supple, and more correct. His commanding style also defeats both of these styles by being more intentionally humorous than either.

TWAIN'S HUMOR IS, or at least one expects it to be, the most distinctive turn of his signature as a writer. Yet like the style that enfolds it, Twain's humor in *Life* is that of a respectable, even genteel, writer. It is remarkably varied but also notably tame. The most memorable comic moments are probably those in which he turns his text over to a vernacular speaker. Some of these speakers, like Uncle Mumford, are people he actually met on his trip; others, like the New Orleans undertaker, are invented. Twain is not a snob, but there is always a clear distance between him and such speakers. As traveler and writer he is obviously above them in knowledge, wealth, culture, prestige, and class.

The humor he creates through their talk arises not only from what they say but also from the fact that they speak in peculiar, often incorrect idioms. Twain introduces Uncle Mumford this way: "Uncle Mumford has been thirty years a mate on the river. He is a man of practical sense and a level head; has observed; has had much experience of one sort and another; has opinions; has, also, just a perceptible dash of poetry in his composition, an easy gift of speech, a thick growl in his voice, and an oath or two where he can get at them when the exigencies of his office require a spiritual lift" (*LOM* 188). Despite the palpable affection here, Twain's description is tinged with condescension. Operating out of the same propriety evident in "Old Times," he edits out of Uncle Mumford's "stenographically reported" remarks not only irrelevant interjections but also profanity (*LOM* 206). Mumford's observations remain piquant (seeing the lack of whitewash at Grand Tower, he explains, "People who make lime run more to religion than whitewash" [*LOM* 187]), but he is inevitably stigmatized by his vernacular speech. Anticipating the day when the mate will be forced to dress in the official uniforms of the Anchor Line, Twain says, "Then he will be a totally different style of scenery" (*LOM* 188), betraying the fact that for him Mumford is already a part of the scenery, a part of the local color.

When he does not reduce amusing vernacular speakers to mere regional types, Twain tends to use them as objects of satire. The fast-talking seller of oleomargarine is wonderfully funny: "Why, we are turning out oleomargarine *now* by the thousands of tons. And we can sell it so dirt-cheap that the whole country has *got* to take it—can't get around it you see. Butter don't stand any show—there ain't any chance for competition. Butter's had its *day*—and from this out, butter goes to the wall" (*LOM* 283). His fellow drummer who markets American cottonseed oil as imported olive oil is equally amusing: "Maybe you 'll butter everybody's bread pretty soon, but we 'll cotton-seed his salad for him from the Gulf to Canada, and that's a dead-certain thing" (*LOM* 284). But Twain is interested in them as "two scoundrels" (*LOM* 284) for whom "the dollar" is "god," and "how to get it their religion" (*LOM* 282). His moral norms are so conventional as to go unnoticed.

However, most of the humor in *Life* derives from neither regional types nor satiric portraits. Most of it, to begin with, is voiced by Twain himself, and it is what one might call a humor of remarks—a series of comic observations and comments. Dashed off throughout the text, these quips, gibes, jests, and sarcasms pepper the narrative. They both spice and tantalize, creating sudden relish and a longing for more. They are, in all likelihood, what keep the reader reading; they are also rather literary, one sure sign that Mark Twain is now a "scribbler of books."

In his introductory chapters about the river and its history, for instance, Twain pokes at rapacity posing as piety. From the quick and mildly debasing remark that all the early explorers traveled with "an outfit of priests" (*LOM* 45), to the searing comment that La Salle's usurpation of the country was a "robbery" consecrated "with a hymn" (*LOM* 48), he laughingly exposes the hypocrisies recorded in history. At the other end of his anatomy he ironically rewrites Bishop Berkeley's imperialist "Westward the course of empire takes its way" into "Westward the Jug of Empire takes its way," whimsically noting that it "was like a foreigner—and excusable in a foreigner—to be ignorant of this great truth" and to "wander off into astronomy" (*LOM* 412). With sharper irony he observes that the progressive town of Chester, Illinois, has a "penitentiary now, and is otherwise marching on" (*LOM* 185). In New Orleans he slyly notes that an early pirate was treated with "homage and reverence" until he became an alderman, at which sad turn the city "wept" (*LOM* 314). His literary comic tone ranges from the sharp-tongued—"what a dullwitted slug the average human being is" (*LOM* 176)—to the silly—"the billiard-tables were of the Old Silurian Period" (*LOM* 169)—to the fey—"the weather was rainier than necessary" (*LOM* 401). While an occasional chapter like "The House Beautiful" is animated by sustained sarcasm, most often Twain is comic in isolated chirps.

With varying degrees of self-consciousness, but always with an artful flair, he makes use of three recurrent comic techniques: outrageous poses, extended conceits, and fanciful notions. The most memorable pose in *Life* is, of course, that of the innocent, romantic cub. But after the cub's disappearance, Twain from time to time creates himself for a brief shining (verbal) moment as the cub's very opposite: a knowing, hard-nosed adult. Thus he laments not crashing into and destroying another steamboat "for he would have made good literature" (*LOM* 190) and finds a steamboat race with its danger of explosion and death "the most enjoyable of all races"—a "sport that makes a body's very liver curl with enjoyment" (*LOM* 325). His extended conceits, on the other hand, in their obvious, even labored, artistry, deny the insensitivity comically assumed in his tough-guy posture. Faced with a dirty Grand Tower packet, he first remarks that she is "taxable as real estate," then observes that there are "places in New England where her hurricane deck would be worth a hundred and fifty dollars an acre," goes on to say that a "new crop of wheat was already springing from the cracks" in her forecastle, suggests that the companionway, being "of a dry sandy character," is "well suited for grapes," and finally concludes by noting that while the "soil of the boiler deck is "thin and rocky," it is "good enough for grazing purposes" (*LOM* 175). Elaborate as this comedy is, he adds a final comment: sailing on the packet would be like "sailing down the river on a farm" (*LOM* 175). Twain's comedy of fanciful notions lies somewhere between the deliberately insensitive and the designedly artful, in a kind of no man's land of delightful nonsense. He imagines the Mississippi in its pre-exploration period as a commodity which "nobody happened to want," and so it "remained out of the market and undisturbed" (*LOM* 43). Using a similar commercial metaphor, he facetiously regrets that he didn't buy St. Louis "for six million dollars" when he first saw it. It was, he says, "the mistake of my life" (*LOM* 171).

All of this humor is decidedly nonthreatening to conventional values. Indeed, the presentation of vernacular speakers reinforces traditional class lines, the satire condemns the kind of shady business dealing the moral routinely reviled, and the various comic quips generally operate along axes of respectability (or, as in the case of his outrageous posturing, openly declare their playful improbability). In short, Twain's humor in *Life* is funny but tame. It is as reputable as his authorial eminence.

In his humor, as in his stance as authority, as in his strictures on writing, as in his general norms, the Mark Twain of *Life* upholds conventional standards as he creates his "standard work." This, too, marks it as a characteristic performance. To be sure, there were unconventional impulses in him, and in *Life* they occasionally enter the flow of the text, but they never control its main current. The book remains as proper as its writer.

Twain himself probably sensed this. As he occupies the South, at the core of his reexperience of the Mississippi River civilization, he creates a memorable analogue for himself as humorous writer, yet one whose humor, unlike Twain's own in this text, is raucous and crude. At New Orleans he joins a "party of ladies and gentlemen" on a day's pleasure excursion on a river tug to a downstream plantation (*LOM* 337). The outing is, Twain tells us, "a charming experience, and would have been satisfyingly sentimental and romantic but for the interruptions of the tug's pet parrot." The parrot, "always this-worldly, and often profane," is a cynical humorist. His laugh destroys all romance and sentimentality. After touching songs, after "Home again, home again, from a foreign shore," the parrot seems to announce that he "would n't give a damn for a tugload of such rot" (*LOM* 339). Twain himself went a long way toward dispelling the rot of romantic writing—and thinking and acting—but he was not as free as his admired parrot. Creating his standard work as a conventional writer, he was so constrained by his notions of propriety that he couldn't even exercise the parrot's prerogative to swear.

CHAPTER FIVE

Adventurous Homebody

Sam Clemens's happiest years—and Mark Twain's most productive—were his years of domestic establishment at Nook Farm. Living grandly in his palatial home at 351 Farmington Avenue, summering at Quarry Farm in Elmira, Clemens enjoyed his marriage and his growing family. There were dark spots—deaths of family members, overwork for both Livy and Clemens, financial worries, and the uncertain tides of fame—but on the whole, this was an idyllic time. It was also the time in which Clemens became most visibly respectable and conventional, "an immovable fixture," as he said in *Life on the Mississippi*, among the "rocks of New England," a "scribbler of books." This period, 1870–91, saw the creation of Mark Twain's three most popular books of boy adventure: *Tom Sawyer*, *The Prince and the Pauper*, and *Huckleberry Finn*. *Tom* is inscribed to Livy: "To My Wife This book is Affectionately Dedicated" (*TS* 32), and *The Prince and the Pauper* is dedicated with affectionate irony to his daughters: "To Those Good-Mannered And Agreeable Children, Susie and Clara Clemens, This Book Is Affectionately Inscribed By Their Father" (*P&P* 33). *Huckleberry Finn* has no dedication, but flaunts a full-page heliotype of a bust of Mark Twain (*HF* li). All three books thus bear some imprint of the home that centered around Livy, the girls, and Mark Twain.

Twain's boy stories reflect his immersion in the literary culture of New England. Fictions centered on childhood were popular, whether they were the genteel tales of little women and men of the sort Louisa May Alcott penned or slightly more realistic recollections like Thomas Bailey Aldrich's *Story of a Bad Boy* (see Stone). Of course, Twain's stories also reflect Clemens's own actual boyhood, and they bear the stamp of Twain's idiosyncratic sensibility, for he was original even when he wrote in familiar modes. What is surprising about that sensibility is how sentimental it was. Different as the three boy books are, they have in common not only childhood innocence put on trial but also the redemptive force of right human feeling. (This, too, reflects the Clemens family life, at least at its best.) In all three, Twain turns to the sentimental mode of fiction and searches for the true basis of ethical behavior—and for an authentic way to present it. He seeks, that is, both the moral foundation and the aesthetic medium of his art. In exploiting sentimentality Twain participates in one of the most conventional—and popular—literary fashions of his time.

CLEMENS'S WAS AN ERA in transition. The "Sentimental Years," as they have been called (E. Douglas Branch), the years of Clemens's childhood, were giving way to the Age of Realism. Stoicism not sympathy, competition not compassion, survival not self-sacrifice—these were increasingly the prescribed norms for manly behavior, and in literature the imagined real was more apparent than the imagined ideal. Yet the sentimental mode had by no means disappeared. The "mob of scribbling women," in Hawthorne's notorious phrase, went right on scribbling, creating sentimental fictions whose tears and conventionality often concealed powerful subversive notions. Children's books continued the tearful style, and local colorists found good-hearted country folk at home in every region of the country. In politics, stump speeches turned ideas into emotions; in reform, lectures charged morality with passionate feeling; and in religion, camp meetings and revivals continued to awaken great affections. Newspapers sensationalized events daily, and the new department stores arranged merchandise to make it appear palpitant and enticing (Fisher, "Appearing and Disappearing in Public"). Surrounded by all this, Twain's impulse was to lampoon sentimentality. Typical of his mood (or at least one of them) was his attack in *Tom Sawyer*—that book dedicated with feeling to Livy—on "sappy women" who drip tears over the death of Injun Joe from "their permanently impaired and leaky water-works" (*TS* 221).

Writing to his childhood friend, Will Bowen, just as he was seeing *Tom Sawyer* into print, Clemens took him to task for his sentimentality in a well-known letter: "Damnation, (if you will allow the expression,) get up & take a turn around the block & let the sentiment blow off you. Sentiment is for girls—I mean the maudlin article, of course. *Real* sentiment is a very rare & godlike thing.—You do not know anybody that has it; neither do I" (*MTLB* 23). By maudlin sentiment Twain means sentimentality, of course, and in ascribing it to "girls" he participates in the gender typing of his era. Ironically, given that he had just plumbed his own boyhood to write *Tom Sawyer*, he went on to tell Bowen: "As to the past, there is but one good thing about it, & that is, that it *is* the past—we don't have to see it again. There is nothing in it worth pickling for present or future use" (*MTLB* 23). Intent upon giving his friend "a dose of salts," he made an even stronger, more direct and personal assault: "I can see by your manner of speech, that for more than twenty years you have stood dead still in the midst of the dreaminess, the melancholy, the romance, the heroics, of sweet but sappy sixteen. Man, do you know that this is simply mental & moral masturbation? It belongs eminently to the period usually devoted to *physical* masturbation, & should be left there & outgrown. Will, you must forgive me, but I have not the slightest sympathy with what the world calls Sentiment—not the slightest" (*MTLB* 24).

The letter, which runs to over eight hundred words, is probably Clemens's longest and most revealing fulmination on the topic of sentimentality. To minister his dose of salts, he deploys a traditional male rhetoric, peppered with profanity and spiced by the confessional man-to-man reference to forbidden sexual activity. Yet he protests so much that the sting is actually softened by the stagy excess—an excess of virulence that is the obverse counterpart to the sentimentality under attack. While he detests "what the world calls Sentiment," Clemens concedes a wondering admiration for that "very rare & godlike thing," which is "*real* sentiment." The problem, as the letter suggests, is one of expression. It is Bowen's "manner of speech," as much as the subject matter (presumably the past of lost opportunities), that bespeaks his sentimentality, defining it for Clemens as false emotion rather than the "rare & godlike." As Clemens pursues his goal of shaking his friend out of self-pitying doldrums, he reveals Mark Twain's difficulty. For Twain, too, admires "*real* sentiment," but he finds it hard to create, using the expressive conventions of his time.

From *Tom Sawyer*, which transpires in "the dreaminess, the melancholy, the romance, the heroics" of Clemens's own past, through *The Prince and the Pauper*, with its elegantly imagined sixteenth century, to

Huckleberry Finn, which grittily revisions *Tom Sawyer*'s world, Twain struggles to make sentiment seem authentic. He strives to create cred-ible fictions of the heart, or to put it less sentimentally, he tries to repair the "leaky water-works."

Recuperated in recent scholarship as a powerful tactic in cultural dis-course, nineteenth-century sentimentality is not only a literary mode but also a philosophical outlook. In *Sentimental Twain: Samuel Clemens in the Maze of Moral Philosophy*, a study valuable for its exposition of sentimen-tal philosophy as well as for its treatment of Twain, Camfield defines sentimentalism as a "plastic and vital cosmology" (19) predicated on "an anti-authoritarian belief in the innate goodness of each human being and a belief in each person's access to that goodness through intuitive knowl-edge" (17). He shows convincingly how Twain wrestled with this con-cept. Part of Twain's resistance to the sentimental may arise from asso-ciating it with women ("Sentiment is for girls," he assured Bowen). As a literary mode, sentimentality was in fact employed chiefly by women. The recent reevaluations of the mode have revealed that it was a complex literary strategy. It has been defined in significantly different ways: as an author's attempt to play on the reader's emotions or as the reader's emotions themselves—such responses as sighing, weeping, or intensely caring. More negatively, it may be seen as violating standards of artistic proportion, presenting emotions in excess of their occasions, or trans-gressing norms of truth by oversimplifying, typing, and so falsifying some common sense of reality. More neutrally, sentimentality may be said to depend on formal conventions, a set of stylistic traits ranging from dic-tion to character type to formulas for emotion. The cultural import of sentimentality has been seen, contradictorily, as a confirmation of the sta-tus quo and as a subversion of it.[1] Not surprisingly, for Mark Twain the is-sue of sentimentality loomed much more simply: sentimental emotion was excessive, trite in expression, or falsely at odds with true feeling (or all three at once). Somewhat surprisingly, however, despite Twain's frequent and virulent attacks upon the sentimental, he is himself a sentimentalist.

Paradoxically, the more he settled into comfortable middle-class do-mesticity, a complex financial, social, and emotional circumstance, the more he began to write fictions that lifted him out of that world. Imaginatively he entered not only into the past but into masculine realms whose ambiance was largely at odds with his own feminized sphere of domestic tranquility. *Roughing It* was the first such move, but it depicted a western male world whose pleasures, however real, were finally left behind without regret. Writing of it was an affectionate yet distancing act of exculpation. "Old Times" continued the same imaginative process of recall, indulgence, definition, and then distancing. It, too, re-created an all-male world, a realistic compound of striving, failure, and muted success. But as the papers themselves acknowledge, the time of the pilot was past. The fictive worlds of *Roughing It* and "Old Times" seemed to offer freedom, danger, and waywardness, but even as he wrote of them, the proper Mark Twain inscribed his interest in boundedness, safety, and respectability. In his boy books, he manages to indulge his attraction to the unfettered and the unprescribed, on the one hand, and his need for conventions and traditional conduct, on the other. Boyhood as Twain conceives of it is the perfect in-between state: it enables one to be both child and adult, free and bound, wayward and respectable, both in danger and safe at home.

The idea of "adventure" loomed large for Twain, but his notion of adventure seems as tame as his interest in it was strong. Exciting, remarkable things befall—or are created by—Tom Sawyer, and Huck's experiences are, as all readers of both books notice, even more unexpected and threatening. Yet in both cases one is sure that everything will come out all right in the end. For Twain's conception of adventure seems to be closer to harmless play than danger. The opening of *Roughing It*, one of his most extended passages on adventure, turns risk into safety through comic exaggeration. The narrator begins by envying his brother's prospect of "travel" and then turns to coveting his likely "adventures," especially the possibility that he will be "hanged or scalped, and have ever such a fine time" (*RI* 1–2). Though nothing of the sort ever comes close to happening in *Roughing It*, the West—the real one as opposed to the fictionalized one—did pose such risks. The realm of St. Petersburg, the world of reconstructed boyhood, did not. As Twain imagines it, the world of *Tom Sawyer* does have its dark side (DeVoto 306; Towers, "Strategies of Transcendence"), but such nightmare danger always gives way to daylight. Twain's imagining of adventure stops far short of putting its hero seriously at risk. What, then, is the nature of Tom's "adventures"?

There is by now a body of what one might call "adventure theory," and its concepts help put *Tom Sawyer* into perspective. Several key notions seem especially important for understanding Twain's novel.[2] First, though it is obvious, it is nonetheless true that adventure has most often—certainly up to the twentieth century—been thought of as male. Second, adventure seems to be associated with the exertion of force, male force, whether physical, sexual, or psychological (or some combination or sublimation of the three). Third, and this too seems obvious, adventure serves as a test of character in which the adventurer masters difficult experience to achieve some important end. Fourth, adventure provides occasion for, indeed calls forth, a high degree of creativity. Fifth, it recreates in safe contexts experiences banished from the ordinary activities of society—the violent, for instance, or the illicitly erotic; it indulges what is otherwise liminal in the social world. (This may go a long way toward explaining the appeal of adventure tales to the imagination of the domestic and respectable Sam Clemens, though his versions of them, Mark Twain's fictions, remain highly conventional even as they sport with the socially unacceptable.) The upshot of adventure, thus constituted, has been provocatively summarized by Martin Green in *The Adventurous Male:* abstractly considered, adventure is, he says, "a series of events that outrage civilized or domestic morality and that challenge those to whom those events happen to make use of powers that civil life forbids to the ordinary citizen" (4).

Tom Sawyer's adventures do, at least superficially, pit him against "civilized or domestic morality," and he does tap personal prowess normally repressed or diverted in society. He lies, cheats, steals, and fights on the one hand, and exercises cunning, duplicity, and psychological force on the other. Predictably, in keeping with the form, Twain genders Tom's actions along conventional lines. His adventures—misbehaving at home, church, and school, playing soldier and pirate, running away from home, searching for stolen treasure, and exploring the unknown—reflect the traditional male; his ties to home mirror the traditional female. Significantly, however, despite the manifold attractions of adventure, Twain finally endorses the domestic. If Tom enters liminal spaces for fun and self-definition, he always returns to the central social world for final self-realization. He is an adventurer whose heart is firmly at home. Twain's tale exploits the opposing spheres of adventure and domesticity in conventional ways, but he has an unconventional commitment—unconventional for a male, that is—to the domestic as the center of true value.[3] As he uses the stock opposition between home life and adventure, however, he confronts a problem that envelops both, the problem for which he took Will Bowen to task: the need to avoid sentimental expression.

Twain's treatment of St. Petersburg is notably mild, tempered at every turn by his nostalgia. Despite his obvious affection for the community, however, a number of critics have insisted on condemning it for multiple failings.[4] Here, put comprehensively, is the case against the community: "St. Petersburg festers with lies, smugness, hypocrisy, human cruelty, murder, and greed" (Maik 207). This hardly squares with Twain's own notion that the book was "simply a hymn, put into prose form to give it a worldly air" (*MTL* 2:477). There is, admittedly, something somewhat off-key about the hymn. The problem is not the moral lapses itemized by so many critics but rather the "style" of community discourse—the way the town expresses itself.[5] Three episodes in the book signal Twain's interest in the expressive modes of his society: the Sunday morning church service, including its Sunday school; the school graduation recitation; and the legal and social proceedings surrounding Muff Potter and Injun Joe. Different as these episodes are, Twain exposes in each a radical separation between formulaic utterances and genuine emotions. The three episodes constitute the core of Twain's attack on the sentimental.

Significantly, the first scene that introduces the adult community in *Tom Sawyer*, the gathering at church, is awash in sentimentality. The Sunday school superintendent, Mr. Walters, holds forth with what Twain calls "much effusion" (*TS* 63). Judge Thatcher, visiting dignitary, strives for a similarly impressive rhetoric as he awards Tom the prize Bible for apparently having mastered numerous biblical verses, though his efforts at eloquence are tempered by his condescending use of the colloquial in addressing Tom. As he talks down to him, he intensifies and elevates his speech through ponderous repetition and the pronouncement of moral clichés:

> And you never can be sorry for the trouble you took to learn them; for knowledge is worth more than anything there is in the world; it's what makes great men and good men; you'll be a great man and a good man yourself, someday, Thomas, and then you'll look back and say, It's all owing to the precious Sunday-school privileges of my boyhood—it's all owing to my dear teachers that taught me to learn—it's all owing to the good Superintendent, who encouraged me, and watched over me, and gave me a beautiful Bible—a splendid elegant Bible, to keep and have it all for my own, always—it's all owing to right bringing up! (*TS* 64)

The tone is sanctimonious, and the speech, which ostensibly congratulates Tom, actually celebrates his teachers and the institutions they represent.

The minister, the Rev. Mr. Sprague, reads, prays, and delivers his sermon in a single style of discourse: he strives for "impressiveness" by uttering the "gravest sentiments" (*TS* 70). In passing, Twain links the grandiosity of the minister's official style with the artificiality of literary readings, noting that the minister was "always called upon to read poetry" at "sociables" where his performance invariably moves women to exclaim, "Words cannot express it; it is too beautiful, too beautiful for this mortal earth" (*TS* 67). Although the minister's sermon contains "prosy" argument, he fills it with "grand and moving" pictures aimed at "pathos" to point a moral "lesson" (*TS* 68). Nonetheless, many in the congregation fall asleep. They nod off because they have heard it all before and they have heard it in the same words, the same syntax, the same rhythms, in short, the same style. It is the prevailing nineteenth-century style in which moral sentiments are purveyed through elevated diction, lovely figures, intense repetition, pathetic pictures, and a rhetoric of abstractions. It is the sentimental style that rarefies and attenuates experience to the point of falsification, vaporizing ideas in the hot atmosphere of extreme emotion. Twain shows it at work in St. Petersburg in church, school, and the legal system, as well as in ordinary conversation. More than anything else, this style is what is wrong with the community.

In the memorable school examination, Twain exposes the same spurious sentimentality and displays an even deeper animus toward it. The ora-
tions and readings given by the school children are generally in the sentimental mode. The original compositions in particular show how the
educational system invites students to think and write on trite topics in
an excessively emotional style. Expounding on such stock subjects as
Friendship, Memories of Other Days, Religion in History, Dream Land,
Melancholy, Filial Love, Heart Longings, and the Advantages of Culture, the essays are, Twain insists, full of the "gush of 'fine language',"
"prized words and phrases," and "sermons" that the "moral and religious
mind could contemplate with edification." Twain sums up the core of
the problem with these themes by pointing to their "glaring insincerity"
(*TS* 160). It is hard to make too much of this episode, for Twain himself
goes to considerable lengths to expose the falsity of the enterprise. By
pointedly announcing that he has taken his examples of the sentimental
mode—"without alteration" (163)—from Mary Ann Harris Gay's book
The Pastor's Story and Other Pieces; or, Prose and Poetry (1871), he makes it
clear that the issue is not one of the past and not even one of schooling
alone. Since the "moral and religious mind" to which the sentimental effusions are addressed is the prevailing consciousness of Twain's time,
what is at stake is the mind of America itself.

For Twain, that mind has created a false culture and an inauthentic
people. He is at pains in *Tom Sawyer* to show the disadvantages of such a
culture and such a mentality; at the same time, he seeks to find a surer
footing for his society. Apologizing for unpalatable "homely truth," he
expounds on the difficulty of banishing the sentimental fashion (*TS* 160),
but then he arranges the events of his story—the world he creates and
controls—to take revenge on the teacher who inspires and sanctions
such wrongheaded, wrong-hearted ways of thought and expression; he
attacks Dobbins. In several ways, Dobbins is the most objectionable official in St. Petersburg; he is the exception to the rule that the townsfolk
are, by and large, good country people. For Twain depicts him not only
as a schoolroom tyrant but also as something of a sadist who derives pleasure from beating the children. He mocks him first by making him just
tipsy enough to be unable to draw an accurate map of America. And then

he humiliates him through the famous gilding of his head and the lifting of his wig to expose the glitter. The gilded head is, of course, an apt emblem of just the superficial style Twain is assailing, and there is a suggestion of emasculation in the symbolic action.

In the figure of Dobbins, Twain suggests a link between sadism and sentimentality. Excessive violence and excessive emotional expression, both indulged for personal pleasure, seem to be two sides of the same coin. Or perhaps more accurately, sentimentality gilds violence. Although he would not explore this linkage fully until *Huckleberry Finn*, Twain tentatively probes the twining of sentimentality and violence in the doubling of Tom and Injun Joe. As more than one reader has felt, Injun Joe looms as the dark side of Tom. Tom plays pariah, Injun Joe is a true outcast; Tom feigns bloody deeds, Injun Joe commits them; Tom dreams of treasure, Injun Joe steals it; Tom fantasizes a life of crime, Injun Joe lives one; Tom longs for revenge, Injun Joe murders for it. Even Tom's possessive puppy love has its dark counterpart in Joe's talk of mutilating and violating the Widow Douglas. And curiously, Tom's melancholy, his morbid, excessive feelings of slight and neglect, are matched by Joe's bitter outbursts against mistreatment at the hands of Doc Robinson and the husband of the Widow Douglas. Through Injun Joe, Twain reveals the dark side of the world of male adventure.

On trial in the case of Muff Potter, then, is in some sense the character of Tom Sawyer. In exposing Injun Joe, Tom is close to confronting his own dark side. But, of course, Injun Joe is not brought to justice at the trial (Twain keeps his plot tense), and Twain's interest focuses instead on the town's reactions. He notes that when Muff groans, many "men were moved, and many women's compassion testified itself in tears" (*TS* 170). This sympathy comes from the same men and women who have clamored for Muff's blood and even contemplated lynching him. When Muff is acquitted, thanks to Tom's testimony, Twain reports that "the fickle, unreasoning world took Muff Potter to its bosom and fondled him as lavishly as it had abused him before." Then somewhat self-consciously checking his cynicism, Twain adds, "But that sort of conduct is to the world's credit; therefore it is not well to find fault with it" (*TS* 173). What is not to the world's credit in Twain's accounting, however, is the emotional excess displayed first in the town's virulent condemnation of Muff and then in its equally intense embrace of him after his acquittal. Both outbursts exceed their occasions.

After Injun Joe's death, the town unwittingly puts into practice the sentimentality enshrined in its religious sermons, schoolroom exercises, and courtroom histrionics. In an aside whose oddity suggests its significance, Twain gratuitously announces: "This funeral stopped the further growth of one thing—the petition to the Governor for Injun Joe's pardon. The petition had been largely signed; many tearful and eloquent meetings had been held, and a committee of sappy women had been appointed to go in deep mourning and wail around the governor and implore him to be a merciful ass and trample his duty under foot" (*TS* 221). Here Twain gives his most serious indictment of the consequences of the sentimental mode that grips the community of St. Petersburg. Enthralled by their own emotionalism, the citizens defy common sense, abandon reason, and argue against justice. What begins in the book as a hollow style of personal expression becomes by the end a mistaken collective means of subverting the social order.

Although it ties neatly together with Twain's exposure of the town's fundamental problem, the petition incident disrupts the flow of the narrative and seems somewhat out of place. The explanation for its inclusion is probably Twain's personal anger over a murder case in New York in 1873, just when he was beginning *Tom Sawyer*. In brief, after a man named William Foster was tried and sentenced to death for murder, his father, the murdered man's widow, members of the convicting jury, and some prominent public figures petitioned the governor to commute the sentence from death to life imprisonment. Published in the New York *Tribune*, these pleas for clemency struck Twain as outrageous. He wrote a letter to the editor in which he sarcastically pretended to be moved by accounts of the murderer's character that ignored his bloody crime and celebrated instead his unbelievable rectitude: "The generous tears will flow—I cannot help it." Dropping his pose as sentimentalist, however, he railed: "A criminal juror must be an intellectual vacuum, attached to a melting heart and perfectly macaronian bowels of compassion" ("Foster's Case" 166–67). The same anger at mawkishness evident in his letter informs *Tom Sawyer*, muted into amusement in all but the attack on those "sappy women" who would have the governor pardon Injun Joe.

While church, school, and courtroom are presided over by men, the social world of *Tom Sawyer* is largely a world of women. They create, in the words of Cynthia Griffin Wolff, a "world that holds small boys in bondage" (641). The boys defy this world of routine, discipline, order, convention, propriety, and manners—a world of women in which, as Huck says with disgust, "They'll all comb a body" (*TS* 177). To escape from this feminized world, the boys run away to the woods, to Cardiff Hill, to the river, and to the cave, seeking adventure. Twain's book thus appears to be a nearly prototypical expression of male aversion to female civilizing (see Baym). It seems to celebrate male adventuring as a necessary self-defining activity for boys who would one day be men.

Yet Twain accords the women of Tom's world one important, indeed crucial, function. If in many trivial ways they seem to harass and to smother the boys, they nonetheless provide what Twain himself sees as an indispensable instruction: they are the shapers of right feeling.

Because they themselves thrive within an atmosphere of high emotionalism, a heated air of perpetual tears and lamentation, the women of St. Petersburg seem to be a part of the community's problem rather than its solution. In his trenchant study of Twain, Forrest G. Robinson has argued that the people of St. Petersburg, including its women, are all caught up in what he calls "bad faith"—the "reciprocal deception of self and other" ("Social Play" 168), a social dynamic in which "varieties of deception" are given "the tacit, often unconscious approval of the society as a whole" (167). As instructors of the young, the women of this world might seem to inculcate only such "bad faith," yet there is something genuine about their emotionality. Their excess of feeling always contains a core of truth, so that despite the pleasure they find in their displays of sentiment—thus in one sense inauthenticating the emotion itself and seeming to make them participants in "bad faith"—their performances of feeling are never entirely bogus. In fact, they teach the boys the true basis of good conduct in this fiction, which is not an adherence to rules for their own sake, or even for the sake of the social order, but rather a compassionate consideration of the feelings of others. They inculcate this ethic chiefly by teaching their charges to take the feelings of others into account. Tom explains early on that Aunt Polly "never licks anybody—whacks 'em over the head with her thimble—and who cares for that, I'd like to know. She talks awful, but talk don't hurt—anyways it don't if she don't cry" (*TS* 47). Crying is Aunt Polly's weapon in the battle to do her duty by Tom, to bring him up right. Feeling is the agent as well as the end of her moral instruction. After Tom has been out almost all night, Twain reports, "His aunt wept over him and asked him how he could go and break her old heart so; and finally told him to go on, and ruin himself and bring her gray hairs with sorrow to the grave" (*TS* 103). Evoking guilt in Tom by making him see—and feel—her anguish, Aunt Polly's general point is not that Tom should stop sneaking out at night but that he should stop hurting her.

The centrality of such ethical feeling is underscored by Twain's plotting in his manuscript notes. His first plan was to track Tom's life from youthful innocence to adult maturity; he noted these four stages: "1, Boyhood & youth; 2 y & early Manh; 3 the Battle of Life in many lands; 4 (age 37 to 40), return to meet grown babies & toothless old drivelers who were grandees of his boyhood" (qtd. in *TS* 8–9). With this outline apparently in view, he had, he said, "pumped" himself "dry" by about page 400. In Hamlin Hill's intriguing conjectural analysis, the pivot between Twain's planned book and the one he ended up writing is the moment when Tom leaves Jackson's Island and returns to Aunt Polly's with his message for her written in red chalk on the sycamore scroll. According to Hill, the message may well have been the farewell that would send Tom off to the projected third stage of his adventures, "the Battle of Life in many lands" ("Composition and Structure of *TS*" 387–88). But Twain could not take Tom away from Aunt Polly (it would break her heart). Significantly, once his creative tank was full again, the message he has Tom write to Aunt Polly, far from announcing Tom's departure from her, becomes evidence that he is truly attached to her.

Whether or not Twain's reason for not sending Tom off to many lands was the tie to Aunt Polly, the scroll itself takes on great significance. It is one of three texts Tom writes in the course of his adventures. Tom has been described as a "yarn spinner" who is expected by his audience to embellish his tales, inviting disbelief as much as credence (Wonham, "Undoing Romance" 232). But Tom's three *written* texts seem to be performances of a different kind. In each he seeks not to show off or entertain but to say something honest. Each text turns upon one of the three major plotlines in the book: Tom in love, Tom in trouble with his conscience, and Tom in the throes of adventure. Together, the three texts constitute Tom's own efforts at genuine, as opposed to sentimental, expression.

Tom's first written document is his love note to Becky. Scrawled on his school slate, this message actually interprets the picture he has just drawn of a house, a tall man, and Becky. Without saying so, he has sketched his vision of their future of domestic bliss, typically making the house too grand and himself too large, and his text certifies and explains the imagined estate: "*I love you*" (*TS* 80). What more could he say in fewer, simpler words? In his second attempt at sincere expression, the oath to keep quiet about the true murderer of Doc Robinson, Tom fails. Although Huck admires "the sublimity" of the language, the oath signed in blood falsifies its pledge in its extravagantly expressed desire for death and destruction: "Huck Finn and Tom Sawyer Swears they will keep mum about This and They wish They may Drop down dead in Their tracks if They ever Tell and Rot" (*TS* 100). The oath is Tom's slangy equivalent of the sentimental style, and its very excess, its obvious insincerity, its unreality, all foretell that the oath will be broken. (The subject-verb error also suggests that only one of the boys is really swearing.) Tom's third text, the message on the scroll, the one upon which the entire plot of the book apparently hinged, is the most illuminating. For Tom never puts his true message into words. Intending to reassure Aunt Polly, to keep her "from grieving," he writes (or at least so he reports, for the text is not reproduced): "*We ain't dead—we are only off being pirates*" (*TS* 144). The message is a bare statement of fact without any of the posturing or inflation that shows up in the oath. It means more than it says, however, for it shows not only that Tom misses Aunt Polly but also that he is, for once, taking her feelings into account. Obliquely, without putting it into words, the message convincingly inscribes Tom's love and indicates how far he has taken to heart the need to consider her feelings.

The revelation of the scroll is a turning point in Tom's relations with Aunt Polly. While she first chides him for his deception of her and then doubts the truth of his explanation ("It's a blessed, blessed lie," she tells herself, a "good lie" [*TS* 151–52]), she ends up reveling in the clear evidence of Tom's love. Precipitated by Tom's having led her to believe in—and even to relate to Sereny Harper—the bogus dream he concocts on the basis of his actual late-night visit, her chiding is especially significant: "O, child you never think. You never think of anything but your own selfishness. You could think to come all the way over here from Jackson's Island in the night to laugh at our troubles, and you could think to fool me with a lie about a dream; but you couldn't ever think to pity us and save us from sorrow" (*TS* 150). Although the phrases "pity us" and "save us from sorrow" sound sentimental, they actually ask for honest compassion and the readiness to act—protectively—out of it. They define the proper code of manly conduct taught by the women of St. Petersburg. In responding to Aunt Polly's instructive complaint, Tom for once not only drops all evasion, deceit, and self-justification but also speaks directly, openly, and honestly. What he says is simply that he acted out of true feeling: "Because I loved you so" (*TS* 151). After this encounter (chap. 19), which culminates in the discovery of the scroll, the confirmation of Tom's love, Aunt Polly never again scolds Tom. She recedes from the story as if her work were done.

When in 1897 he returned in memory to the Hannibal of Sam Clemens's youth, over two decades after he first published *Tom Sawyer*, Twain recorded in "Villagers of 1840–3" both the childishness of the sentimentality of Sam's old home and his approval of it:

> All that sentimentality and romance among young folk seem puerile, now, but when one examines it and compares it with the ideals of to-day, it was the preferable thing. It was soft, sappy, melancholy; but money had no place in it. To get rich was no one's ambition—it was not in any young person's thoughts. The heroes of these young people—even the pirates—were moved by lofty impulses: they waded in blood, in the distant fields of war and adventure and upon the pirate deck, to rescue the helpless, not to make money; they spent their blood and made their self-sacrifices for "honor's" sake, not to capture a giant fortune; they married for love, not money and position. It was an intensely sentimental age, but it took no sordid form. (*AI* 100)

Anyone reading this as an after-the-fact gloss on *Tom Sawyer* must be struck by the difference between Twain's recollection that no one sought money and Tom's mighty efforts to secure it. But Tom is not really money-hungry. Under the influence of romantic notions of pirates and robbers, he begins searching only for "hidden treasure" (*TS* 175)—not money. But as so often happens in Twain's fantasy of boyhood, what begins as play turns real: Injun Joe has gold stolen by the historically quite real gang of cutthroat robbers once led by John Murrell, and Tom eventually gets it. From the first mention of digging for treasure, however, Twain mitigates the taint of the enterprise by having Tom and Huck innocently imagine how they will use their riches. Huck says he wants "pie and a glass of soda every day" and to see "every circus that comes along," while Tom wants a "new drum," a "sure-'nough sword," a "red neck-tie"—his list is noticeably longer than Huck's—a "bull pup," and to "get married" (*TS* 177). By making marriage (to Becky, of course) the aim of the treasure hunt, Twain links his love story to the adventure story and exculpates Tom from any hint of the avarice he would later come to denounce.

The other terms of his recollection are all strikingly true to the hymn to boyhood that Twain actually composed. In his remembrance Twain validates idealistic postures, though he is silent about the ways they were expressed, and the terms he uses are in keeping with the spirit of Aunt Polly's moral instruction. To rescue the helpless, to sacrifice for honor, and to wed for love are all impulses very much in line with Aunt Polly's imperatives to pity and to save from sorrow. They are also impulses discussed, approved, and sometimes even enacted by Sam and Livy. There is more than a childish version of their love encoded in *Tom Sawyer*, the book that grew out of that love. It records some of their most cherished mutual ideals. Apparently it was Livy who wrote in the margin of the manuscript (interestingly in the slang of Mark Twain), "Tom licked for Becky" (Hill, "Composition and Structure of *TS*" 385), thereby suggesting that Tom assume the traditional posture of manly self-sacrifice, but this was also the stance Sam himself had taken in their courtship. The emphasis upon rescue (Tom to rescue Becky from exposure, humiliation, and punishment; Tom to rescue her from violation by Injun Joe as well as suffering and death in the cave) recalls Sam's dream letter to Livy in which he tried to save her from a nameless destroyer who threatened her with a fate worse than death (see my chap. 3). Indeed, the general stance imagined and created for Tom as one to pity and protect women is close

to the role Sam cast for himself during his courtship. Tom ends up acting out Aunt Polly's ideals because in *Tom Sawyer* the sentiments underlying the sentimentality, struggling in some sense to displace it, were endorsed by Sam and Livy as well as by Mark Twain.

A number of perceptive critics have attempted to place—or to replace—*Tom Sawyer* in its most natural genre, the nineteenth-century boy
book (Gribben, "Boy-Book Elements"; and See). As it evolved during
that century, the boy book recast its hero from paragon of virtue (the
model boy Tom hates) to innocent rapscallion or, as he was most often
called, bad boy. In most cases the badness is only superficial, for there is
goodness at the core. With as yet undetermined degrees of indebtedness,
Twain writes to form, exaggerating his bad boy's badness for comic effects and multiplying the instances of it until it becomes indelible. When
Becky tells Tom that she knows his name is Thomas Sawyer, he replies,
"That's the name they lick me by. I'm Tom, when I'm good" (*TS* 80). He
receives several lickings—and seems to deserve even more—but Twain
entitles his tale "The Adventures of Tom Sawyer," not Thomas, which is
to say that the story is finally a chronicle of the good boy Tom.

In one sense everyone realizes this, though early readers with a strict
sense of propriety were sometimes alarmed by the apparent badness.
However, that line of critical interpretation, which strains to uncover the
moral corruption of St. Petersburg, sometimes ends up disliking Tom. In
effect, such critics talk about their version of Thomas. Perhaps the most
common way of describing Tom as a good bad boy is to say that he "does
not hold any values which are at root different from those of the community" (Fetterley, "Sanctioned Rebel" 301). Such shared values are evident in Tom at every turn in his adventures, but it is important to see
how Twain tries to anchor these conventional norms.

Tom's struggle with his conscience over Muff Potter is the best example. The episode is a prime instance not only of Tom's internalized social standards, his essential conventionality, but also of his growing sense
of responsibility, his nascent maturity. Twain speaks repeatedly of Tom's
"gnawing conscience" (*TS* 107). But what finally moves Tom to overcome his fear of reprisal from Injun Joe and tell the truth in court is his
sympathy for Muff Potter. "Don't you feel sorry for him, sometimes?"

Tom asks Huck on the very day he sneaks off to tell the whole story to Muff's lawyer (*TS* 168). In a scene that anticipates the famous moment in *Huck Finn* in which Jim thanks Huck for his friendship just as Huck is setting off in the canoe to turn him in, Twain has Muff express his gratitude to Tom and Huck:

> "You've been mighty good to me, boys—better'n anybody else in this town. And I don't forget it, I don't. Often I says to myself, says I, 'I used to mend all the boys' kites and things, and show 'em where the good fishin' places was, and befriend 'em what I could, and now they've all forgot old Muff when he's in trouble; but Tom don't, and Huck don't—*they* don't forget him,' says I, 'and I don't forget them.' Well, boys, I done an awful thing—drunk and crazy at the time—that's the only way I account for it—and now I got to swing for it, and it's right. Right, and *best*, too I reckon—hope so, anyway. Well, we won't talk about that. I don't want to make *you* feel bad; you've befriended me. But what I want to say, is, don't *you* ever get drunk—then you won't ever get here. Stand a little furder west—so—that's it; it's a prime comfort to see faces that's friendly when a body's in such a muck of trouble,—and there don't none come here but yourn. Good friendly faces—good friendly faces. Git up on one another's backs and let me touch 'em. That's it. Shake hands—yourn'll come through the bars, but mine's too big. Little hands, and weak—but they've helped Muff Potter a power, and they'd help him more if they could." (*TS* 168–69)

Despite the skillful rendering of the vernacular here, Twain lets the speech slip into the sentimental when Muff asks first to look on the boys' "good friendly faces" and then to touch those faces and when he says, "Little hands, and weak—but they've helped Muff Potter a power." Yet the exchange is moving enough, and it forces home the central point: one must honor his right feelings. Tom's feelings, stirred by Muff, are driving him to do what his conscience tells him to. For unlike *Huckleberry Finn*, in which Twain presents the conflict, in his now famous words, between "a sound heart and a deformed conscience," in *Tom Sawyer* the sound heart is the conscience.

That's why Aunt Polly's training in right feeling is so important. Tom's interactions with her foster and eventually certify his good heart; they define the goodness within his bad boyness. Tom's feeling is his conscience, and it moves him in the end to save Muff. In a lesser vein, it also moves him to protect, comfort, and rescue Becky. His right feeling even tempers his sense of relief at the death of Injun Joe: "Tom was touched, for he knew by his own experience how this wretch had suffered. His pity was moved" (*TS* 220). Most important of all, Tom's carefully nurtured, incessantly instructed good heart prompts him to talk Huck into returning to the Widow Douglas. Tom cons Huck into coming back—as Twain slyly suggests, "Tom saw his opportunity" (*TS* 235)—not because he believes in a contemptible respectability, as some critics have suggested, but because, having learned from his own experience with Aunt Polly, he takes pity on the widow in her "great distress" (*TS* 233) and tries to "save" her "from sorrow." But, of course, as one bad boy talking to another, he can hardly say so.

"Saying" is the central and finally unresolved problem in this otherwise triumphant story. The community cannot say authentically what it feels, and neither can Tom, most of the time. Most tellingly, neither can Mark Twain. His dissatisfaction with spurious emotion and with honest emotion falsely expressed problematizes his own efforts to write convincingly of emotional states. In his illuminating commentary on the form of *Tom Sawyer*, Henry Wonham has suggested that by exploiting the difference between the romantic narrator and Tom, whose stories are informed by tall tale exaggeration and skepticism, Twain manages "to question the method of his novel as he writes it" ("Undoing Romance" 239). Finding a similar dialectic between narrator and protagonist, Lowry in effect turns Wonham's reading around, noting not that the dual device questions the romantic but that it often "invites delight in the very fantasy of melodramatic possibility it parodies" (79). Neither of these analyses explores the relationship between Tom's evolving moral character and Twain's— or his narrator's—own style of writing. Twain faces a kind of paradox: he finds strong emotion hard to believe in, difficult to authenticate, yet crucial to individual and social existence. While he exposes the emotional excess of St. Petersburg and makes fun of it, he nonetheless posits right feeling, good-heartedness, as the necessary ground of individual being, the foundation of morality. It is what Tom learns—and learns to act on. Yet when Twain himself wants to write of emotional states, more often than not he turns to a language that is as hollow as that used by the people of St. Petersburg. To put it another way, the community's problem is also Mark Twain's: neither can put emotions into adequate words.

There are many moments in *Tom Sawyer* in which Twain tries to create a credible fiction of intense emotion. When he wants to convey Tom's sudden sympathy for Becky, for instance, as she faces exposure for tearing the page of Dobbins's anatomy book, he writes, "Tom shot a glance at Becky. He had seen a hunted and helpless rabbit look as she did, with a gun leveled at its head" (*TS* 155). There is no burlesque or satire here. However, "haunted" and "helpless" overload the case, and the image of a rabbit staring into the gun that will kill it is improbable. Twain is just as serious—and just as unsuccessful—when he describes the fear that Tom and Huck feel after they have seen the murder of Dr. Robinson: "The two boys flew on and on, toward the village, speechless with horror. They glanced backward over their shoulders from time to time, apprehensively, as if they feared they might be followed. Every stump that started up in their path seemed a man and an enemy, and made them catch their breath; and as they sped by some outlying cottages that lay near the village, the barking of the aroused watch-dogs seemed to give wings to their feet" (*TS* 98). While he creates a nice sense of flight here and effectively deploys gestures that signal fear, the clichés make the trauma seem fake, and the rhetorical intensity smacks of artificiality. In the cave episode, the emotional climax of the book, Twain's rendering of terror, tenderness, and love is no more powerful. Becky gives way to "tears and wailings" (*TS* 213); Tom's "fright" weakens "every muscle in his body" (*TS* 215); and the two together wander "hand in hand and hopeless" (*TS* 213). Even as Tom gives Becky a kiss before starting on his final search, he does so "with a choking sensation in his throat" (*TS* 216).

More convincing than his trite and sentimental expressions of emotion are the tokens Twain creates to signify essential feeling. Sometimes they are comic, as with Tom's cherished brass knob from an andiron; sometimes they are quaintly local, as with Mary's gift of a genuine Barlow knife; and sometimes they are natural, touching, and central to the novel's concerns, as with Tom's sycamore scroll. Twain invents tokens, icons (the *t* on the wall of Injun Joe's hideout), and dramatic gestures

(Aunt Polly's thimble-thwacking) to convey.the emotions he cannot put into words.

What all this signifies is how strongly Twain himself was writing as an emotionalist, indeed as the kind of sentimentalist he objected to. Twain himself is caught in the problem of expression he mocks in St. Petersburg. He is often in the grip of excessive feeling in this book and just as often relies on conventional expression. While he sometimes manages a realistic rendering of setting, character, and dialogue, Twain writes most often in this fiction in a mode of excess. *Tom Sawyer* is full of tearful, touching circumstances, on the one hand, and fearful, threatening ones, on the other, and Twain conveys both in a sentimental style. Surprisingly Twain even follows in the footsteps of Harriet Beecher Stowe (his new neighbor) in evoking religious consolation:

> Fatigue bore so heavily upon Becky that she drowsed off to sleep. Tom was grateful. He sat looking into her drawn face and saw it grow smooth and natural under the influence of pleasant dreams; and by and by a smile dawned and rested there. The peaceful face reflected somewhat of peace and healing into his own spirit, and his thoughts wandered away to bygone times and dreamy memories. While he was deep in his musings, Becky woke up with a breezy little laugh—but it was stricken dead upon her lips, and a groan followed it.
>
> "Oh, how *could* I sleep! I wish I never never had waked! No, no, I don't, Tom! Don't look so! I won't say it again."
>
> "I'm glad you've slept, Becky; you'll feel rested, now, and we'll find the way out."
>
> "We can try, Tom; but I've seen such a beautiful country in my dream. I reckon we are going there." (*TS* 227)

Such intimations of immortality were the stock-in-trade of nineteenth-century sentimental writers. Twain also dramatizes the gothic horrors from which "such a beautiful country" may ultimately redeem—or, in the language of Twain's own thinking, rescue—one: "The children fastened their eyes upon their bit of candle and watched it melt slowly and pitilessly away; saw the half inch of wick stand alone at last; saw the feeble flame rise and fall, rise and fall, climb the thin column of smoke, linger at its top a moment, and then—the horror of utter darkness reigned!"

(*TS* 214). However one values this, the moment is carefully staged in words and rhythms to convey the fixation of fear, and it has a forceful, if sensational, climax in the final exclamation: "the horror of utter darkness reigned!" It is a momentary triumph of Twain's excessive style. If one enjoys it, one likes *Tom Sawyer*. If it disturbs one, then as Twain himself says at the end of Tom's Sunday school fiasco, it is best to "draw the curtain of charity over the rest of the scene" (*TS* 65).

TWAIN HIMSELF was far from dropping the curtain on scenes of intense emotion. Throughout his career his humor was counterbalanced by his fondness for extreme sentiment, and his next major fiction after *Tom Sawyer*, *The Prince and the Pauper*, is awash with tender feelings. *The Prince and the Pauper* is often seen as an anomaly in Twain's canon, but it is in most ways a characteristic performance. Certainly its attention to children, its historical setting, its conventional morality, its pretensions to reform, its generally conservative politics, and even its exploitation of emotional excess are all typical. And as Stahl has pointed out, the story has roots in Clemens's remembrance of his own father, a recollection that would enter into many of Twain's writings (76). The romance has been seen as Twain's surprising concession to gentility, a temporary capitulation created by the force of New England culture from which Twain would eventually recover to write more powerful, more unconventional, more subversive books. But such a reading distorts the true nature of Clemens's creative self: gentility was inherent in Mark Twain. It informs, as we've seen, both "Old Times" and *Life*. *The Prince and the Pauper* reflects Twain's continuing interest in the efficacy of tender human feeling. In terms of his development from *Tom Sawyer* to *Huckleberry Finn*, however, it marks two important shifts, one formal, the other conceptual. Formally, as he never had before, Twain crafts a pure melodrama that is a perfect outlet for his sentimentality; intellectually, he begins to question the congruence of social law and private feeling.

Twain felt that his tale posed special challenges for him: "I must go warily seeing this is such a wide departure from my accustomed line" (qtd. in Andrews 191). But he did not go warily. He wrote with unusual speed and special delight. The most important fact about the composition of the book is that Twain found so much pleasure in it. Again and again he testified to his enjoyment. Happily he explained to Mother Fairbanks, "What am I writing? A historical tale, of 300 years ago, simply for the love of it" (*MTMF* 218). Cheerfully he told Howells, "I have reached (MS) page 326 on my historical tale of 'The Little Prince & the Little Pauper' & if I knew it would never sell a copy my jubilant delight in writing it would not suffer any diminution" (MTHL 1:290). Cautiously he informed Orion (cautiously, because he liked to sell his brother on his hard work), "I am grinding away now, with all my might, & with an interest which amounts to intemperance, at the 'Prince & the Pauper'" (*MTBus* 143). Gaily he confessed to Howells, "I take so much pleasure in my story that I am loth to hurry, not wanting to get it done" (MTHL 1:291). Twain, who most often cursed his way through the writing of a book, was experiencing a prolonged fit of joy.

He was joyful for once because he was deeply engaged in pure fantasy, pleasurable wish fulfillment, and because for once he had no qualms about rendering his wishes in extravagant terms. His form dictated them. When he saw the illustrations drawn by Frank T. Merrill, he told his publisher: "It is a vast pleasure to see them cast in the flesh, so to speak— they were of but perishable dream-stuff, before" (*MTLP* 140). Whatever the value of *The Prince and the Pauper* as literature, the book reveals the stuff of Twain's dreams. The core of those dreams is crystallized in William Stafford's playful poem, "A Story That Could Be True." Slighted by people everywhere, Stafford's hero—significantly a "you" that thus includes us all—muses on the question, "Who are you really, wanderer?" Stafford provides this explanation:

> and the answer you have to give
> no matter how dark and cold
> the world around you is:
> "Maybe I'm a king." (4)

Twain's tale is about unacknowledged royal identity. It is about kingship, both literal and moral, since for Twain one can attain majesty by character as well as noble descent. Switching the prince and the pauper, he inaugurates an archetypal story of the true self's concealment, trial, and final vindication. He employs the timeless folklore plot of the worthy self, unrecognized by the world, indeed persecuted by it, who finally achieves power and prominence. (This dimension of the plot is explored most fully by Regan [*Unpromising Heroes*] and Spengemann [*MT and Backwoods Angel*]). If this is every child's secret dream, it was also to a surprising degree Sam Clemens's life story—or so Mark Twain liked to believe.

Perhaps because it is dream stuff, *The Prince and the Pauper* displays Mark Twain's sensibility starkly. It demonstrates the moral cast of his imagination, his absorption in primal conflicts, his obsession with the home and its antithesis, adventure, and most of all, his inveterate combination of humor and melodrama. Indeed, humor and melodrama are the twins of his genius.

Twain said he preferred *The Prince and the Pauper* to his first boy fiction: "I like this tale better than *Tom Sawyer*—because I haven't put any fun in it. I *think* that is why I like it better. You know a body always enjoys seeing himself attempting something out of his line" (qtd. in *P&P* 1 n. 2). What is out of his line in *The Prince and the Pauper* is not the melodrama, for, as we have seen, *Tom Sawyer* is full of emotional excess, but the humor, which is most often simply cute. For instance, Twain takes the humor of physical discomfort, a staple of western humor he often traded in, and purges it of its subversive crudity and violence. Thus in an elaborately worked-up scene, he shows poor Tom Canty, uneasily masquerading as the prince, suffering during his first royal dinner the agonies of an itchy nose. Twain observes, all too cutely, "Alas, there was no Hereditary Scratcher!" (*P&P* 100). His humor is equally coy and tame when he has Tom drink the "fragrant rose-water" in the finger bowl (*P&P* 100). In general he creates out of Tom's accidental enthronement as prince a humor of captivity, the kind of humor he practiced briefly when at the end of *Tom Sawyer* he turned Huck over to the Widow Douglas to be vexed by manners, rituals, routines, and required dress. But while all of this in *Tom Sawyer* evoked a serious conflict between respectability and roguery, in *The Prince and the Pauper* it does no more than invite one to smile at Tom's inevitable ignorance.

The humor Twain creates from Edward's predicament is most often just as harmless and cloying. Twain enjoys—and expects his readers to enjoy—the true prince's hopeless efforts to cook for the two little girls who find him in a barn and for their mother who receives him with "pity" out of her "womanly heart" (P&P 217), but the fact that Edward burns "the cookery" (P&P 219) is neither very funny nor in any way provocative. When Edward gratefully beds down for warmth and friendship with a calf that is, Twain says, not "embarrassed by sleeping with a king" (P&P 213), the humor is sticky-sweet. Since Edward insists on proclaiming himself king in one perilous circumstance after another, to one threatening mob after another, the humor of his incongruous outbursts seems to carry the potential for electrifying class difference, but again Twain defuses these clashes, softens his humor and retreats from seriousness, by having Edward dismissed as merely mad. There are two moments of comedy that threaten to undermine the prevailing coyness. When Tom asks the royal court if the dead King Henry will "keep" until the funeral and when Miles Hendon sings a bawdy ballad about a married woman loved by another man, Twain's humor threatens to transgress the boundaries of propriety, but Tom's question is passed over and Hendon's song is never finished. Twain keeps his tale cute.

If the humor of *The Prince and the Pauper* is somewhat out of Twain's line, its melodrama is right up his alley. As we have seen, *Tom Sawyer* is charged with melodrama, and, although it is seldom discussed this way, *Huckleberry Finn* is a kind of tear-jerker. Looked at realistically, almost nothing rings true in *The Prince and the Pauper*. Rescued from Offal Court, mistaken for the prince, Tom Canty "sighed pathetically and murmured to himself, 'In what have I offended, that the good God should take me away from the fields and the free air and the sunshine, to shut me up here and make me a king and afflict me so?'" (P&P 161–62). Fields, free air, and sunshine in Offal Court? Being awakened in a barn by a rat, Edward "smiled, and said, 'Poor fool, why so fearful? I am as forlorn as thou. 'Twould be a shame in me to hurt the helpless, who am myself so helpless'" (P&P 215). The prince conversing with a rat? The melodramatic cast of this book is so evident it is taken for granted, but it is important. While Twain mutes the melodrama of *Tom Sawyer* by grounding it in a specific world rendered in authenticating detail (and by criticizing the sentimental mode itself), in *The Prince and the Pauper* he openly pursues the stock effects of melodrama. (Like the fantasy of the plot, the melodrama contributed to the great pleasure Twain found in writing his tale.)

The melodramatic form frees Twain from the opposition he struggled with in *Tom Sawyer* between authentic feeling and its false expression, for in melodrama the true is always articulated in stylized, extravagant utterances. *The Prince and the Pauper* is almost pure melodrama: it presents hyperbolic figures, lurid events, and masked identities; it polarizes and simplifies good and evil, depicts extreme emotional states, displays overt villainy persecuting innocent goodness, and finally celebrates the triumph of virtue.

A theatrical impulse has been described as the very heart of melodrama (Bentley), and such an impulse is insistently at work throughout Twain's tale. It is a book of histrionic scenes (almost a picture-book for Susy and Clara): small ones are staged for horror or pathos; large ones are turned into spectacles for the sake of grandeur. Typical of Twain's inflation is the scene in which Miles Hendon, already locked unjustly in the stocks, the "sport and butt of a dirty mob," sacrifices himself to save Edward (only a more extreme version of Tom Sawyer's sacrifice for Becky):

> "Let the child go," said he; "ye heartless dogs, do ye not see how young and frail he is? Let him go—I will take his lashes."
>
> . . . .
>
> Hendon was removed from the stocks, and his back laid bare; and whilst the lash was applied the poor little king turned away his face and allowed unroyal tears to channel his cheeks unchecked. "Ah, brave good heart," he said to himself, "this loyal deed shall never perish out of my memory." (*P&P* 286–87)

Twain gives this extravagantly touching scene a final melodramatic twist as Edward first whispers to the repilloried Miles, "Kings cannot ennoble thee, thou good, great soul, for One who is higher than kings hath done that for thee," and then, in grotesque parody of his lost power, touches Hendon's "bleeding shoulders" lightly with the very "scourge" used on him and proclaims, "Edward of England dubs thee earl!" (*P&P* 288).

Perhaps the most important dimension of Twain's melodrama, one that leads to its central themes, is the given nature of good and evil. Critics have seen in the education of Tom and Edward an indication of Twain's emerging interest in the formative power of environment. In some ways, *The Prince and the Pauper* does reflect Twain's growing suspicion that "environment determines morality" (Blair, *MT & Huck Finn* 137). But the fact is, as he imagines them, Tom and Edward are both inherently good. To be sure, both become better, but their innate goodness is there from the first. It is a good centered—like Tom Sawyer's—in the heart. Tom Canty is moved to pity as well as to love his mother and sisters, and despite his father's brutal insistence, he resists the immorality of stealing. When he assumes the throne and begins to administer justice, his "compassion" takes "control" of him and he judges in response to his "heart-strings" (*P&P* 171). While Edward has much to learn about the suffering of his people and the severity of the law, he too is instinctively kind. In the beginning he sends away his servants to save Tom from embarrassment as he eats; and feeling the injury done to him by the palace guard, he sets off to avenge it, thereby precipitating the switch of prince and pauper. When he is told (falsely) that Miles Hendon is wounded, Edward not only threatens revenge on the person who has injured him but, out of compassion, hastens to aid him (*P&P* 188).

Evil is as inherent and inexplicable as goodness in Twain's tale, for at one end of the class scale John Canty's wickedness exceeds the spur of his environment, while at the other end Miles's brother, Hugh, is possessed by an evil that defies both birth and upbringing. Twain's overt moral— "learning softeneth the heart and breedeth gentleness and charity" (*P&P* 70)—depends for success upon the readiness of an already good heart.

While Twain follows melodramatic conventions in his creation of character, and while Tom and Edward learn chiefly the kind of heart-lessons Tom Sawyer acquired, there is a significant new departure in this book. Whereas in *Tom Sawyer* the heart is the conscience and at one with the law, in *The Prince and the Pauper* Twain begins to imagine the separation of heart and law. Repeatedly and melodramatically, he depicts laws that violate right human feeling. Witnessing such horrors constitutes the core of Edward's education, and once he is restored to the throne, he frequently retells his experience to "keep its sorrowful spectacles fresh in his memory and the springs of pity replenished in his heart" (*P&P* 334). To show the severity of old English law was Twain's plan from the beginning, but as he worked it out in the fiction itself, he made the heart the measure of legal injustice. Notably different from the ethical harmony between private feeling and public code in *Tom Sawyer*, this turn in Twain's thinking clearly anticipates the central moral conflict of *Huck Finn*.

If the disjuncture between heart and law opens a potentially radical fissure in the social fabric, it is one Twain closes simply by believing that good kings will create good laws. *The Prince and the Pauper*, is, as Tom Towers has observed, a "forthright expression of a cultural and political conservatism" ("MT's Once and Future King" 194). Its conservative bent is especially evident in Twain's treatment of the classes. He imagines the commoners of Edward's England with disgust. The most pervasive evil from which first Tom and then Edward suffer is the mob; the innocent twin heroes are repeatedly subjected to crowds that are filthy, drunken, irrational, violent, and sadistic. The hordes not only trample identity but also threaten life itself. On the other hand, Twain depicts royals and aristocrats as no more than vain and rigid, and at the same time he makes them attractive in their splendor. He reveals an affinity for the upper classes that matches his contempt for the lower.

Significantly, the one moment in which a mob of commoners is shown to have a capacity for good occurs when Miles takes Edward's lashing. Then, and only then, the mob—a "forlorn and degraded" one, Twain says—is moved to silence and passivity out of respect (*P&P* 287). It even protects Miles from the taunts and blows of a latecomer who has not witnessed the noble self-sacrifice. Thus Twain suggests the possibility of redemptive feeling in ordinary folk, but this single moment hardly offsets the many others in which the mob's wild, irrational violence holds sway. In terms of the book's moral scheme, if the law needs a heart, the heart, at least the heart of the multitudes, needs a law. Far more than a mere concession to gentility, *The Prince and the Pauper* encodes Twain's own political conservatism.

In her groundbreaking study, *Dark Twins*, Susan Gillman points out that in Twain's early works the law is an agent of control that resolves confusions about identity (21). In *The Prince and the Pauper*, however, it is not really the law that restores Edward to the throne and Tom to his position as commoner. The law is powerless to declare which boy is the rightful heir. That truth must be *spoken* by both Edward and Tom—and then certified not by the possession of the Royal Seal but by knowledge of its location. Speech and knowledge constitute empowerment (one that finally vanquishes the force of violence and deceit, though, interestingly, no evil person in the story is ever converted to the good). Tom breaks his silence out of guilt over the betrayal of his mother (his heart is awakened by her suffering, much as Tom Sawyer's is by Aunt Polly's woes), out of pity for Edward, and out of a sense of justice. Edward proclaims his estate out of a sense of right, out of a desire to be himself, and out of an intent to use his kingship to ameliorate harsh law. Both speak from the heart.

Melodrama typically creates a world in which goodness is muted for a time, only to announce itself in the end. Twain's tale is true to form, as the true, the good, and the right are finally spoken, but his use of this convention carries in context a special import: speech is power. It is speech that enables Tom to pass as Edward in the very beginning, and it is speech that draws and binds Miles to Edward. While Edward's self-proclamations often incite the anger of the mob, they also give it pause. Tom Sawyer's talk gave him power with the other boys, but had little force beyond that. In *The Prince and the Pauper*, however, Twain, inveterate talker, platform speaker, fantasized the power of words. Words in this book not only identify their speakers; they also empower them. And, of course, within the historical setting, no matter who he is, the king's *word* is law.

Bruce Michelson's engaging analysis of Twain's romance as "a tale of self-loss and vanishing" (143) almost persuades one that Twain is Tom Stoppard, but Michelson ignores the restoration of identities and the reestablishment of morality that Twain so carefully stages. Twain ends his historical melodrama with virtue rewarded. Miles is certified as knight and peer, earl of Kent, with the hereditary privilege of sitting in the king's presence, and he weds at last his beloved Edith. Tom becomes the king's ward to dwell at Christ's Hospital—and serve as chief of its governors—where henceforth the inmates are to be clothed, sheltered, nourished, and have their "hearts fed" (*P&P* 332). Looked at another way, after enforced adventures, Edward repossesses his home (as does Miles), while Tom is given a new one, one that enables him to take in the homeless.

All these just arrangements, predicted by the very form of the tale, come about in large measure, as Stahl has suggested, because of the ability of the boys to act on their own, to supersede their fathers (83–84). Yet Twain's fairy tale of fathers and sons is also a tale whose resolution depends on good mothers—or perhaps more accurately, good mothering. It is, after all, Tom's guilt over betraying his loving mother that starts the chain reaction that ends in Edward's restoration as well as the elevation of Tom and Miles. Miles himself, who feeds, clothes, tucks in, and protects Edward, is a curiously androgynous figure, a father-mother to the prince who anticipates Huck's Jim.

Amidst the happy moral reckoning of the story's close, however, the resolution that Twain calls "Justice and Retribution," there is one stunning miscarriage. Hugh, whose possession of Edith poses a sexual issue not to be faced by Twain (except in Miles's song: "But another man he loved she" [*P&P* 150]), is appropriately banished to the continent (presumably to France, always for Twain the most licentious of countries), where he dies. But John Canty, in most ways the arch emblem of evil, is simply "never heard of again" (*P&P* 333). Like Pap in *Tom Sawyer*, he is not dead, or imprisoned, but absent. Twain's imagination, even in its most secure moral fantasy, remains haunted by the threat of an evil father still at large in the world. (It is as if he had conjured up a terrifying force too potent to destroy.) Only the release of this dark figure departs from the conventions of his melodramatic form.

If *Tom Sawyer* critiques emotional excess while falling prey to it, *The Prince and the Pauper* indulges it without reservation. Twain's fantasy is airy melodrama, pure and unalloyed, ballasted only a little by the facts and trappings of history. Both boy adventures affirm the heart as the source of morality, a vision common to nineteenth-century sentimentalists. In *Adventures of Huckleberry Finn*, Twain would plumb that conception, complicating and problematizing it, and he would hit upon new ways to make emotional excess, which seems almost the inevitable corollary to a heart-based morality, creditable. He would, to return to the terms he used in admonishing Will Bowen, find ways to create *"Real* sentiment," that "rare & godlike thing," rather than the "maudlin article."

CHAPTER SIX

Southwestern Sentimentalist

In writing *Tom Sawyer* Mark Twain got stuck. After making a large beginning, some one hundred pages or so, in the winter of 1872–73 and then adding another three hundred pages in the spring and summer of 1874, Twain felt he had "pumped" himself dry by early September. He was content to turn to other tasks, some literary, most not. Among the literary was the conception and execution of the seven-part "Old Times on the Mississippi." Having published the final installment of that series in the *Atlantic* in May 1875, he returned to *Tom Sawyer*, completing his first draft by early July. "Old Times" thus occupies a space in Twain's creative work that places it in the middle of *Tom Sawyer*, not, one imagines, as a distraction from that work but as a reinvigorating return from a different perspective to precisely the river along whose banks Tom plays out his adventures. Writing "Old Times" may well have refilled Twain's creative tank. A similar process of creative cross-generation occurred with *Adventures of Huckleberry Finn*, of course, for although Twain began that text right after the completion of *Tom Sawyer*, *Huck Finn* was a long time a-borning—some seven years—and the midwife in that process was Clemens's return to the river in the spring of 1882 and the book Twain wrote about it. Scholarship has amply testified to the symbiotic relationship between *Life on the Mississippi* and *Huck Finn*, noting that parts of Huck made their way into *Life* and that events chronicled in it were in turn transmuted in Twain's fiction.[1]

Life on the Mississippi is the gateway to *Huck Finn*, but it does more than reveal the quotidian material out of which Twain created his masterwork. *Life* also discloses the twin aspects of the Mark Twain persona that give shape and moral point to his novel. For in *Life* two moments of

definitive self-representation occur—or more precisely, are created—
when Mark Twain finally revisits Hannibal.

The return to Hannibal was a highly self-conscious act, one long contemplated, designed to allow Mark Twain to capitalize on Clemens's past
on the river. The arrival at Hannibal is carefully staged, but it nonetheless reveals a great deal of the event's resonance for Sam Clemens and its
import for Mark Twain. Disembarking at 7:00 A.M. on a Sunday, when
everyone is still in bed, Twain occupies the town not as it is but as it has
remained in his memory. His sight is shaped by his fond recollections,
and his reentry becomes a rebirth: "I stepped ashore with the feeling
of one who returns out of a dead-and-gone generation" (*LOM* 370). He
feels, he says, what "the Bastille prisoners must have felt when they used
to come out and look upon Paris after years of captivity" (*LOM* 371).
Although he is referring to the inevitable mix of the familiar and the
strange after long absence, the metaphor of release from the Bastille suggests that he has been imprisoned while away, imprisoned in remote
places, imprisoned perhaps in adulthood. Indeed, as he reenters Hannibal he suddenly feels "like a boy again" (*LOM* 371), and acting as the boy
he once was, he climbs Holliday's Hill, the magical place that was playground for the real Sam and paradise for his fictional avatars, Tom and
Huck. From the top of that special spot he rediscovers a sameness—and
with it a pleasure that betokens a wholeness impervious to time: "From
this vantage ground the extensive view up and down the river, and wide
over the wooded expanses of Illinois, is very beautiful,—one of the most
beautiful on the Mississippi, I think; which is a hazardous remark to
make. . . . No matter, it was satisfyingly beautiful to me, and it had this
advantage over all the other friends whom I was about to greet again: it
had suffered no change" (*LOM* 372).

Having thus regained for a moment some lost sense of participation in
an unaltered natural world, he then faces the facts of change. People have
moved away, aged, or died; the town has grown in population, expanded
in space (all but obliterating some cherished places), and become more
commercial. Twain proceeds to seek out the new as well as the old, and
as he responds emotionally to their intermingling, he creates two differ-

ing representations of himself. First, viewing the town from Holliday's Hill, "a good deal moved," he says to himself, "'Many of the people I once knew in this tranquil refuge of my childhood are now in heaven; some, I trust, are in the other place" (*LOM* 371). Then somewhat later, having descended from the hilltop and entered the new church that has replaced the Old Ship of Zion he once attended, again "mightily stirred," he observes the Sunday school pupils and reports: "I contemplated them with a deep interest and a yearning wistfulness, and if I had been a girl I would have cried for they were the offspring, and represented, and occupied the places of boys and girls some of whom I had loved to love, and some of whom I had loved to hate, but all of whom were dear to me for the one reason or the other, so many years gone by—and, Lord, where be they now!" Recognized as Mark Twain, he is persuaded to address the boys and girls: "I talked a flutter of wild nonsense to those children to hide the thoughts which were in me, and which could not have been spoken without a betrayal of feeling that would have been recognized as out of character with me" (*LOM* 380).

In the first instance, positioned on the hill, place of truant play and unfettered imagining, Twain laughs at his former townspeople. In the second, standing in church, place of prescribed devotion and structured thought, he mourns his absent townspeople. In the first, he is the irreverent humorist; in the second, he is a man of tender feeling. Significantly, he imagines the two selves he dramatizes here as gendered: in his joking he is a boy; in his impulse to cry he is a girl. Further, the positions assumed in each case, a hilltop at the edge of the community, a church at its center, suggest that as humorist he is free of social codes, while as emotionalist he is guided by them. Clearly for Twain there were two parts to Mark Twain, and just as clearly for him, only one was fully "in character," as that character had been defined by his audience. He indulges himself as unconventional, ironic humorist; represses himself as traditional, nostalgic remembrancer. He suppresses his feeling self partly because he conceives of it as female, partly because he understands how Mark Twain has been perceived. The highly emotional Twain would, he realizes, be seen as out of character since the figure of speech, to return to R. Jackson Wilson's formulations, seen in his texts by his readers is only the humorist. But in the very process of saying so, he inscribes the other part of his persona into the text. What Twain's tale of return does, at a significant moment in his career, is to add to the textual self, and the self in the minds of his readers, his own self-conceiving: he is, for himself if not for his audiences, both an unconventional humorist and a conventional man of feeling.

Taken together, the two episodes reveal the twin parts of Clemens's creative self: the confident humorist and the apologetic sentimentalist. These two linked impulses, the drive toward humor and the inclination to sentimentality, are both evident in *Huck Finn* at every turn; they create its greatness and make possible its moral scheme.

Adventures of Huckleberry Finn has usually been placed in the tradition of Southwestern humor, that body of comic sketches and stories that swept the country in the 1840s and 1850s, only to peter out after the Civil War (although vestiges of the humor crop up throughout the twentieth century in such writers as Faulkner, Erskine Caldwell, and William Price Fox). The tradition arose from actual frontier life, from political controversy, from class conflict, and from oral storytelling, among other forces. Twain knew it well and consciously wrote pieces exploiting many of its literary conventions. He also understood the regional appeal and potential offensiveness of Southwestern humor. Writing a review of George Washington Harris's work in 1867, he praised Sut Lovingood's yarns but speculated that, while a collection of them would "sell well in the West," the "Eastern people" would "call it coarse and possibly taboo it" (*MTTB* 221). Virtually every commentator on Southwestern humor notes that it was a male genre generated by a man's world. It has been pointedly contrasted to the popular literature of New England: the "gap between the genteel literature which was being enjoyed by pale young ladies in New England drawing rooms" and the "masculine humor" of this tradition was "immense" (Cohen and Dillingham xv). Although Twain wrote some pieces that fit the tradition perfectly, *Huck Finn* does not; it is a far more complex hybrid that draws into itself many elements of other, non-Southwestern forms of writing. Most notable among these alien aspects is Twain's sentimentality. While it might have been enjoyed in genteel drawing rooms, it would have been wholly out of place in the law offices, saloons, and print shops where Southwestern humor was consumed. But, of course, *Huck Finn* was not, by and large, enjoyed by the genteel, for its sentimentality was obscured by its burly humor. As he indulged his twin impulses, Twain crossed genres and crossed up his readers.

Although there were eight years between Twain's initial work on *Huck Finn* and its first publication, the book was largely written in two bouts of enthusiasm. After finishing *Tom Sawyer*, Twain launched into what he then called "Huck Finn's Autobiography," switching from the third person of *Tom Sawyer* to Huck's narrating first, and thinking as he turned out four hundred pages that he liked it "only tolerably well" and that he might even "pigeonhole or burn the MS when it is done" (*MTHL* 1:144). Why, one wonders, burn it? Twain habitually kept a lot of inferior writing. The second burst of creativity, little less than a seizure, came in the summer of 1883 after his return to the Mississippi and to Hannibal. With glee he informed Howells:

> I haven't piled up MS so in years as I have done since we came here to the farm three weeks & a half ago. Why, it's like old times, to step straight into the study, damp from the breakfast table, & sail right in & sail right on, the whole day long, without thought of running short of stuff or words. I wrote 4000 words to-day & I touch 3000 & upwards pretty often, & don't fall below 2600 on any working day. And when I get fagged out, I lie abed a couple of days & read & smoke, & then go it again for 6 or 7 days. I have finished one small book, & am away along in a big one that I half-finished two or three years ago. I expect to complete it in a month or six weeks or two months more. And *I* shall *like* it, whether anybody else does or not. (*MTHL* 1:435, Twain's emphasis)

Still well short of completing his story at this point, he is notably defiant about it, as if he were sensing that something in it would prove offensive. A month later his final report on the summer's remarkable output playfully celebrates its illicit creation:

> I've done two seasons' work in one, & haven't anything left to do, now, but revise. I've written eight or nine hundred MS pages in such a brief space of time that I mustn't name the number of days; *I* shouldn't believe it myself,

& of course couldn't expect you to. I used to restrict myself to 4 & 5 hours a day & 5 days in the week; but this time I've wrought from breakfast till 5.15 P.M. six days in the week; & once or twice I smouched a Sunday when the boss wasn't looking. Nothing is half so good as literature hooked on Sunday on the sly. (*MTHL* 1:438)

These casual notes to an always-approving Howells suggest two things. First, for whatever reasons, in writing *Huck Finn* Twain was both exhilarated and obsessed. (Since Huck's tale is one in which reality presses upon him, Twain's joy in telling it did not come, as it did with *The Prince and the Pauper*, from the pleasure of fantasy.) And second, in writing *Huck Finn* Twain felt himself in opposition, to his imagined readers—"*I* shall *like* it, whether anybody else does or not"—and even to his muse and censor, Livy—"I smouched a Sunday when the boss wasn't looking." Twain seems to have intuited that he had created a radical text.

Oddly, the most obvious and pervasive aspect of *Huck Finn*, its insistent humor, has not yet received adequate analysis and definition. Karnath observes that Twain's "masterpiece has not been regarded as a comic work" (216). Its sources in the traditions of Southwestern humor have been traced (Lynn, *Southwestern Humor*), and its ties to the Literary Comedians have been outlined (Sloane), but these hardly capture, let alone define, the book's veritable riot of laughter. The novel is our classic of American humor precisely because it contains so many kinds of humor. Even a rudimentary taxonomy would have to include the humor of physical discomfort, the humor of class conflict, the humor of caricature, the humor of innocence, the humor of social satire, the humor of tomfoolery, the humor of imposture, the humor of ignorance, the humor of silliness, the humor of gender, the humor of conflicting values, the humor of miscommunication, the humor of manners, the humor of pretension, the humor of exaggeration, the humor of language, and the humor of physical violence. The categorization here is partial, but it can at least begin to suggest the multiplicity of humors at work in Twain's novel. They range in their effect from the lightly whimsical to the savagely critical. Far more important than any one kind of humor is the overall effect created by Twain's various comic turns. Although the force of the humor varies from scene to scene, there is a cumulative impact: sinewing steadily throughout the book, shifting from the indulgent to the denunciatory, the humor destabilizes the world of the text and subverts everyone and everything in it.

Twain's humor invades and disrupts the central value systems and institutions of his time—and ours. It problematizes religion, manners, morals, society, culture, race, class, gender, and, ultimately, individual identity itself. Twain himself probably grasped the subversive power of his novel only slightly, enjoying its composition on forbidden Sundays and anticipating that some readers would dislike it. But, working through the mask of Huck, he freed himself more than ever before (and more than he ever would again) to sport with the world as he knew it, to laugh it, sometimes gently, sometimes violently, to smithereens. The humor of this book is liberated, for with differing degrees of severity it breaks taboo after taboo. Such transgression was no doubt the source of both the joy and the obsession Twain felt as he composed. The book itself is also liberating, for as it deploys humor to trample conventions, it draws its readers into complicity with its violations. It is no wonder that various readers at different times have recoiled from *Huck Finn*, finding it vulgar, or irreligious, or racist, or sexist, finding it, in short, objectionable in one way or another. And it is no wonder that those who embrace the book have often defended it by not taking its humor seriously. *Huck Finn* is, in Cox's perceptive phrase, "a hard book to take" (386).

But Mark Twain is not a nihilist. Despite the corrosive force of his humor, he struggles toward affirmation. Like a typical Victorian as he doubts the truth of religion, the validity of manners, the efficacy of wealth, the adequacy of traditional morality, the authenticity of culture, and the stability of identity, he nonetheless longs to ground life on some bedrock. To vary slightly Hawthorne's famous explanation of Melville's metaphysical dilemma, Twain can neither believe nor accept his disbelief. Even as his humor destabilizes the familiar world, creating what George C. Carrington Jr. has called a universe of "disorder" and "turbulence" (see chap. 1), Twain tries to reestablish an ethical order. He does so by writing a sentimental melodrama of the heart.

Despite its reputation as a major text of American realism, *Huck Finn* is actually something of a potboiler.[2] Certainly its main events—Pap's imprisonment of Huck, Huck's escape, the encounter with the cutthroat thieves on the *Walter Scott*, the feud, the shooting of Boggs, the facedown between Sherburn and the mob, the attempt to defraud the Wilks girls, and the final effort to steal Jim out of slavery—are all sensational. The plot of an innocent boy helping a kindly slave is worthy of Harriet Beecher Stowe. And then there is the enveloping atmosphere of terror. Hamlin Hill has concluded that fear was the "controlling emotion" of Twain's life (*God's Fool* 269), and whatever the truth of this, Twain makes fear the dominant emotion in Huck's experience. Huck is always threatened by something or someone. The novel is rife with dangers and dark plottings; it is driven by the ferocious and the sinister. Twain's presentation of emotion is often as exaggerated as the events that generate it. Feeling is insistently magnified, whether joyful—"It most killed Jim a-laughing" (*HF* 168)—or fearful—"it most scared the livers and lights out of me" (*HF* 259). Twain's sensationally episodic, emotion-filled thriller transpires in—and is unified by—a universe that is radically polarized, a universe of melodrama of the kind he imagined in *The Prince and the Pauper*.

Melodrama habitually envisions a world of stark, radically simplistic antitheses, a universe in which moral right and wrong, good behavior and bad, the socially responsible and the socially corrupt, the individually authentic and the individually false, are projected as obvious, inevitable oppositions constitutive of life itself. *Huck Finn* is imagined in such terms. Of the many polarizations Twain's melodramatic imagination creates, perhaps the most important is the dichotomy between the manly and the feminine. Now that the original text has been fully restored in the California edition, this fundamental opposition is most evident in the contrast between the burly raftsmen and the delicate Emmeline, a contrast highlighted by their juxtaposition in chapters 16 and 17.

There is something slightly unreal about Huck's encounter with each. He observes the raftsmen for only a short time, and he knows Emmeline only through her family, her painting, and her poetry. Yet the two have a presence in the novel that exceeds Huck's experience of them. Twain presents them with such clarity and intensity, with such comic force, that they become as indelible in the novel as they were basic to his own imagining. At the deepest level, the contrast he draws between them no doubt arises from the impress of Clemens's parents, his compassionate, emotional mother, and his coldhearted, threatening father.[3] But the differences he creates also reflect the divergent worlds he had lived in: most recently, the sphere of domesticity, of the morally civilized and the culturally refined; earlier, the realm of the frontier, of the ethically wild and the culturally crude. Deep in Twain, these oppositions give structure to his novel. He presents their representatives as comic caricatures, of course, but his burlesque does not negate their function as normative counters. (Burlesque is, after all, a way of participating in what one mocks.) The world of Huck's enforced adventuring vibrates between the extremes they embody.

Twain draws the essential contrasts starkly: Emmeline is melancholy; the raftsmen are jubilant (they jump up and crack their heels); she is morbid; they are fecund; she is vulnerable; they are invincible; she is tender; they are tough. She simpers; they swagger. Both perform. And the postures assumed in each case, as well as their accompanying emotions, are palpably bogus (though their falsity is largely lost on Huck). Twain dramatizes here conflicting modes of self-identifying discourse—soft-talk versus tall-talk, the sentimental as opposed to the sadistic—which bespeak profound aesthetic, moral, and ontological differences. To the extent that these oppositions have a common basis in a preoccupation with death, the one lamenting it, the other threatening it, Twain seems to suggest that the entire culture is moribund. It is dying because its capacity for authentic feeling has atrophied.

In varying degrees the gendered attitudes and attributes staged in Huck's encounters with the raftsmen and Emmeline inform and define all the other characters in the novel. On one side of the Great Gender Divide, the Widow Douglas, who never says a word in the book, is reported to call Huck a "poor lost lamb" (*HF* 2), a misconstruction of his character and circumstance conversant with Emmeline's sentimentality, and clearly Aunt Sally is gripped by excessive emotionality. On the other side of the Divide, Colonel Sherburn sadistically guns down Boggs and then announces his prowess in terms extravagant enough to match the raftsmen's brags: "Why, a *man's* safe in the hands of ten thousand of your kind" (*HF* 190).

The duke and the king, who dominate the center of the novel (as if it were their story), embody the worst of both sexes. In their performances they are not only sentimental but also sadistic. Twain makes them parodies of the conflicting modes enacted by the raftsmen and Emmeline. They travesty manly prowess as they prate a fake Shakespeare of kingship and practice sword fighting, only to fall into the river. And they abuse the sentimental style first as they vie with each other for greater fallen grandeur—"Drot your pore broken heart," the King exclaims in vexation. "What are you heaving your pore broken heart at *us* f 'r? (*HF* 161)— and then as they play their scams from the King's heartrending performance as a reformed pirate through the Duke's composition and printing of maudlin poetry (the title of his poem is "Yes, crush, cold world, this breaking heart" ([*HF* 174]) to their joint tear-filled impersonation of the Wilks brothers. Their viciousness, muted somewhat by Twain's burlesque, matches their false emotionality; they use sentimentality to mask their amoral violence. While Twain thus measures his characters in terms of the polarization endemic to his melodramatic imagination, he is as a consequence even more hard-put to counter his nihilistic humor. To put his problem simply: easy and important as it is to pillory false sentiments, whether manly or feminine, how does one create genuine emotions?

At his best in *Huck Finn*, Twain makes use of several strategies. In the case of Jim, many of whose most powerful and moving speeches are blatantly sentimental, the need that gives rise to his utterance goes a long way toward authenticating his feelings. Consider his famous denunciation of Huck in the fog episode, as the evidence of the leaves and brush on the raft make it clear to him that Huck has played a trick:

"What do dey stan' for? I's gwyne to tell you. When I got all wore out wid work, en wid de callin' for you, en went to sleep, my heart wuz mos' broke bekase you wuz los', en I didn' k'yer no mo' what become er me en de raf'. En when I wake up en fine you back agin, all safe en soun', de tears come en I could a got down on my knees en kiss' yo' foot I's so thankful. En all you wuz thinkin 'bout wuz how you could make a fool uv ole Jim wid a lie. Dat truck dah is *trash*; en trash is what people is dat puts dirt on de head er dey fren's en makes 'em ashamed." (*HF* 105)

Although partly concealed by the dialect, the terms Jim uses are the stuff of stage melodrama from the plaintive "all wore out wid work, en wid de callin' for you" through the extravagant "my heart wuz mos' broke" to the final stock avowal "de tears come." The extremity of his emotion is revealed in his improbable insistence, "I didn' k'yer no mo' what became er me en de raf'," a notion which, if taken seriously, diminishes Jim's character and negates not only his desire for freedom but also his status as a loving husband and father.[4]

Yet despite its clichés and its palpable exaggeration, the speech rings somehow true. Its authenticating power comes partly from the dialect, which recasts the familiar, trite phrases just enough to give them freshness, but mostly from a sense of legitimacy. The speech seems appropriate, first because Huck has abused their friendship and treated Jim shabbily, and second because the system of slavery has—until this moment—silenced Jim by denying him the right to assert his feelings to a white person. Jim breaks the long silence of chattel-hood, of non-being, laying claim at last to his humanity, and the enormous urgent rightness of this act validates his utterance, no matter how caught in cliché it is, no matter how extravagant it seems.

In a similar way, Jim's grieving over his wife and children flirts with but finally evades the sentimental. The moment of revelation—Huck discovers that Jim cares "as much for his people as white folks does for theirn" (*HF* 201)—begins with Huck's own rather intensified report of Jim's behavior. Twice he says Jim was "moaning and mourning," and then he quotes Jim's repeated lament, keeping its true-sounding dialect, but structuring it for maximum emotional effect through repetition: "Po' little 'Lizabeth! po' little Johnny! it mighty hard; I spec' I ain't ever gwyne to see you no mo', no mo'!" (*HF* 201). With its haunting refrain, "no mo', no mo'," Jim's expression of anguish—or Huck's version of it—has all the tenderness and melancholy of a traditional slave Sorrow Song. Jim's final account of his response to the discovery that his little daughter is deaf and dumb announces tears and presents a loving gesture—both the stuff of melodrama—to render not only grief but also self-incrimination: "O, Huck, I bust out a-cryin', en grab her up in my arms en say, 'O de po' little thing! de Lord God Almighty fogive po' ole Jim, kaze he never gwyne to fogive hisself as long's he live!'" (*HF* 202). Again the dialect tones down the highly charged conventional phrasing. However, just as the need to assert his selfhood bolsters Jim's passionate speech to Huck in the fog scene, so here Jim's strong emotions are authenticated by the power of his repressed paternal love.

In these two moments Twain achieves what he sought—and missed—in *Tom Sawyer* and *The Prince and the Pauper*: an authentic language of the heart. He transforms the material of melodrama, using it not as it traditionally functions to overstate the obvious but to suggest in a vivid, compacted moment what is hitherto unknown—and not believed—by both Huck and his society: Jim's human dignity in the first instance, his loving fatherhood in the second. Twain exploits a sentimental language in situations that, by virtue of their intensity, turn its extremity into credible expression; he makes the excess of the language consonant with the enormity of the generating circumstance. He does more. By having Jim express himself in the language of the heart, he aligns him with the soft-talking women of his tale rather than the hard-talking men. In fact, Twain feminizes Jim almost as much as Stowe does Uncle Tom, though, unlike her, he also de-Christianizes his slave. He also shows that Jim's emotional centering is, like that of the women, in the domestic. (Of course, as a slave Jim has little access to the public sphere.) In Jim, Twain recuperates not only the power of the heart parodied in Emmeline's verse but also the value of the family violated in the raftsman's tale of Charles William Albright.

The strategies he deploys to authenticate Jim's emotions are viable precisely because of Jim's status as dehumanized "other." In Jim's case, the language of the heart functions chiefly to restore what the society of the antebellum South, the postbellum South, and indeed of the entire United States, then to now, tends to deny: the kinship and equality of an African American. But Twain's liberation of Jim in this way is itself problematical. If the expressive mode of that humanity as well as the sentiments it expresses are bogus and debased (as the burlesque of sentiment suggests), then Jim has gained participation in nothing more than a generally, perhaps generically, damned human race. Do Jim's emotional outbursts emancipate him from the nonpersonhood of chattel slavery only to leave him enslaved within the expressive and normative systems of a fraudulent white culture? To truly free Jim Twain needs to authenticate in some way the validity of that culture's claims to compassionate emotion.

"If I'd a knowed what a trouble it was to make a book I wouldn't a tackled it," Huck tells us in his famous closing (*HF* 362). The kind of book he has made is a hair-raising, tear-jerking adventure story that most often centers in the palpitations of the heart. Odd as it sounds, Huck often writes to the moment in a manner reminiscent of eighteenth- and nineteenth-century novels of sentiment. Unlike the extended analysis typical of those novels, however, Huck always reports on his emotional states briefly. Famous for his flat, matter-of-fact style—and for the empiricism it seems to suggest (Manierre)—he actually situates a surprising amount of his narrative in his own emotions: "I set perfectly still, then, listening to my heart thump, and I reckon I didn't draw a breath while it thumped a hundred" (*HF* 100); "I took one slow step at a time, and there warn't a sound, only I thought I could hear my heart" (*HF* 133). Such moments of tension, fear, and expectation—of the *felt* apprehension of experience—are characteristic of Huck's narrating. Through Huck, Twain writes a *comedy* of tense, confused, and turbulent emotion. He turns Huck's anxieties into cause for laughter, not fear. Often he has him speak of his feelings in comically literalizing metaphors: "My heart jumped up amongst my lungs" (*HF* 48); "my heart shot up in my mouth" (*HF* 259); "My heart fell down amongst my lungs and livers and things" (*HF* 311). Twain's humor insistently qualifies Huck's emotionalism, disguising, or more precisely, transforming, his writing to the heart's moment.

Huck's emotional states run a gauntlet from boredom to excitement to depression, from fear to vexation to pleasure, from curiosity to engagement to joy. Like Jim, as he narrates the varying conditions of his heart, he sometimes appropriates the expressive mode of the women, despite his fame as the quintessential male hero on the run from the entangling skirts of a smothering domesticity (Baym). Only once perhaps does he notably make use of the male mode, and when he does so it is not the brag and swagger (postures quite foreign to Huck) of their style but its capacity to express joy that he emulates: "So, in two seconds, away we went, a sliding down the river, and it *did* seem so good to be free again and all by ourselves on the big river and nobody to bother us. I had to skip around a bit, and jump up and crack my heels a few times, I couldn't help it" (*HF* 259).

Having evaded in the opening both the world of domesticity at the Widow Douglas's house and the world of male brutality at Pap's cabin, Huck ventures free for a time only to be entangled in the Wilks episode in the collision between these spheres. Critics have long acknowledged that this encounter is a pivotal one for Huck, stirring his latent sympathies, prompting him to overcome his characteristic passivity, compelling him to act (Fiedler, *Love and Death* 583–84; Towers, "Love and Power" 33–35). The episode restages some overly familiar plottings of melodrama: the collapse of a loving family, the plight of orphaned girls, the machinations of villainous men, the mystery of contested identities, the threat of mob violence, and the effort of an unlikely hero to rescue and defend vulnerable young womanhood. The events are theatrical in the extreme—from tearful greetings to violent denunciations, from vows of secrecy to public tests of veracity. In the end they reach a wildly sensational climax in the graveyard in the dark of night amidst raging storm under lightning-streaked skies as the agitated crowd exhumes the corpse of Peter Wilks, hoping to read on the dead body itself the signs that will reveal at last the true and the fraudulent, the marks that will define unequivocally the good and the bad. This is pure melodrama.

Yet Twain's rendering of all this is so permeated with humor that it borders on parody. The tearful scenes are undercut by Huck's disgust at their fraudulence as well as their excess. "I never see two men leak the way they done," he observes before denouncing the King's protestations of sorrow and trial and gratitude as "tears and flapdoodle," "rot and slush" (*HF* 212–13). The "family" reunion at dinner, a hearth and home scene reminiscent of Dickens, is similarly exposed when Huck notes the "humbug talky-talk" taking place "just the way people always does at a supper, you know" (*HF* 221).

The evil of the Duke and the King is comically incompetent in the extreme (yet still menacing). They parade ridiculous lies so improbable that only a town of chuckleheads could give them credence for more than the time it takes to hear them, if that, given that the fabrications are conveyed in a language whose ludicrously mistaken terms—*orgies* for *obsequies*—proclaim their falsity. The plot to steal the money also turns comic as the bag of gold gets moved around, in slapstick fashion, from cellar to bedroom to coffin. The funeral service, a standard occasion for theatrical lamentation, is a farce: it is conducted by an unctuous undertaker humorously described by Huck as having "no more smile to him than there is to a ham"; it is interrupted by the "most powerful racket" of a dog attacking a rat; and it is conducted throughout with music from a "colicky" melodeon (*HF* 232–33). In the Wilks affair even Huck, who is usually an adroit liar, botches it as he tries to conceal the cause of Mary Jane's departure by stretching the mumps to include "measles, and whooping cough, and erysipelas, and consumption, and yaller janders, and brain fever" (*HF* 245). But just when the comedy seems to have destroyed the melodrama, Twain has the mob cry out, "Le's duck 'em! le's drown 'em! le's ride 'em on a rail," and shout, "If we don't find them marks, we'll lynch the whole gang!" (*HF* 256). And as Twain's storm breaks overhead, Huck, writing to the moment from the heart, concludes, "This was the most awful trouble and most dangersome I ever was in. . . . Here was nothing in the world betwixt me and sudden death but just them tattoo-marks" (*HF* 257). Even as he mocks sentimentality, laughs at sensationalism, and burlesques melodrama, Twain exploits them for their standard effects.

In the figure of Mary Jane, Twain recuperates the tearful style he ridicules in Emmeline—and in the antics of the Duke and the King. Mary Jane is an emotional vortex: she cries over the arrival of the false uncles, cries over their apparent generosity, cries over the separation of the slave family, and cries over Huck's goodness in planning to rescue her and her sisters. Pointedly, Twain sometimes makes her sound a little like one of Emmeline Grangerford's poems. "O, dear, dear," she exclaims, "to think they ain't *ever* going to see each other any more!" (*HF* 238). Yet for all of their lachrymose effusiveness, Mary Jane's emotions, like Jim's, are authentic. Unlike Emmeline's, Mary Jane's emotions have a true foundation in experience (she does not lament dead strangers). She is emotional, but her emotions are presented as honestly heartfelt. At least one critic has suggested that her ethic of generosity, of putting love before principle, is not only the equivalent of Huck's when he decides to go to hell by rescuing Jim from slavery but is even the cause of that moral decision (Towers, "Love and Power"). Certainly her insistence to her sister Joanna that "the thing is for you to treat him *kind*" (*HF* 225) both echoes Huck's own earlier strictures about what is wanted "above all things" on a raft—"for everybody to be satisfied, and feel right and kind toward the others" (*HF* 165)—and anticipates his later feelings for Jim. In the very episodes in which he mercilessly assaults varieties of false sentimentality through the Duke and the King, Twain is struggling to affirm "*real* sentiment, that "rare and godlike thing."

To endorse Mary Jane's good heart, Twain has Huck contract a case of puppy love that leads him to celebrate her goodness as well as her beauty. Huck's exclamations ring true not only because they arise from his experience but also because they are usually couched in the vernacular: "She had the grit to pray for Judas," "there warn't no back-down to her," and "in my opinion she was just full of sand" (*HF* 244). Huck sums up his admiration for her courage and fortitude and loveliness and goodness by saying, "She lays over them all" (*HF* 244). Here Huck's vernacular covers his own sentimentality.

But it is not always so effective. At times when Twain lets Huck utter his strong emotions, their expression depends on clichés and threatens to become more syrupy than sweet. A case in point is Huck's final thought of Mary Jane as he runs from the graveyard to the raft: "But at last, just as I was sailing by, *flash* comes the light in Mary Jane's window! and my heart swelled up sudden, like to bust, and the same second the house and all was behind me in the dark, and wasn't ever going to be before me no more in this world" (*HF* 258). The sentimentality of Huck's swelling heart is checked somewhat—but also intensified—by his extravagant colloquial "like to bust," but even his incorrect grammar cannot quite contain the maudlin excess of the melancholy "wasn't ever going to be before me no more in this world." Ironically it, too, recalls the mournful Emmeline, who entitled one of her paintings *Shall I Never See Thee More Alas* (*HF* 137).

Decisive things happen to Huck in the Wilks episode. In a novel crafted of echoes, parallels, and repetitions (see Doyno 223–52), Mary Jane's announcement of Huck's own previously articulated desire for *kindness* turns Huck's longing (it is more an emotional state than a rational principle in Huck) back against himself, leading him to act on behalf of the vulnerable sisters. It also sets the stage for the imminent conflict between his "sound heart" and his "deformed conscience." Both Huck's success in articulating his affection for Mary Jane through his emotion-laden colloquialisms and the difficulties he has because of the taint of the Emmeline style also anticipate that heroic struggle. In one sense, the problem—for Twain at least—is how to find the words to convey Huck's heartfelt emotions.

From almost every perspective, the heart of Huck's heartrent narrative is the famous and increasingly controversial "All right, then, I'll go to hell" passage. Analyses, especially those of Smith, have focused on the way Twain brilliantly internalizes in Huck and allows him to put into words the "perverted moral code of a society built on slavery." In Smith's account, the clash between this code and Huck's heart is "depicted by means of a contrast between colloquial and exalted styles," and he notes that the style of the official morality, of the deformed conscience, is "the rhetorical equivalent of the ornaments in the Grangerford parlor" (*Development* 122). But the clash is anything but a clear-cut verbal opposition. As he deploys the exalted style in Huck's narrative, Twain subverts it. The rhetorical heft of "letting me know my wickedness was being watched all the time from up there in heaven" is shattered by the comically literalized (and Pap-Finnized) sense of divine ordination: "the plain hand of Providence slapping me in the face" (*HF* 268). On the other hand, less obvious, or at least less often commented on, is Twain's elevation of Huck's vernacular.

Twain makes Huck's first response to the discovery that Jim is gone a powerful description of action rendered in simple, direct colloquial language: "I set up a shout—and then another—and then another one; and run this way and that in the woods, whooping and screeching; but it warn't no use—old Jim was gone. Then I set down and cried; I couldn't help it" (*HF* 266–67). To generate further emotion, however, to jerk a tear or two, Twain then stretches Huck's typical syntax and charges it with subordinate constructions that suspend and so intensify the unfolding feeling: "After all this long journey, and after all we'd done for them scoundrels, here was it all come to nothing, everything all busted up and ruined, because they could have the heart to serve Jim such a trick as that, and make him a slave again all his life, and amongst strangers, too, for forty dirty dollars" (*HF* 268). Over and over as the debate between heart and social code is fought out, terrifying Huck ("I was so scared"; it "made me shiver" [*HF* 269]), Twain intensifies Huck's vernacular, pushing it toward the rhetorically sentimental: "I would do the right thing and the clean thing"; "I was full of trouble, full as I could be"; "I felt as light as a feather, right straight off, and my troubles all gone" (*HF* 269).

In the famous passage in which Huck, thinking about the trip down river (the word *thinking* is reiterated four times), revisions Jim, Twain further intensifies the vernacular, most notably through rhythmic structuring. First, he deploys the balance of antithesis: "and I see Jim before me, all the time, in the day, and in the night-time, sometimes moonlight, sometimes storms"; and then, he resorts to a lyric repetition generated by coequal, continuous gerunds: "and we a floating along, talking, and singing, and laughing" (*HF* 270). While seeming to be straightforward reporting—first this, then that, then that—the passage evokes activities in such a way as to build from the neutral (floating) to the joyful (laughing). Twain brilliantly elevates Huck's vernacular utterance without fancifying his words. He poeticizes his speech to make it match the tenderness, the quickness, and the depth of his heart.

The heartfelt in *Huck Finn* is always a matter of two things: individual ontology and idiosyncratic rhetorical mode. Feeling, as Twain presents it, emanates from and bears the stamp of individual subjectivity. Thus Jim's most powerful feelings arise from his need to break free of the confinements, the imposed silences and constricted self-actualizations, of slavery. Mary Jane's cries of the heart, on the other hand, come from her temperament (she is a passionate redhead) and from her heightened emotionality. Huck's good-hearted feelings well up from his core of sympathy, from his compassion, from his ability to feel with and for others. While sharing a reliance on many of the rhetorical conventions associated with sentimental women, each of these three most heart-moved characters expresses emotion in a distinctive manner. Jim's dialect refashions the clichés it uses; Mary Jane's intensity squeezes the saccharine from her sentiments (in some sense her energy authenticates her emotions despite their often trite expression, turning what is languid in Emmeline into something vital); and Huck's vernacular, with its incorrect grammar, odd phrasings, and poetic rhythms, vivifies his feelings. Different as Twain makes these characters, ontologically and rhetorically, in making them all susceptible to the heartfelt, he establishes the moral center of the novel.

Increasingly, however, his affirmations of sound-heartedness have come under attack. There is by now something of a tradition that critiques the concept of emotion as a guide to conduct. The position is nicely summed up by Lee Clark Mitchell: "The problem is a logical one, and results from an inherent conflict between concepts Huck unwittingly elides in his concern to feel right. The phrase collapses together antithetical categories by implying that emotion can legislate a standard of reason, that ethical issues can be measured affectively" ("Authority of Language" 85).[5] Basing morality on emotion seems to remove it from logical analysis, to insulate it from community adjudication, and to drain it of rational principle. Further, and perhaps most devastatingly, it seems to make morality entirely a matter of individual responsiveness, thus opening the prospect of something like ethical anarchy. These are unmistakably trenchant objections, yet equally unmistakable is Twain's trust in the heart. And far from imagining that such trust could rupture into moral chaos, he seems to feel secure not only in the heart's correctness but also in its commonality. Has he let his own heart cloud his mind?

Perhaps. One thing to note, however, somewhat deconstructively, is that in the character and actions of Mary Jane Twain himself dramatizes at least some of the dangers of relying exclusively upon the heart. Mary Jane is clearly duped—mistaken and misguided—when she lets her affection prompt her to sponsor the Duke and the King's charade as her uncles. She has, of course, a certain psychological need to do so, to somehow fill the familial void left by the death of her father. Unlike Huck's heart-driven need to help Jim, Mary Jane's endorsement of the Duke and the King is instantaneous, perhaps irresponsibly spontaneous. Huck's heart, on the other hand, receives a long tutelage before it impels him to act.

Despite modifying counterexamples, Twain's confidence in the heart is luminously at the center of the novel. This triumph of the heart has everything to do with Twain's insistent melodrama. Peter Brooks has argued convincingly that for certain nineteenth-century realists, notably Balzac and Henry James, the rendering of the surface of life was insufficient; their imaginations strained to evoke a morality eroded by the loss of traditional faith and by the corrosive force of rational skepticism. Brooks calls the realm they seek to animate the "moral occult," and he defines it as "the domain of operative spiritual values which is both indicated within and masked by the surface of reality. The moral occult is not a metaphysical system; it is rather the repository of the fragmentary and desacralized remnants of sacred myth. It bears comparison to the unconscious mind, for it is a sphere of being where our most basic desires and interdictions lie, a realm which in quotidian existence may appear closed off from us, but which we must accede to, since it is the realm of meaning and value" (5). In Brooks's analysis, this realm of occluded meaning and value is called forth in realistic texts by melodrama. "The melodramatic mode," he says, "in large measure exists to locate and to articulate the moral occult" (5).[6] Twain's melodrama, with its polarization of good and evil and especially its sentimental valorization of the heart, seems to arise from his instinctive belief in some such realm of morality. While he certainly does not suggest in *Huck Finn* that the plain hand of Providence guides human affairs (whether with a slap or not), he does seem to feel that wickedness is being watched, if not by God, if not by a moral society, still by some internal individual monitor that knows the right and wrong of things. He trusts the heart because it is in touch with a hidden realm of moral meaning and value.

Such an orientation is at the core of Twain's conventional character. It is the legacy of Sam Clemens's Protestant upbringing; it is linked to the moral values Twain assumed as reformer in the West; it is consonant with the best values of his Victorian traveling; it is consistent with the promise of Clemens's courtship; it is of a piece with the ethical systems of *Tom Sawyer* and *The Prince and the Pauper*; it is the empowering source of Mark Twain's late performances, both written and oral, as Sage; and it informs the self-representations of his final autobiographical dictations. In short, it is the heart of proper Mark Twain.

Twain's melodrama with its sentimental affirmations and his humor with its denigrations are constantly commingled in *Huck Finn*. The two together create the fundamental dynamic of the novel: what is undercut

through the disruptive humor is reestablished through sentimental melodrama, only to be subjected once again to humor, which in turn calls for
yet another reassertion through melodrama, and so on. What Twain's
humor strips down, his sentimentality builds up; and what his sentimentality elevates, his humor brings down. The humorous and the sentimental arise from conflicting impulses in Twain and express antithetical
notions that paradoxically serve the same psychic end. On the one hand,
the humor negates its objects, suggesting that the world is morally mean-
ingless, while on the other, the melodrama values its subjects, positing
an ethical order. But both the humor and the melodrama originate in
the release of the repressed for author and (sympathetic) reader alike: the
humor unleashes anarchic urges that violate taboo to bring pleasure; the
melodrama sets loose primal desires that break through a rational skepticism to provide a moral order. As the book vacillates between blatant
comedy and muted emotionalism, a vision of nihilism alternates with a
vision of meaning. Each begets—necessitates—the other, and there is
no end to their exchange as long as Twain himself is divided between annihilating humorist and affirming melodramatist.

This essential division creates yet another problem with the ending of
Huck Finn. Who is to get the last word? Twain's self-representations in
Life on the Mississippi, the portal to *Huck Finn*, foretell his answer, but the
final adjustments in the novel actually create a precarious balance.

In the final sequence at the Phelps farm, the Great Evasion, Twain recuperates the domesticity that his comic plotting has mocked in the earlier sections of the novel.[7] Although concern over the treatment of Jim
has obscured it, the fact is that the Phelps household is presented—its
tolerance of slavery notwithstanding—as a pretty good country place.
Aunt Sally and Uncle Silas are good country people. The hypocrisy of
Miss Watson, the brutality of Pap, and the pretension of the Grangerfords
are all replaced here with honesty, kindness, and simplicity. Even the civilizing that Huck chafed under at the Widow's gives way to unbridled
freedom at the Phelps farm, as Tom and Huck establish dominion in a
lenient world of love (and muddleheadedness). Huck's journey thus finds
its terminus within a hospitable home and loving family. In the midst of
the slapstick of the Evasion, Twain waxes sentimental over domestic love.

The heart receives its final celebration in the Phelps episode. Jim, of course, sacrifices himself, gives up his freedom, to save Tom, and however misplaced his loyalty may seem, there is no mistaking its nobility. Nor is there any gainsaying Twain's endorsement of it. He directs his irony at those who can only conceive of Jim's goodness in racist terms—the doctor, for instance, who insists Jim "ain't a bad nigger" and says that "a nigger like that is worth a thousand dollars," and the farmers who decide to acknowledge Jim's sacrifice by promising not to "cuss him no more" (*HF* 352–54). Within this racist world, however, Twain creates a final sense of the power of the heart. Although Tom and Huck toy with the emotional Aunt Sally throughout the Evasion, in the end Huck cannot evade the commanding force of her love.

Her visible love bends him to her will, and he curbs his impulse to run off to see about the wounded Tom in order to avoid causing her further pain. He acts, reluctantly to be sure, in keeping with the injunction given to Tom Sawyer by Aunt Polly: "pity us" and "save us from sorrow." Huck reports the decisive encounter with Aunt Sally at length, and the indirection of his discourse subsumes much of the emotional excess even as it signals it:

> And then when I went up to bed, she come up with me, and fetched her candle, and tucked me in, and mothered me so good I felt mean and like I couldn't look her in the face; and she set down on the bed and talked with me a long time, and said what a splendid boy Sid was, and didn't seem to want to ever stop talking about him; and kept asking me every now and then, if I reckoned he could a got lost, or hurt, or maybe drownded, and might be laying at this minute, somewheres, suffering or dead, and she not by him to help him; and so the tears would drip down, silent, and I would tell her that Sid was all right, and would be home in the morning, sure; and she would squeeze my hand, or maybe kiss me, and tell me to say it again, and keep on saying it, because it done her good, and she was in so much trouble. (*HF* 349–50)

Evoking rather than directly asserting, Huck's indirect discourse manages to have things two ways: it announces the sentimental and makes it distant enough to seem acceptable. Twain climaxes the heart-full episode by picturing Aunt Sally in the stock image of the loving, sacrificing mother of sentimental Victorian fiction. As Huck discovers by sneaking out of bed and down the drainpipe three times, she sits up all night, with a candle burning in the window, waiting for Sid (aka Tom). The emotion of this powerful image is released through Huck's flat, matter-of-fact account with its stream of conjunctives: "And the third time, I waked up at dawn, and slid down, and she was there yet, and her candle was most out, and her old gray head was resting on her hand, and she was asleep" (*HF* 350). On a miniature scale, this enshrining view matches in its precision, its tenderness, and its simple lyricism Huck's more famous description of sunrise on the river. Both passages are so charged with affection as to become celebrations.

Twain thus brings *Huck Finn* to the doorstep of a most unexpected closure. His melodramatic urge sentimentally cherishes the home, the family, and, above all, the good heart of a loving mother. But, of course, for Mark Twain this is "out of character," and he can no more let it stand than he could let himself be seen moved to tears over Sunday school in Hannibal. And so the humorist gets the last word: "But I reckon I got to light out for the Territory ahead of the rest, because aunt Sally she's going to adopt me and sivilize me and I can't stand it. I been there before" (*HF* 362). Huck's vexation counters—but hardly counterbalances—the sentimental representations that precede it. His last word is not the whole story, nor is Mark Twain's disavowal of sentimentality the whole truth.

CHAPTER SEVEN

Sage

During the 1880s Sam Clemens launched himself vigorously into public affairs and speculative business ventures as well as literary undertakings. He confidently assaulted the world, expecting—and often achieving—success at every turn. This decade, in the very middle of which *Huckleberry Finn* appeared, was perhaps the most spectacular in Clemens's life. No matter what the custodians of high culture thought, *Huck* sold well, and Mark Twain's fame continued to spread—indeed, he continued to spread it. He toured for four months with George Washington Cable as one of the "twins of genius" (the only one who *was* a genius, in his private estimation). He appeared frequently for after-dinner and special occasion speeches, making over ninety such appearances, almost triple the number of such outings he made in the previous decade. His books were popular, and the market for them was steady. He was satisfied with both the sales of his books and their content; he explained to Howells what he told himself about his work: "Everybody reads it, & that's something—it surely isn't pernicious, or the most respectable people would get pretty tired of it" (*MTHL* 2:586).

In the 1880s he increasingly appeared as more than just a famous author and lecturer. As a mugwump, stumping for Cleveland, he was active as a serious politico; as co-owner of the Charles L. Webster Company, issuing Grant's *Memoirs*, he was a talked-about publisher; as the principal backer of the Paige typesetting machine, steadily raising capital, he was a notable entrepreneur; and as the friend of presidents, generals, and captains of industry, as well as other writers, he was a public man of prominence and perhaps even influence. He exuded confidence—and he made news. The publicity surrounding Grant's heroic efforts to finish his memoirs, for Mark Twain to publish, for instance, was matched only by the public sensation over the profits that finally accrued.

He clearly rode high tides, but some had treacherous undertows. He formed a company and sent his own emissary to the sultan of Turkey to secure an exclusive franchise for a railroad from Constantinople to the Persian Gulf. However, the company was a paper one, and his emissary, Grant's son Jesse, only got as far as London. He dispatched his personal ambassador to meet with Pope Leo XIII to arrange for the publication of a definitive biography. His ambassador, Charles L. Webster, was received, and in due time the biography appeared with the pope's "Encouragement, Approbation, and Blessing," only to fail commercially (qtd. in Kaplan, *Mr. Clemens and MT* 289).

His extravagant ventures in the 1880s reflected his personal sense of power and authority. His multifarious roles consumed his time, energy, and eventually his money, but they were obviously satisfying. For a time he believed that he was a business whiz, political power, and public force for the good. The postures of authority, morality, propriety, and command assumed in his writings seemed to be confirmed in his life.

Ironically, in the midst of his prosperity and confidence, Clemens experienced a growing intellectual uncertainty. In his notebooks during the 1880s and 1890s, he explored privately some philosophical truths that troubled him. Sometime early in this period, probably in the first half of the 1880s, he worked out three statements of his metaphysical belief. He never published these manifestos, probably because they were so personal, but they document his general view of the human circumstance. In brief, his credo (he begins the first of the three, "I believe") is this: he believes in God; he believes that God created the universe; he does not believe in either scriptural revelation or divine intervention in human affairs; he is uncertain whether or not there is an afterlife; he believes that morality is created by humankind; he believes that religion is irrelevant to a hereafter but that it may provide consolation in this life; and he believes that Christianity, by emphasizing "the humaner passages of the Bible," has created "the highest and purest and best" people in "modern society" (*WIM* 56–59). Thus formulated, his belief is a modification of traditional religious outlook, radical in its disconnection of God from human life and in its skepticism about afterlife, but highly orthodox in its moral emphasis. His affirmation of "the highest and purest and best" is wholly in keeping with the proper Mark Twain. However, as he extended his reflections and focused just on humankind in such later manuscripts as "The Character of Man" (1885), "Letter from the Recording Angel" (c. 1887), and "Man's Place in the Animal World" (1896), his notions took a distinctly cynical turn. While acknowledging some noble qualities in humanity—gentleness, love, courage, devotion, among them—traits which he had surreptitiously (or not so surreptitiously) imparted to Huck, he dwells on all that is base: malice, cowardice, hypocrisy, greed, revenge, self-interest, cruelty, indecency, vulgarity, and obscenity. Afraid or re-luctant to publish these ideas directly as his own, Clemens eventually ex-pressed many of them in Mark Twain's fictions.

He worked many of his new ideas into his next two major fictions, *A Connecticut Yankee in King Arthur's Court* (1889) and *Pudd'nhead Wilson* (1894). The two texts are linked opposites. *A Connecticut Yankee* is a first-person narrative; *Pudd'nhead Wilson* is a third-person omniscient. Whereas *A Connecticut Yankee* moves imaginatively back in time to sixth-century Arthurian England, *Pudd'nhead* is set in the antebellum river world of Hannibal. And while *A Connecticut Yankee* is vast in its scope and broadly comic, *Pudd'nhead* has a restricted focus and is acidly satiric. Yet the two fictions share this: an insistent urge to reveal dark truths about society, humanity, and life itself.

To tell the dark truths that were perplexing him, Twain tried out a posture that he would assume in his major fiction, his nonfiction, and his public appearances for the rest of his life: he became the Victorian Sage.

THE SAGE IS BOTH a familiar and elusive figure in nineteenth-century Anglo-American writing. The groundbreaking study of the role, John Holloway's *Victorian Sage: Studies in Argument*, defines the Sage very gen-erally as one who undertakes in fiction or nonfiction "to express notions about the world, man's situation in it, and how he should live" (1). His aim, according to Holloway, is "to make his readers see life and the world over again, see it with a more searching, or perhaps a more subtle and sensitive gaze" (296). More recently, in *Elegant Jeremiahs: The Sage from Carlyle to Mailer*, George P. Landow has seconded Holloway's sense of the Sage and provided an exhaustive taxonomy of the Sage's techniques that emphasizes his preoccupation with "diagnosing the spiritual condition of an age" (18). The archetype of the Sage was the biblical prophet, but the Victorian Sage was more often than not a secular spokesperson, less concerned with the future than the present. Speaking with absolute assurance, with a personal certitude born of—indeed necessitated by—the collapse of traditional authorities, the Sage offers warnings about the evils of the time and wisdom about those things that are timeless. While the Sage may speak on many subjects, ultimately every Sage attempts "to define some crucial aspect of the human" (Landow 43).

The best-known Sages, those writers who shaped the tradition, are Carlyle, Emerson, Newman, George Eliot, Thoreau, Arnold, and Ruskin. But another group of late-nineteenth-century American reformers also held forth in the manner of the Sage, though seldom with the artistry of the major literary Sages. This group is variously known as the Best Men, the Genteel Reformers, or the Liberal Reformers. They might also be called the Genteel Sages. The group included Thomas Bailey Aldrich, Charles Warren Stoddard, Charles Eliot Norton, Edmund Clarence Stedman, Richard Watson Gilder, and George William Curtis. Like Clemens, they experienced what historian Jackson Lears has described as ontological weightlessness (32–47); they wondered anxiously who they were, what was real in their culture, and what their lives meant. And so, like Clemens, they struggled to formulate credos, to define themselves anew, and to reform society. They faced an unsettling doubt of authority. Simply put, accelerating change seemed to invalidate the traditional norms and sanctions of Victorian culture. Authority, whether religious, political, or social, was no longer self-evident. In fact, for many, including those who longed for it as well as those who challenged it, authority of any kind no longer seemed legitimate. It was up to a Sage to provide the sanctions jeopardized by this loss of authority. The Genteel Sages were all either established or, like Clemens himself, newly arrived members of the middle to upper classes. Often experiencing, or fearing, social displacement, the result perhaps of what Richard Hofstadter has termed the "status revolution," these men were outraged moralists, frequently bitter, often frustrated, seldom hopeful, who brought to bear on the realities of a machine culture the ethical shibboleths of a preindustrial age

(Hofstadter 131–73; see also Higham, and Lasch, "Moral and Intellectual Rehabilitation"). They believed in personal propriety, in property rights, in democratic government, in laissez-faire capitalism, in a moral order, and in the centrality of ethical character to good government (Tomsich; Sproat). They tried to reform the Gilded Age by returning it to traditional standards of simple right conduct. Clemens makes an odd bedfellow with them, being free of their high-toned piety, but in his Mugwump and Entrepreneurial phase his general outlook was theirs. And like them, he appropriated to himself the authority of the Sage.

Assuming the posture of Sage seems, at least in the perspective of this study, a natural culmination of the various conventionalities at work in Mark Twain's writings. Certainly the role of Sage is a perfect one for the serious side of the Mark Twain persona: the moralist within the humorist who wanted to instruct his audiences. It is also one that fits the traveler who amused himself abroad by judging the people and cultures of other civilizations. The courtship postures he assumed as man of the world, man of feeling, and man of letters coalesce in the Sage who knows the world well enough to analyze and criticize it, has the tenderness to care about reforming it, and possesses the skill as writer to make his pronouncements convincing. Even the desire to create a standard work on Mississippi River life by exposing what was false in its style of civilization is of a piece with the Sage's intent to establish norms for society to follow. And surely Twain's interest in the basis of right conduct, though worked out under the guise of boy adventure, is indicative of the Sage's serious thinking on fundamental aspects of the human. Underlying these expressions of the proper Mark Twain, informing them all, is his feeling of authority and his conviction of personal rectitude.

A Connecticut Yankee is Twain's first full-scale performance as Sage. His impulse to become a Sage in that work had a particular impetus: he was angry at Matthew Arnold.[1] The preeminent English Sage, Arnold had annoyed Twain with his remark about him as "the jovial, genial man of our middle-class civilization" (qtd. in Budd, *Social Philosopher* 119), with his criticism of the style of Grant's *Personal Memoirs*, and with his attack on "Civilization in the United States," especially his indictment of the American "addiction to the 'funny man'" (qtd. in Baetzhold 119). Twain replied in speeches when he could and plotted more full-scale rebuttals, filling his notebooks with jottings against Arnold, England, monarchy, and aristocracy, some of which eventually worked their way into *A Connecticut Yankee*.[2] More important, however, than any specific material prompted by the tiff with Arnold is the frame of mind Twain first found himself in—and then imparted to Hank.

To set things straight, Twain gave Hank precisely the stance of superiority, authority, and certitude that Arnold himself employed as Sage. In a sense, Twain undertook to out-Arnold Arnold, though he did so with one crucial difference. "I prophesied myself baldheaded," Hank says as he travels with Arthur (*CY* 315), and the remark is revealing in two ways. First, it points to the role Hank quite self-consciously assumes as Sage, and second, it indicates that he is a specific adaptation of the general species. He is a *comic* Sage. If in some sense Twain undertook to meet Arnold on his own ground, he nonetheless preserved his commitment to humor, fielding as his champion a Sage who utters wisecracks as well as wisdom. To make the "funny man" Arnold had objected to into a Sage was, of course, to turn the tables on Arnold with a vengeance. For Twain, however, at least in the 1880s, humor itself had a "serious purpose," one that made it a perfect counterpart to the Sage's effort "to make his readers see life and the world over again." The aim of humor, he wrote to Yale when the university awarded him an honorary master of arts degree, is "the deriding of shams, the exposure of pretentious falsities, the laughing of stupid superstitions out of existence" (*N&J* 3:299). Thus both serious pronouncement and comic flippancy drove toward the same end: the establishment of truth.

Hank Morgan, Twain's truth sayer, is both voice and character. As a character, he is a severely unstable person, a compound of conflicting opposites: pragmatist and sentimentalist, revolutionary and reactionary, democrat and autocrat, optimist and pessimist, a man of reason and a man of heart, a hater of control and a lover of power, a self-belittling common man and a self-vaunting showman. Troubling to some critics, these oppositions actually make him a prototypical modern figure. Lacking a constant core of being, Hank's identity is, like that of the modern self that comes into prominence at the turn of the century, ontologically uncertain and experientially discontinuous. His inconsistencies probably reflect Twain's growing intuitions about the self, intuitions that find definitive expression in *Pudd'nhead Wilson.* In any case, he gives this version of modern selfhood a paradoxical role in his tale. Hank both undermines all established authority, thereby fomenting in the imagined sixth century the very crisis of Twain's own era, and relocates in himself the authority missing in the culture, Twain's as well as his, thereby resolving the critical impasse.

As voice, Hank becomes the mouthpiece for Twain the Sage. Holding forth with confidence, Hank expresses at one time or another the leading ideas of the Genteel Sages, most of which were the commonplaces of Twain's time among the respectable middle class. Like the Genteel Sages, he advocates responsible democracy in politics, laissez-faire capitalism in economics, and traditional courtesies, especially sexual delicacy in speech and behavior, as well as polite respect in social arrangements. He believes, broadly speaking, in Victorian civilization. His convictions make him, as Louis J. Budd has shown, the proponent of a very traditional liberalism (*Social Philosopher* 111–44). Asked at one moment by Arthur to prophesy the immediate future, Hank cleverly distinguishes between prophets who can see only into the near future—"stump-tail prophets," he derisively calls them—and those who can penetrate the mysteries of far-distant times (*CY* 314–15). Being from a time over thirteen centuries away, Hank sets himself up as a long-seeing Sage, but judged from a nineteenth-century perspective in terms of the common ideas he espouses, he is only a stump-tail.

Hank describes himself as an all-American pragmatist, a "Yankee of the Yankees—and practical" (*CY* 50), and he often dismisses idealist epistemology with fervent conviction: "Words realize nothing, vivify nothing to you, unless you have suffered in your own person the thing which the words try to describe" (*CY* 324–25). Of course, he confronts a paradox that looms before any would-be reformer: he wants to alter the factual world, to change the shape of things as they are, through language, which is always at least one remove from things as they are (and may even be entirely disconnected) and through conceptions, which are themselves mediated by language.

Despite his sometimes misleading assertions to the contrary, in his efforts to revolutionize the world in which he finds himself, Hank is, as Jeffrey L. Duncan, has argued, "a rank idealist" (207). He believes in the supremacy of conceptions, and he tries to achieve reform through the power of his ideas articulated in words. In this, too, he is at one with the Genteel Sages. His latent idealism is visible in his conversations with Sandy (he finally elicits from her not the facts of her experience but some abstract configuration of it) as well as in his willingness to let his own identity and power derive from such conceptualizations as the boss, prophet, and magician. While continuing to express astonishment at Arthurian idealists, he accepts and exploits the efficacy of the "unproven word" (*CY* 282). The grandest expression of his own philosophical idealism, however, one that is both comic and tragic, is his "Proclamation" in the face of the Church's interdict. "*A Republic is hereby proclaimed,*" he announces to a people who do not even know what a republic is, "as being the natural estate of a nation when other authority has ceased" (*CY* 469). Here Hank's idealist metaphysic reveals itself to the full: the world is what he imagines it to be, what his *words* say it is.

Hank's tactics of persuasion are in keeping with his philosophical idealism, for he relies upon words—not empirical evidence—to effect change. Here is Hank holding forth as Sage:

> The truth was, the nation as a body was in the world for one object, and one only: to grovel before king and Church and noble; to slave for them, sweat blood for them, starve that they might be fed, work that they might play, drink misery to the dregs that they might be happy, go naked that they might wear silks and jewels, pay taxes that they might be spared from paying them, be familiar all their lives with the degrading language and postures of adulation that they might walk in pride and think themselves the gods of this world. (*CY* 111)

Seemingly directed at the subjugation of the lower classes in Arthur's England, the deliberate generality of this assertion allows it to torque with egalitarian fervor against the privileged of any time. In the name of truth Hank deploys not analysis or exposition but emotion, fielding verbs of oppression, "grovel," "slave," and exploiting extravagant clichés of violent suffering: "sweat blood," "drink misery," "go naked." The whole is structured in terms of melodramatic contrasts between the conditions of the lower and upper classes: starving/eating, working/playing, misery/happiness, nakedness/sumptuous attire, degradation/elevation. The whole is also cast into a rhythmic, poetic syntax. Voiced with absolute authority, it is an effective piece of rhetoric.

Twain's performance as Sage, his intent to enlighten his audience, to make them see "the world over again," is even more blatant when he has Hank concern himself directly with circumstances and concepts that specifically postdate the sixth century. Hank's well-known remarks about the French Revolution reverberate with the Sage's corrective instruction:

> There were two "Reigns of Terror," if we would but remember it and consider it: the one wrought murder in hot passion, the other in heartless cold blood; the one lasted mere months, the other had lasted a thousand years; the one inflicted death upon ten thousand persons, the other upon a hundred millions; but our shudders are all for the "horrors" of the minor Terror, the momentary Terror, so to speak; whereas, what is the horror of swift death by the axe, compared with life-long death from hunger, cold, insult, cruelty and heart-break? what is swift death by lightning, compared with death by slow fire at the stake? A city cemetery could contain the coffins filled by that brief Terror which we have all been so diligently taught to shiver at and mourn over; but all France could hardly contain the coffins filled by that older and real Terror—that unspeakably bitter and awful Terror which none of us has been taught to see in its vastness or pity as it deserves. (*CY* 157–58)

Animated by an urgent didacticism—the aim to teach what "none of us has been taught," the confident proclamation unfolds through a powerful set of symmetrical inequalities. It strives to persuade through its series of stark contrasts, through its emotional, kinesthetic diction, through its compounding syntax, and through such grotesque images as "swift death by lightning" as opposed to "death by slow fire at the stake." As he preaches his message with moral fever, Hank's style becomes ornate, elevated, and oratorical.

As presumed author of his own narrative, Hank writes in two styles; he uses both a low or vernacular mode and a high or genteel one. Some critics have claimed that a clear shift—from low to high—occurs in the course of the narrative and that the shift signals that Hank "has begun, unconsciously, to accept the most inhumane and aristocratic values of

Arthurian society" (Berthold 57). But, in fact, from the time of his arrival in Camelot, Hank looks contemptuously at aristocrat and commoner alike, denouncing them with a cynicism that reflects Twain's own darkening views. There is no real shift in his style and the values it manifests; style and value remain divided from the beginning to the end of his tale. More often than not, however, Twain turns to the high style as the medium for Hank's pronouncements as Sage.

As reforming Sage, Hank relies on the power of his words—elegantly arranged in the elaborate syntax of his high style. But in his urgency to create and transform reality through his linguistic utterances, he sometimes goes too far. He overstates his cases. It is as if his distrust of words, despite his commitment to them, forces him to heap them up, to persuade through excess. He frequently evokes pathos through verbal extravagance until, as often as not, the very thing he seeks pity for turns insubstantial. Here, for instance, is a part of his effort to bring home the horror of slavery, represented to him by a chained slave gang he encounters while traveling with the pilgrims to the Valley of Holiness:

> None of these poor creatures looked up as we rode along by; they showed no consciousness of our presence. And they made no sound but one; that was the dull and awful clank of their chains from end to end of the long file, as forty-three burdened feet rose and fell in unison. The file moved in a cloud, of its own making.
>
> All these faces were gray with a coating of dust. One has seen the like of this coating upon furniture in unoccupied houses, and has written his idle thought in it with his finger. I was reminded of this when I noticed the faces of some of those women, young mothers carrying babes that were near to death and freedom, how a something in their hearts was written in the dust upon their faces, plain to see, and lord how plain to read! for it was the track of tears. (*CY* 244)

From the opening designation of the slaves as "poor creatures," through the lurid image of "young mothers carrying babes that were near to death," to the dramatic final cliché, "the track of tears," Hank's description is designed to stir emotion. Through intense sights and sounds defined by valuative adjectives, "awful clank of their chains," he tries to tap his audience's feelings, to reach their hearts. His success is dubious, however, for the whole passage is too clearly staged. The interrupting recollection of tracing a finger over dust-coated furniture distances one from the immediate scene and seems both irrelevant and dispassionate. It betrays the fact that the whole is self-consciously "written up." The extended metaphor of signs written in dust finally consumes the reality of human suffering that it is meant to convey.

Time and again Hank creates, as he himself says, "another scene that was full of heart-break" (*CY* 333). There are several reasons for this. To begin with, as we have seen in this study, Twain himself is a sentimentalist as well as a humorist. He is susceptible to tears in church as well as Olympian ironies on Holliday's Hill. He believes, as his courtship so dramatically reveals, in gentle feeling as a sign of fine character. And, as *Huckleberry Finn* makes clear, he also believes in the heart as the sure guide to right conduct. Beyond these personal alignments, he participates in a tradition that valorizes emotion as the means of radical reform. As Philip Fisher has pointed out (*Hard Facts* 99–104), from about 1740 to 1860 the sentimental mode was the major literary tactic in the politically radical representation of Anglo-American writing. Sentimentality was the agent of insurrection employed to effect the extension of humanity to persons and classes oppressed by the culture. Children, slaves, women, political radicals, old people, and the insane were all sentimentalized in order to be humanized. Mark Twain, who usually feigned literary ignorance to emphasize his own democratic origins and interests, knew this mode well. It was the favorite mode of the lesser New England literati and of the Genteel Sages, and, of course, the single most effective piece of reforming sentimental fiction in the nineteenth century, *Uncle Tom's Cabin*, was written by his neighbor. To be sure, Twain's sentimentality in *A Connecticut Yankee* is neither as insistent nor as excessive as Stowe's, and it is relieved by a wild humor, but like hers, it is predicated on the twin assumptions that the heart is the key to social change and that the sentimental mode is the way to reach it.

In making Hank a sentimental reformer, Twain placed himself in a significant tradition, indulged an important dimension of his own sensibility, and reflected an inveterate impulse of the Genteel Sages. But there is even more at work in his preference for sentimentality as the medium of reform argument.

Twain makes Hank a champion of manhood: he repeatedly condemns what he sees as unmanly and celebrates his glimpses of what he takes to be manly. Most often his condemnations are directed at servility, weakness, fear, or the willingness to endure injustice out of a sense of helplessness; his celebrations are occasioned by defiance, strength, courage, or the readiness to risk death in order to correct wrong. Reflecting the gender bias of his time (indeed, of *both* his times), he proclaims that only the unmanly would suffer or permit oppression. In all this, his thinking flows along very traditional lines. But Twain also gives Hank the kind of heart lessons Aunt Polly gave Tom Sawyer and instills in him the essential soft-heartedness he made so evident in Huck Finn. In effect, dealing in this novel with an adult rather than a child, Twain dramatizes a manhood centered in large measure on compassionate feeling.

Hank himself sometimes apologizes for his soft emotions, playing them off against traditional male thinking. "You can't reason with your heart," he says, suggesting that he wishes he could; "it has its own laws, and thumps about things which the intellect scorns" (*CY* 229). At other moments, however, he seems sufficiently resigned to his own emotionality to define it as an indisputable element of general human nature: "We don't reason, where we feel; we just feel" (*CY* 140). Just as Twain had disguised his own (feminine, he thought) sentimentalizing in *Huck Finn* with a recurrent burlesque of sentimentality, so he makes Hank a rough-and-tumble traditional male in order to cover the gentle heart within him. However, for all of his burly talk, his aggressive impulses, and his predisposition to violence, Hank is Twain's fullest portrait of a man strengthened—indeed, made a man—by his soft emotions. Possessing such manhood, Hank becomes the champion of manly character as heart-governed character. He praises it in aristocrat and commoner alike, even finding King Arthur, as he says, "sublimely great" as he ignores personal danger to carry the young girl dying of smallpox to the arms of her weeping mother (*CY* 332).

The cultural influences at work in Twain's depiction of manly character remain to be determined. If there was a crisis of masculinity in America in the closing decades of the nineteenth century, as historians have maintained, Twain seems significantly caught up in it. Building on the impulses of his own character as well as conventional Victorian ideals, he makes Hank both a "manly" man and a "womanly" man. To be more precise, he unites in Hank attributes usually associated with character formed and sustained by the doctrine and practice of separate spheres: Hank reflects not only the traditionally masculine traits of individualism, aggression, and competitiveness but also the equally traditional feminine qualities of connectedness, sympathy, and cooperation. He is interested in the homeplace as well as the marketplace; he is a loving husband and father as well as an ardent capitalist. He waxes sentimental over home and family even as he strives to create a capitalist, industrial economy most often thought to be antithetical to the domestic. As advocate of civilization—itself a conflicted discourse invoked by different groups in Twain's time to rationalize contesting notions of manhood (see Bederman)—Hank, no less than Harriet Beecher Stowe, would have the heart at the center of public life as well as home life.[3]

His sentimental style, then, is of a piece with his basic conception of manhood. To put it baldly, he often writes from the heart to the heart, and imagines such a transaction to be a sign of manly character. Speaking as authoritative Sage, he announces: "A man *is* a man, at bottom. Whole ages of abuse and oppression cannot crush the manhood clear out of him" (*CY* 346). His vision of the revolutionizing power of manhood is probably as close as he ever comes to achieving every Sage's aim of defining "some crucial aspect of the human." Plot reinforces pronouncement on the issue of manhood, for Hank's plan for revolution centers on his Man Factory. If the phrase itself seems to hint at a dehumanizing production of the human, the plan nonetheless signals Hank's belief in the absolute necessity of making men "men" in order to bring about change. Especially striking in all this is the moral emphasis. Like the other Sages, English as well as American, Hank—or rather Twain—conceives of reform as a matter of personal character. Although he mentions institutions and systems, he finally ignores them in his preoccupation with manhood. For him, as for the other Sages, political, social, and economic change depends on personal character. For him, as for the other Sages, questions of public policy are ultimately issues of individual morality (Tomsich 96ff.).[4]

Like the other Sages, then, he lectures his age, assuming the authority of a cultural elite and expecting to move the masses to his idealist visions through ornate rhetoric, sentimental representation, and an appeal to moral character centered in a good heart. Hank fails, of course, and to a degree Twain fails with him. Although in the contemporary reviews there was some praise for *A Connecticut Yankee*'s democratic principles, there was also a great deal of carping about irreverence (see *CH* 148–81). The performance as Sage, in several senses a trial for Twain, seems to have misfired. His wisdom was not embraced. With a curious prescience, he has Hank confess, "I have done some indiscrete things in my day, but this thing of playing myself for a prophet was the worst" (*CY* 315). He is not a very sagacious Sage.

Ironically, at the very moment he was discovering himself as Sage through Hank, Twain was ever more firmly embracing the conventional. However, part of his difficulty may lie not in his ideas but in his reliance on a sentimental style. To the extent that he substitutes extreme rhetoric, excess emotion, and syntactic poetry for rational analysis, he in fact reflects a flaw common to many Victorian Sages. As Camille R. La Bossiere has argued convincingly in *The Victorian "Fol Sage,"* such displacements of the logical often served to "make the work of the public teacher of wisdom nugatory" (9). Twain himself seems to have been dissatisfied with Hank's performance as Sage. As defeat closes in around Hank during the Battle of the Sandbelt, Twain has him both acknowledge the shortcoming of idealist thought—"How empty is theory in the presence of fact!"—and lament his reliance on emotion as a means of persuasion, calling his sympathy for the nobles and his appeal to them to surrender for the sake of their families so many "mistimed sentimentalities" (*CY* 480–81). Perhaps the mode of persuasion he had adopted as Sage seemed dubious to Twain in the end.[5]

Writing confidentially to Howells after *A Connecticut Yankee* was finished (in what has now become a famous letter), Twain explained his moral and emotional state: "Well, my book is written—let it go. But if it were only to write over again there wouldn't be so many things left out. They burn in me; & they keep multiplying & multiplying; but now they can't ever be said. And besides, they would require a library—& a pen warmed-up in hell" (*MTHL* 2:613). Clearly the desire to tell truths has replaced the urge to relate tales; the Sage has superseded the storyteller. While his pen cooled down in the years following *A Connecticut Yankee*, the impulse to comment on life and human nature—to criticize, inform, clarify, and instruct—did not abate. And in his final major fiction, *Pudd'nhead Wilson*, Twain found a new mode of address for himself as Sage.

ALTHOUGH SELDOM NOTED, a key fact about *Pudd'nhead Wilson* is that it is set in Dawson's Landing. If the St. Petersburg of *Tom Sawyer* and *Huck Finn* recalls Hannibal as both a heavenly paradise for boys and the seat of tyranny tantamount to czarist control, Dawson's Landing gives it another curious turn. The name refers to Clemens's childhood school teacher, John D. Dawson. The name "Dawson's Landing" thus suggests not only a site of riverbank loading and unloading but also a school teacher's arrival—or even a school teacher's platform. Reimagining his boyhood home yet again, Twain thinks of it this time as a place of instruction. Accordingly, he makes his title character, Pudd'nhead Wilson, a writer of almanacs filled with whimsical humor, pragmatic wisdom, and what Twain calls "a little dab of ostensible philosophy" (*PW* 25). Like Hank before him, Wilson functions as an outlet for Twain as Sage.

While he toyed with epistemology in *A Connecticut Yankee*, playing idealism off against empiricism, in *Pudd'nhead Wilson* Twain mystifies knowledge and in the process problematizes the role of teacher or Sage. Hank Morgan had thirteen centuries of future history at his disposal, and so he felt himself to be, and performed as, an all-knowing Sage (and a know-it-all Yankee). But in *Pudd'nhead Wilson* Twain makes knowledge hard to attain, for he is at pains to show that the real is always carefully secreted. From its opening, "A Whisper to the Reader," in which he playfully imagines Dante pretending to watch the erection of Giotto's Campanile when he is, in fact, on the lookout for Beatrice, to the conclusion, in which a full confession of hidden crimes is obtained, he centers his tale on the attempt to discern concealed truth through vigilant surveillance.

Twain plots his tale around the fact of secrecy, and he designs the acts and metaphors of the text to emphasize concealment. He imagines Dawson's Landing as a community of cloaked identities and hidden histories, a world in which everyone dissembles and nothing is what it appears to be. The F.F.V.s hoodwink the town, concealing their rapacious self-interest beneath a cloak of decorum and disguising their displacement of God with self behind a mask of piety. Roxy hides her subversive insurgency, posing as the compliant mammy of southern myth, and after she has switched the infants, the true slave passes as free, while the real heir unwittingly lives as a slave. Wilson himself conceals his intelligence from the town that dubs him a pudd'nhead. And on a lesser note, the foreign twins obscure parts of their personal history. In a powerful metaphor that endows the hidden self with economic power and religious holiness, Twain has Judge Driscoll exclaim the code by which his society lives: "A man's secret is still his own property, and sacred" (*PW* 78).

The text underscores the duplicitous nature of the individual and of the community by foregrounding acts of deceit. Twain uses the stock stuff of melodrama to figure the world of seeming: the changing of the babies, the assumption of disguises, the putting on of social roles, the feigning of ignorance as well as the pretending to knowledge, the acting out of calculated parts in both domestic spheres and social arenas, and the general, insistent staging of appearances. The concealed identities hide the profound social truths of concern to Twain in this text. He sees and structures his story to let the reader see that the moral society is made immoral by race slavery, that the ordered social world is disordered by miscegenation, that humane concerns are subverted by speculative desires, that a democratic body politic is ridden with aristocratic biases, and that a benevolent paternalism is actually a rapacious patriarchy. As Susan Gillman has observed, the book is finally about the "problem of knowledge"; it is about "the mechanisms by which we persuade ourselves that the constructed is the real" ("Sure Identifiers" 89, 103).

Given that so much is concealed, it is no wonder that Twain casts his hero as a detective. Wilson seems to become a detective somewhat by chance after his fatal remark about killing half a dog has relegated him to pudd'nhead-hood in the eyes of the town, but the urge to know—and to have the power that comes from knowing—is deep in his character. After the practice of law is closed to him by the prejudice of the town, he survives as a part-time surveyor and accountant. His real interest, however, lies in surveying his fellow townspeople, and his true bookkeeping is fingerprinting. He is a police chief's dream. Patient as his own microscope, dispassionate as a machine, and methodical to a fault, he sets about gathering what he calls each person's "natal autograph," one that its owner cannot disguise (*PW* 108–9), thus hoping at some level of consciousness to penetrate the cloud of mystery that veils the town. He is an inveterate, compulsive observer, a spy upon the community, who keeps his own secrets even as he works to discover those of others. Much of the plot hinges on the fact that he repeatedly peers from a window in his house through a window in Judge Driscoll's to observe the secret affairs transpiring there. He wants to see without being seen; he is the detective as Peeping Tom. (The mix of surveillance with voyeurism is hinted at when what Wilson thinks he sees is "a young woman where properly no young woman belonged"—and goes right on looking [*PW* 32].) He tries to oversee people and events. At a crucial juncture his seeing actually creates what is seen, since it is his seeing the similarities between the slave and free babies that gives Roxy the idea of switching them. To see is to control, as vision becomes supervision, so there is a logic in Wilson's becoming mayor as he solves some of the crimes that plague Dawson's Landing.

Although Clemens's interest in detectives is usually attributed to his times, to such real and fictive things as the Pinkertons, dime novels, and Sherlock Holmes, it is also congruent with his peculiar psyche and his formative childhood experience. On the highly personal level, the other side of Clemens's famed love of being conspicuous was his obsession with privacy. Making a spectacle of himself as Mark Twain for his wife, family, friends, readers, and audiences, Clemens nonetheless resented intrusions into his private life. He insisted that for all his public living there was, as he once said to Livy's mother, "a secret chamber or so in my being which no friend has entered" (*L3* 91).

Many of his own darkest discoveries about life seem to have come about through acts of peeping. He peeps from hiding to discover a dead man in his father's office (*IA* 139); he peeps—through the keyhole—to witness the autopsy performed on his father (Wecter 116). And the medium of knowledge remains the same when things turn the other way: practicing, he confesses in his autobiography, his part as a bear for a play, prancing

about naked, he is peeped at by two giggling girls (*AMT* 37–40). Fundamental realities are thus discovered, in Twain's remembering, through
furtive, covert glimpsing. The concealed is discovered from concealment, as the young Sam spies on the world. Some such sense of how the
hidden is found out seems to arise in Mark Twain whenever he imagines
Sam's childhood past (*Tom Sawyer* and *Huck Finn* are full of peeping).
Three years after Clemens published *Pudd'nhead Wilson*, living in far-off
Switzerland but still dreaming of Hannibal, he wrote an extended series
of notes about the people of his hometown. Simply called "Villagers of
1840–3," these notes not only record thumbnail sketches of over one
hundred of his former townspeople, as Clemens tries to fix identities in
his remembrance as surely as Wilson tries to define them in his fingerprinting, but also reveal how Clemens came to know them. They show
Clemens himself at work as a Peeping Tom.

Twain's emphasis on the problem of knowing the truth compounds
the difficulty of performing as Sage. The Sage faces a double bind: as
Twain's text makes clear, he confronts the near impossibility of discovering the truth when it is both deliberately and accidentally concealed;
on the other hand, he is tasked to convey truth once it has been obtained
in a way that will be compelling to a world accustomed to deceit. Hank
finds it easy to know truth, and for most of his narrative he has confidence in direct pronouncement as a medium for conveying it. However,
in *Pudd'nhead* Twain casts his Sage differently. Twain's messages, the
truths that the Sage in him longed to teach, may have been burning within,
as he suggested to Howells just after he completed *A Connecticut Yankee*,
but in writing *Pudd'nhead*, he did not vent them directly; in fact, he
damped them down in several ways. Writing first the extravagant farce
from which he finally extracted *Pudd'nhead* was one way. Confused and
wasteful, that process allowed him to express all manner of outrageous—
and often gauche—notions. However, as he changed his fiction from
farce to tragedy, as his tale shifted from unnatural freaks, the Siamese
twins, to a natural human, David Wilson, he exerted more emotional and
conceptual control. He also employed a different mode. Having had his
first long say as Sage through the voice of Hank Morgan, he abandoned
such direct pronouncement in *Pudd'nhead Wilson* in favor of the indirec-

tions of irony. His teaching thus changes from simple assertions requiring only assent to complex observations and representations calling for interpretation.

His ironic mode is the perfect medium for conveying the world of mystery he imagines in *Pudd'nhead Wilson*. Recognizing from his own past that village life and character are hidden, that only a peeping child or an adult detective can glimpse their realities, he uses irony both to realize and to resolve his vision. It realizes it by presenting a discourse of multiplicity, a verbal text in which the said (indeed several, often different "saids") and the unsaid (indeed several, often different "unsaids") must be negotiated. His irony creates a linguistic world in which the characters— and readers—must weigh statements to detect whether they mean what they say or mean exactly the opposite, just as the characters—and readers—must examine costumes and social roles to see whether they disclose the real or cloak something hidden. His irony resolves his vision, however, in that, properly apprehended, it clarifies.

Such an ironic mode—and *Pudd'nhead Wilson* is his most sustained ironic performance—poses risks for the Sage, as Twain well knew. In two telling self-reflexive moments, he dramatizes the danger. Wilson's ironic dog joke befuddles the townsmen who hear it, with disastrous consequences, and his almanac witticisms, when shown about by Judge Driscoll as proof of Wilson's superior intellect, fail to amuse and enlighten. The townspeople, Twain says, "read those playful trifles in the solidest earnest, and decided without hesitancy that if there had ever been any doubt that Dave Wilson was a pudd'nhead—which there hadn't—this revelation removed that doubt for good and all." The problem, Twain points out, is that "irony was not for those people." But then to compound the ironies at work here he explains the Judge—who does understand irony—very much in the aphoristic manner of Wilson's calendar: "That is just the way, in this world; an enemy can partly ruin a man, but it takes a good-natured injudicious friend to complete the thing and make it perfect" (*PW* 25).

Writing an ironic text, Twain the Sage risks not only the incomprehension of his readers but also the miscalculations of even friendly interpreters. The ultimate irony in all this is that the text exposes ironies lost on Twain himself. He may teach in his ironic mode of the social con-

struction of reality. He may impart messages about race slavery, miscegenation, male dominance, racial hostility, class pride, and material obsession, but what he fails to detect, ironically, are all the manifestations
of his own latent racism, sexism, and elitism.[6]

Although the calendar headings, which I will take up in a moment,
are the clearest signs of Twain's urge to hold forth as Sage, his carefully
plotted story also conveys his teachings. In his opening note to *Those
Extraordinary Twins*, the famous note in which he belittles his talent as a
novelist, defining himself as only a "jack-leg," Twain significantly lays
claim to three areas of knowledge as a writer: he knows "a locality," "an
incident or two," and most of all "some people" (*PW* 119). It is that
knowledge of people, or more generally of human nature, that leads him
to his most important lesson as Sage.

Long ago, Frederick Anderson suggested that David Wilson was mod-
eled on Clemens's brother, Orion ("Introduction," *PW* x). When he
made the connection between Orion and Wilson, Anderson was thinking of Orion's long, indeed lifelong, futile struggle to practice law, but
the figure of Orion was also suggestive to Twain in more profound ways.
In "Villagers," Clemens says Orion was "as capricious as a weather-vane"
(*AI* 106), and while Wilson is, if anything, steady to a fault, what Clemens
thus cryptically recalls about his brother is an aspect of his character that
does, in fact, go to the heart of Wilson and to the philosophical center
of the fiction ironically named for him.

In the figure of Orion, Clemens witnessed—and Mark Twain made
creative use of—a stunning instance of a radically fragmented self. As
he makes clear in his private discussions of him, Orion was not just as
changeable as a weather vane. He was a composite of contradictory selves.
Clemens explains and laughs over this unique phenomenon most exten-
sively in an early letter to Howells (9 Feb. 1879). Urging his friend and
fellow writer to "put him in a book or a play right away," he details much
of his brother's feckless career, from his grand scheme to write a burlesque of *Paradise Lost* to his humble work as a proofreader, from his efforts to succeed as a lawyer (in over four years he is said to have made
only twenty-six dollars while paying annual office rent of sixty) to his
venture into chicken farming (*MTHL* 1:253–55). But Clemens also sees

something more peculiar in Orion than a mercurial temperament that shifts him from task to task. He records several instances in which Orion is said to occupy two different identities *at the same time*. Thus he plans to write both an exposé of religion and a defense of it against the sacrilegious Robert Ingersoll. At one time he is simultaneously a democrat and a republican; at another he is simultaneously a true believer, indeed a deacon and Sunday School teacher in the Congregational Church, and a "confirmed *infidel*" (*MTHL* 1:253).

One recognizes in this account of Orion's many contraries exactly the divisions that Twain used to depict the twins in the original tale, "Those Extraordinary Twins," from which he extracted *Pudd'nhead Wilson*. It is no wonder, then, that, if we are to believe his account of his own creative process, "a stranger named Pudd'nhead Wilson" showed up in the fiction to displace the twins (*PW* 120), for both the twins and the emerging stranger were versions of Orion. With Orion as a model, Twain makes Wilson, a serious—unlike the twins, who are farcical—example of a radically fragmented self that challenges the traditional conception of a unified human identity. To reveal such a figure, to make such a challenge, is Twain's most ironic teaching as Sage.

This face of *Pudd'nhead Wilson* has been perceptively examined from an anthropological point of view, and judiciously assessed in terms of the postmodern, by George E. Marcus. In an illuminating essay, he suggests the ways in which Twain's text employs divided, doubled, and crossed selves to problematize "the main ideological premise of bourgeois, middle-class life in the West—the priority and irreducibility of the autonomous individual as the meaningful, coherent actor in social life" (191).[7] In his reading, while Roxy, Tom, and Tom-and-Chambers are all arresting representations of divided, doubled, or crossed selves, Pudd'nhead Wilson himself is merely "Twain's double," serving as "a kind of reflective panopticon standing for Twain within the novel itself" (203). For Marcus, the "flirting with multiplying selves, beyond doubles" in the text "remains partial" (209), and Twain finally succumbs to "imposing unity on a fragmented self by repeatedly attributing to his creations whole selves in the form of their base and natural characters" (203). But Twain's tale may push further than Marcus's analysis acknowledges. To

see twins, somehow halves of a whole, and then switched twins is to con-
front the dizzying possibility of *four* identities in one. And in Wilson himself, and this brings us back to the originating figure of Orion, Twain creates not just his double but a man who is a multiplicity of selves—three
certainly, maybe even four.

From first to last in the text, Wilson is a compound of two profound
contraries. These opposed selves may be most clearly seen in his first
appearance in Dawson's Landing and his final courtroom performance.
However one reads it, Wilson's fatal remark about wanting to own half
of the barking dog in order to kill his half is an oblique, ironic commentary on the community he is just then entering. Covertly the remark
mocks the society that divides into black and white, slave and free, an
indivisible humanity; further, it critiques the categorizing essentialist
thought by which such divisions are constructed and institutionalized in
science, law, and more broadly still, social mores. It is his attack on the
fictions of law and custom by which the community lives, and it marks
him as a critical antagonist of the society, a fact tacitly recognized when
the town defensively dubs him pudd'nhead. Yet at the story's close, Wilson appears in court, using science and law, precisely the kinds of arbi-
trary constructs his initial remark seems to have mocked, to reestablish
the artificial social order he appeared to have exposed when he first arrived in Dawson's Landing. He functions in the end as an apologist for
the status quo. It is this contradiction, born of a basic antinomy of being,
that leaves the reader reeling with what one critic has called "moral ver-
tigo" (Porter, "Roxana's Plot," 136).

The epigrammatic chapter headings, nominally from Pudd'nhead Wilson's Calendar, generate the sense that Wilson's dual identity is further
divided. Despite their attribution to Wilson, and despite the moment in
the text in which his writing of an almanac is acknowledged, the fact is
that the epigrams just don't *feel* like his. (They feel like Mark Twain's, of
course, which is one reason why critics like Marcus see Wilson as Twain's
double.) It is impossible to square the attitudes expressed in the epigrams,
as well as their tones, with what we see of Wilson in the narrative proper.

With the possible exception of his barking dog joke, nothing Wilson
says suggests the kind of astringent wit in the epigrams. Nothing he does

suggests the wealth of experience from which they seem to emerge. The epigrams constitute truths that range from the trite (*"Nothing so needs reforming as other people's habits"* [*PW* 73]) to the silly (*"We know all about the habits of the ant, we know all about the habits of the bee, but we know nothing about the habits of the oyster. It seems almost certain that we have been choosing the wrong time for studying the oyster"* [*PW* 80]), and from the jaunty (*"Let us endeavor so to live that when we come to die even the undertaker will be sorry"* [*PW* 27]) to the bitter (*"Why is it that we rejoice at birth and grieve at a funeral? It is because we are not the person involved"* [*PW* 40]). They are perhaps most memorable in their dark estimates of life, human nature, and cosmic ordering, and again there is nothing in the narrative, no action of his or statement of his, to suggest that such notions are Wilson's. In fact much of his behavior is at odds with the darkest of the reflections. One cannot imagine the aspiring, upwardly mobile Wilson saying this, for instance: *"Whoever has lived long enough to find out what life is, knows how deep a debt of gratitude we owe to Adam, the first great benefactor of our race. He brought death into the world"* (*PW* 12). Nor can one imagine the dour bachelor Wilson saying, *"Adam and Eve had many advantages, but the principal one was, that they escaped teething"* (*PW* 17). In their pessimism but also in their gaiety they seem incompatible with the textual Wilson. Further, since the epigrams are set as epigraphs to each chapter—presumably selected by the author of the text, Mark Twain—they bestow an extratextual, or perhaps more accurately, a supratextual, identity on Wilson. He exists within and beyond the narrative. His identity, already divided in two within the narrative itself, is thus further partitioned.

The headings themselves may reveal one final split. One can account for this division by mood perhaps, but the epigrams seem to arise from—and point back to—on the one hand, a perception of life, one implicitly born of joy, that is playful, that finds pleasure in things, and on the other, a view of life, one implicitly born of distrust, that is cynical, that finds solace in despair. Wilson, who is firmly divided into three selves, may thus even have four.

More accurately, his identity is not divided into but composed of such multiple selves. Twain clearly confronts us with three: the apologist self of the close, the antagonist self of the opening, and the transtextual self of the calendar. They correspond closely to the divisions of self he later recorded in his private notebook as he solved what he called "a haunting mystery"—the conundrum of human identity. Setting aside the process by which he arrives at it, his conception is simply this: that the self is actually composed of three selves, a self in command during wakefulness, a self in charge during sleep, and a spiritualized self (*MTN* 350–52). Although imprecisely defined—Susan Gillman has perceptively analyzed this "hierarchy of selves" and found it "confused" (*Dark Twins* 52)— Twain's three selves are clearly analogues for the conscious, for the unconscious, and for some other part of being that is free of the bodily connections that bind both the conscious and the unconscious. He thus laid out in his notebook the same divisions of self he had written into Wilson's character three years earlier, for the apologist Wilson is a conscious self, the antagonist Wilson an unconscious one (who breaks aggressively through the constraints of the conscious mind once in his barking dog joke), while the transtextual self matches Twain's disembodied, spiritualized self. The point, however, is not to make an exact tie between the representation of Wilson and Twain's later triadic theory of identity, but to see that in addition to its manifold social concerns *Pudd'nhead Wilson* has a provocative, quite serious, ontological aspect— what might even be called, theoretical problems notwithstanding, a philosophical message.

Twain's desire to instruct, to be the new Dawson of Dawson's Landing, is most obvious in the calendar headings. They, more than anything, reveal his growing impulse to appear before the world, whether in fiction-making or speech-making, as a dispenser of wisdom, a Sage. Softened by whimsy, by folksiness, even, paradoxically, by the occasional shock of the untenable, the epigrams are coined to instruct as they amuse. Minuscule Mark Twain texts, they are meant to enlighten through entertainment. Since they originate less in the textual character of Wilson, more in the Twain-Who-Would-Be-Sage, it makes sense that they would be extracted, as they have been, from *Pudd'nhead Wilson* by later editors (who thus replicate a part of Twain's own creative process) and published separately. They have been given the status of independent texts. In popular culture they are thought of as the sayings of Mark Twain, while in the culture of letters they are sometimes dignified as his philosophy. Taken together, however, they are various enough to leave a stronger impression of momentary caprice than coherent worldview. Twain was proud of them, and of course he wrote another set to serve as chapter headings for his own final travel book, *Following the Equator*, thus encircling the world with his wisdom.

EFFECTIVE AS THEY ARE, and even extended as they would soon become, Twain's epigrams hardly constitute an adequate outlet for his desire to instruct as Sage. In the 1890s, despite the seclusion he sought after the death of Susy, and in the final decade of his life, despite family illnesses, Livy's death, and his own growing infirmities, Clemens performed happily as Sage in four venues, three public, one private. Publicly he wrote seriously as an essayist for the magazines, held forth magisterially as an after-dinner speaker, and spoke off the cuff in endless interviews. Privately he worked to fictionalize his philosophical outlook in the various manuscript versions of the Mysterious Stranger.[8]

The Mysterious Stranger is Twain's last major effort to shape his ideas, his beliefs and suppositions, into an instructive fiction. Never bringing any of his imaginings to final polish and conclusion, he left three manuscripts and a fragment. He worked on versions of his fiction, off and on, during a period of almost eleven years—from 1897 to 1908. Deciphering the chronology of the compositional process and the authority of each text is a bit of detective work that Twain—or rather, Pudd'nhead Wilson—would have relished (see Tuckey, *MT and Little Satan*). The three manuscripts, known now as the "The Chronicle of Young Satan," "Schoolhouse Hill," and "No 44, The Mysterious Stranger," differ significantly in specific setting, narrative voice, and final vision. (The earliest draft, the "St. Petersburg Fragment," was eventually incorporated into "The Chronicle of Young Satan.") Despite their differences, however, underlying all three versions are these drives: to reveal truths, to judge, and to teach.

Twain himself explained the impetus behind this writing quite clearly to Howells: "What I have been wanting was a chance to write a book without reserves—a book which should take account of no one's feelings, no one's prejudices, opinions, beliefs, hopes, illusions, delusions; a book which should say my say, right out of my heart, in the plainest language & without a limitation of any sort." The "say" he wanted to say right out of his heart was about "Man, & how he is constructed, & what a shabby poor ridiculous thing he is, & how mistaken he is in his estimate of his character & powers & qualities & his place among the animals" (*MTHL* 2:698–99). As it turned out, he would add to his central attack on man a condemnation of the moral sense, an insistence on the controlling force of training, a dark panorama of history, and a solipsistic explanation of human existence itself. To voice this vision he invented the Mysterious Stranger, an unfallen Satan, who visits earth to enlighten its inhabitants darkly. The figure has been examined so carefully in criticism that he is now anything but mysterious. His chief traits are superiority, omniscience, creative power, exemption from feeling, and dismissive contempt. He is, in the words of William M. Gibson, a "truth-speaker momentarily banished from heaven" ("Introduction," *MTMS* 15). Given the supernatural knowledge he is supposed to possess, the Mysterious Stranger is the ultimate expression of Twain as Sage.

Certainly through his Stranger Twain planned to perform the Sage's most basic function in the most radical way he could imagine: "to make his readers see life and the world over again" (Holloway 296). It is ironic, then, that this most powerful vehicle for Twain's didactic impulse remained silent, at least in Twain's lifetime, his dark messages sounding only in Twain's own mind. Various explanations have been advanced to account for Twain's inability to complete any of his three versions of the Mysterious Stranger. They range from a paralyzing personal despair (DeVoto, *MT at Work* 105–30) to his art having lost contact with reality (Paine, *MTB* 3:1519) to a disgust with humanity so strong as to leave him uninterested in writing about it any further (Smith, *Development* 184–88). But there is also an aesthetic problem, of which Twain himself seems to have been aware. In his letter to Howells he explained the form of his piece. "It is in tale-form," he said, and then he added with a confidence that betrays some anxiety, "I believe that I can make it tell what I think" (*MTHL* 2:698). His problem was finding a way to embed Satan's pronouncements ("what I think") in an engaging story (his "tale-form"). As artist—and he was an artist to the end—he was worried about the adequacy of his form for the task he was imposing on it; he was worried about the success of his craft.[9] His uneasiness emerges again at the close of his letter. "I hope it will take me a year or two to write it," he said, giving himself time enough, and then he added, "& that it will turn out to be the right vessel to contain all the ordure I am planning to dump into it" (*MTHL* 2:699).

Of the three versions of the Mysterious Stranger, "The Chronicle of Young Satan" probably comes closest to expressing the Sage's ideas, with perhaps two exceptions. Twain is not able in this story either to announce or give dramatic enactment to his notion of the tripartite self, nor does he manage to present in any way his sense that life itself is nothing more than a dream dreamed by the individual. These ideas are realized most fully in his third try, "No. 44, The Mysterious Stranger." The "Chronicle" does, however, otherwise convey a great deal of the "ordure" Twain hoped to load it with. It emerges in four ways: as direct pronouncement, as spectacle staged by Satan, as indirect discourse reported by Theodor Fischer, and as enactment through the events of the story. The direct pronouncements are most often rhetorically effective; the spectacles are sometimes pale, since they are reported by Theodor without much vivifying detail (oddly, they have little pictorial quality); the indirect discourse provides clarity but lacks the sharpness of direct speech (and after a while the reports sag through repetition); the enactments are generally compelling, especially those that convey the sense of life as a determined chain of choices and acts and those that represent human cruelty. These presentational strategies enable Twain to express his dark vision of human nature, history, and life in general with considerable variety and power. By making the character of Satan known to the three boys (and hence the reader) but not to the villagers, he is able to generate some mystery and several conflicts. He structures his story rather loosely along three plot lines: the doctrinal and financial tribulations of Father Peter, the familial, social, and emotional difficulties of Marget, and the success and seeming downfall of the wicked Father Adolf. When he ends his manuscript, the first two plots are resolved, and only the fate of Father Adolf remains in question. Further, by the termination of his draft Twain has more or less expressed his central ideas; he has had his "say"; the Sage has spoken. All but out of plot and having voiced his major ideas, he really has nowhere to go with the story; he can only repeat his basic conceptions. It is no wonder, then, that the tale trails off into extraneous episode.

The "Schoolhouse Hill" version is the least developed of the three. Twain evokes a familiar place, one more rendering, albeit a sketchy one, of Hannibal, introduces Satan and defines his nature, and shows him at work within the community, demonstrating his intellect at school (and his power in combat after school), rescuing townspeople stranded in a blizzard, and illuminating his host family and their domestics. Twain's emphasis is more on the town's reactions than on Satan. In this relatively brief manuscript, he is just starting his tale. The story is never unfolded, and he never gets to convey more than one or two of the truths—"what I think"—that he wants to announce as Sage. However, his working notes suggest how difficult it was for him to combine his ideas with his story. He somewhat desperately contemplates having Satan turn religious in order to have him preach. (In the other two versions, Satan is openly antireligious.) Twain makes this notation to himself:

> Proposes to join Pres. ch. Can't.
> Starts cch of Society for Eradication of the Moral Sense.
> He preaches. (*MTMS*, "Appendix B," 430)

This seems as unpromising as plot as it is promising for argument. It reveals the improbable measures Twain was driven to imagine in order to have his "say" through Satan as ultimate Sage.

The most fanciful of the stranger tales, "No. 44," is the best plotted. Since its plot carries many of Twain's messages, there is much less pronouncement in this version than in the "Chronicle," and what there is tends to be made in the form of quick remarks as opposed to Young Satan's long diatribes. Even No. 44's true nature is concealed here to become a matter of speculation on the part of August Feldner right up to the moment in which the dissolving Satan explains that he is nothing more than August's dream. (In both of the other versions, several people know who Satan really is.) Twain manipulates four plotlines: the mystery of No. 44's identity, a tale of conflicts within the print shop, a fantasy of duplicated selves, and a farce of crossed lovers. The narrative often jars in its sudden shifts and its gaps (Twain simply never gets around to resolving either the fate of the duplicates or the twisted love tale), but these also impart a kind of energy to the story. However, the character of 44 creates some problems for Twain. He makes this Satan the liveliest, most human, of all three versions of his stranger, for he depicts him as insistently boyish, a kind of magical Tom Sawyer. His temperament provokes August into complaining that he is "careless, capricious, unstable, never sticking to a subject, forever flitting and sampling here and there and yonder, like a bee" (*MTMS* 313). The character 44 is given to levity, to circus antics that rival, he says, Barnum and Bailey. He appears at different times playing a Jew's harp and dancing to his own tune, parading "like a princeling 'doing a cake-walk,'" and performing a minstrel show, replete with costume, blackface, and banjo (*MTMS* 299, 303, 354–56). Such frivolity and boyish showing off tend to undercut his authority when he utters Twain's dark truths. Further, since he is fully defined as an actor within all the multiple plots (unlike Young Satan of the "Chronicle," who remains at the margin of events, even when he controls them), 44 is seldom disengaged enough to elaborate dispassionately the truths Twain has in view.

The tension in Twain between his desire to spin a tale and his urge to state truths is well illustrated in this narrative by his use of the duplicates. Creating them, he complicates his story and makes it suggest a part of his triadic theory of self, but only a part. To get the full notion into the story, he is forced to have August Feldner simply report that Satan has told him that "each human being contains not merely two independent entities, but three—the Waking-Self, the Dream-Self, and the Soul" (*MTMS* 342). (For a different ordering of the multiple selves, see Kahn 137–50.) Further, to get his ideas into his narrative, he also turns other characters into his spokespersons. Perhaps sensing that 44's gaiety disqualifies him as an advocate of dark truths, Twain gives some of his ideas to August's duplicate, Schwarz, who bemoans his own mortal flesh—"this loathsome sack of corruption in which my spirit is imprisoned" (*MTMS* 369)—in terms that echo what the Satan of the "Chronicle" says of humankind in general: "Man is a museum of disgusting diseases, a home of impurities; he comes to-day and is gone to-morrow, he begins as dirt and departs as a stench" (*MTMS* 55). Yet in the end Twain makes his jovial Satan utter in all seriousness his famous annihilating, empowering, solipsistic explanation of human existence.

All three versions of the Mysterious Stranger are flawed in one way or another. All three betray the strain between pronouncement and dramatic representation; all three reveal the tension between Twain the Sage and Twain the storyteller. However, each has vivid moments in which some of the Sage's truths come clear. Many of the truths themselves are replays of Twain's credos and his speculations on the multiplicity of individual human identity, and many reiterate ideas argued somewhat tediously in his *What Is Man?* (a piece largely drafted in 1898, but not published until 1906). But Twain not only repeats notions expressed earlier. He also recapitulates thoughts common in western philosophy and current in his own day. As Sage, he proved highly conventional. Such ordinary conceptions as human selfishness, a problematic moral sense, the deterministic force of heredity and environment, doubt—or denial—of God and immortality, and the lodgment of reality in individual consciousness are not new. Even his notion of man as a machine, the key concept in *What Is Man?* and one asserted in the Stranger manuscripts, has, as Sherwood Cummings has pointed out, a history at "the folk level" (*MT and Science* 208). Needless to say, his complaints about human cruelty, immortality, cowardice, and vanity are even more familiar, being, among other things, the stuff of pulpit oratory. Ironically, the ideas that Twain took so seriously, and thought shocking, are commonplace. The proper Mark Twain was more proper than even he realized.

CHAPTER EIGHT

Personage

In April 1902 Mark Twain published in the prestigious *North American Review* one more utterance as Sage, "Does the Race of Man Love a Lord?" It was a topical essay, occasioned by the enthusiastic public response to Prince Heinrich of Germany's goodwill visit to the United States. As usual, Twain used the immediate event for wide-ranging reflections on human nature in general. He writes in a mode of rational analysis, and his argument, in brief, is that humankind not only loves lords (and other persons of distinction) but also envies them, because everyone longs for power and conspicuousness (*MTC2* 513). Contact with nobility yields the pleasure of "reflected glory" (*MTC2* 515), but the issue, Twain argues, transcends the lines of blood or social class: "Rank holds its court and receives its homage on every round of the ladder, from the emperor down to the rat-catcher; and distinction, also, exists on every round of the ladder, and commands its due of deference and envy" (*MTC2* 514). Twain insists that the head of any body, the "lord of a group," from millionaires to saloon politicians, commands respect, and so his or her notice pleases (*MTC2* 520); "we" are all susceptible to "flattering attentions" because "at bottom we are all alike and all the same" (*MTC2* 516). In the midst of this general argument, he suddenly provides an arresting example: "We all like these things [attentions, homage, distinctions] . . . and I felt just so, four years ago in Vienna (and remember it yet), when the helmeted police shut me off, with fifty others, from a street which the Emperor was to pass through, and the captain of the squad turned and saw the situation and said indignantly to that guard: 'Can't you see it is the Herr Mark Twain? Let him through.'" Twain remarks that while this event occurred four years ago, "it will be four hundred before I forget the wind of self-complacency that rose in me" (*MTC2* 517). The episode is double-edged. On the one hand, in offering himself as an example of universal human vanity Twain gently mocks himself, while on the other, despite his self-deprecation, he parades his fame with undisguised pride. What the passage reveals is that the Sage understands—and happily calls attention to—the fact that Mark Twain is a celebrity.

Mark Twain had, of course, been famous for years. He made a living by being in the public eye as writer, newspaper correspondent, comic lecturer, gadfly, after-dinner speaker, and man-with-a-notion about everything. (His daughter Clara wondered in *My Father, Mark Twain* how he "could manage to have an opinion on every incident, accident, invention, or disease in the world" [217].) But in the late 1890s, triggered by the steady spread of his writings, by his much-publicized bankruptcy, and by his world lecture tour, he became something more than a well-known person. He became a personage—not just a famous person but a person of importance, of consequence, of eminence. He had, to return to the terms of his own essay on popular adulation, become the "lord of a group," and he enjoyed his conspicuousness and power. He believed in his own preeminence, avowing privately in 1907 in his autobiographical notations: "I am quite well aware that for a generation I have been as widely celebrated a literary person as America has ever produced, and I am also privately aware that in my own peculiar line I have stood at the head of my guild during all that time, with none to dispute the place with me" (*AMT* 349). During the last two decades of his life, he was increasingly recognized as what he believed he was: America's foremost man of letters.

At least from the time of his marriage, Clemens had chosen to live as one of the privileged. Writing to his father, Howells explained his own circumstance—and what he took to be his friend's: "[Mark Twain] and his wife and Elinor and I are all of accord in our way of thinking: that is, we are theoretical socialists, and practical aristocrats" (qtd. in *MTHL* 2:579). One may question whether Clemens was even in theory a socialist, but he unmistakably enjoyed living as an aristocrat. Paradoxically perhaps, while his failing business affairs and eventual bankruptcy jeopardized the financial foundation of his privileged life, his decision to live abroad to economize actually brought him even more celebrity. During his so-called years of exile, 6 June 1891 to 15 October 1900, he was lionized abroad. When he wanted to (and for a time after Susy's death he did not want to), he was able to meet and be entertained by the cultural elite of Europe. He was most celebrated during his twenty months in Vienna, to which he moved in the fall of 1897, but even at the very beginning of his long sojourn in Europe he was invited to dine with so many people of distinction and so many people of royal blood that Jean was moved to exclaim, "Why, papa, if it keeps going on like this, pretty soon there won't be anybody left for you to get acquainted with but God" (*MTOA* 125).

In his public performances during the last fifteen years of his life, from the quick interview to the formal speech, Twain conducted himself as a personage. Playfully, he took himself seriously, and in turn, despite his fun, he was taken seriously. As he entered "the kingdom of personality" (Cox, *Fate* 297), he managed to amuse without offending—to appear as a seemly sage, full of opinions but generally holding forth well within the bounds of respectability. Indeed, as several studies have pointed out, the late Twain gauged public opinion and trimmed his sails the way the wind was blowing.[1] To put it in the terms with which this study opened, in his later years the bounded Twain was more visible than the transgressive. This is especially true in the final two major texts of his career, *Following the Equator* and the selections from his autobiography published in the *North American Review*.

UNDERTAKEN WITH SOME reluctance in the first place and denounced with vehemence after the fact, Twain's last lecture trip (the basis for *Following the Equator*) must have brought home to him as nothing before just how famous he was. He made the trip to make money to repay—in full, as he announced to the papers—the debts incurred though the failure of the Paige typesetter and the Charles L. Webster Publishing Company. The world tour was ambitious—from Paris (he liked to think of Europe as the starting point in order to have made a true circumnavigation of the globe on his return to England) to the United States to Canada to Australia to New Zealand to India to Ceylon to Mauritius to South Africa to England, all in just over twelve months (14 July 1895 to 31 July 1896). Accompanied by Livy and Clara, he recalled the trip as one in which he "lectured and robbed and raided for thirteen months" (*AMT* 263–64).

Although he had a great many health problems, publicly the tour was nothing less than a triumphal procession.[2] He was honored and feted everywhere. His notebooks brim with entries like the following from the Indian leg of the journey:

> Invited with family to lunch with Lord Sandhurst, Governor of Bombay, of Government House, Malaber [sic] Point, tomorrow. (MTN 272)
>
> Two interesting hours with Prince Kumar Shri of Pulitava. (MTN 273)
>
> This evening went to Belvidere and dined with the Lieut. Governor of Bengal—Sir Alexander MacKenzie and a dozen—a private dinner party. (MTN 276)
>
> Left Calcutta for Darjeeling in the official car of Mr. Barclay, Chief of Traffic. (MTN 277)

Lunches, dinners, receptions, and even balls were the order of his days. He was not only a social giant, however; he was also a great success as a lecturer. Attended by dignitaries as well as ordinary people, his lectures were often sold out, and the news reports of them were frequently glowing. On the tour that would become *Following the Equator*, Mark Twain was a personage for the world.

However grand his actual tour, turning the experience into his final travel book was an emotional as well as intellectual struggle. He wrote under the double duress of exhaustion from the trip and grief over the death of Susy. In a mortuary frame of mind just before beginning, he announced: "I shall write the book of the voyage—I shall bury myself in it" (*MTHHR* 235). Having completed it, he later explained to Howells, "I wrote my last travel-book in hell; but I let on, the best I could, that it was an excursion through heaven" (*MTHL* 2:690). For all of his before and after gloominess, Twain actually enjoyed the process of composition, as William R. Macnaughton has pointed out, in large part because the form of the travel book posed few constraints and opened itself to many facets of his creative personality (20). Everett Emerson accurately observes that *Following the Equator* is "the most elegant" of Twain's travel books, and he goes on to suggest that much of its grace was achieved through careful revision governed by Twain's consciousness of "the image of himself that he wanted to project" (*Authentic* 207).

The image he creates is not only that of a proper gentlemen of conventional morality but also that of a personage known and honored by the world. That stature is implied in the very first sentence of his book: "The starting point of this lecturing-trip around the world was Paris, where we had been living a year or two" (*FE 25*). Twain assumes that the reader knows about this trip, casually announces that it is a spectacular tour around the world, and offhandedly suggests his cosmopolitan life in Paris for "a year or two." Though the indirection is disarming, Twain thus begins his account by implying his fame, his elite life, and the grandeur of his excursion. He keeps his stature before the reader throughout his narrative. In the second chapter, as if marking his own rise to fame, he pointedly recalls two private meetings with General Grant, the first when Mark Twain was "wholly unknown to the public," the second, ten years later, when he was not only "better known" but known well enough to be asked to speak at the army reunion dinner honoring Grant on his return from his own world tour (*FE 37–38*).

Unostentatiously, for he is writing a decorous travel book, he notes his visits—most often by invitation—with mayors, governors, lords, princes, and generals. He makes it clear that he is the acquaintance of earls, lords, famous authors, and prominent politicians. In two charming episodes he even relates encounters with two different Indian gods (Jean's fancy is thus fulfilled), both revered, indeed worshiped, by "multitudinous followers" (*FE 366*). The first god seeks Twain out and surprises him by wanting to discuss "the philosophy of Huck Finn." Stunned by a god conversing about his book, Twain exclaims, "It is a land of surprises— India! I had had my ambitions—I had hoped, and almost expected, to be read by kings and presidents and emperors—but I had never looked so high as That" (*FE 367*). The second god not only receives him when he is "turning away Maharajas" but also asks to exchange autographs (*FE 511*). "I gave him," Twain reports, "a copy of Huckleberry Finn" (*FE 512*). Despite the playfulness of the narrative, and despite the tinge of religious skepticism that informs it, these episodes remind one just how famous Mark Twain is.

Several overtly comic moments also underscore his personage. He is famous enough to be impersonated. He learns of a Mark Twain Club, and the organization seems completely plausible, though he finally discovers it has only one eccentric member who poses as all of its officers and participants. And in a wonderfully zany moment, he describes Indian crows as singling him out (apparently even crows can recognize a celebrity) to make fun of—talking about "my clothes, and my hair, and my complexion, and probable character" and "how I had happened to go unhanged so long" (*FE* 355). He describes one crow as "always chaffing, scolding, scoffing, laughing, ripping, and cursing, and carrying on," always "delivering opinions" with an "impudent air," always cheerful and "satisfied with himself." This crow seems to be an analogue for—a critical yet nostalgic evocation of—the youthful Mark Twain (*FE* 353–54).

Through such comic and serious turns in his narrative, Twain keeps his stature apparent. It is a stature that derives chiefly from his achievements as a writer (hence the gift of his own book to a god), and that identity is reclaimed at the beginning of each chapter of *Following the Equator* in the chapter headings from "Pudd'nhead Wilson's New Calendar." The maxims vary from the morbid to the trenchant to the silly, but they all call attention to Twain the writer. They refocus the fact that he has created a famous character through whom he dispenses wisdom. They also position Twain within his narrative as Sage as well as Personage, Personage *because* Sage, as they encapsulate in memorable phrasing many truths about human nature, society, life, and death. The maxims keep Twain in view as a Victorian moralist, perhaps a dangerous one, certainly one with power. Twain himself comically makes the point. As he analyzes the Jameson raid in South Africa, explaining with pleasure its multiple miscalculations, he notes that Jameson took with him eight heavy Maxim guns, Gatling guns that could fire some 500 bullets a minute, and then he says, "Jameson should have furnished himself with a battery of Pudd'nhead Wilson maxims instead. They are much more deadly than those others, and they are easily carried, because they have no weight" (*FE* 683). Deadly or not, heavy or weightless, Twain's maxims maintain within the text his presence as a writer and thus his fame and his authority.

During his lecture in Melbourne, Twain notes that he was twice interrupted by the question from the audience, "Is he dead, Mark?" He had no ready response, and according to the local papers, he did not even understand the question (Shillingsburg 65). It was, of course, an echo from the past, a repetition of the query he had used in *The Innocents Abroad* to persecute self-important guides anxious to proclaim the glories of European culture created by the genius of its artists. Twain's failure to recognize the question is understandable, but the episode measures more than time; it signals difference.

Although Twain himself thought of *Following the Equator* in relation to *The Innocents Abroad*, as he worried over the title of his new travel book, calling it "Another Innocent Abroad," "The Latest Innocent Abroad," and "The Surviving Innocent Abroad" (Emerson, *Authentic* 207), little of the Twain of *The Innocents Abroad* survives in his final travel narrative. Gone from it, perhaps inevitably, are the youthful exuberance, the strident iconoclasm, and the outlandish comic posturing. Gone is the search for pleasure, the resistance to tourist culture, the serious, conflicted examination of Christianity.

The two journeys themselves were radically different, of course. While the excursion in *The Innocents Abroad* was supposed to be a pleasure trip centered on the splendors of Europe and the places sacred to Christianity in the Holy Land, Twain's journey around the world was a business venture, a lecture tour that took him to some of the newest and some of the oldest cultures in history and to the sites of multiple non-Christian religions. Whereas the "innocents" of the first book were invited to feel subservient to the cultures they encountered, in *Following the Equator* Twain brings the culture of an acclaimed literary performer to the lands he visits; he imports art to colonial provinces. The narrator of *The Innocents Abroad* struggled to create status for himself by contentiously disputing the conduct of his fellow travelers, the reliability of conventional guidebooks, and the accuracy of traditional histories. In *Following the Equator*, however, Twain has no need to establish his authority; it is a given, the product of his literary achievement and of his skill and fame as a lecturer. He comfortably assumes supremacy from the first and exerts it throughout his book. But while much of the original Mark Twain does seem, to answer his Australian auditor's query, dead, there are nonetheless some strong continuities between *The Innocents Abroad* and *Following the Equator*. The stance of authority, fought for in the first book, simply assumed in the second, links the two in an important way. Both books rely principally on a flexible, literary style, one higher than low, though the style of the first is frequently intense while that of the later book is most often matter-of-fact. Both books evoke the inevitable passage of time as a measure of human vanity, and in both Twain creates emblems of transience—the crumbling wall at Tangiers, for instance, in *The Innocents Abroad* and, at Benares in *Following the Equator*, pictures made with colored dust particles dropped into the water—"a symbol," he says, of "Instability" (*FE* 505).

In both narratives, as counterpoint to the consciousness of time's annihilating power, he affirms some of the beauties and joys of life itself. Interestingly, two of these affirmations are prompted by his encounters with those who renounce the world for an ascetic religious life. In *The Innocents Abroad* he is appalled by the Catholic hermits of Mars Saba— those "dead men who walk" (*IA* 478)—and similarly in *Following the Equator* he complains of the Trappist monks near Durban, South Africa, whose life seems to him "a sweeping suppression of human instincts," even "an extinction of the man as an individual," again, a kind of death in life (*FE* 647–48). But the core of commonality between these differing, linked texts lies in their impulse to judge—to evaluate foreign cultures.

In *The Innocents Abroad*, Twain traveled as a cultural imperialist; he championed nineteenth-century western civilization. He reveled in its material progress and believed in its self-proclaimed moral advances. In his credos of the early 1880s—preludes to the Sage's pronouncements— he reaffirmed the moral superiority of present over past, more particularly of Protestant civilization's creation of "the highest and purest and best individuals which modern society has known" (*WIM* 57–58). He generally assumed that technological improvements and increased material prosperity were matched by the ethical standards of civilization—by the qualities of gentleness, charity, mercy, and purity he upheld in *The Innocents Abroad*. In that narrative he praised these virtues when he saw them, and held others, notably the Pilgrims, accountable for possessing them. Even in *A Connecticut Yankee*, despite Hank's inability to create a new society, he preaches—and Twain affirms—the values of traditional nineteenth-century western civilization. When he made his world tour, however, Twain examined civilization itself anew, questioning whether its moral ideals were upheld in its actual practice.

He did not set about this in any systematic way. His evaluations of civilization are scattered throughout *Following the Equator*, apparently arising naturally from his observations of colonial lands. As he encountered the colonial enterprise in action, however, he looked honestly at the process and its results, and although he started his tour as a believer in imperialism, he ended it with reservations. Twain's famed opposition to imperialism is usually dated as emerging in 1900, following his disillusionment with the treaty that ended the Spanish American War (Zwick xx), but the groundwork for that position was clearly laid during his last lecture tour. What he did during that long excursion through colonial lands was nothing less than adjust his "mental baggage to fit the realities he met" (Budd, *Social Philosopher* 169).

In *Following the Equator* he tends to reflect on two things: the process of colonization and the results it has created. As he muses over the treatment of the natives by white colonials in Australia, especially Queensland and Tasmania, and in New Zealand, he emphasizes duplicity, brutality, and violence. Recounting episodes of enslavement and extermination, he discloses, as Maxwell Geismar has pointed out, "the genocide of the native peoples upon which the white man's civilization had always been established" (169). He often explains colonial depredations and atrocities by direct statements that convey matter-of-factly the horrors of history: "They did not kill all the blacks, but they promptly killed enough of them to make their own persons safe. From the dawn of civilization down to this day the white man has always used that very precaution" (*FE* 209). Sometimes he treats colonization with devastating, if contrived, irony, as he does, for instance, when he recommends that native laborers be returned from Queensland to their home islands, since their death rate at Queensland is over ten times that experienced at home during plagues and war: "Common Christian charity, common humanity, does seem to require, not only that these people be returned to their homes, but that war, pestilence, and famine be introduced among them for their preservation" (*FE* 88–89).

When he turns from the process of colonial settlement to its fruits in Australia, he is equally appalled and only slightly less bitter in his irony. Facetiously he itemizes the benefits of western civilization to the natives:

clothes, a Waterbury watch, and some jewelry (*FE* 85); a hat, an umbrella, a belt, a neckerchief, and some profanity (*FE* 86); a necklace, an umbrella, and an imperfection in the art of swearing (*FE* 88). Lands, labor, even lives, he suggests, have been exchanged for a few gauds of civilization.

However, when he looks at both the process and the results of imperial rule in India, he has a different assessment. He sees the imposition of British control as a humane end to ancient factional strife and oppression by local princes. He depicts native resistance as misguided and often brutal, and he heroicizes the British who combat and finally quell such uprisings (see esp. chaps. 54 and 58). He sees English imperialism as "the best service that was ever done to the Indians themselves, those wretched heirs of a hundred centuries of pitiless oppression and abuse" (*FE* 506), because he believes that the English govern by "tact, training, and distinguished administrative ability" in behalf of "just and liberal laws" (*FE* 518). Clearly Twain is divided: in colonial and imperial ventures he finds slaughter and exploitation practiced for the enrichment of the controlling powers; and he finds an end to war and abuse undertaken for the betterment of the native peoples. He foresees that all so-called savage lands will soon come under European control, and he announces that he is "not sorry, but glad" about that future (*FE* 625), for he hopes that the change will bring "peace and order and the reign of law" (*FE* 626).

His estimations of the civilizations he encounters tend to depend upon his construction of the past as well as his experience in the present. He is inclined to see the past of the Australasian aborigines as more benign, satisfying, and peaceful than that of the Indians. He romanticizes the one, demonizes the other. And he finds the Indian present, under British rule, less corrupted by economic interest, by sheer greed, than the current circumstances of both Australia and South Africa. On the purely material plane, whenever he encounters western technology, whether in the form of transport, or housing, or the production of goods, he approves of it. Clearly he imagines pasts incorrectly, misconstrues much of the present, and overvalues the material. Sometimes, however, his judgments of civilization are anchored in moral imagination, informed by an effort to view things from the native perspective. It is not, he observes, "our custom to put ourselves in the other person's place" (*FE* 87); yet this is just what he tries to do. The attempt leads him to such reflections as the following: "The Natives were not used to clothes, and houses, and regular hours, and church, and school, and Sunday-school, and work, and the other misplaced persecutions of civilization, and they pined for their lost home and their wild free life" (*FE* 265). This sounds like an imposition of Huck Finn's dilemma onto the native experience; it is born of Twain's effort to imagine for a moment the point of view of a radically alien other.

The inability to get inside the skin of another is for Twain the root of the evil created by well-intentioned, indeed charitable, white men. Even the "kindest-hearted white man can always be depended on to prove himself inadequate when he deals with savages," he says.

> He cannot turn the situation around and imagine how he would like it to have a well-meaning savage transfer him from his house and his church and his clothes and his books and his choice food to a hideous wilderness of sand and rocks and snow, and ice and sleet and storm and blistering sun, with no shelter, no bed, no covering for his and his family's naked bodies, and nothing to eat but snakes and grubs and offal. This would be a hell to him; and if he had any wisdom he would know that his own civilization is a hell to the savage. (*FE* 267)

Twain's judgments of civilization are also guided by his compassion. He tries to feel with—and hence for—the indigenous populations. To assess western civilization's impact, he deploys a series of moral attributes: kindness, mercy, tenderness, and humanity. He expects these to be exerted in the civilizing process, but he discovers that they are not. In using such standards as criteria for judging colonial civilizations, he actually employs the ethical ideals of his own culture to condemn it. He thus steps outside what the age thought of—indeed, what the Twain of *The Innocents Abroad* had thought of—as the clash between civilization and savagery to judge western civilization in terms of itself—and find it wanting.

Twain's estimations of colonial civilization are so sporadic that they do not impose themselves as the central concern of his variegated narrative, but his final focus on the political upheavals in South Africa brings them to the fore at the close. Oddly, his account of the Rhodes-backed Jameson incursion is almost as interested in the military superiority of the Boers as it is in the struggle for control of the country. He simply delights in calculating British ineptitude. But his condemnation of Rhodes himself—and of all that he represents—is stark and powerful, and it leads to one of the most memorable lines in his book: "I admire him [Rhodes], I frankly confess it; and when his time comes I shall buy a piece of the rope for a keepsake" (*FE* 710). Victorian travel writers habitually passed judgments on persons, peoples, and cultures, but Twain involves himself in something more: he undertakes to analyze and evaluate a contemporaneous historical process. He sees it ultimately not just as the dynamic by which Europe extends its power over other continents but as a replication of Europe's own past. Using a traditional moral and religious rhetoric, he defines the true nature of international politics, asserting that "the territorial possessions of all the political establishments in the earth" are, in fact, just "pilferings," and he observes with pointed irony that "robbery by European nations of each other's territories has never been a sin" (*FE* 623). For Twain, contemporary imperialism is nothing more than a continuation of history itself.

Twain's recurrent reflections on serious issues led Howells to write to him with especially lavish praise: "The thing [*Following the Equator*] is enormously good. No man has ever got himself so honestly out as you have always done, and in Following the Equator the sincerity is notable, even for you. At the right times there is a noble seriousness; and at all times, justice and mercy. There isn't a mean thought, a shabby lie, a cowardly bravado in the whole book. Well, I believe that is you" (*MTHL* 2:707). Having argued off and on for almost three decades that Mark Twain was a serious writer, a man of deep humanity, arresting morality, and courageous honesty, Howells must have felt vindicated by such a full expression of the proper Twain as *Following the Equator* provided.

Curiously, Twain himself undertakes to absolve himself, or more precisely, the unruly part of his famed persona. He provides a disquisition on what people venerate and why, and his observations constitute a not too oblique defense of some of his own earlier performances as humorist. His remarks are prompted by his encounter with a scholar of Indian scripture, but he goes beyond the question of religious homage to consider all forms of reverence:

> The ordinary reverence, the reverence defined and explained by the dictionary costs nothing. Reverence for one's own sacred things—parents, religion, flag, laws, and for one's own beliefs—these are feelings which we cannot even help. They come natural to us; they are involuntary, like breathing. There is no personal merit in breathing. But the reverence which is difficult, and which has personal merit in it, is the respect which you pay, without compulsion, to the political or religious attitude of a man whose beliefs are not yours. . . . If the man doesn't believe as we do, we say he is a crank, and that settles it. I mean it does nowadays, because now we can't burn him.
>
> We are always canting about people's "irreverence," always charging this offense upon somebody or other, and thereby intimating that we are better than that person and do not commit that offense ourselves. Whenever we do this we are in a lying attitude, and our speech is cant; for none of us are reverent—in a meritorious way; deep down in our hearts we are all irreverent. There is probably not a single exception to this rule in the earth. (*FE* 514)

The confident dogmatism here is characteristic of Twain in this narrative, and the flash of dark humor—"now we can't burn him"—is all but lost in the sequence of strident pronouncements. Although cast as a reflection about people in general, Twain's argument implicitly justifies his own past performances as an irreverent humorist on the simple grounds that everyone is irreverent. It betrays in Twain an anxious sensitivity to potential criticism. It reveals the proper Twain struggling to exonerate the transgressive one. In doing so, he is thinking more of his past career than his present text, for there is relatively little irreverence in *Following the Equator.*

There is humor, of course, but it is usually either mild and inconsequential or else heavy-handed and pointedly ironic. He spends as much time making fun of such slight topics as the weather, animals, travel, dress, hotels, and landscapes as he does quipping about such serious subjects as governments, class, age, customs, commerce, literature, national character, human nature, and religion. His humor is actually subsumed by the predominating seriousness of the book. Although this travel narrative is generally regarded as a dark book, one permeated by "unmitigated and even invented pessimism" (Bridgman, *Traveling* 128), that darkness arises not because Twain scoffs irreverently or assaults transgressively but because he is poignantly attuned to what is irrevocably sad, unfair, or painful in human experience. There is far more melancholy seriousness than humor in his book. And in most cases what humor there is does not debunk the sacred so much as it plays with the improbable—"I killed sixteen tigers" (*FE* 547)—and smiles at the fanciful—"In Noah's Ark the beds were simply scandalous" (*FE* 630). His comic tone at one extreme is fey—"a cobra bit me but it got well; everyone was surprised" (*FE* 547)—and at the other, sententious and moral: "Be careless in your dress if you must, but keep a tidy soul" (*FE* 223). The moral is, in fact, the overwhelming note in this book. It is so pervasive and powerful that it assimilates not only the irreverent (on those rare moments when irreverence occurs) but also, oddly, the nihilistic. Though true throughout the book, this is quite evident in the maxims. The expectation of wisdom inherent in the form conceals the darkness of an observation like this: "Pity is for the living, envy is for the dead" (*FE* 184), and somehow its potential conceptual blow is softened by the graceful balance of the phrasing. In keeping with the prevailing earnestness of his narrative, Twain closes his book on a note that is Olympian in its generality, Victorian in its morality, genteel and gentle in its humor, and utterly trite in its conception: "Human pride is not worth while; there is always something lying in wait to take the wind out of it" (*FE* 712).

The seriousness of *Following the Equator* was not lost on its first reviewers, some of whom even complained about a want of humor. They found little to object to, however (a few English critics thought Twain was too hard on British colonialism), for Twain had created a stately travel narrative full of conventional wisdom, as befit a personage. (For a representative sampling of reviews, see *CH* 207–27.)

His posture stood him in good stead throughout his remaining time in Europe. He was most often interviewed because he was a famous humorist, but in the interviews themselves he held forth earnestly on current affairs. He was treated abroad as both great writer and wise man. He enjoyed his renown, enjoyed having something to say about the major events of the day, and enjoyed fraternizing with the elite. To the distress of his partisan democratic admirers, then and now, he reveled in European high society. He kept his delight largely to himself, however, confining it to the privacy of his notebooks. There he recorded both the gatherings of the notable he attended and his estimates of the group: "Night before last Madame Letschtishki [*sic*] came & took Clara & me to Ritter von Dutschka's to dine. Twenty persons at dinner: Count von Eulenberg (German Ambassador) & others came in after dinner. A remarkable gathering—no commonplace people present, no leatherheads. Princes & other titled people there, but not *because* of their titles, but for their distinction in achievement. It was like a salon of old-time Paris" (qtd. in Dolmetsch 133). Striking here is his effort to conceal from himself—there is no other audience—the fact that the guests were invited because of their lineage. Here, as in his latter essay "Does the Race of Man Love a Lord?" he prefers to believe that personage derives from "distinction in achievement." Yet as Carl Dolmetsch suggests, there is nothing on record to indicate that the guests were not assembled because of their titles (133). Twain's own elitism is made indelible, in any case, by his clearly satisfied, somewhat disdainful, observation, "no commonplace people present." With a kind of playfulness probably fostered by uneasy guilt, he also records in his notebooks of this period his regret that he himself is "not a prince." He admonishes himself for his feeling even as he acknowledges it, and he excuses himself by imagining a universal longing for such nobility: "It isn't a new regret, but a very old one. I have never been properly & humbly satisfied with my condition. I am a democrat only on principle, not by instinct—nobody is *that*. Doubtless some people *say* they are, but this world is grievously given to lying" (qtd. in Dolmetsch 142).

A prince by desire, perhaps even by conviction of self-worth, Twain accepted the social honors of Europe as they were copiously extended to him until his return to the United States in the fall of 1900. Thereafter, a democrat on principle, he used his status as a celebrity to advocate reform locally (in politics), nationally (in morals and citizenship), and internationally (in foreign policy). Paradoxically, he was a would-be aristocrat who championed democracy, a truly privileged person who suffered for the poor and the oppressed, and a private misanthrope who publicly worked to better humankind. His biographers and critics have long recognized that in his last decade Twain's public personality dominated his life, forming his chief means of expression (to be sure, he continued to write some and to dictate even more). Budd has suggested that in the late Twain's public appearances two things emerged, both quite daring: first, his self-appointed task of regulating, as he himself put it, "the moral and political situation on this planet"; and second, his inveterate desire, as Budd puts it, "to 'advertise'" Mark Twain "attractively" (*Our MT* 201). Principled concern for people thus became entangled with crass self-promotion. But the situation is even more complex, for the efficacy of Twain's humanitarianism—the true thing at last, as opposed to the mere pretense of it that first appeared in the western writings of his early California days—depended directly on his currency as an important person.

The personage Mark Twain was kept before the public through what might be called mini-appearances. During the last decade of his life, he did not publish a single long major work—with the exception of the selections from his autobiography. (However much he may have valued it personally, the text he thought of as a major utterance, *What Is Man?*— finally brought into print in 1906—is not a significant literary work, and in any case it was published anonymously in a private limited edition.) What he did do, however, was appear in public in short stories, brief essays, interviews, and speeches. The essays fall into three categories: essays on politics and social issues, essays on writing (or lecturing), and essays centered on some dimension of his personal life. All three kinds define important aspects of his final public identity. The first group spotlights Twain the reformer, the second brings into focus Twain the artist, and the third calls attention to Twain the private man. All three types crop up in one form or another throughout Twain's long career, but in the 1890s and the first decade of the twentieth century, such essays became more frequent.

While maintaining Mark Twain's public presence through short pieces published in leading journals, Clemens worked to achieve favorable publication arrangements in the short and long term for old as well as new books. His overriding concern was to make money—to recover from his bankruptcy and reestablish his family in luxury (though, in fact, they always lived quite comfortably even during his financial distress). To achieve this he vacillated between two modes of production and distribution: subscription publishing and publishing through an established trade house. He had, of course, made (and lost) his fortune through subscription houses, but he had unshakable confidence that canvassers could sign up more buyers than bookstores could secure. At the same time, however, he was aware, as he said to Henry Huttleston Rogers, who negotiated for him with his potential publishers, that trade houses published "very high-class books" (*MTHHR* 249). To complicate his uncertainty about the best outlet for Mark Twain, he wanted to line up the publication of both new individual texts and a uniform edition of all his works. He planned to make money from both ventures. Working through the ever-patient (and ever-shrewd) Rogers, he jockeyed with the American Publishing Company and Harper & Brothers.

Clemens was far from a free agent in these negotiations. To begin with, as a part of his bankruptcy settlement, the copyright to Mark Twain's books had been assigned to his wife. This was only a strategy to enable Clemens to retain control of his published writings, and it posed no impediment to his disposition of them. More hindersome was the fact that the American Publishing Company owned the rights to five books of Mark Twain's that it had published earlier. This impinged on arrangements with Harper for a uniform edition. In the end, however, Twain had it all ways, arguably achieving through multiple publications of his works even wider circulation. In 1896 Harper announced that it was publishing a uniform edition of Mark Twain and actually brought out the first six volumes. In 1898 and 1899 the American Publishing Company issued, for sale by subscription, twenty-two volumes of Mark Twain's works, graced with his signature and touted as the autograph edition, to which they added another six volumes between 1899 and 1907. They also issued a cheaper popular edition. Through complex contractual arrangements, Harper became Twain's exclusive American publisher in 1904, guaranteeing him an annual income of $25,000, and continued to bring out its version of the uniform edition. In England, Chatto & Windus, his English publisher since the 1870s, after declining to handle the American Publishing Company's cheap popular edition of Twain's collected works, first agreed to market the author's signed deluxe edition provided by the American Publishing Company and then brought out its own uniform library edition of Mark Twain.

Sold by subscription and through reputable trade houses in popular, deluxe, and library collected editions, Mark Twain was made available to lowbrows and highbrows alike. He was certified as a standard author and canonized by the book industry. If, as he explained to Rogers, with his usual air of authority, a "literary reputation" is "a most frail thing" that can be destroyed by "any trifling accident" and with it "its market," Twain did everything he could to keep his own reputation strong, and he worked wonders at keeping the market for his works both broad and quick (*MTHHR* 349). He accomplished what no American author before him had: through self-promotion, clever (and fortuitous) manipulation of publication, and the genius of his writings, he moved himself into the center of American literary culture while continuing to do a lively business at its margins.

As Alan Gribben has observed in his perceptive review of Twain's lifelong mythologizing of himself, toward the end of his career Twain was gripped by "a terrific possessiveness about his posthumous image" ("Autobiography as Property" 46). This led him to guide the creation of a capsule biography for the uniform edition, to squelch insofar as he could the attempts of others—such as Will M. Clemens (no relation)—to write his life story, and finally to select and guide an authorized biographer in Albert Bigelow Paine. Twain believed fiercely that a "man's history is his own property until the grave extinguishes his ownership in it" (*MTHHR* 447 n. 2). Concern for his posthumous image also informed his careful monitoring of public sentiment on volatile issues and caused him to withhold from publication some of his polemical writings on them. But if he thus suppressed and edited himself with an eye on posterity, he also took care to *present* a self for present and postmortem viewing. Such self-presentation informs *Following the Equator*, but his final major piece of image making is his autobiography.

"ALL MY BOOKS," Twain once confessed, "are autobiographies." To an unusual degree this is true, as he mined his past for his fictions and recorded versions of his present for his travel books. At the same time, from at least 1870 on, he began to write sketches of his life experiences and his family that are more directly autobiographical. The impulse found new impetus in Vienna from 1897–98 and acquired a new mode in Florence in 1904 when he began to dictate (he had tried dictation briefly in 1885). Finally in 1906 he started the series of almost daily dictations that would continue to within a few months of his death. Always self-conscious, always performing versions of himself, Twain took naturally to autobiography, especially during his later years when he was worrying over his present and future image. As Michael Kiskis has observed, however, most of Twain's autobiography was "composed during periods of creative, personal, and emotional stress" (*MTOA* xxx). The result of Twain's writing and dictating portions of his life story off and on for some forty years is, in the words of one critic, "one of the most perplexing compilations in American letters" (De Eulis 202).

Part of the problem is the form of Twain's autobiography. It is a series of fragments, written or dictated at different times, that replaces chronology with free association prompted by present events as well as past memories. It incorporates, though it has never been published this way, a range of documents, some personal to Twain, others just the flotsam of everyday life. Twain intended to add some parts of his autobiography as notes to his already published works in order to extend their copyright (see *MTHL* 2:779). He also intended to have his self-told life story published in successive installments only after his death, the first installment of which would omit characterizations of his acquaintances, while the second, third, and fourth would leave out what he thought were his more heretical opinions. He designated certain chapters to be sealed and unpublished for one hundred years. Rather clearly visible in these designs is not only a desire to perpetuate Mark Twain but also a large sense of self-importance.

Given the complications, not to say, the peculiarities, of Twain's forays into autobiography, as well as his directions about them, there may never be a definitive text of this work, despite the ingenuity and energy of the editors at the Mark Twain Project. Fortunately, however, Twain himself may have given us a final version of his autobiographical self. En-

ticed as ever by money ($30,000 in this case), he agreed to publish in the
North American Review in twenty-five installments "Chapters from My
Autobiography." They were selected and edited by George Harvey, editor of the *Review* and the senior editor at Harper who was handling Mark
Twain, but, as Kiskis has pointed out, Twain was "involved in the choices
for the installments, had final control over the revisions that were made
to the texts, and gave his approval for their publication" (*MTOA* xxiv).
The "chapters" appeared from September 1906 to December 1907. If
they are not the definitive version of the autobiography, they are certainly the final, extended public representation of Mark Twain.

In naming these selections "The Autobiography of Mark Twain,"
Clemens confounds the customary triad of autobiographical composition: author, narrator, subject. Who is which? Reversing the usual relationship in which Clemens did the living, Twain the writing, here Clemens seems to become the writer, the biographer of Mark Twain, who
seems to have a life of his own—at least until the term *autobiography* dis-
solves the difference between the two. It is tempting to say that the narrator and the subject are both Twain, making Clemens just the author,
but what the "Autobiography of Mark Twain" actually presents are the
facts (and fictions) of Clemens's life. To complicate things further, this
autobiographical text presents itself throughout as unreliable. Its author
repeatedly subverts his story by suggesting that it may not be the truth.
The last line summarizes the deliberately uncertain status of the whole:
"Now, then, that is the tale. Some of it is true" (*MTOA* 242). And yet
these problematics are perfectly characteristic of Mark Twain. They point
once more to the all but inextricable unity of Clemens and his persona.
Here the pseudonym does not subvert the autobiographical act. The text
does tell the life of Clemens, but it tells it through the eyes and style of
Mark Twain. The two are, in the end, in *this* end, one. Further, the autobiography is not an especially humorous performance, thus reinforcing
the view that the pseudonym Mark Twain signals the entire range of the
creative self, the serious, sentimental, and conventional as well as the
comic, caustic, and unorthodox. The autobiography, perhaps more than
any other text of Mark Twain's, makes it clear that we need to enlarge our
sense of the persona to at least the proportions of its actual practice.

Although Clemens's life was in reality a spectacular instance of success against heavy odds (followed by failure, capped yet again by success), the autobiography does not shape itself around the traditional pattern of rising in the world. Nor does it isolate any turning point or conversion experience. (Twain specifically denies that there are any.) And if, as Susanna Egan has argued, post–Civil War American autobiographies are typically cast as "history in the making, with the self, in varying degrees of objectivity, as participant," then Twain's autobiography is atypical for its time (71). It does not place the self in history; it is not concerned with the self as master or victim or even exemplar of historical process. Even Henry James, whose memoirs are so firmly lodged in the development of his own artistic consciousness, offers a fuller sense of historical force than Twain. Twain simply ignores history or shrinks it to the dimensions of the personal. Thus, to take only a few obvious examples, in his life story slavery becomes the childhood experience of black folkways and interracial companionship; the Civil War is refracted into Mark Twain's visits to and conversations with General Grant; westward expansion is reduced to anecdotes of Mark Twain's time in Nevada and California; reconstruction is skirted altogether except for allusions to personal friends, such as Cable, who were in the thick of its ideological struggles; and urbanization and industrialization are either overlooked or realized only as affording modern conveniences for Mark Twain. (In the *North American Review* version, Twain even omits his highly publicized opposition to imperialism.) Despite the fact that he was in so many ways a Representative Man of his era, Twain chooses to place his autobiographical self largely outside of his times. He thus removes from his self-portrait the shaping influence of historical process, making himself appear independently self-created.

Ignoring chronology, Twain also presents himself as fully formed from the first of his narrative. Although he does begin the first chapter with scattered remarks about ancestors (including Satan), he jumps almost at once to his literary use of his mother's cousin and then moves in his second chapter to unconnected events separated by as much as fifty-seven years, with several other discrete episodes slipped in between. Thus by the second chapter his method of autobiography is fully under way: "It is a deliberate system, and the law of the system is that I shall talk about the matter which for the moment interests me, and cast it aside and talk about something else the moment its interest for me is exhausted. It is a system which follows no charted course and is not going to follow any such course. It is a system which is a complete and purposed jumble" (*MTOA* 4).

The randomness of his system defies the causality common to most autobiographies. Essentially a collection of nonchronological fragments that begin, unfold, and conclude willy-nilly, his form is designed to thwart the emergence of any coherent pattern and with it a meaning to his life. He is as unconcerned with presenting, or discovering, a unified self (despite his emphasis in *What Is Man?* on idiosyncratic temperament) as he is with displaying a multiple self (despite his complex representations in *Pudd'nhead Wilson* of individual identity). His guiding principle is "the matter which for the moment interests me." Such a conception of auto-biography is massively egotistical as it privileges the present interest of the writer above all other considerations. It also presupposes that what is of interest to Mark Twain will inevitably be of interest to his readers.

Thus enacted in the very form of Twain's autobiography is the ab-solute autonomy of self. The self is the narrative fragments, and each is assumed to be equally revelatory, defining, and engaging. This heralding of the independent self is common to the Victorian mode of male auto-biography, which tends to diminish community and silence the voices of others (see Danahay). On the other hand, Twain's peculiar version of self-creating actually employs groups and places others in dialogue with the self. His autobiography is in its way consummately *social*.[3] His narra-tive voice is often that of the storyteller, and storytelling presumes and creates an audience. But the people he surrounds and involves himself with in his text—from family, to friends, to publishers, to presidents—are used on the whole only to highlight the many facets of Mark Twain. With so much functioning to illuminate him, what Mark Twain is finally revealed?

A remarkably conventional one. Whatever the range and quirkiness of his complete autobiographical writings and dictations, in the selections published in the *North American Review* Twain's life is defined as more mainstream than divergent, his self more conventional than radical. He appears as a winsome, slightly eccentric, but thoroughly respectable Victorian.

As with many Victorians, he achieves his upright, public self through a series of repressions. Suppressed in, or edited out of, this autobiography are, among other things, his antagonism toward his father, the actual facts of his aborted duel, his violent aggression toward imagined enemies, his business dealings, notably those leading to his bankruptcy, and his sexuality. And muted, though as we shall see, not entirely suppressed, is his religious skepticism. More generally still, the autobiography conceals his domineering personality. What *is* presented, then, is the conventional person: the loving husband, the doting father, the successful writer, the tender sentimentalist, the staunch moralist, the urgent sage, the famous personage. While these roles may not, indeed do not, disclose the whole man, they do define fundamental aspects of him; they reveal the proper Mark Twain.

In the well-known preface he prepared for his autobiography (not one he used in the *North American Review* version) he imagined, to protect as well as to liberate himself, that he was "speaking from the grave" (*MTA* 1:xv). He also proposed a model of free expression:

> The frankest and freest and privatest product of the human mind and heart is a love letter; the writer gets his limitless freedom of statement and expression from his sense that no stranger is going to see what he is writing.
>
> It has seemed to me that I could be as frank and free and unembarrassed as a love letter if I knew that what I was writing would be exposed to no eye until I was dead, and unaware, and indifferent. (*MTA* 1:xv–xvi)

In his autobiography Twain does not attain anything like the intimacy and candor of a conventional love letter, for the fragments of his life are always *told*, sometimes, when he was writing, to an imagined audience, always, when he was dictating, to a real one—to some gathering of his stenographer, secretary, authorized biographer, and even upon occasion his business manager. (Throughout his later years, special audiences, whether made up of his domestic circle, his "aquarium" of young girls, or his male cronies, fed his sense of personage.) But in one sense the autobiography is a love letter—a love letter to Livy. He memorializes her with affection and tenderness, evoking many of the same terms of praise and devotion he had used in his courtship correspondence. Again, she is both "girl and woman," a loving innocent full of "limitless affection" and unfailing "charity," a saintly person of "perfect character" (*MTOA* 23); and again, she is the object not only of his love but of his "worship" (23). Twain's use of the love letter as analogue for his autobiographical narrative recalls the postures Clemens assumed in his courtship. Significantly, the one that seemed so real at that time because it was weighted with his visible imperfections, the role of prodigal returning to the fold, is gone now, replaced by a resolute skepticism, while the other major postures, ones that proclaimed his achieved, constant character, his roles as Man of the World, Man of Feeling, and Man of Letters, are all confirmed in the autobiography. Indeed, his life story as he tells it testifies that he has lived as the man he assured Livy he was. The first full expression of himself as a proper gentleman is reenacted in the autobiography.

The conventionality of the autobiography has not escaped notice. For all of his promises of personal and conceptual fireworks, Twain actually created a fairly staid set of narrative fragments. Certainly, as Cox has pointed out, there is "little of a revelatory or shocking nature in all the dictations" (*Fate* 306). And there is nothing at all that shocks or surprises in the selections Twain actually published, unless one is taken aback by their very orthodoxy.

Predictably, those passages that seem to lie deepest in Twain's past, to define in some way his core, his recollections of the Quarles farm, are repossessed and re-created—repossessed through their re-creation—in a highly stylized manner. This, too, is indicative of the conventional in Mark Twain. Their vivid particularity, the sensuous specificity, the astounding details of his descriptions are all knit together in a self-conscious, complex syntax, governed by the rhetorical refrain, "I know," and its variants, "I can see" and "I can remember" (*MTOA* 120–23). The passage, probably the most admired in the entire autobiography, is a successful set piece of ostentatious prose of the sort practiced so long ago in the love letters (and repeated in one form or another in many of the major works). Bathed in nostalgia, Twain's litany of lost, "blessed" (*MTOA*

120) things depends on the romantic assumption that "the eye of the artist is the eye of the child" (Chernaik 80). This is a very traditional notion, to say the least, one that infatuated Romantics and Victorians alike. To approximate that innocent vision, Twain incorporates Susy's biography of him into his own autobiography.[4] Just as George Harvey selects and edits Twain's chapters, so Twain chooses and presents excerpts from Susy's text. (He does leave her style, with all its misspellings, for it conveys her untutored youth, certifies her innocence.) His appropriation of Susy's observations allows him to pay eulogistic tribute to her, to recover the wonder of a child's perspective, to celebrate himself (for Susy's remarks are full of admiration even when they chide him), and to display to the full his loving fatherhood. Through Susy he enshrines himself within the family nexus as a loving husband, father, neighbor, and friend. It is a very Victorian act.

It is also through Susy that Mark Twain frames his own skepticism. His report of her innocent, wondering question "What is it all for?" (*MTOA* 28) echoes throughout his story. And at times he uses her as access to his own deeper doubts. He reports her account, for instance, of familiar childhood play: "Sept. 10, '85.—The other evening Clara and I brought down our new soap bubble water and we all blew soap bubbles. Papa blew his soap bubbles and filled them with tobacco smoke and as the light shone on them they took very beautiful opaline colors," and then he adds to it his own sentimental moral reflection: "It is human life. We are blown upon the world; we float buoyantly upon the summer air a little while, complacently showing off our grace of form and our dainty iridescent colors; then we vanish with a little puff, leaving nothing behind but a memory—and sometimes not even that. I suppose that at those solemn times when we wake in the deeps of the night and reflect, there is not one of us who is not willing to confess that he is really only a soap-bubble, and as little worth the making" (*MTOA* 152–53). From the initial metaphor, through the trite language, to the final idea of human transience, this is a stock piece of Victorian melancholy.

Twain could hardly be more conventional—and hence safer—in his musings. Yet he is so uneasy about his cynical reflections that he seeks (or rather creates) multiple sanctions for them. First, his thoughts are prompted by—and softened by—Susy's play, and then he reaches for the exemption of universality—"there is not one of us who is not willing to confess"—to depersonalize his despair. Such a moment as this in the autobiography reveals (though the revelation is neither new nor shocking) just how conventional Mark Twain is: conventional enough to write effectively using familiar tropes, conventional enough to reflect moralistically on the vanity, the brevity, and insignificance of life, and conventional enough to feel guilty about the religious challenge of his reflections (as far as one can tell, he was pleased with their expression).

Had Twain been less conventional, he might have reveled in the doubt he shared with so many other Victorians.[5] In his *North American Review* autobiography, however, he only toys with orthodox religious belief, tweaking the noses, as it were, of true believers with his humorous—and therefore, he must have felt, safe—remarks about Providence. This version of his quarrel with God is staged as little more than a quibble conducted through quips.

The quips are both frequent and varied. Explaining the horrors that plagued his childhood—fears of death, nightmares of mutilation, remembrances of violence—he observes facetiously, "They were inventions of Providence to beguile me to a better life." Then he exploits his past innocence to mock the framework of such thought: "It would not have surprised me, nor even over-flattered me, if Providence had killed off that whole community in trying to save an asset like me. Educated as I had been, it would have seemed just the thing, and well worth the expense" (*MTOA* 155). The adult Twain often uses Providence for his humorous criticisms, disarmingly including himself in those he attacks: "It is the will of God that we must have critics, and missionaries, and Congressmen, and humorists, and we must bear the burden" (*MTOA* 37). Sometimes an anecdote is shaped around the mistaken notion of attributing to God what is done by man. In this vein he complains that his family, in the habit of giving credit "to Providence" for every good event out of "automatic religion," thanks God for providing ducks when it is he who buys them (*MTOA* 173–74). As he relates this story, he creates an unusually ugly picture:

There was a stranded log or two in the river, and on those certain families of snapping-turtles used to congregate and drowse in the sun and give thanks, in their dumb way, to Providence for benevolence extended to them. It was but another instance of misplaced credit; it was the young ducks that those pious reptiles were so thankful for—whereas they were *my* ducks. I bought the ducks.

When a crop of young ducks, not yet quite old enough for the table but approaching that age, began to join the procession, and paddle around in the sluggish water, and give thanks—not to me—for that privilege, the snapping-turtles would suspend their songs of praise and slide off the logs and paddle along under the water and chew the feet of the young ducks. (*MTOA* 174)

Vying comically here with Providence for the respect due to one in control, Twain raises, however obliquely, the fundamental question of causality and opens the lens on a savage nature. At such moments what seems good-humored play has a dark nether side. Relating a variant of a familiar Twain joke, he says that in his boyhood people were always thwarting Providence by saving him from death: "I was drowned seven times after that before I learned to swim—once in Bear Creek and six times in the Mississippi. I do not now know who the people were who interfered with the intentions of a Providence wiser than themselves, but I hold a grudge against them yet" (*MTOA* 212). The final ironic inversion—resenting those who saved his life—implies a preference for death over life that is openly announced elsewhere in the autobiography, most poignantly perhaps when the grieving father says that even if he could he would not bring back the dead Susy to suffer "the cares, the sorrows, and the inevitable tragedy of life" (*MTOA* 58).

In a dazzling, provocative study of the autobiography, G. Thomas Couser explores Twain's conception of a narrative that would open itself to "the subtlest impulses of consciousness and memory" (96). Echoing Twain's own metaphor of narrative as a river stream ("narrative should flow as flows the brook" [*MTA* 1:237]), Couser observes this: "Alternating between rapids and leisurely eddies, the narrative would resist, if not negate, the chronology and teleology of life-writing that point toward the subject's death" (96). While the act of narrating might as it transpires provide such a resistance, Twain's actual narrative engages rather than avoids his own mortality. Light as they are, his jokes about Providence, especially in their cumulative force, undercut the prevailing religious teleology.

His published autobiographical chapters are haunted by death. Most obviously, Livy and Susy cast the dark shadow of death over the entire autobiography, but Twain goes out of his way to chant the names of the dead: Olivia Clemens, Susy Clemens, Jane Clemens, Orion Clemens, Henry Clemens, Pamela Moffett, Samuel Moffett, General Grant, Harriet Beecher Stowe, Dean Sage, Thomas Bailey Aldrich, Bret Harte, Frank Stockton, James Redpath, Charles Dudley Warner, John Garth, Will Bowen, Sam Bowen, Ed Stevens, Irving Ayres, George Butler, Ruel Gridley. His litany expands as the narrative unfolds until the story of Twain's life begins to feel saturated with death. As counterpoint perhaps to naming the dead—and thus honoring them—Twain paradoxically offers from time to time a generalized reflection on the meaning of all life that emphasizes its futility, thus indirectly suggesting that everyone dies in vain:

> A myriad of men are born; they labor and sweat and struggle for bread; they squabble and scold and fight; they scramble for little mean advantages over each other; age creeps upon them; infirmities follow; shames and humiliations bring down their prides and their vanities; those they love are taken from them, and the joy of life is turned to aching grief. The burden of pain, care, misery, grows heavier year by year; at length, ambition is dead, pride is dead; vanity is dead; longing for release is in their place. It comes at last— the only unpoisoned gift earth had for them—and they vanish from a world where they were of no consequence; where they achieved nothing; where they were a mistake and a failure and a foolishness; where they have left no sign that they have existed—a world which will lament them a day and forget them forever. Then another myriad takes their place, and copies all they did, and goes along the same profitless road, and vanishes as they vanished—to make room for another, and another, and a million other myriads, to follow the same arid path through the same desert, and accomplish what the first myriad, and all the myriads that came after it accomplished— nothing! (*MTOA* 28)

Whatever stays against death narrating his autobiography may have provided, Mark Twain's immortality lay, as he perceived, in his literary achievement. It was the rock upon which he was tenoned and mortised. In "The Turning Point of My Life," a comic bit of autobiography published just two months before his death, he does what he refuses to do in the autobiography proper: he offers an explanation of his life's centering. "To me," he writes, "the most important feature of my life is its literary feature" (*MTC2* 931). Although its deliberately nonchronological, nonpatterned, nonpivotal form denies overall significance to the life, the chapters published in the *North American Review* do return time and again in one way or another to his career as a writer—to his life's "literary feature." He does not, to be sure, explore the creative process itself. He no more enters into that subjective arena than into his own psychological makeup and emotional states. Despite his belief that the true life of a person resides in the flow of ideas and feeling in consciousness, his autobiography is notably lacking in inwardness.[6] But he refers to the sources of his works, to their subjects, to their publications, to their receptions, and to their earnings so recurrently that not even the determined randomness of his form can conceal the importance of his identity as author. It flits through the times and places of his narrative like a ghost whose presence is always felt. The figure of Mark Twain, the writer, is arguably at the center of his wandering memoirs, informing all the other facets of his life. Both husbandhood and fatherhood are tied to his authorship: he discovers Livy because he is traveling abroad as a writer; Susy undertakes his biography because he is a famous author whose character, she believes, is misperceived by the world. Given the importance of authorship to his life story, as he tells it, there is an aptness about the first of the two events with which he concludes his *North American Review* narrative. That penultimate episode also marks an important metaphorical turn in the awareness of death that pervades the autobiography.

In the first half of his final chapter, Twain revisits what he felt was the greatest catastrophe in his literary career—the Whittier birthday speech. In returning to that episode he exercises a power inherent in his form, one fundamental to the autobiographical act: the ability to rewrite one's life. As we saw earlier, the original speech, given in December 1877 at the dinner held by the *Atlantic Monthly* to honor Whittier at seventy, was perceived by Twain—with a lot of guidance from Howells—as a disaster of incalculable magnitude. Twain felt its consequences keenly, believing that he had offended Emerson, Longfellow, and Holmes, the objects of his burlesque, as well as Whittier, the guest of honor. He believed for a time that the speech itself was of inferior quality. And he believed that he had disgraced himself as a member of polite society. Believing all this, he feared that his *literary* career was in jeopardy, and, as noted in chapter 2, he may even have gone abroad in the spring of 1878 to escape what he imagined to be a continuing storm of public protest. His anxiety is worth recalling. "My misfortune," he wrote to Howells, "has injured me all over the country; therefore it will be best that I retire from before the public at present" (*MTHL* 1:212). Given his delusions and, as he says as he retells the episode and reprints the speech, his actual pain (*MTOA* 230), there is at least symbolic truth as well as humor to his saying, "I shall never be as dead again as I was then" (*MTOA* 235). Insofar as his autobiography records the life of Mark Twain the writer, this is his moment of death.

The Whittier fiasco epitomized the cultural conflict between elite gentility and democratic commonality. Twain is customarily taken to be at one with the latter. Yet his distress over his performance was so great precisely because he cared about being genteel. He had, or so it seemed to him (and Howells), failed himself, failed as a gentleman, betrayed his innate sense of propriety, however accidentally and momentarily, and so lapsed in social grace. Precisely because all this mattered to him, he exaggerated the proportions of his blunder. Howells deepened his sense of monumental error. "Every one with whom I have talked about your speech," he wrote Twain, "regards it as a fatality" (*MTHL* 1:213). But this report of the death of Mark Twain was premature. He recovered at the time, of course, and went on to greatness as a writer. And in the autobiography, having suffered his death in the retelling, he resurrects himself—for himself—by reclaiming the very proprieties of character he once feared he had lost. Rereading his speech, he testifies that there is no "coarseness" in it, no "vulgarity." It is, he says, "smart" and "saturated with humor" (*MTOA* 237). Twain thus restores himself to the living, rewrites the past, and removes a supposed blemish from his person. At the near end of his autobiography, he reestablishes his character as a proper gentleman.

Ironically, the final story he tells plays directly against that character. The tale, in brief, is that he once sold another man's dog (for three dollars), reclaimed it for its true owner (returning the three dollars), and then accepted a reward (three dollars again) for his service. Told with stylish innocence, often displaying Twain as inspired idiot, the story ends the autobiography with a tale that may be tall ("some of it is true," Twain says [*MTOA* 242]). It shows Twain at the last as an accomplished literary humorist, but that very act raises a question about the humor of the autobiography. To put the issues in terms appropriate to the form: what kind of a humorist is Twain in his life story?

The final comic tale, made important by its very position, discloses the essential nature of the humorous Mark Twain of the autobiography. There is an orality about its narrative (but then the autobiography itself often feels spoken, as indeed much of it was), and it does show off Twain as master of illogic, non sequitur, and deadpan stupidities. The tale also takes yet another comic swipe at religious ideology, since Twain undertakes his dog dealing to provide what the Lord hasn't (*MTOA* 239). But the humor overall really turns upon Twain's protestations of morality. "I was always honest," he says. "I know I can never be otherwise" (*MTOA* 242). The joke at the heart of the anecdote turns on the question of how honest Twain has been in his dog dealing. In somewhat broader terms, however, what entertains here is the spectacle of Mark Twain, celebrated writer, famous person, moralist to the nation, playing a con game. The humor derives from Twain's stature.

Throughout his autobiography, Twain's humor makes light of his character; it turns upon—by turning against—his personage. He presents himself through remarks and through anecdotes as other than what his readers expect him to be, other than what most segments of the autobiography show him to be. Thus he comically contests his prestige, his morality, his social standing, his power, and his eminence—the very conditions of achievement and character that authorize the autobiography in the first place. Such humor at the expense of the very proprieties and attainments he cares so much about does not subvert them, however. We continue to believe in the proper Twain even as he proclaims and reveals his improprieties. His revelations of questionable self are just jokes, made funny to the degree that they are improbable. Ironically, then, the more he uses humor to display an improper self, the more he actually evokes the presence of the proper one. To put it another way, Mark Twain actually flaunts his propriety by comically declaring his impropriety.

Icon

Two events late in Clemens's life, each in its own way extremely odd, underscore his sense of Mark Twain's propriety. The first was a matter of behind-the-scenes maneuvering; the second was very much an onstage public performance. The two together confirm yet again the proper Mark Twain.

Some seven years before Clemens published selections from Mark Twain's autobiography (though well after he had begun writing it), he had a hand in producing a brief biography of Mark Twain. The episode is as curious as any in his career. At the request of his publisher, Frank Bliss, he sketched an outline of his life and sent it to his nephew, Samuel Moffett. Moffett—and this was the agreed-upon arrangement—elaborated the bare facts of the outline, decorated the narrative with laudatory remarks, and published the piece as written by himself. Clemens's original outline of his life—slightly altered by Livy[1]—is devoid of evaluations, but Moffett's version of it is rife with positive assessments. Clemens endorsed Moffett's celebratory account. It was published first in *McClure's Magazine* and then reprinted in the final volume of Mark Twain's collected works brought out in 1899 by the American Publishing Company, thus making it appear to be the last word on Mark Twain. For the original version, which is identical to that published in the collected edition, Clemens expressed his approval in a prefatory note not included in the reprinting: "This biographical sketch suits me entirely—in its simplicity, directness, dignity, lucidity—in all ways" ("Editor's Note" 523). Presumably, that "in all ways" decorously included the commendatory descriptions of Mark Twain's character and achievements.

If "ghost written" doesn't exactly explain this text, it comes close. Perhaps "ghost guided" is closer, but one way or another Clemens left his behind-the-scenes stamp on "Mark Twain: A Biographical Sketch." Kaplan observes that the sketch contained "much" that Clemens "said himself—in the freedom of anonymity—and nothing that he disapproved" (*Mr. Clemens and MT* 356). The sketch is a significant retrospective envisioning of Mark Twain by Sam Clemens as it etches the various conventionalities evident in the major texts of his career. Class consciousness, indeed upper-class bias, emerges at once: Samuel Clemens (the sketch mixes Clemens and Twain haphazardly) is said to have inherited "good blood" (315–16), and "Mark Twain's parents" are linked to both notable and noble people: on his father's side to the regicide judge Gregory Clement (mistakenly called "Clemens" in the article) and on his mother's to the aristocratic Lamptons (called "Lambtons") of Durham, England.[2] Education is both valued and deflected from the traditional, for Twain is praised for having "made the world his university" (317), and learning to pilot the Mississippi is said to require "a labor compared with which the efforts needed to acquire the degree of Doctor of Philosophy at a University are as light as a summer course of modern novels" (319). The office of pilot is heralded, as ever, for its "grandeur" and "majesty" (319)—its holders celebrated as "aristocrats" (322). The importance of domesticity emerges briefly but emphatically as Clemens is praised for having "one of the most ideal marriages in literary history," and Mark Twain is celebrated as a man "of family" (327). Reflecting values at odds with Twain's occasional reputation as buffoon and vulgarian but fully in accord with Clemens's deepest self-conceiving, the sketch notes a steady improvement in Mark Twain's character, claiming "spiritual growth," growth in "knowledge" and growth in "culture." He is finally said to be "an accomplished scholar and a man of the world" (329–30). Twain is elevated to the position of Sage: a "prophet of humanity" (329). And in terms that might make a ghost—or a ghost writer—blush, he is proclaimed a "master" (332) and a "classic" (333).

With economy, this biography, like the sprawling autobiography, centers on Twain's life as a literary man. Its governing idea is the one Clemens tried repeatedly to impart to his family, to his friends (most notably and successfully to Howells), and to his various audiences: the "humorist" evolved into the "philosopher" (328). Betraying in its very terms an acceptance of genteel critical standards, the sketch praises Mark Twain's writings for their "charm" (318), their "fidelity to human nature" (333), their "universal quality" (332), and their "power of moral uplift" (330). His humor is described as "sympathetic and buoyant" (318). Its aim is defined as something more than making people laugh; its "more important purpose" is "to make them think and feel" (333). Nearly acknowledging Twain's sentimentality, the sketch praises his power of "passionate sympathy" (329). His works, especially *Joan of Arc*, are said to possess a timeless power to "reach the elemental human heart" (329).

The biography concludes with an encomium whose earnest morality and overt sentimentality embody the very qualities of character and art that are claimed as Twain's:

> And with the progress of the years Mark Twain's own thoughts have become finer, his own feelings deeper and more responsive. Sympathy with the suffering, hatred of injustice and oppression, and enthusiasm for all that tends to make the world a more tolerable place for mankind to live in, have grown with his accumulating knowledge of life as it is. That is why Mark Twain has become a classic, not only at home, but in all lands whose people read and think about the common joys and sorrows of humanity (333).

The sketch says directly, albeit through the seeming voice of another ("seeming" because some of Twain shows in the writing as well as the ideas), what Clemens believed himself and wanted his audiences to believe about Mark Twain: that he is a serious man of propriety as well as a humorist of unpredictability. This biographical self-portrait echoes those positive descriptions of Twain provided through the years by those closest to him: it confirms (or at least repeats) Livy's sense of him as a serious moralist; Susy's insistence on his kind, sympathetic nature; Howells's celebration of his earnestness and humanity.

This casting of the persona Mark Twain as an icon of respectability had, despite its dual publication, only a limited readership. Still animated by the desire for the world to see the proper Mark Twain, Clemens staged a complicated public display of his persona that everyone interested in him came to know well: he appeared as the Man in the Pure White Suit.

Clemens first conceived of wearing white out of season in October 1906 while he was staying in Dublin, New Hampshire. Sadly he reflected on the seasonal change of attire customary for men: "One of my sorrows, when the summer ends, is that I must put off my cheery and comfortable white clothes and enter for the winter into the depressing captivity of the shapeless and degrading black ones" (*MTOA* 137). The terms of his lament are curious: in black he is both in captivity and degraded. At this time his secretary, Isabel Lyon, noted in her diary that he was "filled with the idea" of wearing "white clothes all winter" (qtd. in Budd, *Our MT* 207). To this end, he ordered new white suits, but with his usual flair for the theatrical he made his first highly public appearance in unseasonal white on December 7, 1906, when he spoke before a joint congressional committee on copyright. Howells remembered the moment: "The first time I saw him wear it [his white serge suit] was at the author's hearing before the Congressional Committee on Copyright in Washington. Nothing could have been more dramatic than the gesture with which he flung off his long loose overcoat, and stood forth in white from his feet to the crown of his silvery head. It was a magnificent coup" (*MyMT* 96). His speech was anything but a coup, however. In it Twain argues for the ownership of ideas, claiming the right to possess intellectual property, but he makes his points in a rambling commentary that bounces back and forth between abstract argument and personal anecdote. The humor running through the speech is distinctly odd as it turns now against his audience, then against publishers, then against himself with little sting to any of its bites; it even flirts with the off-color when he compares setting a copyright limit to restricting families to "twenty-two children by one mother" and then observes that there are "only one or two couples at one time in the United States that can reach that limit" (*MTSpk* 535). Equally off-key (though a different key) is his remark that he has "carefully raised" his two daughters "as young ladies, who don't know anything and can't do anything" (*MTSpk* 534). Given the unfocused, not to say discordant, nature of his talk, it may well be, as one critic has suggested, that the "central issue of copyright was almost entirely obscured" by his "performance"—in particular by his "dress" (Gillman, *Dark Twins* 184). Indirectly, however, his speech provides a clue to that dress, for at one point, as he suggests the intellectual constitution of material things, citing a "skyscraper," the "railway," the "telephone," and—just for fun—the "washtub," he observes that all of these are "*symbols* which *represent ideas*" (*MTSpk* 537, his emphasis). So are his white garments.

What did the white suit signify? The question has puzzled Twain's audience from his time to ours. Twain was acutely aware of the symbolic import of clothes, and he sometimes invested them with multiple meanings:

> I can't bear to put on black clothes again. I wish I could wear white all winter. I should prefer, of course, to wear colors, beautiful rainbow hues, such as the women have monopolized. Their clothing makes a great opera audience an enchanting spectacle, a delight to the eye and to the spirit—a garden of Eden for charm and color. The men, clothed in odious black, are scattered here and there over the garden like so many charred stumps. If we are going to be gay in spirit, why be clad in funeral garments? (qtd. in *MTB* 3:1341–42)

Casually here through his metaphors he locates in the difference between color and blackness a profound set of antinomies: female versus male, beauty versus ugliness, creativity versus sterility, primal innocence versus charred experience, wholeness as opposed to mutilation, eros as opposed to death. Having put on white as something of a whim, one fraught with defiance yet vague in import, Twain lost little time in defining the significance of his garb. Interviewed by the press when he appeared in white before the congressional committee, he explained his new dress: "I suppose everyone is wondering why I am wearing such apparently unseasonable clothes. I'll tell you. This is a uniform. It is the uniform of the American Association of Purity and Perfection, of which I am president, secretary and treasurer, and the only man in the United States eligible to membership" (*MTSpk* 530). The suggestion of a club of one is both a good joke and a powerful claim to distinction. In describing his suit as a uniform signifying "Purity and Perfection," Twain is in equal measure comic and self-vaunting. Throughout his career Twain did believe in his "purity"—that is, his moral probity. His white suit suggests such rectitude. He soon came to refer to his white clothes as his "don'tcareadamn suit" (qtd. in Kaplan, *Mr. Clemens and MT* 380), and his label captures both his resistance to convention—he doesn't care a damn—and his regard for it, a suit being a sign of respectability. Thus he laid claim for himself to a kind of freedom within propriety.

In an autobiographical dictation he ruminated further on the meaning of his attire: "I am considered eccentric because I wear white clothes both winter and summer. I am eccentric, then, because I prefer to be clean in the matter of raiment—clean in a dirty world; absolutely the only cleanly-clothed human being in all Christendom north of the Tropics. And that is what I am" (*AMT* 370). Here surely the literal becomes figurative through the moral and social implications of "clean" and "dirty." Throughout his career, Twain tended to equate "clean" with the civilized, the socially superior, the sexually innocent, and the morally correct, while "dirty" for him suggested the savage, the socially inferior, the sexually improper, and the morally corrupt.[3] Most often these antithetical qualities were gendered in his thinking: the first set as female, the second as male. To be civilized, as he understood it—that is, superior in class, proper in sexuality, and correct in morals—was to be, whether female or male, conventional in the extreme. If the transgressive Mark Twain distanced himself from society by attacking it, the bounded Mark Twain both attached himself to and departed from society by claiming to possess its virtues more fully than society itself does. Paradoxically, in wearing white out of season, he violated the conventional and proclaimed his conventionality at one and the same time.

Clearly he protested too much. He was no doubt in some unascertainable degree what Howells teasingly called him, a "whited sepulchre" (*MTHL* 2:823), covering with his pure white clothes some real or imagined impurities. Kaplan has suggested that they signified his "obsession with guilt, with forbidden and therefore unclean thoughts" (*Mr. Clemens and MT* 380). More recently, Evan Carton has argued that Twain's white suit not only manifests his claim to "stainlessness" but also invites those who see him in it "to examine him for a 'blemish'" (158), and he offers his own explanation of the blemish: Twain's complicity in "slavery," the "lust for wealth," and more broadly still, "whiteness" (168). This interpretation of the white suit ingeniously reads it as inverted symbolism (stainlessness becomes the signifier of blemishes, innocence becomes guilt, good becomes bad). At the other extreme Budd commonsensically emphasizes the literal: the suit's power "to break the winter gloom" ("Deconstructing" 7). Budd also points out that, whatever the white suit meant to Clemens, his public seized on it as "another sign" of Mark Twain's "individuality" (*Our MT* 210). If the suit concealed anything, however, it was probably neither unclean thoughts nor involvement in slavery, wealth, and whiteness, but even more encompassingly, the famous, transgressive humorist. In black, we recall, he felt both captive— that is, trapped in the role his public perceived, the one he tried repeatedly to redefine—and degraded, which is to say, denied the eminence and power that a recognition of his serious, nonrebellious self should have bestowed.

But to become preoccupied with the hidden interior of Clemens/ Twain is to miss the visible truth of the symbolic charade. It announced that Mark Twain was a figure of morality, and in time as he wore his white suit when pontificating humorously in public forums, it was recognized as the garb of the Sage. In wearing out-of-season white, Clemens not only violated the conventions of male dress but also seemed to cross gender lines by putting on a woman's color. (He would have preferred, he said, to dress in rainbow colors as women did.) He thus obliquely acknowledges the feeling person paradoxically expressed, suppressed, and understood as both female and "out of character" for Mark Twain in *Life on the Mississippi.* Throughout his life Clemens believed that women were the custodians of social propriety, of morality, and of civilization itself.[4] This is not to say that he thought men were excluded from these things, but only that women were their primary guardians. Men of fine character and feeling, gentlemen, were also for Clemens arbiters of the social, the moral, and the civilized. Significantly, when he put on his symbolic attire, Clemens chose to dress up—to be more elegant and refined—not down, as Whitman had in posing for the frontispiece of the first edition of *Leaves of Grass.* He did not want Mark Twain to be seen as one of the roughs. On the contrary, he chose to present him as a gentleman of sartorial splendor.

The symbolic declaration of propriety and prominence made by donning his white suit signals the neglected dimension of his creative self. Besides being transgressive in his writings, Mark Twain is also bounded. Not just the man on Holliday's hill, the humorist at the margins of proper society, he is also the man in the church, the tender man of conventional feelings—feelings that he takes to be feminine. If Mark Twain is, as he surely is, a subversive comic writer, he is also—and this has been the burden of this book—a humorist of orthodox values and ideas. The white suit bespeaks this; it signals the bedrock of conventionality in the persona Mark Twain. When Clemens put on his whites, he proclaimed Mark Twain to the world as nothing less than an eminent Victorian: pure, proper, moral, and civilized.

Whatever people made of his white suit, the symbol that would dominate his final years and literally see him to his grave, the self-assessments of the ghost-written biography took hold. After he died, obituary after obituary sounded the same notes of evaluation struck by Clemens himself—or struck by Moffett and then sanctioned by Clemens. The reports of Mark Twain's death—of his real one—lauded him for his fine character as well as his artistry, defining him as a man of probity, his works as texts of profundity. Clemens's own long campaign to rewrite Mark Twain from comic fool to moral philosopher had succeeded. As one postmortem tribute put it, Twain's humor was "the humor of a deep thinker, a gentle but penetrating observer, a philosopher who loved mankind while seeing all its weaknesses" ("The Death of Mark Twain," *Chatauquan* 9).[5] Mark Twain could hardly have said it better himself; indeed, as we've seen, he had said it himself (except for that "loved mankind"). Surely in this way too the reports of his death were an exaggeration, but not by any means a complete distortion. The man so many thousands viewed in his white suit in the casket in the Brick Presbyterian Church in New York was— and still is—visible in the works of Mark Twain.

NOTES

Introduction

1. In the beginning of his *Our Mark Twain: The Making of His Public Personality*, Louis J. Budd makes a similar point, one that his study amply illustrates: "effective naysaying carries over into affirmation" (xv).

2. The idea of the gentleman in America has a complex history (see Cady and Gilmour) and important regional variations (see Taylor), but according to one cultural historian, the American gentleman was an "invention of a national imagination in need of ideals" (Castronovo 15). Twain's idea of the gentleman will come up several times in this study, but his fundamental view was set forth as early as 1867 in a sketch published in the New York *Sunday Mercury* in which he distinguishes between the old ideal of the patrician gentleman of fine moral character and the new type of moneyed social gentleman whose character is dubious at best (see "The Winner of the Medal," ts, MTP). For three other early formulations that also contrast the moral and social gentleman, see chapter 33 of *The Gilded Age* (1873), the short sketch "Francis Lightfoot Lee" (1877), and the June 1, 1870 entry in Twain's notebook. Twain's own moral emphasis remained constant throughout his career, as the 1906 dictation, "The American Gentleman," makes clear (*MTE* 33–34).

3. Twain's defenders were by no means limited to these three; indeed, he seems to have prompted defense from many friends and constant readers, eliciting corrective public praise from people as different as the minister (and close friend) Joseph Hopkins Twichell (see "Mark Twain") and the Columbia literature professor (and casual friend) Brander Matthews (see *The Tocsin of Revolt*).

4. Defining varieties of humor, James Russell Lowell once pinpointed the core of any humorist as the kind of doubleness embodied in Clemens by Mark Twain. Lowell insisted that the "advantage of the humorist" was a "duality in his mind"; the humorist cannot, he argued, "be a man of one idea—for the essence of humor lies in the contrast of two" (83).

5. John Gerber's seminal study of Twain's comic masks ("Mark Twain's Use of the Comic Pose") locates, in addition to three poses of inferiority—Sufferer,

Simpleton, and Tenderfoot—four postures of superiority—Gentleman, Sentimentalist, Instructor, and Moralist—that are variously related to the conventional Twain I am concerned with here. But for Gerber these four poses are
comic devices, while I see the proper Twain enacting serious ideas and values.
Florence's lively and perceptive recent study of Twain's early works defines the
persona in them as "multifaceted" (3), but like those critics who focus chiefly on
Twain the transgressive humorist, he ends up seeing the multifaceted Twain as
a writer "who uses the plasticity of humor to unsettle our notions of a fixed world"
(16). Twain sometimes does this, but I hope to show that sometimes he does just
the opposite: he reinforces conventional notions and defines a stable world.

6. The classic studies of American humor remain Rourke (*American Humor*),
Blair (*Native American Humor*), and Blair and Hill (*America's Humor*), to which
one needs to add Walker's more recent study of women's humor, *A Very Serious
Thing*. The standard study of both Southwestern humor and of Twain's use of it
is Lynn (*Mark Twain and Southwestern Humor*); his account is usefully enlarged
by Budd ("Gentlemanly Humorists") and Cox ("Humor of the Old Southwest").

7. His expressed dislike of Mark Twain here must be taken with a grain of salt,
however, since Clemens was trying to avoid having Mark Twain write articles for
the *American Publisher*, the house organ of the American Publishing Company,
which Clemens had arranged to be edited by Orion.

Chapter One

1. The impulse to create a self other than himself, to enlarge himself into a
figure of cultural significance, seems to have been innate in Clemens, though after the invention of Mark Twain what was instinctive became self-conscious.
The impulse is strikingly evident in an 1853 letter from the then seventeen-year-
old Clemens to his brother (no doubt written with an eye on publication in his
brother's Muscatine *Journal*) about a trip to Independence Hall; the letter contains this bit of playful posturing: "A small pine bench or pew in this Hall bears
this inscription—'Washington, Franklin and Bishop White sat on this Bench.'
Of course, I 'sot down' on it. I would have whittled off a chip, if I had got half a
chance" (*L1* 23). Brief as it is, the passage dramatizes the self in terms of contrasts
that anticipate Mark Twain: civilization and the backwoods, the grand and the
lowly, restraint and revolution, propriety and irreverence, proper behavior and
unruly impulse. For illuminating analyses of Twain's later self-mythologizing, see
the various essays in Davis and Beidler.

2. Warren uses "failing westward" in the poem "Last Laugh" (*Now and Then*) to define John Marshall Clemens's career. The poem itself is an intriguing capsule biography and interpretation of Mark Twain.

3. The studies of both Foucault and Peter Gay have made the case that the Victorians were preoccupied with sexual matters and that they in fact created the modern obsession with sex, but the Victorian interest in sex did not alter the social decorum that enjoined silence on the subject.

4. The most extensive discussion of John Marshall Clemens is in Wecter (chaps. 1–9), but the best assessment of his influence on his son is Rubin (34–81). Malin offers some provocative speculations about the father-son relationship.

5. Clemens's flirtation with suicide remains an opaque event in his western life. At least two bits of evidence, both somewhat problematical, suggest a suicidal state of mind. The first, in a letter to Orion and Mollie in October 1865, seems more rhetorical than sincere: "You are in trouble, & in debt—so am I. I am utterly miserable—so are you. . . . If I do not get out of debt in 3 months,—pistols or poison for one—exit *me*" (*L1* 324). The second, a marginal note made in 1909 in a copy of the *Letters of James Russell Lowell*, recalls, with the questionable precision of a sixty-nine-year-old man in failing health, an "experience of 1866": "I put the pistol to my head but wasn't man enough to pull the trigger" (*L1* 325 n. 6).

6. In 1897–98, writing an installment of his autobiographical memoirs, "Early Days," Clemens with a combination of pride and self-deprecation cited the regicide Gregory Clement (he misnamed him Geoffrey) as one of his ancestors (*MTOA* 4–5). Early in 1891, he sought and obtained a facsimile of the warrant to execute Charles I and proudly noted the signature of this ancestor on it; and in the same year Olivia obtained from his English publisher, Andrew Chatto, two pictures of the judge at Charles I's trial as Christmas presents for her husband (Welland 158).

7. For detailed accounts of the conflicts I summarize here, see *MTEnt* (24–30), Benson (106–113), Mack (307–26), Fatout (196–213), *L1* (273–303), and my own "Mark Twain Fights Sam Clemens' Duel."

8. Walker's career is examined in Greene and in Wallace (142–240). For Twain's admiration of Walker, see Duckett (19–20).

9. Twain again seriously evokes the powerful, manly eye in "The United States of Lyncherdom" and "A Double-Barreled Detective Story."

10. In the last retelling of the duel, the autobiographical dictations, Twain adds a new ending to his previous accounts by explaining that there was a new Nevada law against dueling and that a Judge North was so "anxious to have some

victims for that law" that he would put Twain "in prison" without pardon for "two years" (*AMT* 118). In fact there was no new law, only an old one that was never seriously enforced (see *MTEnt* 28–29), but in making up this particular end to the aborted duel Twain transforms himself from aggressor to victim, expressing in the process both the sense of persecution and the self-pity characteristic of the feelings evoked in him by his father's Tennessee lands.

11. In *San Francisco's Literary Frontier* (chap. 5) Walker provides a good account of the coterie of writers and artists who affected bohemianism, though he tends to downplay the importance of the bohemian stance. For an intriguing discussion of the import of bohemian acting and writing as a class-driven challenge to conventional culture, especially its definitions of masculinity, see Knoper (chap. 1). In his history of bohemianism Parry observes that the "desire to escape from the painful reality of an uncertain social position has been . . . one of the chief distinguishing reasons for Bohemianism" (5).

12. Edgar Branch, in particular, often links the early with the later Twain, observing that some of his West Coast exposés voice "the same indignant humanitarianism that he later directed against the church, imperialism, and war" (*Literary Apprenticeship* 144). In even more sweeping terms, Lennon launches her study of Twain in the West to show that he was "an essentially politically motivated writer and thinker" whose politics were formed by "a confluence of specifically Western experiences" (xvii).

13. For a useful overview of "The Male Tradition and the Female Tradition" of American humor, see Walker's *A Very Serious Thing* (chap. 2). Fender notes both Twain's uneasiness in depicting women and his frequent aggression toward them (chap. 6). In his fine study of Twain and the feminine aesthetic, Stoneley explores not only Twain's traditional stereotyping of women but also his valorizations of women and his incorporation of the feminine into his writings.

14. Twain was so troubled by her sexuality that he recalled it some forty-three years later when he wrote *Letters from the Earth* (41).

15. Frear believed that Burlingame was "during his nineteen days stay in almost daily association with Twain" (112). In the introduction to his collection of Twain's speeches, Paine explained Burlingame's importance this way: "Burlingame's example, companionship, and advice, coming when it did, were in the nature of a revelation to Samuel Clemens, who returned to San Francisco, consciously or not, the inhabitant of a new domain" (viii).

16. Standard accounts of Burlingame's career can be found in Williams and in Morse; for a more recent assessment, see Tsai.

17. Budd points out that the Burlingame treaty not only catered to commercial interests but also ensured a cheap supply of coolie labor (*Social Philosopher* 31–32); it thereby codified the outlook articulated by Twain himself in his original Sandwich Island letters.

18. Ignoring Bladensburg, the traditional dueling ground five miles outside of Washington, Burlingame specified the Canadian side of Niagara Falls, knowing that it would be dangerous for Brooks to travel there through an angry North. There is also some evidence that Burlingame may have left Washington secretly for Hamilton, Ohio, in order to avoid any further negotiation of the duel that might bring it to pass. The fullest account of all this is in Campbell and in Bigelow.

19. After Smith's seminal analysis (*Development* 52–70), the most ambitious interpretation of the text as a process of initiation is Gunn's argument that Twain's narrative traces "the stages of individuation," rites of passage reflecting Joseph Campbell's notion of monomyth, that lead to "self-actualization and maturation as a contributing member of society" (564). This should be compared to Karnath's argument that "the greenhorn is initiated into nothing" (214).

20. The new California edition of *Roughing It* issued by the Mark Twain Project provides the contents of Orion's lost journal, taken from a letter to his wife, Mollie, identifies in its Explanatory Notes Twain's earlier newspaper articles, and documents his use of the Sandwich Island letters.

21. Michelson's provocative reading is in many ways a culmination of the critical emphasis on disruption in *Roughing It*, for he sees the narrative itself as one that "defies logic, obeys no rules, goes everywhere except to its own conclusion" (63) and argues that "illusions and delusions" must "prevail as the order of the day" (65) as Twain is "cured of notions like 'reality' and 'truth'" (68) to escape into "places away from the real, and from culturally grounded laws of selfhood and storytelling" (74). While earlier critics saw the disorders registered in the text as reflections of the region, Michelson sees them as preferences of the author.

22. I am indebted here to Bridgman's analysis of the entire Greeley correspondence, including his illuminating insights into this ominous phrase (*Traveling* 39–48).

23. Criticism has tended to celebrate Twain's depiction of these vernacular speakers as a part of a presumed affirmation of values at odds with the dominant culture (again Smith, *Development* 52–70, is central here), but Twain's actual presentation suggests not his affinity for them but his distance from them. In his review of the book, Twain's neighbor Charles Dudley Warner understood that Twain used these figures to capture the life of the region, reporting "the odd

characters he meets and the people of the new countr[i]es he describes, exactly as they were, slang and all" (qtd. in Introduction to *RI* 885). Sewell has correctly pointed out that "Twain's relation to the colloquial or vernacular language was ambivalent throughout his life" (16).

24. Cracroft's two articles form the most complete account of Twain's attitude toward the Mormons as well as his use of them in *Roughing It*.

Chapter Two

1. Cultural analysis had become so significant to Victorians that by 1825 the English *Quarterly Review* announced that the chief value of travel was "the view which it gives us of the state of society and the moral condition of large masses of people." This was, the *Review* cautiously conceded, "perhaps more important" than information about "geographical discovery" ("African Discoveries," 518).

2. Collected in *Mark Twain's Travels with Mr. Brown*, this correspondence has received little critical attention. Most comments have focused on the Twain-Brown comic axis rather than on the content of the letters themselves (see, e.g., Rogers 42–43). Emerson provides one commentary that does briefly take up subject matter (*Authentic* 40–41).

3. For a powerful analysis of the age's use of the savage-civilized dichotomy, see Bederman. She is primarily concerned with the deployment of the dichotomy in the cultural construction of manhood. For illuminating commentary on Twain and manhood in *The Innocents Abroad*, see Stahl (chap. 1), Messent (chap. 2), and Stowe (chap. 7).

4. The eminent Victorian Sigmund Freud suggested that "the use of soap" was "an actual yardstick of civilization" (*Civilization and Its Discontents* 40). For recent studies that explore the connections between hygiene and morality in Victorian culture, see Haley, Mort, and Stallybrass and White.

5. Walker points out in his study of literary (and nonliterary) travelers to the Holy Land that many hoped to answer their "questions of faith or *lack of faith*" (*Irreverent Pilgrims* 31, emphasis added). This strikes me as a formulation that may well illuminate Clemens's own circumstance.

6. Michelson sees Twain's emotion at the site of the Crucifixion partly as a polite strategy of balance (or compensation for the overt satire unleashed at palpable fraud elsewhere in the Church), partly as the expression of "a dire need to *feel*," and partly as the consequence of the fact that Twain "can at least believe in death" (60–61, his emphasis). Twain's notebook entry only further complicates

our reading of this moving moment in the context of so many sham ones, for it expresses skepticism as a wish for faith: "O for the ignorance & the confidingness of ignorance that could enable a man to kneel at the Sepulchre & look at the rift in the rock, & the socket of the cross & the tomb of Adam & feel & know & never question that they were genuine" (*N&J1* 368).

7. The loss of faith, as well as the struggle to recover it, has long been a standard element in the analysis of Victorian culture (Buckley, Houghton). For Clemens's own religious struggles, see Ensor, Cummings (*MT and Science*), Emerson ("MT's Quarrel with God"), and various articles by Brodwin.

8. Smith provides the most thorough discussion of the dinner and its aftermath ("That Hideous Mistake"), but his account should be supplemented by Lynn (*William Dean Howells*) and Lowry.

9. Ferguson suggests that Clemens went abroad at least in part because of what he took to be the disaster of his speech (192), but Blair contests the idea (*MT & Huck Finn* 159–60). Kaplan echoes Ferguson (*Mr. Clemens & MT* 213), as do the editors of Twain's notebooks for this period (*N&J2* 41).

10. When Twain first imagined this opening, he was both gleeful and secretive, wanting to keep the three-part joke fresh for publication (*MTHL* 1:249; *MTLP* 109). The idea of nontravel may have had its origin in the widely publicized walk Clemens took with Twichell from Hartford to Boston in November 1874. After a brave start—they made some thirty-four miles in a day and a half—they gave up and took the train (*MTHL* 1:36–37).

Chapter Three

1. Twain recounted the courtship in his autobiography and turned it into something of a legend, one which his relatives and later biographers loved to retell. For Twain's version, see *AMT* 183–90; for family variations, see Samuel Webster (*MTBus* 98) and Ida Langdon ("My Uncle Mark Twain" in Jerome and Wisbey, *MT in Elmira* 51–53). Paine, Ferguson, and Kaplan give essentially the same account, but Hoffman challenges several familiar aspects of the story, stressing in particular Jervis Langdon's early acceptance of Clemens and Olivia's equally speedy acquiescence (*Inventing MT* 139–69).

2. Although I believe that we should view the courtship letters as Mark Twain creations, I will nonetheless follow the biographical and critical convention of referring to them as Clemens's. Kauffman provides a compelling theoretical framework for viewing love letters that underscores their status as *created* texts.

She suggests that such letters, written out of a desire that is endlessly transcribable, are by virtue of their originating circumstance—the separation of the lovers—performative rather than mimetic pieces that create the absent beloved one as well as the present writer, offering illusion and artifice to be embraced by both the writer and receiver of the love letter (17–27).

3. For courtship practices, see Rothman; Davidson's introduction to *The Book of Love* is also useful in this regard.

4. The lecture is reproduced in *MTSpk* (27–36); for an extensive analysis of the text and its context, see Lorch and Boewe.

5. Harris provides an illuminating analysis of the different reading strategies employed by Olivia and Clemens, and she does so in part by examining their divergent approaches to Dickens, as well as Shakespeare (*Courtship* 106–34). Without contesting her conclusions, I would only add to them that in some moods Olivia and Clemens may have found a common ground for their shared reading in a mutual appreciation of effectively rendered emotion.

6. Harris provides the best account of Clemens's interest in science during this period, and she convincingly distinguishes his approach from Olivia's (*Courtship* 46–69); but also see Hill ("Mark Twain's Lectures on Science") and Cummings (*MT and Science*).

7. The incident, described in detail by Kaplan (*Mr. Clemens and MT* 88–90), illustrates not only how literary Clemens's correspondence was but also how easily the ostensibly private could be served up for public consumption.

8. There is a family tradition, one often repeated in scholarship, that Olivia lacked a sense of humor. She was, her cousin Hattie Lewis recalled, "rich, beautiful and intellectual, but she could not see through a joke, or see anything to laugh at in the wittiest sayings unless explained in detail" (qtd. in *L2* 249). The notion that Olivia was without a sense of humor should be dispelled by her commonplace book, in which she recorded varied bits of humor as well as praise of humor by famous writers (ms. DV161.MTP).

9. For Clemens's idealization of Jervis Langdon and Langdon's manipulation of him, see Steinbrink (*Getting to Be MT* 41, 68). Steinbrink sees Langdon as "an adumbration of the father" Clemens "lost as a boy," while I view him as a variant of the Good Father first found in Anson Burlingame.

10. Clemens and Olivia used Holmes's *The Autocrat at the Breakfast-Table* as a kind of courting book, with Clemens apparently reading the book first, annotating it, and then giving it to Livy (Gribben, *MT's Library* 1:317). His annotations are often intended to be humorous, and apparently Olivia enjoyed them (they are reproduced in Booth).

11. In her study of Twain's preferred images, Harris examines this letter as an indication that Olivia will "provide the stability that his public life lacks," that the home she creates will be "the innermost circle of the sphere around which his multiple personalities will revolve" (*Escape from Time* 117).

12. The fullest argument for Olivia's lifelong influence on Mark Twain, sometimes a convincing account, sometimes a bit of a stretch, is Skandera-Trombley's *Mark Twain in the Company of Women*.

Chapter Four

1. For three very different readings of Boston culture, see Green (*The Problem of Boston*), Buell, and O'Connell.

2. The definitive account of the pilots' association is Branch (*MT and the Starchy Boys*).

3. For a careful study of the proper Bostonian's attention to money, see Kolko; for Clemens's own interest in it in association with piloting, see Branch ("'Old Times': Biography and Craftsmanship"); and for an unusual reading of the "Old Times" papers themselves in terms of "the economics of the aesthetics of piloting," see Horwitz.

4. Arguing, contrary to most biographical and critical studies, that Mark Twain had a "fundamentally unitary self," Branch offers this intriguing explanation of the apparent oppositions in Twain: "His sense of self in relation to *future* experience was positive, strong, and aggressive. . . . But his recall of *past* experience is known to have often been skewed toward the negative: memories of past embarrassments, frustrations, and wounded feelings were never entirely laid to rest" ("'Old Times': Biography and Craftsmanship" 80–82). This view may well resolve—or at least explain—many of the contradictory elements in *Life*. For a different approach that emphasizes a protean Mark Twain, see Brown.

5. In "Why I Killed My Brother," Robinson reads this episode biographically, finding Clemens's "unconscious hostility toward his brother" projected onto Brown and his own "repressed feelings of self-reproach" targeted in the pilot, making him the object of "righteous wrath" (176). Cox associates Brown with Pap Finn and sees the conflict as marking the transition from the "humor" of "Old Times" to the "essential pathos" of *Life on the Mississippi* (*Fate* 162–64).

6. There are discrepancies between the version Twain gives here in *Life* and the ascertainable facts, and there is one crucial piece of missing evidence: no scholar has been able to verify that Sellers's notices were ever signed "Mark Twain" (a notice signed simply "I. Sellers" is extant). One critic has suggested

that the account in *Life* is "an authentic tall tale" (Cox, *Fate* 164–66). An alternate explanation of the origin of the pseudonym argues that it was either a bar tot—charging two drinks—or a term derived from Clemens's habit of having two drinks in a row (Fatout 34–66). The definitive review of all this, one that provides important new evidence, is Kruse ("Mark Twain's *Nom de Plume*").

7. Critics have tried to discern the essence of Twain in the pseudonym itself, as if the literal could encompass the figurative and a simple term of river work could reveal the full range of a complex literary personality. The term has been read as a signal for safe water, for dangerous water, or more ambiguously as both. Cardwell reviews all this ("Clemens' Magical Pseudonym"). I side with those who opt for the cry as a sign of safety—in the context of this study, one more small signal of the conventionality in Mark Twain.

8. Since Marx's seminal essay ("The Pilot and the Passenger"), the cub's learning to read the river has become the site of critical controversy. Burde maintains that he learns through "intuition" (882), while Branch contends that he learns through "empirical training" ("The Pilot and the Writer" 33). Cummings ("The Science of Piloting") argues for both, as I do here.

9. Horwitz also links the cub's learning to the writer's through this passage, but he feels that "the writer's manner of knowing cannot be fully detailed" (109–10).

Chapter Five

1. The critical literature on sentimentality is now voluminous. For its characteristic effects I have drawn on Stevick, Fred Kaplan, and Fisher (*Hard Facts*); for its cultural significance, Douglas, Tompkins, and the essays in Samuels.

2. Much of the critical literature that illuminates adventure is only peripherally concerned with it. In defining adventure, I draw on ideas of Bataille, Cawelti, Day, Detienne, Green (*Adventurous Male*), Simmel, and Nerlich.

3. The Victorian home functioned as both refuge from the world and as preparatory school for it. It was often, as Houghton long ago pointed out, a kind of secular church in which children, especially bad boys, were taught altruistic emotions that could replace weakening traditional Christian ethics (347). Women were the crucial shapers of children into moral adults (Ryan 45–85). For Twain's own imagining of the home, see Krauth ("MT at Home in the Gilded Age") and Harris (*Escape from Time* 117–18).

4. For a succinct and illuminating account of the history of *Tom Sawyer* criticism, see Scharnhorst. Mitchell reviews the popularity of the novel, finding in its mesh of "contrary forces" (*TS* xii) the grounds for its perennial appeal, yet puz-

zling over its artistic lapses and the morality of its "darker reaches" (*TS* xiv). I hope to show that the novel's popular appeal and its conventional morality derive from its sentimentality.

5. Citing no fewer than ten certain—or likely—sources, Emerson points out that *Tom Sawyer* reflects not only Clemens's actual boyhood but also "Mark Twain's reading" (*Authentic MT* 80–81). For sources, see also "Introduction" and "Textual Notes" in *TS*, as well as Blair (*MT and Huck Finn* 50–70). Given this consciousness of other texts, it is not surprising that Twain attends to modes of expression in his own.

Chapter Six

1. For standard accounts of the writing of *Huck Finn*, see Blair (*MT & Huck Finn*, 249–59) and Blair's introduction to *Huck Finn* (xxiii–l). More interpretative recent commentaries are Doyno and Quirk (10–41).

2. Sundquist provides a useful overview of old and new approaches to realism (3–24). For specific commentary on *Huck Finn*, see Bell (39–69) and Quirk (83–105). Bell in particular challenges the idea that the novel is realistic, but his terms are quite different from mine here.

3. Clemens's remembrance of his father as austere and intimidating is documented in chapter 1; for his fond recollection of his mother as emotional and compassionate, see "Jane Lampton Clemens," *AI* 82–92. The various versions of the autobiography also draw the same contrasts.

4. The character of Jim and the concomitant issue of Twain's racism (or antiracism) have become central considerations in recent interpretation of the novel. For a firm, if contradictory, grounding on these topics, see the essays in Leonard et al., eds., *Satire or Evasion? Black Perspectives on "Huckleberry Finn,"* Quirk ("Is *Huckleberry Finn* Politically Correct?" 147–62), Messent (chap. 5, "Racial Politics in *Huckleberry Finn*" 86–109), and Fishkin, *Was Huck Black?*

5. The critical literature on *Huckleberry Finn* is now several times longer than the novel itself, and illuminating insights abound in it. From different perspectives, these commentaries are especially useful in considering the heart/conscience conflict: Cox (*Fate* 156–84), Bennett ("The Conscience of *Huck Finn*"), Gabler-Hover ("Sympathy Not Empathy"), Opdahl ("When Feelings Go Bad"), and Camfield (*Sentimental Twain* 141–50).

6. The connection Brooks makes between melodrama and some lost—but still felt and longed for—system of values shows up in several other important studies. Janet Gabler-Hover links the ethical vision of nineteenth-century American

novelists, including Twain, to a fading tradition of rhetorical idealism (*Truth in American Fiction*), and in his study of sentimentality in nineteenth- and twentieth-century literature, Fulweiler points to what he terms the Victorian "psychomachia": a split between a "cold rationalistic spirit" and a "warm, yearning need" for "relationship" to and "participation" in a lost world of values associated with both nature and the nuclear family (22–23).

7. Cox's long-familiar but still provocative reading of the end of the novel as a burlesque of moral sentiment (*Fate* 180–84) is echoed in Bell's recent suggestion that we "read the problematic of the ending of *Huckleberry Finn* as an extended, terminal deflection of the feeling built up in the first thirty-one chapters—into one last (and in this case finally tiresome) joke" (64). Both of these approaches (and others like them) ignore the clear moments of nonburlesque Twain creates in the end.

Chapter Seven

1. Twain's tiff with Arnold is traced in Hoben and in Baetzhold (chaps. 6 and 7). The Arnold material is readily available in *General Grant by Matthew Arnold with a Rejoinder by Mark Twain* and in "Civilization in the United States."

2. Twain first replied on 27 April 1887 in his speech to the Connecticut Army and Navy Club, and then a second time on 25 June 1888 in his letter to Yale accepting an honorary M.A. (*N&J3* 299; for his various planned rebuttals, see entries in notebooks 27 and 28, *N&J3*).

3. For accounts of the "crisis in masculinity," see Bederman, Leverenz, and the essays collected in Carnes and Griffen, ed., *Meanings for Manhood*. Paradoxically, troubled men in America sought more robust expressions of their masculinity, on the one hand, and softer signs of it, on the other. Hank's divided character is thus very much a part of Twain's cultural milieu. Stahl provides an especially illuminating analysis of the sexual politics in the novel (85–120). Future attempts to come to grips with Twain's notions of manhood will have to grapple with his infatuation with the military recently documented so fully in Leon.

4. Individual morality certainly remained central in the age of reform, but there is a discernible shift among progressives in tactical emphasis away from moral suasion to empirical data (Hofstadter 174–214; Lasch, *New Radicalism* ix–xviii).

5. Although he later defended his sage as a "natural gentleman," as a man of "good heart" and "high intent" (*LLMT* 257), Twain also described him as a "perfect ignoramus" (qtd. in *CY*, ed. Ensor 309). After finishing the manuscript of *Yankee*, he worried that some of his sharp didacticism might be too strong; he

urged Howells to excise "blasts of opinion which are so strongly worded as to repel instead of persuade" (*MTHL* 2:609).

6. These attitudes are perceptively—and thoroughly—explored in the various essays collected in *Mark Twain's "Pudd'nhead Wilson": Race, Conflict, and Culture*, ed. Gillman and Robinson.

7. For two different readings of the philosophical orientation of Twain's fictional treatment of the individual self, see Johnson and Horn. Blues provides a consistently sensible and illuminating discussion of the relation of this self to community.

8. During this period, he also created what he himself sometimes mistakenly thought of as his best book, *Personal Recollections of Joan of Arc*. The book has generally been ignored in criticism. Concentrating on Joan herself, Michelson reads it provocatively as an "escape from selfhood" (203), but in fact Joan has a self (though not a psychology). Her self is constituted by a veritable compendium of the traditional Victorian virtues for a woman (Warren 154–56; Stahl 126). Clearly an inferior work, the novel reveals the conventionality of Twain traced in this study, but unlike the major works in which Twain's orthodoxy is embedded in compelling narratives (and often complicated by opposing tensions), in *Joan* the ordinary is rendered uninteresting. Cox rightly observes that Joan of Arc is "the total embodiment" of "conventional values," but failing to see that such conventionality also informs Twain's greatest works, including, as I hope I've shown, his comic ones, Cox concludes that Joan is a threat to Twain's humorous identity (*Fate* 264). On the contrary, she is just one more expression, sadly a tedious one, of the proper Mark Twain. In the context of the Sage, what is noteworthy about Joan is that Twain is intrigued by someone who is apparently given the gift of prophecy, like Hank Morgan in his retrospective visionary moments, and who has "intellectual superiority to all other human beings" (Camfield 202), thus anticipating the even more powerful figure of Little Satan in the Mysterious Stranger manuscripts.

9. Once the textual matters surrounding the Mysterious Stranger have been settled, critics have tended to examine the tale—or tales—for philosophical orientation. Their readings range from hopeless nihilism (Smith, *Development* 185–88) to optimistic existentialism (Kravitz 133–48). Michelson's emphasis on the story as the late Twain's free play, as an expression of "a free mind" (219), is refreshing in its verve but only defines another form of ideology: one that insists on being free of ideology. My interest here is different, and perhaps less ambitious, for I do not try to define Twain's philosophical outlook, only to adumbrate the tension between uttering ideas and storytelling.

Chapter Eight

1. The daring of the late Twain remains in dispute. Anderson ("Introduction," *Pen*) and Geismar (188–239) both argue that Twain boldly spoke out on controversial issues, but Leary and Hill (*God's Fool* 40) maintain that he cautiously checked the pulse of public opinion, publishing only what would match it and repressing what would not.

2. Shillingsburg concludes her definitive study of the tour with the assertion that, despite its real difficulties and despite his later grim recollections of it, Twain "enjoyed nearly the whole experience" (230).

3. For an especially illuminating discussion of Twain's creative process, including his use of audience, see Kiskis ("Collaborative Autobiography").

4. Kiskis has explored the importance of Susy's biography for Twain's autobiography, noting in particular that Twain's lack of form reflects "the disorder of Susy's own biographical method" and more generally that Twain "often followed Susy's lead" ("Susy Clemens" 48).

5. The same uneasiness, paradoxically marking the same basic conventionality, guides Twain's treatment of his most famous antireligious text, *Letters from the Earth*, for, of course, he felt that the heterodox ideas expressed in those writings were too blasphemous for his public. Hill has pointed out that the ideas vented there were "commonplace thoughts for Mark Twain" (*God's Fool* 248). Some measure of the truth of this may be taken by comparing *Letters* to Twain's various lifelong screeds on the Bible (see the texts in *WIM* and *The Bible according to Mark Twain*). Most of Twain's hostile attitudes were the commonplaces of the free-thought movement of Twain's own time (see Austin). Robert Ingersoll, whom Twain knew and admired, made something of a career declaiming them to interested audiences. Twain's reticence about what he took to be his heresy actually bespeaks his bedrock orthodoxy. As Baender has observed, "secret skeptics," like Mark Twain, felt "honorable in maintaining their private beliefs while submitting to the compromise of an outer decorum" (*WIM* 33). By concealing his unorthodox views, Twain could, among other things, preserve his very conventional sense of honor.

6. In a segment of autobiography not included in the *North American Review*, Twain wrote, "Life does not consist mainly—or even largely—of facts and happenings. It consists mainly of the storm of thoughts that is forever blowing through one's head." But then excusing himself from recording such subjectivity, he insists that not even "fifteen stenographers hard at work" could begin to keep up with the storm of ideas and impressions (*MTA* 1:283).

Coda

1. Kaplan notes that Clemens submitted his manuscript to Livy "who made a few small but characteristic changes" (*Mr. Clemens and MT* 355).

2. References here and throughout are to the text published in *The Writings of Mark Twain*, vol. 22, rather than to the less accessible version that appeared in *McClure's*. There are few critical commentaries on this sketch, but Lowry gives one extended analysis that explores it in relation to "Franklin's paradigm of self-making" (128). My interest is in the sketch as an evaluative assessment of the self-made literary figure.

3. He fetishizes "clean" and "dirty" very much as Toni Morrison has suggested the white creative imagination does "white" and "black": to evoke "erotic fears or desires" and to establish "fixed and major difference where difference does not exist or is minimal." In terms that seem especially apt for Mark Twain, she adds, "Fetishization is a strategy often used to assert the categorical absolutism of civilization and savagery" (68).

4. Wecter (chap. 2) outlines the cultural circumstances that shaped Clemens's thinking about gender, while Harris (*Escape from Time*, chap. 7) elaborates on the creative resonance of such thinking for Mark Twain. Criticism has divided sharply over Twain's attitudes toward and representation of women. The negative brief is filed forcefully by Joyce Warren; the positive case is made constructively by Skandera-Trombley. For an extended review of Twain and women, see Fishkin ("MT and Women").

5. I am indebted to Thomas Tenney, who kindly allowed me to read through his extensive collection of Twain obituaries.

BIBLIOGRAPHY

Works by Mark Twain

Mark Twain Papers. Bancroft Library, University of California, Berkeley.

Samuel L. Clemens's autobiographical dictations. Mark Twain Papers.

Adventures of Huckleberry Finn. Ed. Walter Blair and Victor Fischer. Berkeley: University of California Press, 1985.

The Adventures of Tom Sawyer, Tom Sawyer Abroad, Tom Sawyer, Detective. Ed. John C. Gerber, Paul Baender, and Terry Firkins. Berkeley: University of California Press, 1980.

The Autobiography of Mark Twain. Ed. Charles Neider. New York: Harper and Brothers, 1959.

The Bible according to Mark Twain. Ed. Howard G. Baetzhold and Joseph B. McCullough. Athens: University of Georgia Press, 1995.

Clemens of the "Call": Mark Twain in San Francisco. Ed. Edgar M. Branch. University of California Press, 1969.

The Complete Essays of Mark Twain. Ed. Charles Neider. Garden City, N.Y.: Doubleday, 1963.

A Connecticut Yankee in King Arthur's Court. Ed. Allison R. Ensor. New York: Norton, 1982.

Contributions to the "Galaxy," 1868–1871, by Mark Twain. Ed. Bruce R. McElderry Jr. Gainesville, Fla.: Scholars' Facsimiles and Reprints, 1961.

Early Tales and Sketches, Volume 1 (1851–1864). Ed. Edgar Marquess Branch and Robert H. Hirst. Berkeley: University of California Press, 1979.

Early Tales and Sketches, Volume 2 (1864–1865). Ed. Frederick Anderson, Lin Salamo, and Bernard L. Stein. Berkeley: University of California Press, 1975.

"Editor's Note." *McClure's Magazine* 23.6 (1899): 523.

Following the Equator: A Journey around the World. 1897. New York: Dover, 1989.

The Forgotten Writings of Mark Twain. Ed. Henry Duskis. New York: Philosophical Library, 1963

"Foster's Case." *Mark Twain: Life as I Find It: Essays, Sketches, Tales and Other Material.* Garden City, N.Y.: Doubleday, 1961.

"Francis Lightfoot Lee." *Pennsylvania Magazine* 1.3 (1877): 343–47. Rpt. in *Mark Twain's Collected Tales, Sketches, Speeches, and Essays, 1852–1890*, ed. Louis J. Budd. New York: Library of America, 1992.

Goldmines and Guttersnipes: Tales of California by Mark Twain. Ed. Ken Chowder. San Francisco: Chronicle Books, 1991.

Huck Finn and Tom Sawyer among the Indians and Other Unfinished Stories. Ed. Dahlia Armon and Walter Blair. Berkeley: University of California Press, 1989.

The Innocents Abroad, Roughing It. Ed. Guy Cardwell. New York: Library of America, 1984.

Letters from the Earth. Ed. Bernard DeVoto. New York: Harper and Row, 1962.

Life on the Mississippi. Ed. James M. Cox. New York: Penguin, 1984.

The Love Letters of Mark Twain. Ed. Dixon Wecter. New York: Harper and Brothers, 1949.

Mark Twain, Business Man. Ed. Samuel C. Webster. Boston: Little, Brown, 1946.

Mark Twain: Collected Tales, Sketches, Speeches, and Essays, 1852–1890. 2 vols. Ed. Louis J. Budd. New York: Library of America, 1992.

Mark Twain–Howells Letters. 2 vols. Ed. Henry Nash Smith and William M. Gibson. Cambridge: Harvard University Press, 1960.

Mark Twain in Eruption. Ed. Bernard DeVoto. New York: Harper and Brothers, 1940.

Mark Twain of the "Enterprise." Ed. Henry Nash Smith. Berkeley: University of California Press, 1957.

Mark Twain on the Damned Human Race. Ed. Janet Smith. New York: Hill and Wang, 1962.

Mark Twain, San Francisco Correspondent: Selections from His Letters to the Territorial Enterprise, 1865–66. Ed. Henry Nash Smith and Frederick Anderson. San Francisco, 1957.

Mark Twain Speaking. Ed. Paul Fatout. Iowa City: University of Iowa Press, 1976.

Mark Twain to Mrs. Fairbanks. Ed. Dixon Wecter. San Marino, Calif.: Huntington Library, 1949.

Mark Twain's Aquarium: The Samuel Clemens Angelfish Correspondence, 1905–1910. Ed. John Cooley. Athens: University of Georgia Press, 1991.

Mark Twain's Correspondence with Henry Huttleston Rogers. Ed. Lewis Leary. Berkeley: University of California Press, 1969.

Mark Twain's Fables of Man. Ed. John S. Tuckey. Berkeley: University of California Press, 1972.

Mark Twain's Hannibal, Huck, and Tom. Ed. Walter Blair. Berkeley: University of California Press, 1969

Mark Twain's Letters. 2 vols. Ed. Albert Bigelow Paine. New York: Harper and Brothers, 1917.

Mark Twain's Letters from Hawaii. Ed. A. Grove Day. Honolulu: University Press of Hawaii, 1975.

Mark Twain's Letters to His Publishers. Ed. Hamlin Hill. Berkeley: University of California Press, 1967.

Mark Twain's Letters to Mary. Ed. Lewis Leary. New York: Columbia University Press, 1961.

"Mark Twain's Letters to San Francisco *Call* from Virginia City, Nevada Territory, July 9th to Nov. 19th 1963." Ed. A. E. Hutcheson. *Twainian,* Jan.–Feb. 1952, May–June 1952.

Mark Twain's Letters to Will Bowen: "My First and Oldest and Dearest Friend." Ed. Theodore Hornberger. Austin: University of Texas Press, 1941.

Mark Twain's Letters, Volume 1 (1853–1866). Ed. Edgar Marquess Branch, Michael B. Frank, and Kenneth M. Sanderson. Berkeley: University of California Press, 1988.

Mark Twain's Letters, Volume 2 (1867–1868). Ed. Harriet Elinor Smith and Richard Bucci. Berkeley: University of California Press, 1990.

Mark Twain's Letters, Volume 3 (1869). Ed. Victor Fischer and Michael B. Frank. Berkeley: University of California Press, 1992.

Mark Twain's Letters, Volume 4 (1870–1871). Ed. Victor Fischer and Michael B. Frank. Berkeley: University of California Press, 1995.

Mark Twain's Mysterious Stranger Manuscripts. Ed. William M. Gibson. Berkeley: University of California Press, 1969.

Mark Twain's Notebook. Ed. Albert Bigelow Paine. New York: Harper and Brothers, 1935.

Mark Twain's Notebooks and Journals, Volume 1 (1855–1873). Ed. Frederick Anderson, Michael B. Frank, and Kenneth M. Sanderson. Berkeley: University of California Press, 1975.

Mark Twain's Notebooks and Journals, Volume 2 (1877–1883). Ed. Frederick Anderson, Lin Salamo, and Bernard L. Stein. Berkeley: University of California Press, 1975.

Mark Twain's Notebooks and Journals, Volume 3 (1883–1891). Ed. Robert Pack Browning, Michael B. Frank, and Lin Salamo. Berkeley: University of California Press, 1979.

Mark Twain's Own Autobiography: The Chapters from the "North American Review." Ed. Michael J. Kiskis. Madison: University of Wisconsin Press, 1990.

Mark Twain's San Francisco. Ed. Bernard Taper. New York: McGraw-Hill, 1963.

Mark Twain's Satires and Burlesques. Ed. Franklin R. Rogers. Berkeley: University of California Press, 1967.

Mark Twain's Travels with Mr. Brown. Ed. Franklin Walker and G. Ezra Dane. New York: Alfred A. Knopf, 1940.

Mark Twain's Which Was the Dream? and Other Symbolic Writings of the Later Years. Ed. John S. Tuckey. Berkeley: University of California Press, 1967.

"Old Times on the Mississippi." *Great Short Works of Mark Twain.* Ed. Justin Kaplan. New York: Harper and Row, 1967.

The Prince and the Pauper. Ed. Victor Fischer and Lin Salamo. Berkeley: University of California Press, 1979.

Pudd'nhead Wilson and Those Extraordinary Twins. Ed. Sidney E. Berger. New York: Norton, 1980.

Roughing It. Ed. Harriet Elinor Smith and Edgar Marquess Branch. Berkeley: University of California Press, 1993.

Sketches of the Sixties, Being Forgotten Material Now Collected for the First Time from the "Californian," 1864–67. Ed. John Howell. San Francisco, 1926.

A Tramp Abroad. New York: Harper and Brothers, 1907. Vols. 3 and 4 of *The Writings of Mark Twain, Author's National Edition.* 25 vols. 1907–18.

Traveling with the Innocents Abroad: Mark Twain's Original Reports from Europe and the Holy Land. Ed. Daniel Morley McKeithan. Norman: University of Oklahoma Press, 1958.

"Visit of Mark Twain/Wit and Humor." *Sydney* (Australia) *Morning Herald,* 17 Sept. 1895, 5–6. Rpt. in Louis J. Budd, ed., "Mark Twain Talks Mostly about Humor and Humorists." *Studies in American Humor* 1 (1974): 4–22.

The Washoe Giant in San Francisco. Ed. Franklin Walker. San Francisco: George Fields, 1938.

What Is Man? And Other Philosophical Writings. Ed. Paul Baender. Berkeley: University of California Press, 1973.

"The Winner of the Medal." New York *Sunday Mercury,* 3 March 1967. Typescript in Mark Twain Papers, Bancroft Library, University of California, Berkeley.

The Writings of Mark Twain. Autograph ed. 22 vols. Hartford, Conn.: American, 1899.

Secondary Sources

"African Discoveries." *Quarterly Review* 33 (1825): 518.

Anderson, Frederick. Introduction. *A Pen Warmed-Up in Hell: Mark Twain in Protest.* New York: Harper and Row, 1972. 1–17.

———. Introduction. *Pudd'nhead Wilson/Those Extraordinary Twins.* By Mark Twain. San Francisco: Chandler, 1968. xii–xxxii.

———, ed. *Mark Twain: The Critical Heritage.* London: Routledge and Kegan Paul, 1971.

Andrews, Kenneth R. *Nook Farm: Mark Twain's Hartford Circle.* Cambridge: Harvard University Press, 1950.

Arnold, Matthew. "Civilization in the United States." *The Complete Prose Works of Mathew Arnold.* Ed. R. H. Super. Ann Arbor: University of Michigan Press, 1974. 350–69.

———. *General Grant by Mathew Arnold with a Rejoinder by Mark Twain.* Ed. John Y. Simon. Carbondale: Southern Illinois University Press, 1966.

Austin, Mary Minor. "Free Thought." *The Mark Twain Encyclopedia.* Ed. J. R. LeMaster and James D. Wilson. New York: Garland, 1993. 305–6.

Baender, Paul. Introduction. *What Is Man? And Other Philosophical Writings.* By Mark Twain. Berkeley: University of California Press, 1973. 3–34.

Baetzhold, Howard G. *Mark Twain and John Bull.* Bloomington: Indiana University Press, 1970.

Bakhtin, Mikhail. *Rabelais and His World.* Trans. Helene Iswolsky. Bloomington: Indiana University Press, 1984.

Banta, Martha. "The Boys and the Bosses: Twain's Double Take on Work, Play, and the Democratic Ideal." *American Literary History* 3 (Fall 1991): 487–520.

Bassett, John E. "Life on the Mississippi: Being Shifty in a New Country." *Western American Literature* 21 (Spring 1986): 37–45.

Bataille, Georges. *Eroticism: Death and Sensuality.* Trans. Mary Dalwood. 1962. San Francisco: City Lights, 1982.

Batten, Charles L., Jr. *Pleasurable Instruction: Form and Convention in Eighteenth-Century Travel Literature.* Berkeley: University of California Press, 1978.

Baym, Nina. "Melodramas of Beset Manhood: How Theories of American Fiction Exclude Women Authors." *The New Feminist Criticism: Essays on Women, Literature, Theory.* Ed. Elaine Showalter. New York: Pantheon, 1985. 63–80.

Bederman, Gail. *Manliness and Civilization: A Cultural History of Gender and Race in the United States, 1880–1917.* Chicago: University of Chicago Press, 1995.

Beisner, Robert L. *Twelve against Empire: The Anti-Imperialists, 1898–1900.* New York: McGraw-Hill, 1968.

Bell, Michael Davitt. *The Problem of American Realism: Studies in the Cultural History of a Literary Idea.* Chicago: University of Chicago Press, 1993.

Bennett, Jonathon. "The Conscience of Huckleberry Finn." *Philosophy* 49 (1974): 123–34.

Benson, Ivan. *Mark Twain's Western Years.* Stanford: Stanford University Press, 1938.

Bentley, Eric. *The Life of Drama.* New York: Atheneum, 1964.

Berkove, Laurence I. *Ethical Records of Twain and His Circle of Sagebrush Journalists.* Quarry Farm Papers 5. Elmira, N.Y.: Elmira College Center for Mark Twain Studies, 1994.

Berthold, Dennis. "The Conflict of Dialects in *A Connecticut Yankee.*" *Ball State University Forum* 18 (1977): 51–58.

Bigelow, John. *Retrospection of an Active Life.* 3 vols. New York: Baker and Taylor, 1909.

Blair, Walter. *Mark Twain and Huck Finn.* Berkeley: University of California Press, 1960.

———. *Native American Humor, 1800–1900.* New York: American Book, 1937.

Blair, Walter, and Hamlin Hill. *America's Humor: From Poor Richard to Doonesbury.* New York: Oxford University Press, 1978.

Blues, Thomas. *Mark Twain and the Community.* Lexington: University Press of Kentucky, 1970.

Boewe, Mary. *The American Vandal Goes A-Courting; or, Mark Twain's First Elmira Lecture and Its Romantic Aftermath.* Quarry Farm Papers 4. Elmira, N.Y.: Elmira College Center for Mark Twain Studies, 1993.

Booth, Bradford A. "Mark Twain's Comments on Holmes' *Autocrat.*" *American Literature* 21 (1950): 456–63.

Branch, E. Douglas. *The Sentimental Years, 1836–1860.* 1934. New York: Hill and Wang, 1965.

Branch, Edgar Marquess. *The Literary Apprenticeship of Mark Twain.* Urbana: University of Illinois Press, 1950.

———. "Mark Twain: The Pilot and the Writer." *Mark Twain Journal* 28 (1985): 28–43.

———. *Mark Twain and the Starchy Boys.* Quarry Farm Papers. Elmira, N.Y.: Elmira College Center for Mark Twain Studies, 1992.

———. "'Old Times on the Mississippi': Biography and Craftsmanship." *Nineteenth-Century Literature* 45 (June 1990): 73–87.

Brashear, Minnie M. *Mark Twain: Son of Missouri.* Chapel Hill: University of North Carolina Press, 1934.

Brettell, Caroline B. "Introduction: Travel Literature, Ethnography, and Ethnohistory." *Ethnohistory* 33.2 (1986): 127–38.

Bridgman, Richard. *The Colloquial Style in America.* New York: Oxford University Press, 1966.

———. *Traveling in Mark Twain.* Berkeley: University of California Press, 1987.

Brodhead, Richard H. *Cultures of Letters: Scenes of Reading and Writing in Nineteenth-Century America.* Chicago: University of Chicago Press, 1993.

Brodwin, Stanley. "Mark Twain in the Pulpit: The Theological Comedy of Huckleberry Finn." *One Hundred Years of "Huckleberry Finn."* Ed. Robert Sattelmeyer and J. Donald Crowley. Columbia: University of Missouri Press, 1985. 371–85.

———. Mark Twain's Theology: The Gods of a Brevet Presbyterian." *The Cambridge Companion to Mark Twain.* Ed. Forrest G. Robinson. New York: Cambridge University Press, 1995. 220–48.

———. "The Theology of Mark Twain: Banished Adam and the Bible." *Critical Essays on Mark Twain, 1910–1980.* Ed. Louis J. Budd. Boston: G. K. Hall, 1983. 176–93.

———. "The Useful and the Useless River: *Life On The Mississippi* Revisited." *Studies in American Humor* 2 (1976): 196–208.

Brooks, Peter. *The Melodramatic Imagination: Balzac, Henry James, Melodrama, and the Mode of Excess.* New Haven: Yale University Press, 1976.

Brooks, Van Wyck. *The Ordeal of Mark Twain.* 1920. New York: E. P. Dutton, 1970.

Brown, Maurice F. "Mark Twain as Proteus: Ironic Form and Fictive Integrity." *Papers of the Michigan Academy of Science, Arts, and Letters* 51 (1966): 515–27.

Buckley, Jerome H. *The Victorian Temper: A Study in Literary Culture.* Cambridge: Harvard University Press, 1951.

Budd, Louis J. "Deconstructing Mark Twain's White Suit." *Publications of the Arkansas Philological Association* 9 (1983): 1–15.

———. "Editor's Notes." *Studies in American Humor* 2 (January 1976): 144–45.

———. "Gentlemanly Humorists of the Old South." *Southern Folklore Quarterly* 17 (1953): 232–40.

———. *Mark Twain, Social Philosopher.* Bloomington: Indiana University Press, 1962.

———. *Mark Twain: The Ecstasy of Humor.* Quarry Farm Papers 6. Elmira, N.Y.: Elmira College Center for Mark Twain Studies, 1994.

———. *Our Mark Twain: The Making of His Public Personality.* Philadelphia: University of Pennsylvania Press, 1983.

Buell, Lawrence. *New England Literary Culture: From Revolution through Renaissance.* Cambridge: Cambridge University Press, 1986.

Burde, Edgar J. "Mark Twain: The Writer as Pilot." *PMLA* 93 (1978): 878–92.

Buzzard, James. *The Beaten Track: European Tourism, Literature, and the Ways to "Culture," 1800–1918.* New York: Oxford University Press, 1993.

Cady, Edwin Harrison. *The Gentleman in America: A Literary Study in American Culture.* Syracuse: Syracuse University Press, 1949.

Camfield, Gregg. *Sentimental Twain: Samuel Clemens in the Maze of Moral Philosophy.* Philadelphia: University of Pennsylvania Press, 1994.

Campbell, James E. "Sumner, Brooks, Burlingame, or the Last of the Great Challenges." *Ohio Archaeological and Historical Quarterly* 34 (1925): 435–73.

Cardwell, Guy A. "Life on the Mississippi: Vulgar Facts and Learned Errors." *ESQ* 19.4 (1973): 283–93.

———. *The Man Who Was Mark Twain: Images and Ideologies.* New Haven: Yale University Press, 1991.

———. "Samuel Clemens' Magical Pseudonym." *New England Quarterly* 48 (1975): 175–93.

Carnes, Mark C. and Clyde Griffen, eds. *Meanings for Manhood: Constructions of Masculinity in Victorian America.* Chicago: University of Chicago Press, 1990.

Carrington, George C., Jr. *The Dramatic Unity of "Huckleberry Finn."* Columbus: Ohio State University Press, 1976.

Carton, Evan. "Speech Acts and Social Action: Mark Twain and the Politics of Literary Performance." *The Cambridge Companion to Mark Twain.* Ed. Forrest G. Robinson. New York: Cambridge University Press, 1995. 153–74.

Castronovo, David. *The American Gentleman: Social Prestige and the Modern Literary Mind.* New York: Ungar, 1991.

Cawelti, John G. *Adventure, Mystery, and Romance: Formula Stories and Popular Culture.* Chicago: University of Chicago Press, 1976.

Chernaik, Warren L. "The Ever-Receding Dream: Henry Adams and Mark Twain as Autobiographers." *First Person Singular: Studies in American Autobiography.* Ed. A. Robert Lee. New York: St. Martin's Press, 1988. 72–103.

Clemens, Clara. *My Father, Mark Twain.* New York: Harper and Brothers, 1931.

Clemens, Susy. *Papa: An Intimate Biography of Mark Twain.* Ed. Charles Neider. Garden City, N.Y.: Doubleday, 1985.

Cohen, Hennig, and William B. Dillingham. Introduction. *Humor of the Old Southwest.* 2d ed. Athens: University of Georgia Press, 1975. xii–xxviii.

Couser, Thomas. *Altered Egos: Authority in American Autobiography*. New York: Oxford University Press, 1989.

Covici, Pascal, Jr. *Mark Twain's Humor: The Image of a World*. Dallas: Southern Methodist University Press, 1962.

Cox, James M. "A Hard Book to Take." *One Hundred Years of "Huckleberry Finn": The Boy, His Book, and American Culture*. Ed. Robert Sattelmeyer and J. Donald Crowley. Columbia: University of Missouri Press, 1985. 386–403.

———. "Humor of the Old Southwest." *The Comic Imagination in America*. Ed. Louis D. Rubin Jr. New Brunswick, N.J.: Rutgers University Press, 1973. 101–12.

———. Introduction. *Life on the Mississippi*. By Mark Twain. New York: Penguin, 1984.

———. "Life on the Mississippi Revisited." *The Mythologizing of Mark Twain*. Ed. Sara deSaussure Davis and Philip D. Beidler. Tuscaloosa: University of Alabama Press, 1984.

———. *Mark Twain: The Fate of Humor*. Princeton: Princeton University Press, 1966.

Cracroft, Richard H. "Distorting Polygamy for Fun and Profit: Artemus Ward and Mark Twain among the Mormons." *Brigham Young University Studies* 14 (1974): 272–88.

———. "The Gentle Blasphemer: Mark Twain, Holy Scripture, and the Book of Mormon." *Brigham Young University Studies* 11 (1971): 119–40.

Cummings, Sherwood. *Mark Twain and Science: The Adventures of a Mind*. Baton Rouge: Louisiana State University Press, 1989.

———. "Mark Twain's Theory of Realism; or, The Science of Piloting." *Studies in American Humor* 2 (January 1976): 209–21.

Danahay, Martin A. *A Community of One: Masculine Autobiography in Nineteenth-Century Britain*. Albany, N.Y.: State University of New York Press, 1993.

Davidson, Cathy. Introduction. *The Book of Love: Writers and Their Love Letters*. New York: Simon and Schuster, 1992.

Davis, Sara deSaussure, and Philip D. Beidler, eds. *The Mythologizing of Mark Twain*. Tuscaloosa: University of Alabama Press, 1984.

Day, William Patrick. *In Circles of Fear and Desire*. Chicago: University of Chicago Press, 1985.

De Eulis, Marilyn Davis. "Mark Twain's Experiments in Autobiography." *American Literature* 53 (May 1981): 202–13.

"The Death of Mark Twain." *Chautauquan* 59 (June 1910): 9–10.

Detiene, Marcel. *Dionysus Slain.* Baltimore: Johns Hopkins University Press, 1979.

DeVoto, Bernard. *Mark Twain's America.* 1932. Rpt. as *Mark Twain's America and Mark Twain at Work.* Boston: Houghton Mifflin, 1967.

Dickens, Charles. *American Notes and Pictures from Italy.* 1893. New York: Macmillan, 1903.

Dickinson, Leon T. "Mark Twain's Revisions in Writing *The Innocents Abroad.*" *American Literature* 19 (1947–48): 139–57.

Dolmetsch, Carl. *"Our Famous Guest": Mark Twain in Vienna.* Athens: University of Georgia Press, 1992.

Douglas, Ann. *The Feminization of American Culture.* New York: Knopf, 1977.

Doyno, Victor A. *Writing "Huck Finn": Mark Twain's Creative Process.* Philadelphia: University of Pennsylvania Press, 1991.

Duckett, Margaret. *Mark Twain and Bret Harte.* Norman: University of Oklahoma Press, 1964.

Duncan, Jeffrey L. "The Empirical and the Ideal in Mark Twain." *PMLA* 95 (1980): 201–12.

Eagleton, Terry. *Criticism and Ideology.* 1976. Rpt., London: Verso, 1978.

Eble, Kenneth E. *Old Clemens and W.D.H.: The Story of a Remarkable Friendship.* Baton Rouge: Louisiana State University Press, 1985.

Egan, Susanna. "'Self'-Conscious History: American Autobiography after the Civil War." *American Autobiography: Retrospect and Prospect.* Ed. Paul John Eakin. Madison: University of Wisconsin Press, 1991. 70–94.

Emerson, Everett. *The Authentic Mark Twain: A Literary Biography of Samuel L. Clemens.* Philadelphia: University of Pennsylvania Press, 1984.

———. "Mark Twain's Quarrel with God." *Order in Variety: Essays and Poems in Honor of Donald E. Stanford.* Ed. R. W. Crump. Newark: University of Delaware Press, 1991. 32–48.

Ensor, Allison. *Mark Twain and the Bible.* Lexington: University Press of Kentucky, 1969.

Fatout, Paul. *Mark Twain in Virginia City.* Bloomington: Indiana University Press, 1964.

Fender, Stephen. *Plotting the Golden West.* London: Cambridge University Press, 1981.

Ferguson, DeLancey. *Mark Twain: Man and Legend.* Indianapolis: Bobbs-Merrill, 1943.

Fetterley, Judith. "Disenchantment: Tom Sawyer in *Huckleberry Finn.*" *PMLA* 87 (1972): 69–74.

————. *The Resisting Reader: A Feminist Approach to American Fiction*. Blooming-ton: Indiana University Press, 1978.

————. "The Sanctioned Rebel." *Studies in the Novel* 3 (1971): 293–304.

Fiedler, Leslie. "An American Abroad." *Partisan Review* 33 (1966): 77–91.

————. "Foreword: Subversive Mark Twain." *Mark Twain: Selected Writings of an American Skeptic*. Ed. Victor Doyno. New York: Prometheus Books, 1995. xi–xv.

————. *Love and Death in the American Novel*. 1960. Cleveland: World, 1962.

Fisher, Philip. "Appearing and Disappearing in Public: Social Space in Late-Nineteenth-Century Literature and Culture." *Reconstructing American Literary History*. Ed. Sacvan Bercovitch. Cambridge: Harvard University Press, 1986. 55–88.

————. *Hard Facts: Setting and Form in the American Novel*. New York: Oxford University Press, 1987.

Fishkin, Shelley Fisher. *Lighting Out for the Territory: Reflections on Mark Twain and American Culture*. New York: Oxford University Press, 1996.

————. "Mark Twain and Women." *The Cambridge Companion to Mark Twain*. Ed. Forrest G. Robinson. New York: Cambridge University Press, 1995. 52–73.

————. *Was Huck Black? Mark Twain and African American Voices*. New York: Oxford University Press, 1993.

Florence, Don. *Persona and Humor in Mark Twain's Early Writings*. Columbia: University of Missouri Press, 1995.

Foner, Philip S. *Mark Twain, Social Critic*. New York: International, 1958.

Foucault, Michel. *The History of Sexuality*. Trans. Robert Hurley. New York: Vintage, 1980.

Frear, Walter Francis. *Mark Twain and Hawaii*. Chicago: Lakeside Press, 1947.

Freud, Sigmund. *Civilization and Its Discontents*. Trans. James Strachey. New York: W. W. Norton, 1962.

————. *Jokes and Their Relation to the Unconscious*. Trans. James Strachey. New York: W. W. Norton, 1963.

Frye, Northrop. *Anatomy of Criticism: Four Essays*. Princeton: Princeton University Press, 1957.

Fulweiler, Howard W. *"Here a Captive Heart Busted": Studies in the Sentimental Journey of Modern Literature*. New York: Fordham University Press, 1993.

Gabler-Hover, Janet A. "Sympathy Not Empathy: The Intent of Narration in *Huckleberry Finn*." *Journal of Narrative Technique* 17 (Winter 1987): 67–75.

————. *Truth in American Fiction: The Legacy of Rhetorical Idealism*. Athens: University of Georgia Press, 1990.

Ganzel, Dewey. *Mark Twain Abroad*. Chicago: University of Chicago Press, 1968.

Gay, Peter. *The Bourgeois Experience: Victoria to Freud*. Vol. 1: *Education of the Senses*. New York: Oxford University Press, 1984. Vol. 2: *The Tender Passion*. New York: Oxford University Press, 1986.

Geismar, Maxwell. *Mark Twain: An American Prophet*. Boston: Houghton Mifflin, 1970.

Gerber, John C. *Mark Twain*. Boston: G. K. Hall, 1988.

———. "Mark Twain's Search for Identity." *Essays in American and English Literature Presented to Bruce Robert McElderry Jr*. Ed. Max F. Schulz. Athens: Ohio University Press, 1967.

———. "Mark Twain's Use of the Comic Pose." *PMLA* 77 (1962): 297–304.

———. "The Relationship between Point of View and Style in the Works of Mark Twain." *Style in Prose Fiction*. New York: Columbia University Press, 1959. 142–71.

Gibson, William M. *The Art of Mark Twain*. New York: Oxford University Press, 1976.

———. "Mark Twain and Howells: Anti-Imperialists." *New England Quarterly* 20 (1947): 435–70.

Gillman, Susan. *Dark Twins: Imposture and Identity in Mark Twain's America*. Chicago: University of Chicago Press, 1989.

———. "'Sure Identifiers': Race, Science, and the Law in *Pudd'nhead Wilson*." *Mark Twain's "Pudd'nhead Wilson": Race, Conflict, and Culture*. Ed. Susan Gillman and Forrest G. Robinson. Durham, N.C.: Duke University Press, 1990. 86–104.

Gilmour, Robin. *The Idea of the Gentleman in the Victorian Novel*. London: George Allen, 1981.

Green, Martin. *The Adventurous Male: Chapters in the History of the White Male Mind*. University Park: Pennsylvania State University Press, 1993.

———. *The Problem of Boston: Some Readings in Cultural History*. New York: Norton, 1966.

Greene, Laurence. *The Filibuster*. Indianapolis: Bobbs-Merrill, 1937.

Gribben, Alan. "Autobiography as Property: Mark Twain and His Legend." *The Mythologizing of Mark Twain*. Ed. Sara de Saussure Davis and Philip D. Beidler. Tuscaloosa: University of Alabama Press, 1984.

———. "'I Did Wish Tom Sawyer Was There': Boy-Book Elements in *Tom Sawyer* and *Huckleberry Finn*." *One Hundred Years of "Huckleberry Finn*." Ed. Robert Sattelmeyer and J. Donald Crowley. Columbia: University of Missouri Press, 1985. 149–70.

———. "The Importance of Mark Twain." *American Quarterly* 37 (Spring 1985): 30–49.

———. *Mark Twain's Library: A Reconstruction.* 2 vols. Boston: G.K. Hall, 1980.

———. "'When Other Amusements Fail': Mark Twain and the Occult." *The Haunted Dusk: American Supernatural Fiction, 1820–1920.* Ed. Howard Kerr, John W. Crowley, and Charles L. Crow. Athens: University of Georgia Press, 1983. 171–89.

Gunn, Drewey Wayne. "The Monomythic Structure of *Roughing It.*" *American Literature* 61.4 (1989): 563–85.

Gutwirth, Marcel. *Laughing Matter: An Essay on the Comic.* Ithaca, N.Y.: Cornell University Press, 1993.

Haley, Bruce. *The Healthy Body and Victorian Culture.* Cambridge: Harvard University Press, 1978.

Harris, Susan K. *Mark Twain's Escape from Time: A Study of Patterns and Images.* Columbia: University of Missouri Press, 1982.

———. *The Courtship of Olivia Langdon and Mark Twain.* New York: Cambridge University Press, 1996.

Hauck, Richard Boyd. *A Cheerful Nihilism: Confidence and "The Absurd" in American Humorous Fiction.* Bloomington: Indiana University Press, 1971.

Higham, John. "The Re-Orientation of American Culture in the 1890s." *Writing American History.* Bloomington: Indiana University Press, 1973. 77–102.

Hill, Hamlin. "The Composition and Structure of *The Adventures of Tom Sawyer.*" *American Literature* 32 (January 1961): 379–92.

———. Introduction. *Roughing It.* By Mark Twain. New York: Penguin Books, 1981. 7–24.

———. *Mark Twain: God's Fool.* New York: Harper and Row, 1973.

———. "Mark Twain's 'Brace of Brief Lectures on Science.'" *New England Quarterly* 34 (1961): 228–39.

Hoben, John B. "Mark Twain's *A Connecticut Yankee:* A Genetic Study." *American Literature* 18 (November 1946): 197–218.

Hoffman, Andrew J. *Inventing Mark Twain: The Lives of Samuel Langhorne Clemens.* New York: William Morrow, 1997.

———. "Mark Twain and Homosexuality." *American Literature* 67.1 (1995): 23–49.

———. *Twain's Heroes, Twain's Worlds.* Philadelphia: University of Pennsylvania Press, 1988.

Hofstadter, Richard. *The Age of Reform: From Bryon to F.D.R.* New York: Random House, 1960.

Holloway, John. *The Victorian Sage: Studies in Argument.* London: Macmillan, 1953.

Horn, Jason Gary. *Mark Twain and William James: Crafting a Free Self.* Columbia: University of Missouri Press, 1996.

Horwitz, Howard. *By the Law of Nature: Form and Value in Nineteenth-Century America.* New York: Oxford University Press, 1991.

Houghton, Walter E. *The Victorian Frame of Mind, 1830–1870.* New Haven: Yale University Press, 1957.

Howe, Daniel Walker, ed. *Victorian America.* Philadelphia: University of Pennsylvania Press, 1976.

Howells, William Dean. *My Mark Twain: Reminiscences and Criticism.* New York: Harper and Brothers, 1910.

———. "Recollections of an *Atlantic* Editorship." *Atlantic Monthly* 100.5 (Nov. 1907): 594–606. Rpt., *Criticism and Fiction and Other Essays,* ed. Clara Marburg Kirk and Rudolph Kirk, 185–205. New York: New York University Press, 1959.

Jerome, Robert D., and Herbert A. Wisbey Jr., eds. *Mark Twain in Elmira.* Elmira, N.Y.: Mark Twain Society, 1977.

Johnson, James L. *Mark Twain and the Limits of Power: Emerson's God in Ruins.* Knoxville: University of Tennessee Press, 1982.

Kahn, Sholom J. *Mark Twain's Mysterious Stranger: A Study of the Manuscript Texts.* Columbia: University of Missouri Press, 1978.

Kaplan, Fred. *Sacred Tears: Sentimentality in Victorian Literature.* Princeton: Princeton University Press, 1987.

Kaplan, Justin. Introduction. *Great Short Works of Mark Twain.* New York: Harper and Row, 1967. vi–xii.

———. *Mr. Clemens and Mark Twain.* New York: Simon and Schuster, 1966.

Karnath, David. "Mark Twain's Implicit Theory of the Comic." *Mosaic* 9 (1978): 207–18.

Kauffman, Linda S. *Discourses of Desire: Gender, Genre, and Epistolary Fictions.* Ithaca, N.Y.: Cornell University Press, 1986.

Kaufman, William. "The Comedic Stance: Sam Clemens, His Masquerade." *Mark Twain: A Sumptuous Variety.* Ed. Robert Giddings. London: Vision Press, 1985.

Kiskis, Michael J. Introduction. *Mark Twain's Own Autobiography: The Chapters from the "North American Review."* By Mark Twain. Madison: University of Wisconsin Press, 1990.

———. "Mark Twain and Collaborative Autobiography." *Studies in the Literary Imagination* 29 (Fall 1966): 27–40.

———. "Susy Clemens as the Fire for Mark Twain's Autobiography." *Mid-Hudson Language Studies* 10 (1987): 368–84.

Knoper, Randall. *Acting Naturally: Mark Twain in the Culture of Performance.* Berkeley: University of California Press, 1995.

Kolko, Gabriel. "Brahmins and Business, 1870–1914: A Hypothesis on the Social Basis of Success in American History." *The Critical Spirit: Essays in Honor of Herbert Marcuse.* Ed. Kurt H. Wolff and Barrington Moore Jr. Boston: Beacon Press, 1968. 343–63.

Krauth, Leland. "Mark Twain: At Home in the Gilded Age." *Georgia Review* 28 (1974): 105–13.

———. "Mark Twain Fights Sam Clemens' Duel." *Mississippi Quarterly* 33 (1980): 144–53.

Kravitz, Bennett. *Dreaming Mark Twain.* New York: University Press of America, 1996.

Kruse, Horst H. *Mark Twain and "Life on the Mississippi."* Amherst: University of Massachusetts Press, 1981.

———. "Mark Twain's Nom de Plume: Some Mysteries Resolved." *Mark Twain Journal* 30.1 (1992): 2–32.

La Bossiere, Camille R. *The Victorian "Fol Sage": Comparative Readings on Carlyle, Emerson, Melville, and Conrad.* Lewisburg, Pa.: Bucknell University Press, 1989.

Landow, George P. *Elegant Jeremiahs: The Sage from Carlyle to Mailer.* Ithaca, N.Y.: Cornell University Press, 1986.

Lasch, Christopher. Introduction. *The New Radicalism in America, 1889–1963.* New York: Vintage, 1965. ix–xxiii.

———. "The Moral and Intellectual Rehabilitation of the Ruling Class." *The World of Nations.* New York: Knopf, 1973. 80–91.

Lears, T. J. Jackson. *No Place of Grace: Antimodernism and the Transformation of American Culture, 1880–1920.* New York: Pantheon Books, 1983.

Leary, Lewis. "The Bankruptcy of Mark Twain." *Southern Excursions: Essays on Mark Twain and Others.* Baton Rouge: Louisiana State University Press, 1971. 75–86.

Lennon, Nigey. *The Sagebrush Bohemian: Mark Twain in California.* New York: Paragon House, 1990.

Leon, Philip W. *Mark Twain and West Point.* Toronto: ECW Press, 1996.

Leonard, James S., Thomas A. Tenney, and Thadious M. Davis, eds. *Satire or Evasion? Black Perspectives on "Huckleberry Finn."* Durham, N.C.: Duke University Press, 1992.

Leverenz, David. "The Last Real Man in America: From Natty Bumppo to Batman." *American Literary History* 3 (Winter 1991): 753–81.

Lorch, Fred W. "Mark Twain's Lecture of 1968–1869: 'The American Vandal Abroad.'" *On Mark Twain: The Best from "American Literature."* Ed. Louis J. Budd and Edwin H. Cady. Durham, N.C.: Duke University Press, 1987.

Lowell, James Russell. "Humor, Wit, Fun, and Satire." Rpt. in *Literary Criticism of James Russell Lowell*, ed. Herbert F. Smith, 78–94. Lincoln: University of Nebraska Press, 1963.

Lowry, Richard S. *"Littery Man": Mark Twain and Modern Authorship*. New York: Oxford University Press, 1996.

Lynn, Kenneth S. *Mark Twain and Southwestern Humor*. Boston: Little, Brown, 1959.

———. *William Dean Howells: An American Life*. New York: Harcourt Brace Jovanovich, 1971.

McCloskey, John C. "Mark Twain as Critic in *The Innocents Abroad*." *American Literature* 25 (1953): 139–51.

Mack, Effie Mona. *Mark Twain in Nevada*. New York: Scribner, 1947.

Macnaughton, William R. *Mark Twain's Last Years as a Writer*. Columbia: University of Missouri Press, 1979.

Maik, Thomas A. "The Village in *Tom Sawyer*: Myth and Reality." *Critical Essays on "The Adventures of Tom Sawyer."* Ed. Gary Scharnhorst. New York: G. K. Hall, 1993. 201–7.

Malin, Irving. "Mark Twain: The Boy as Artist." *Literature and Psychology* 11 (1961): 78–84.

Manierre, William R. "Huck Finn, Empiricist Member of Society." *Modern Fiction Studies* 14 (Spring 1968): 57–66.

Marcus, George E. "'What did he reckon would become of the other half if he killed his half?': Doubled, Divided, and Crossed Selves in *Pudd'nhead Wilson;* or, Mark Twain as Culture Critic in His Own Time and Ours." *Mark Twain's "Pudd'nhead Wilson": Race, Conflict, and Culture*. Ed. Susan Gillman and Forrest G. Robinson. Durham, N.C.: Duke University Press, 1990. 190–210.

Marx, Leo. "The Pilot and the Passenger: Landscape Conventions and the Style of *Huckleberry Finn*." *American Literature* 28 (May 1956): 129–46.

Matthews, Brander. "Memories of Mark Twain." *The Tocsin of Revolt and Other Essays*. New York: Scribner, 1922. 251–94.

Messent, Peter. *Mark Twain*. New York: St. Martin's Press, 1997.

Michelson, Bruce. *Mark Twain on the Loose*. Amherst: University of Massachusetts Press, 1995.

Mills, Barris. "'Old Times on the Mississippi' as an Initiation Story." *College English* 25 (1964): 283–89.

Mitchell, Lee Clark. Introduction. *The Adventures of Tom Sawyer*. By Mark Twain. New York: Oxford University Press, 1993.

———. "'Nobody but Our Gang Warn't Around': The Authority of Language in *Huckleberry Finn*." *New Essays on "Adventures of Huckleberry Finn."* Ed. Louis J. Budd. New York: Cambridge University Press, 1985. 83–106.

———. "Verbally *Roughing It:* The West of Words." *Nineteenth-Century Literature* 44 (June 1989): 67–92.

Moffett, Samuel. "Mark Twain: A Biographical Sketch." *The Writings of Mark Twain*. Autograph Edition. Hartford, Conn., 1899. 22:314–33.

Morrison, Toni. *Playing in the Dark: Whiteness and the Literary Imagination*. New York: Random House, 1992.

Morse, Hosea Ballou. *The International Relations of the Chinese Empire*. 3 vols. London: Longmans, Green, 1918.

Mort, Frank. *Dangerous Sexualities: Medico-Moral Politics in England since 1830*. London: Routledge and Kegan Paul, 1987.

Nerlich, Michael. *The Ideology of Adventure*. Minneapolis: University of Minnesota Press, 1987.

O'Connell, Shaun. *Imagining Boston: A Literary Landscape*. Boston: Beacon Press, 1992.

Opdahl, Keith. "'The Rest Is Just Cheating': When Feelings Go Bad in *Adventures of Huckleberry Finn*." *Texas Studies in Literature and Language* 32.2 (1990): 277–93.

Paine, Albert Bigelow. Introduction. *Mark Twain's Speeches*. New York: Harper and Brothers, 1919.

———. *Mark Twain: A Biography*. 3 vols. New York: Harper and Brothers, 1912.

Parry, Albert. *Garrets and Pretenders: A History of Bohemianism in America*. 1933. Rev. ed. New York: Dover, 1960.

Pemble, John. *The Mediterranean Passion: Victorians and Edwardians in the South*. New York: Oxford University Press, 1987.

Pettit, Arthur G. *Mark Twain and the South*. Lexington: University Press of Kentucky, 1974.

Porter, Carolyn. "Roxana's Plot." *Mark Twain's "Pudd'nhead Wilson": Race, Conflict, and Culture*. Ed. Susan Gillman and Forrest G. Robinson. Durham, N.C.: Duke University Press, 1990. 121–36.

Porter, Dennis. *Haunted Journeys: Desire and Transgression in European Travel Writing*. Princeton: Princeton University Press, 1991.

Pratt, Mary Louise. *Imperial Eyes: Travel Writing and Transculturation*. New York: Routledge, 1992.

Purdie, Susan. *Comedy: The Mastery of Discourse*. Toronto: University of Toronto Press, 1993.

Quirk, Tom. *Coming to Grips with "Huckleberry Finn": Essays on a Book, a Boy, and a Man*. Columbia: University of Missouri Press, 1993.

Regan, Robert. "The Reprobate Elect in *The Innocents Abroad*." *American Literature* 54 (1982–83): 240–50.

———. *Unpromising Heroes: Mark Twain and His Characters*. Berkeley: University of California Press, 1966.

Robinson, Forrest G. *In Bad Faith: The Dynamics of Deception in Mark Twain's America*. Cambridge: Harvard University Press, 1986.

———. "Patterns of Consciousness in *The Innocents Abroad*." *American Literature* 58 (1986): 46–63.

———. "'Seeing the Elephant': Some Perspectives on Mark Twain's *Roughing It*." *American Studies* 21 (1980): 43–64.

———. "Social Play and Bad Faith in *The Adventures of Tom Sawyer*." *Critical Essays on "The Adventures of Tom Sawyer."* Ed. Gary Scharnhorst. New York: G. K. Hall, 1993. 160–78.

———. "Why I Killed My Brother: An Essay on Mark Twain." *Literature and Psychology* 30 (1980): 168–81.

———, ed. *The Cambridge Companion to Mark Twain*. New York: Cambridge University Press, 1995.

———. "The Innocent at Large: Mark Twain's Travel Writing." *The Cambridge Companion to Mark Twain*. Ed. Forrest G. Robinson. New York: Cambridge University Press, 1995. 27–51.

Rodney, Robert M. *Mark Twain "Overseas."* Washington, D.C.: Three Continents Press, 1993.

Rogers, Franklin R. *Mark Twain's Burlesque Patterns: As Seen in the Novels and Narratives, 1855–1885*. Dallas: Southern Methodist University Press, 1960.

Rothman, Ellen K. *Hands and Hearts: A History of Courtship in America*. Cambridge: Harvard University Press, 1987.

Rourke, Constance. *American Humor: A Study of National Character*. New York: Harcourt Brace, 1931.

Rubin, Louis D., Jr. *The Writer in the South*. Athens: University of Georgia Press, 1972.

Ryan, Mary. *Cradle of the Middle Class: The Family in Oneida Country, New York, 1790–1865*. New York: Cambridge University Press, 1981.

Salomon, Roger B. *Twain and the Image of History*. New Haven: Yale University Press, 1961.

Salsbury, Edith Colgate. *Susy and Mark Twain*. New York: Harper and Row, 1965.

Samuels, Shirley, ed. *The Culture of Sentiment: Race, Gender, and Sentimentality in Nineteenth-Century America*. New York: Oxford University Press, 1992.

Scharnhorst, Gary. Introduction. *Critical Essays on "Tom Sawyer."* New York: G. K. Hall, 1993.

Scott, Arthur L. *Mark Twain at Large*. Chicago: Henry Regery, 1969.

See, Fred G. "*Tom Sawyer* and Children's Literature." *Essays in Literature* 12 (Fall 1985): 251–71.

Sewell, David R. *Mark Twain's Languages: Discourse, Dialogue, and Linguistic Variety*. Berkeley: University of California Press, 1987.

Shillingsburg, Miriam Jones. *At Home Abroad: Mark Twain in Australasia*. Jackson: University Press of Mississippi, 1988.

Simmel, Georg. *On Individuality and Social Forms*. Chicago: University of Chicago Press, 1971.

Skandera-Trombley, Laura E. *Mark Twain in the Company of Women*. Philadelphia: University of Pennsylvania Press, 1994.

Sloane, David E. E. "*Adventures of Huckleberry Finn*": *American Comic Vision*. Boston: Twayne, 1988.

———. *Mark Twain as a Literary Comedian*. Baton Rouge: Louisiana State University Press, 1979.

Smith, Henry Nash. *Mark Twain: The Development of a Writer*. Cambridge: Belknap/Harvard University Press, 1962.

———. *Mark Twain's Fable of Progress: Political and Economic Ideas in "A Connecticut Yankee."* Rutgers, N.J.: Rutgers University Press, 1964.

———. "That Hideous Mistake of Poor Clemens." *Harvard Library Bulletin* 9 (1955): 145–80.

Spengemann, William C. *The Adventurous Muse: The Poetics of American Fiction, 1799–1900*. New Haven: Yale University Press, 1977.

———. *Mark Twain and the Backwoods Angel: Innocence in the Works of Samuel L. Clemens*. Ohio: Kent State University Press, 1966.

Sproat, John G. "*The Best Men*": *Liberal Reformers in the Gilded Age*. New York: Oxford University Press, 1968.

Spurr, David. *The Rhetoric of Empire: Colonial Discourse in Journalism, Travel Writing, and Imperial Administration*. Durham, N.C.: Duke University Press, 1993.

Stafford, William. *Stories That Could Be True: New and Collected Poems*. New York: Harper and Row, 1977.

Stahl, J. D. *Mark Twain, Culture and Gender: Envisioning America through Europe*. Athens: University of Georgia Press, 1994.

Stallybrass, Peter, and Allan White. *The Politics and Poetics of Transgression*. Ithaca, N.Y.: Cornell University Press, 1986.

Steinbrink, Jeffrey. *Getting to Be Mark Twain*. Berkeley: University of California Press, 1991.

———. "Why the Innocents Went Abroad: Mark Twain and American Tourism in the Late Nineteenth Century." *American Literary Realism* 16 (1983): 278–86.

Stevick, Philip. "Sentimentality and Classic Fiction." *New Views of the English and American Novel*. Ed. R. G. Collins and Kenneth McRobbie. Winnipeg: University of Manitoba Press, 1971. 23–31.

Stone, Albert E. *The Innocent Eye: Childhood in Mark Twain's Imagination*. New Haven: Yale University Press, 1961.

Stoneley, Peter. *Mark Twain and the Feminine Aesthetic*. New York: Cambridge University Press, 1992.

Stowe, William W. *Going Abroad: European Travel in Nineteenth-Century American Culture*. Princeton: Princeton University Press, 1994.

Stringfellow, Frank, Jr. *The Meaning of Irony: A Psychoanalytic Investigation*. Albany: State University of New York Press, 1994.

Sundquist, Eric J. Introduction. *American Realism: New Essays*. Baltimore: Johns Hopkins University Press, 1932.

Tanner, Tony. *The Reign of Wonder: Naivety and Reality in American Literature*. Cambridge: Cambridge University Press, 1965.

Taylor, William R. *Cavalier and Yankee*. New York: Braziller, 1961.

Tenney, Thomas A. *Mark Twain: A Reference Guide*. Boston: G. K. Hall, 1977.

———. "Mark Twain's Early Travels and the Travel Tradition in Literature." Ph.D. diss., University of Pennsylvania, 1971.

Tompkins, Jane. *Sensational Designs: The Cultural Work of American Fiction, 1790–1860*. New York: Oxford University Press, 1985.

Tomsich, John. *A Genteel Endeavor: American Culture and Politics in the Gilded Age*. Stanford: Stanford University Press, 1971.

Towers, Tom H. "'I Never Thought We Might Want to Come Back': Strategies of Transcendence in *Tom Sawyer*." *Modern Fiction Studies* 21 (Winter 1975–76): 509–20.

———. "Love and Power in *"Huckleberry Finn."* *Tulane Studies in English* 23 (1978): 17–37.

————. *"The Prince and the Pauper:* Mark Twain's Once and Future King." *Studies in American Fiction* 6 (1978): 194–202.

Trilling, Lionel. *Sincerity and Authenticity.* Cambridge: Harvard University Press, 1972.

Trollope, Anthony. *An Autobiography.* 2 vols. London: William Blackwood and Sons, 1883.

Tsai, Shih-shan Henry. *China and the Overseas Chinese in the United States, 1868–1911.* Fayetteville: University of Arkansas Press, 1983.

Tuckey, John S. *Mark Twain: The Youth Who Lived On in the Sage.* Quarry Farm Papers 2. Elmira, N.Y.: Elmira College Center for Mark Twain Studies, 1994.

————. *Mark Twain and Little Satan: The Writing of "The Mysterious Stranger."* West Lafayette, Ind.: Purdue University Studies, 1963.

Turner, Arlin. "Mark Twain and the South: An Affair of Love and Anger." *Southern Review* 4 (1968): 493–519.

Twichell, Joseph H. "Mark Twain." *Harper's Magazine* 92 (May 1896): 817–27.

Veeder, William. *Henry James, the Lessons of the Master: Popular Fiction and Personal Style in the Nineteenth Century.* Chicago: University of Chicago Press, 1975.

Wadlington, Warrick. *The Confidence Game in American Literature.* Princeton: Princeton University Press, 1975.

Walker, Franklin. *Irreverent Pilgrims: Melville, Browne, and Mark Twain in the Holy Land.* Seattle: University of Washington Press, 1974.

————. *San Francisco's Literary Frontier.* 1939. Seattle: University of Washington Press, 1969.

Walker, Nancy A. *A Very Serious Thing: Women's Humor and American Culture.* Minneapolis: University of Minnesota Press, 1988.

Wallace, Edward S. *Destiny and Glory.* New York: Coward-McCann, 1957.

Warren, Joyce W. *The American Narcissus: Individualism and Women in Nineteenth-Century American Fiction.* New Brunswick: Rutgers University Press, 1984.

Warren, Robert Penn. *Now and Then: Poems, 1976–1978.* New York: Random House, 1978.

Wecter, Dixon. *Sam Clemens of Hannibal.* 1952. Rpt., Boston: Houghton Mifflin, 1961.

Welland, Dennis. *Mark Twain in England.* London: Chatto and Windus, 1978.

Whympter, Edward. *Scrambles amongst the Alps in the Years 1860–69.* London: John Murray, 1871.

Williams, Frederick Wells. *Anson Burlingame and the First Chinese Mission to Foreign Powers.* New York: Scribner, 1912.

Wilson, James D. *A Reader's Guide to the Short Stories of Mark Twain.* Boston: G. K. Hall, 1987.

———. "Religious and Esthetic Vision in Mark Twain's Early Career." *Canadian Review of American Studies* 17 (1986): 155–72.

Wilson, R. Jackson. *Figures of Speech: American Writers and the Literary Marketplace from Benjamin Franklin to Emily Dickinson.* New York: Knopf, 1989.

Wolff, Cynthia Griffin. "*The Adventures of Tom Sawyer:* The Nightmare Vision of American Boyhood." *Massachusetts Review* 21 (1980): 637–52.

Wonham, Henry B. *Mark Twain and the Art of the Tall Tale.* New York: Oxford University Press, 1993.

———. "Undoing Romance: The Contest for Narrative Authority in *The Adventures of Tom Sawyer.*" *Critical Essays on "The Adventures of Tom Sawyer."* Ed. Gary Scharnhorst. New York: G. K. Hall, 1993. 228–41.

Ziff, Larzer. "Authorship and Craft: The Example of Mark Twain." *Southern Review* 12 n.s. (1976): 246–60.

Zwick, Jim, ed. *Mark Twain's Weapons of Satire: Anti-Imperialist Writings on the Philippine-American War.* Syracuse: Syracuse University Press, 1992.

INDEX